NEHRU'S BANDUNG

ANDREA BENVENUTI

Nehru's Bandung

Non-Alignment and Regional Order in Indian Cold War Strategy

SPEAKING TIGER

SPEAKING TIGER BOOKS LLP
125-A, Ground Floor, Shahpur Jat
New Delhi – 110049

First published in the UK in 2024 by C. Hurst & Co.(Publishers) Ltd.
First published in India in 2024 by Speaking Tiger Books

Every effort has been made to identify copyright holders and obtain their permission for the use of copyright material. Notification of any additions or corrections that should be incorporated in future reprints or editions of this book would be greatly appreciated.

Material from Prime Ministers Museum and Library (PMML) reprinted with permission.

Material from Geetika Publishers reprinted with permission.

Material from the Wilson Center reprinted with permission.

Material from *Foreign Affairs* © 1954 Council on Foreign Relations, publisher of *Foreign Affairs*. All rights reserved. Distributed by Tribune Content Agency.

Material from Michael Brecher, *India and World Politics: Krishna Menon's View of the World* (London: Oxford University Press, 1968) reprinted by permission of Oxford University Press.

ISBN: 978-93-5447-908-3
10 9 8 7 6 5 4 3 2 1
Printed at Chaman Enterprises, New Delhi

CONTENTS

ACKNOWLEDGEMENTS

I am grateful in different ways to the various archives from which I gathered most of the sources for this book. I owe a particular debt to the archivists at the Prime Ministers Museum and Library and the National Archives of India in New Delhi for their kindness and patience in dealing with all my queries and requests regarding the files and papers in their keeping. I also express my sincere appreciation to the staff of the National Archives of Australia in Canberra, the National Archives of the United Kingdom in London and the National Archives and Records Administration in Washington, DC for their help during my research visits. I am also indebted to the University of New South Wales for funding my research trips to India, the United States and Britain, as well as archival fieldwork in Canberra.

I would also like to thank my colleagues Brian P. Farrell, S. R. Joey Long, Karl Hack, Shannon Brown, Charles Burgess, Marek Rutkowski and Fumihito Yamamoto for providing the inspiration to explore India's role and influence in the reordering of post-1945 Asia at a time when antagonistic visions of regional order clashed over the future character of the Asian state system. The idea of this book came to me as I was working with them on a two-volume book project called *Chasing Dragons: Western Military Power and Reordering Modern Asia*, to be published by Bloomsbury in London. The project, funded by the National University of Singapore and the Singapore Ministry of Education, aimed to explore the role of twentieth-century great powers in shaping and reshaping the East Asian regional system from the end of the First World War to the end of the Cold War. Although, or perhaps because, post-independence India was not included in the 'mix' of major powers covered in this project, I considered that this country, while no great power, was by no means an insignificant player in 1950s Asia and thus required independent examination in a separate work. Finally, I wish to take this opportunity to remember the late Professors M. S. Rajan and K. R. Singh of Jawaharlal Nehru University, who, many years ago, sparked my interest in Indian foreign policy during my first visit to the Indian subcontinent in the early 1990s.

At Hurst Publishers, I wish to thank Senior Editor Lara Weisweiller-Wu and Managing Editor Mei Jayne Yew for their tremendous patience and invaluable expertise in ensuring that this book project would see the light of day. I must also express my sincere gratitude to Taylor & Francis and DeGruyter for granting me permission to draw from three previously published works, namely: 'Constructing Peaceful Coexistence: Nehru's Approach to Regional Security and India's Rapprochement with Communist China in the mid-1950s,' *Diplomacy & Statecraft* 31: 1 (2020), pp. 91–117, DOI: 10.1080/09592296.2020.1721063, available at https://www.tandfonline.com; 'Nehru's Bandung Moment: India and the Convening of the 1955 Asian-African Conference,' *India Review* 21: 2 (2022), pp. 153–80, DOI: 10.1080/14736489.2022.2080489, available at https://www.tandfonline.com; 'Frustrating the Americans and Befriending the Communists: Nehru's Policy in the Early Asian Cold War, 1947–1954,' in Farrell, Brian P., Long, S. R. Joey and Ulbrich, David (eds), *From Far East to Asia Pacific: Great Powers and Grand Strategy 1900–1954* (Berlin: DeGruyter, 2022), pp. 251–80, DOI:10.1515/9783110718713-012. Last but not least, I am indebted to the two anonymous reviewers for their thorough reading of the manuscript and their insightful comments.

Most of all, I would like to thank my family for their unstinting love and for directly or indirectly making this book possible. My brother, Francesco, unfailingly supported me through my life and facilitated my first trip to India in 1991. My late parents, Giulio and Fernanda, not only believed in me and enabled me to pursue my passions, but also made my first visit to India possible, during which my 'discovery' of this mesmerising country began in earnest. Moreover, I would like to remember the late Mool Chand Kapoor and his wife, Malka Rani Kapoor, who generously hosted me for 4 months during my first stay in New Delhi and caringly introduced a young Italian student to the delights and wonders, as well as complexities, of Indian life. I want to dedicate this book to them all.

Finally, a heartfelt thank you goes to my wife Karla, with whom I share a passion for India. Karla has filled my many travels through this fascinating country with joy. Her love, friendship, patience and encouragement have made this book journey all the more pleasurable.

GUIDE TO TRANSLITERATION AND NAMES

This book generally follows the Pinyin spelling of Chinese names, except for archival or historical references, and peoples and places outside of the People's Republic of China. Chinese names are Romanised in this case according to the old Wade-Giles system.

As regards Indonesian names, this book adheres to the Republican Spelling System, which was introduced in 1947 and lasted until 1972 when President Suharto replaced it with the so-called Perfected Spelling. The only exception in the book is the name of Jakarta, which was spelt 'Djakarta' before Suharto's reform of the orthographic system. Moreover, as Indonesians often lack a family name and many have only one name, this book uses the names by which they were commonly known. For instance, Indonesian Prime Minister Ali Sastroamidjojo had no family name; hence, this book will refer to him as Ali Sastroamidjojo (first name and patronymic) unless in quotations, and in citations he is simply referred to as Sastroamidjojo.

As for Burmese names, most people in Burma have only given names, not surnames. This book will often refer to Burma Prime Minister U Nu. Strictly speaking, U is a title (it means 'uncle'), but it has generally become integral to the name 'Nu' in foreign usage. This book, therefore, will use 'Nu' and 'U Nu' interchangeably. This book also uses the word 'Burma' as shorthand for 'Union of Burma,' the country's official name since independence until 1989, when the ruling military junta renamed it Union of Myanmar (or Myanmar). Similarly, the book uses the old name of Burma's capital city: Rangoon, not Yangon. The same logic has been applied to Sri Lanka, known as Ceylon until 1972.

In this book, Indian cities such as Mumbai, Chennai and Kolkata are also referred to by their old names of Bombay, Madras and Calcutta.

NOTE ON INDIAN NOMENCLATURE

This book will occasionally refer to the posts of Secretary-General, Foreign Secretary and Commonwealth Secretary. During the Nehru years, the Ministry of External Affairs (MEA) had three high-ranking officials serving as secretaries under the Minister of External Affairs (Nehru himself). The MEA was then divided into two separate administrative units: a Department of Foreign Affairs, headed by a Foreign Secretary, and a Department of Commonwealth Relations, headed by a Commonwealth Secretary. The position of Secretary-General was created to ensure coordination and supervision between these two departments. It was abolished in 1965 when the two departments ceased functioning as separate administrative bodies within the MEA. For further details, see Jeffrey Benner, *The Indian Foreign Policy Bureaucracy* (Abingdon, UK, and New York: Routledge, 2019).

LIST OF ABBREVIATIONS

ADEA	Australian Department of External Affairs
AHC	Australian High Commission
BHC	British High Commission
CAB	Cabinet Office files (Britain)
CCP	Chinese Communist Party
CIA	Central Intelligence Agency
CMFA	Chinese Ministry of Foreign Affairs
CO	Colonial Office files/Colonial Office (Britain)
CPI	Communist Party of India
CRO	Commonwealth Relations Office (Britain)
DO	Dominions Office and Commonwealth Relations Office files (Britain)
FO	Foreign Office files/Foreign Office (Britain)
FRUS	*Foreign Relations of the United States*
Indel	India's delegation
Indembassy	Indian Embassy
JNLCM	*Jawaharlal Nehru Letters to Chief Ministers*
LSD	Lok Sabha Debates
Memcon	Memorandum of conversation

NAA	National Archives of Australia
NAI	National Archives of India
NARA	National Archives and Records Administration
NAUK	National Archives of the United Kingdom
NEFA	North-East Frontier Agency
NSC	National Security Council
PLA	People's Liberation Army
PMML	Prime Ministers Museum and Library
PNI	*Partai Nasional Indonesia*
PRC	People's Republic of China
PREM	Prime Minister's Office documents (Britain)
RG	Record Group
ROC	Republic of China (Taiwan)
SEATO	Southeast Asia Treaty Organization
SWJN	*Selected Works of Jawaharlal Nehru*
UK	United Kingdom
UN	United Nations
US	United States of America
USSR	Union of Soviet Socialist Republics
WCDA	Wilson Center Digital Archive

LIST OF KEY POLICYMAKERS

AUSTRALIA

Crocker, Walter	High Commissioner to India (1952–55); Ambassador to Indonesia (1955–57); High Commissioner to India and Ambassador to Nepal (1958–62)
Shann, K. C. O. (Keith Charles Owen)	Assistant Secretary, United Nations (UN) Branch, Australian Department of External Affairs (ADEA) (1952–55); Assistant Secretary, Americas and Pacific Branch (1955); Observer to Asian-African Conference (1955)

BRITAIN

Churchill, Winston	Prime Minister (1951–55)
Clutterbuck, Alexander	High Commissioner to India (1953–56)
Eden, Anthony	Foreign Secretary (1951–55); Prime Minister (1955–57)
MacDonald, Malcolm	High Commissioner to India (1956–60)
Middleton, G. H. (George Humphrey)	Deputy High Commissioner to India (1953–56)
Morland, Oscar	Ambassador to Indonesia (1953–56)

Trevelyan, Humphrey	Chargé d'Affaires to the People's Republic of China (PRC) (1953–55)

BURMA

Ba Swe	Prime Minister (1956–57)
Ne Win	Prime Minister (1958–60 and 1962–74)
U Nu	Prime Minister (1948–58 and 1960–62)

CANADA

Reid, Escott	Deputy Under-Secretary for External Affairs (1948–52); High Commissioner to India (1952–57)
St. Laurent, Louis	Prime Minister (1948–57)

CEYLON

Bandaranaike, Sirimavo	Prime Minister (1960–65, 1970–77 and 1994–2000)
Bandaranaike, S. W. R. D. (Solomon West Ridgeway Dias)	Prime Minister (1956–59)
Kotelawala, John	Prime Minister (1953–56)

CHINA

Deng Xiaoping	Vice Premier of the State Council of the PRC (1954–59); General Secretary of the Chinese Communist Party (CCP) Central Committee's Secretariat (1956–66)
Liu Shaoqi	President of the PRC (1959–66)
Mao Zedong	Chairman of the Central Committee of the CCP (1935–56), Chairman of the PRC (1949–59)
Zhou Enlai	Premier of the PRC (1949–76); Minister of Foreign Affairs (1949–58); Standing Committee of the CCP Bureau (1956–76)

EGYPT

Nasser, Gamal Abdel	Prime Minister (1954–62); President of Egypt (1956–70)

FRANCE

Bidault, Georges	Foreign Minister (1953–54)
Ely, Paul	Army General and Chief of Staff of the French Joint Chiefs of Staff (1953–54); Commissioner-General and Commander of French Forces in Indochina (1954–55)
Laniel, Joseph	Prime Minister (1953–54)
Mendès France, Pierre	Prime Minister (1954–55); Foreign Minister (1954–55)
Navarre, Henri	Army General and Commander in Chief of the French Union Forces in Indochina (1953–54)

INDIA

Bajpai, Girija Shankar	Secretary-General, Ministry of External Affairs (MEA) (1947–52)
Desai, C. C. (Chandulal Chunilal)	High Commissioner to Ceylon (1954)
Desai, M. J.	Foreign Secretary, MEA (1961–63)
Dutt, Subimal	Commonwealth Secretary, MEA (1954–55); Foreign Secretary, MEA (1955–61)
Jha, C. S. (Chandra Shekhar)	Joint Secretary, MEA (1947–50); Ambassador to Turkey (1950–54); Joint Secretary, MEA (1954–57); Ambassador to Japan (1957–59); Ambassador to the UN (1959–62); High Commissioner to Canada (1962–63); Commonwealth Secretary, MEA (1964)
Jung, Ali Yavar	Ambassador to Egypt (1954–58)

Katju, Kailas Nath	Minister for Home Affairs (1951–55)
Kaul, T. N. (Triloki Nath)	Joint Secretary, MEA (1953–55)
Menon, V. K. Krishna	High Commissioner to the UK (1947–52); Chairman of the Indian Delegation to the UN (1953–62); Minister without Portfolio (1956–57); Minister of Defence (1957–62)
Metha, G. L. (Gaganvihari Lallubhai)	Ambassador to the United States (1952–58)
Mullik, B. N. (Bhola Nath)	Director, Intelligence Bureau of India (1950–64)
Nehru, B. K. (Braj Kumar)	Joint Secretary, External Finance, Ministry of Finance (1955); Ambassador to the United States (1961–68)
Nehru, Jawaharlal	Prime Minister (1947–64); Minister of External Affairs (1947–64)
Nehru, R. K. (Ratan Kumar)	Foreign Secretary, MEA (1952–55); Ambassador to the PRC (1955–58); Ambassador to the United Arab Republic (1958–60); Secretary-General, MEA (1960–63)
Pandit, Vijaya Lakshmi	Nehru's sister (née Swarup Kumari Nehru); Head of the Indian Delegation to the UN (1946–48); Ambassador to the Soviet Union (1947–49); Ambassador to the United States (1949–51); 8th President of the UN General Assembly (1953–54); High Commissioner to the UK (1954–61)
Panikkar, K. M. (Kavalam Madhava)	Ambassador to China (1948–52); Ambassador to Egypt (1952–54)
Pillai, N. R. (Narayanan Raghavan)	Cabinet Secretary (1950–53); Secretary-General, MEA (1953–59)

Prasad, Rajendra	President of India (1950–62)
Radhakrishnan, Sarvepalli	Vice President of India (1952–62); President of India (1962–67)
Raghavan, N. (Nedyam)	Ambassador to the PRC (1952–55)
Syed Mahmud	Deputy Minister of External Affairs (1954–57)
Tyabji, B. F. H. B.	Ambassador to India (1954–56)

INDONESIA

Burhanuddin Harahap	Prime Minister (1955–56)
Hatta, Mohammad	Vice President of Indonesia (1950–56)
Palar, L. N. (Lambertus Nicodemus)	Ambassador to the UN (1950–53); Ambassador to India (1953–55)
Sastroamidjojo, Ali	Ambassador to the United States (1950–53); Prime Minister (1953–55 and 1956–57); Permanent Representative to the UN (1957–60)
Soekardjo Wirjopranoto	Asian Division, Ministry of Foreign Affairs (1954)
Subandrio	Foreign Minister (1957–66)
Sukarno	President of Indonesia (1945–67)
Sunario	Foreign Minister (1953–54)
Wilopo	Prime Minister (1952–53)

NORTH KOREA

Kim Il Sung	Premier of the Democratic People's Republic of Korea (1948–72); Supreme Commander of the Korean People's Army (1950–91); Chairman of the Workers' Party of Korea (1949–66)

PAKISTAN

Bogra, Mohammed Ali	Prime Minister and Minister of Defence (1953–54); Prime Minister and Minister of Foreign Affairs (1954–55)
Rahim, J. A. (Jalaludin Abdur)	Foreign Secretary (1953–55)
Suhrawardy, H. S. (Huseyn Shaheed)	Prime Minister (1956–57)

REPUBLIC OF CHINA

Chiang Kai-shek	President of the Republic of China (ROC) (1950–75)

SOVIET UNION

Bulganin, Nikolai Alexandrovich	Minister of Defence (1953–55); Premier of the Soviet Union (1955–58)
Khrushchev, Nikita Sergeyevich	First Secretary of the Communist Party of the Soviet Union (1953–64); Premier of the USSR (1958–64)
Malenkov, Georgy Maximilianovich	Premier of the Soviet Union (1953–55); Deputy Premier of the Soviet Union (1955–57)
Menshikov, Mikhail	Ambassador to India (1953)
Molotov, Vyacheslav Mikhaylovich	First Deputy Premier of the Soviet Union (1942–57); Minister of Foreign Affairs (1939–49 and 1953–56)
Novikov, Kirill	Ambassador to India (1950–53)
Stalin, Joseph Vissarionovich	General Secretary of the Communist Party of the Soviet Union (1922–52); Chairman of the Council of People's Commissars (1941–46); Chairman of the Councils of Ministers (1946–53)

UNITED STATES

Allen, George V.	Ambassador to India (1953–54)
Bowie, Robert R.	Director of the Policy Planning Staff, Department of State (1953–55)
Bowles, Chester B.	Ambassador to India (1951–53 and 1963–69)
Cumming, Hugh S.	Ambassador to Indonesia (1953–57)
Dulles, John Foster	Secretary of State (1953–59)
Eisenhower, Dwight D.	President of the United States (1953–61)
Henderson, Loy W.	Ambassador to India (1950–51)
Kennedy, John F.	President of the United States of America (1961–63)
McGhee, George	Assistant Secretary of State for Near Eastern, South Asian and African Affairs, Department of State (1949–51)
Nixon, Richard M.	Vice President of the United States of America (1953–61)
Truman, Harry S.	President of the United States of America (1945–53)

YUGOSLAVIA

Kveder, Dušan	Ambassador to India (1958–62)
Tito, Josip Broz	President of Yugoslavia (1953–80); Prime Minister (1944–63)

Jawaharlal Nehru delivering an address at the Bandung Conference. *Image courtesy of the Museum of the Asian-African Conference, Bandung, Indonesia.*

Prime Minister Ali Sastroamidjojo of Indonesia (left) and Prime Minister U Nu of Burma (centre) with Nehru at the Bandung Conference. *Image courtesy of the Museum of the Asian-African Conference, Bandung, Indonesia.*

INTRODUCTION

The whole object should be to create an atmosphere of cooperation and to put Asia and Africa more in the world picture. During the last few years, the position of Asia in world affairs has gradually changed and the relationship of Asian nations to European or American nations is also a changing one. The old balance no longer holds good and Asia and Asian problems cannot be treated as the sole concerns of non Asian countries.

Jawaharlal Nehru[1]

18 April 1955. The first Asian-African conference opened in Bandung, a hill town of more than half a million people, 150 kilometres south-west of the Indonesian capital, Jakarta. There gathered the leaders of twenty-nine Asian and African nations, the majority of them post-colonial states which had recently gained independence. Together, they made up two-thirds of the world's population. Three leaders stood out from the rest: the Chinese Premier, Zhou Enlai, the Egyptian President, Gamal Abdel Nasser, and the Indian Prime Minister, Jawaharlal Nehru. At the age of sixty-five, Nehru was at the pinnacle of his influence in international affairs and a dominant figure in Indian politics.[2] In office since 1947, he had developed a reputation as a living symbol of anti-colonial struggle and the voice of a resurgent Asia.[3] During the interwar years, he had gained international recognition for speaking out against imperialism and fascism.[4] By the time India gained independence in August 1947—an

event that carried enormous political and symbolic significance with its premonitory signs of the impending decline of European colonial empires in the Afro-Asian world—he had already established himself as an international leader of considerable renown.[5] After India's independence, Nehru's popularity had continued to grow thanks to his policy of non-alignment.[6] Thus, by the time he travelled to Bandung, Nehru enjoyed significant prestige among the newly independent countries of Asia and Africa, which 'looked to India as an example.'[7] Predictably, from the moment his Air India Constellation aeroplane landed at Bandung airport on the afternoon of 16 April, he became one of the conference's main attractions. He drew significant attention from the press. Hundreds of Bandung residents lined the city's main drag, Jalan Merdeka, to cheer him on as he entered the Gedung Merdeka building, the conference's main venue. Leading one of the largest delegations, he was expected to play a prominent role in the conference's proceedings.

Jointly organised by the governments of India, Indonesia, Ceylon, Pakistan and Burma, the Bandung Conference was intended to promote goodwill and friendly relations among Afro-Asian nations and 'to explore and advance' their common interests. Moreover, it aimed to discuss their 'social, economic and cultural problems,' including those 'affecting national sovereignty and of racialism and colonialism.' Lastly, it proposed to assess 'the position of Asia and Africa and their peoples in the world of today and the contribution they can make to the promotion of world peace and cooperation' in an era of escalating Cold War tensions.[8] In brief, the conference afforded the leaders gathered at Bandung a rare opportunity to draw international attention to their nations' needs, goals and perspectives in a world riven by the Cold War and threatened by nuclear destruction. It also signalled their desire to have their voices heard 'in the councils of world affairs, more especially on matters affecting Asian and African countries.'[9]

On a more symbolic level, Bandung foreshadowed 'the awakening of Africa and the arrival of Asia on the international stage.'[10] It should, therefore, come as no surprise that, since the 1950s, the first Asian-African summit has exemplified the emergence of Third World nations as a force for change in post-1945 international relations and, as a result, has generated a lively scholarly interest. Scholars, however, have been divided over Bandung's historical relevance and long-term implications.[11] For some, the first Afro-Asian conference was a watershed in post-1945 international relations. They detect in it the first premonitory stirrings of a radical and transformative vision of global politics. For others, its achievements have been greatly exaggerated. In this latter camp lies, most famously, former Indian diplomat-turned-journalist and historian G. H. Jansen. In assessing the conference's significance a decade after the event, he noted that two meetings took place in Bandung in April 1955. 'One,' he wrote, 'was the real conference, about which not very much is known, about which people care even less, and which has faded away like a bad dream.' The other was an altogether different affair—one that could be described as 'a crystallisation of what people wanted to believe had happened which, as a myth, took on reality in the Bandung Principles and, later, in the Bandung Spirit.'[12]

Even though its accomplishments are contested, few would today deny Bandung's symbolic significance in world politics. Similarly, when it comes to one of its major participants and organisers, few would question India's highly visible international role and considerable influence during the early years of the Cold War. In the same vein, few would dispute Nehru's significant standing at the time among his Afro-Asian contemporaries and within the democratic West, where he came to represent the voice of moderate, democratic and non-communist post-colonial Asia. Yet, despite Bandung's historical importance, Nehru's standing as a world statesman and India's place in Cold War history, far too little attention has been paid to the role played by his Congress party administration in the making of the conference. No existing studies deal with it at length, nor do they draw on extensive archival research. Scholarly works on Indian foreign policy in the 1950s hardly discuss Nehru's role in organising the Bandung Conference.[13] The situation does not get much better when we consider the growing literature on Asian-African internationalism. While shedding light on the historical context in which India's approach to Bandung unfolded, the existing scholarship in this area has failed to provide a comprehensive treatment of this topic.

One notable exception is Jansen's *Afro-Asia and Non-Alignment*, which remains the best and most revealing account of Nehru's attitude towards the convening of the Asian-African conference and the role he played in Bandung.[14] As an Indian diplomat and a journalist, Jansen attended, in one or the other capacity, most of the Afro-Asian and non-aligned conferences of the early Cold War and talked to several Afro-Asian officials and diplomats. More importantly, at the time of Bandung, he was a member of the Indian embassy in Jakarta.[15] As such, he was well-placed to assess Nehru's behaviour and uniquely well-informed about the conference's proceedings and informal backstage discussions.[16] However, although Jansen dealt at some length with Indian diplomacy in and around the 1955 Asian-African conference, the focus of his study, as its title suggests, is not Bandung. Besides, his findings are based mainly on interviews, secondary sources and personal recollections.[17]

Other scholars have also acknowledged the part played by Nehru at Bandung and the contribution he made to shaping the conference proceedings. Yet, their focus on Indian agency is even more limited.[18] In recent years, historians such as Nicholas Tarling, H. W. Brands, Lorenz Lüthi and Amit Das Gupta, as well as international relations experts like Amitav Acharya, have used newly available archival evidence to illuminate aspects of Nehru's diplomacy.[19] Also drawing on declassified sources, Cindy Ewing has briefly covered Nehru's role at the April 1954 Colombo Conference, where he and four other Asian leaders first discussed the idea of an Asian-African conference.[20] More recently, I have begun investigating India's role in convening the Bandung Conference and its contribution to its proceedings in an article published in the *India Review*.[21] The idea for this book comes from this article.

Recognising that little has been written about Nehru's approach to Bandung, this study addresses this gap by providing the first comprehensive account based on declassified archival sources. It will do so by focusing on the policy considerations, concerns and calculations that led the Indian leader to promote the 1955 Asian-African summit. As Nehru was the almost uncontested maker of India's foreign policy between 1947 and 1964, and thus played a central role in shaping policy on this specific issue, he must be the obvious starting point for any study of Indian foreign policy during this period.[22] At the same time, this book also highlights the international factors that drove a sceptical Nehru to support Indonesian calls for such a gathering. Contrary to what one of Nehru's External Affairs advisers claimed nearly 30 years later, he was not 'the prime mover' behind Bandung. Nor was he the champion of Afro-Asianism who had little 'difficulty in persuading the other co-sponsors to fall in with the idea.'[23]

In reality, as this work demonstrates, the label of prime mover belongs to Indonesian Prime Minister Ali Sastroamidjojo; the Asian-African conference was his brainchild, 'not India's baby,' as Nehru's close associate, Krishna Menon, readily admitted at the time.[24] In fact, Nehru did not initially give much importance to Bandung, and his support was not a foregone conclusion when, in late April 1954, Ali Sastroamidjojo proposed holding an Asian-African conference. However, as this book also indicates, the Bandung Conference would not have taken place without India's diplomatic support—due not least to Indonesia's inexperience in organising such a large international event. Only in the second half of 1954 did Nehru come around to the idea. Once he concluded that India should support the Indonesian proposal, he began shaping the meeting's agenda and rationale, as well as picking most of the countries to be invited. It would, of course, be erroneous to suggest that Indonesia's initial idea was transformed into an Indian project *tout court*. Yet, it is no exaggeration to say that Nehru made sure that it was closely aligned with India's foreign policy objectives and reflected its regional designs. Put another way, the 1955 Asian-African conference was to bear a significant, albeit not exclusive, Indian imprint. This being the case, one must wonder why Nehru overcame his initial reservations regarding Ali Sastroamidjojo's proposal. Why did he eventually back the latter's calls for an Asian-African summit? What changed his mind? These fundamental questions are at the heart of India's approach to the Bandung Conference and form the central puzzle of this book.

This book claims three factors pushed Nehru to throw his weight behind the Indonesian proposal. The first was his concern about American policy in Asia. Two aspects of Washington's Asian diplomacy troubled him particularly. One was the US decision to forge a close defence partnership with India's arch-rival, which led to the signing of the United States-Pakistan Mutual Defence Assistance Agreement in May 1954. The other was Washington's resolve to establish an American-led regional alliance to contain communism in South-East Asia. Sceptical of the Soviet Union and China's willingness to stand by the Geneva Conference's settlement on Indochina, the United States moved to establish the South-East Asian Treaty Organization (SEATO) following the signing of the Manila Treaty in September 1954. In taking this course of action, Washington intended to send a clear warning to Moscow and Beijing that it would resist further communist penetration in South-East Asia. However, in Indian eyes, Washington's defence agreement with Karachi not only brought the Cold War to India's borders but also posed a direct threat to its security by eroding its military edge over Pakistan and encouraging the latter to confront India. As for SEATO, its creation presented perhaps a less direct but no less dangerous challenge to India. Viewed from New Delhi, Washington's containment strategy had the potential to undermine the Indochinese settlement so painstakingly negotiated at Geneva, thereby increasing the risk of war by stoking tensions between regional blocs. As perplexing as this may have appeared to Western policymakers at the time, Nehru considered American efforts to check communist penetration in Asia not only destabilising but also profoundly misguided in light of growing Sino-Soviet support for peaceful coexistence.

The second factor contributing to Nehru's change of heart regarding the conference was Beijing's embrace of peaceful coexistence, a policy shift that became increasingly manifest in 1954 and reached its climax at Bandung in 1955. Confronted with renewed international tensions on India's doorstep, Nehru regarded Beijing's apparent decision to give up its erstwhile revolutionary radicalism and embrace the idea of coexistence between Cold War blocs as an opportunity too good to pass up. Accordingly, he attempted to take advantage of this new trend in the Chinese approach to international and regional affairs to secure crucial foreign policy goals. In broad terms, these goals were to end China's international isolation, which Nehru believed was responsible for its revolutionary behaviour; to secure Beijing's long-term commitment to peaceful coexistence; and to neuter the emergence of a potentially hostile power on India's borders. As this book shows, Nehru gradually realised, over the course of the year 1954, that the Jakarta-sponsored conference could provide an excellent opportunity to achieve these objectives. Finally, one further factor prompted him to reconsider his approach to the Indonesian initiative. That factor was Indonesia itself. Ali Sastroamidjojo's government was facing a complex situation at home, and—valuing Ali Sastroamidjojo's non-alignment and considering Indonesia a key partner in India's efforts to foil US plans in Asia—Nehru was hesitant to do anything that might weaken or embarrass him.

However, while these factors help explain Nehru's contingent reasons for supporting Indonesia's diplomatic push for an Asian-African conference, they reveal little about his overall vision and motivations. What did he hope to accomplish with such a gathering? What was his ultimate aim? Here, the book advances a further proposition, arguing that his central aim was to seize the opportunity accorded by the Asian-African conference to promote his vision of 'areas of peace.' What he meant by that was, in essence, a neutralised zone or region in which states rejected Cold War alignments and followed non-alignment as the ordering concept of their foreign policies. As he once put it, there was 'room for a third ideology' (read non-alignment) and for the 'area of peace we have sought to establish and extend between warring blocs.'[25] In Nehru's vision, areas of peace were to be underpinned by what he called the 'Five Principles of Peaceful Coexistence.' While the Five Principles were a Chinese idea originally, Nehru viewed them as 'the foundations of a new approach to international relations.'[26] He contended that, unless Asian nations pursued diplomacy in accordance with these principles, they would be unable to carve out 'areas of peace' and achieve 'collective peace' in Asia.[27] As the book details, in the second half of 1954, Nehru made the Five Principles not only the centrepiece of his China policy but also the cornerstone of his vision of a non-aligned Asia. In this context, Bandung was to serve a dual purpose: first, to secure regional support for the Five Principles as a new code of conduct among Asian nations and, second, to cement

China's commitment to peaceful coexistence, without which peace and stability in Asia would be illusory. If successful, this strategy would also allow India to isolate the United States and counter its containment policy. In other words, as this book clearly underscores, Nehru's agreement to hold an Asian-African conference in Bandung did not stem from a nebulous sense of Afro-Asian solidarity or an emotional commitment to Afro-Asian internationalism. Rather, it emanated from his ambition to promote a 'third way' in an increasingly polarised world and forge a more stable regional order that would increase India's external security and domestic prosperity. In short, Cold War concerns—not Afro-Asian unity—drove his actions.

Drawing on an extensive body of archival material, this book is, first and foremost, a work of diplomatic history. It provides the first detailed attempt to reconstruct Nehru's role in organising the first Asian-African conference and explain the nature, rationale and development of his policy. In so doing, it hopes to contribute to three areas of historical scholarship: Cold War history, Indian foreign policy and Asian-African internationalism. With regard to the first, Cold War scholarship has, in recent years, increasingly emphasised the importance of Third World actors and Third World regions in shaping Cold War dynamics. In this context, this book shifts the focus away from superpower competition as a critical factor in the ordering of Cold War international relations in favour of recognising the role played by influential Third World actors in the unfolding of the Cold War.[28] In so doing, its crucial contribution lies in revisiting India's role and influence in the reordering of post-1945 Asia at a time when antagonistic visions of regional order clashed over the future character of the Asian state system. Although Cold War dynamics in Asia were primarily the result of intense competition between opposing blocs and the collision of their incompatible visions of regional order, India was no mere bystander in the unfolding of 1950s regional politics. By giving voice to the concerns and aspirations of those Asian countries seeking to avoid Cold War alignments, India was able to carve out an influential role for itself.[29] Thus, by placing India at the forefront of Asian politics in the 1950s, this study will enrich and deepen the existing historical literature on the Cold War.

Regarding the second area of scholarship, this book sheds fresh light on India's foreign policy and foreign relations during a period of serious regional tensions. In recent years, the growing availability of archival material on the Asian Cold War has spurred increased scholarly interest in Indian foreign policymaking during the 1950s. It has also provided new insights into various facets of it, from India's relations with the world's major powers to its approach to specific Cold War issues.[30] In this regard, the works of Zorawar Daulet Singh and Anton Harder have been particularly useful in elucidating aspects of Nehru's Cold War vision and tactics. Yet, despite these excellent contributions, no previous study has comprehensively placed Bandung at the confluence of the different strands of Nehru's Cold War diplomacy—notably, non-alignment, Afro-Asianism, accommodation with China and opposition to Cold War military alliances such as SEATO. In so doing, this book has the opportunity to advance our understanding of the foreign policy and foreign relations of India, a country that, as Odd Arne Westad and Voitech Mastny have recently noted, remains a relatively understudied major power in Cold War historiography.[31] Compared to the growing number of scholarly works devoted to the Cold War policies of powers such as the United States and Britain, the study of Indian foreign policy has lagged decidedly behind.

Lastly, with regard to the third area of scholarship, this study also aims to contribute to the expanding historical literature on Asian-African internationalism. Scholars in this field have drawn significant attention to the role of intellectual debates, popular movements, activism, aid politics and alternative Asian-African gatherings in the unfolding of the 'Bandung story.' Thus, they have broken new ground on Bandung and its legacy while providing a broader and more nuanced context in which to situate Indian diplomacy in and around Bandung.[32] However, in acknowledging the importance of these contributions, this study remains focused on the diplomatic dimension of the story, holding that Bandung was first and foremost an inter-governmental conference and its origins lie in the interplay between regional nation-states, their interests and their agendas. That being the case, India's role in the conference is best understood through the lens of diplomatic history. As a result, this study's key contribution to the current literature in this area is its exploration of the role of state agency in shaping Asian-African internationalism.

To describe and explain Nehru's diplomacy in and around Bandung, this book draws on a multitude of Indian and international archival sources. It primarily relies on declassified government files from archives in India, the UK, the United States and Australia. In New Delhi, the Prime Ministers Museum and Library (PMML)—formerly known as Nehru Memorial Library and Museum—provided, first and foremost, access to the Nehru papers. In addition to delivering rich and important insights into Nehru's role as a statesman and decision-maker, these records are indispensable when it comes to comprehending his foreign policy. At the same time, the National Archives of India (NAI) in New Delhi made available the Ministry of External Affairs files on the first Asian-African conference. Outside of India, the National Archives and Records Administration (NARA) at College Park, Maryland, supplied files from the State Department dealing with Asian-related questions as well as American policy in the region. Research in the National Archives of the United Kingdom (NAUK) in Kew covered files principally from the Foreign Office and the Commonwealth Relations Office with reference to Asian questions. The Commonwealth Relations Office, in particular, had specific responsibility for conducting relations with India and South Asia and, as such, is an excellent source of information on Indian politics and foreign policy. In Canberra, the National Archives of Australia (NAA) made available the files from the Department of External Affairs pertaining to India and other Asian countries. As the United States, Britain and Australia had a significant diplomatic presence in the region at the time, the archival evidence from these governments proved extremely valuable to this project. Due to their frequent interactions with local elites, American, British and Australian diplomats in Asia were able to report back to their respective national authorities on the attitudes of Asian governments on crucial Cold War policy issues of the day. While these Western sources are no substitute for regional archival material, they provide an abundance of cables, intelligence reports, memoranda of conversations and political assessments discussing and analysing the politics, policymaking and diplomacy of many Asian nations.

In brief, they are essential for gaining a deeper understanding of regional perspectives and issues. Given that access to government records is severely restricted in most Asian nations,[33] these sources go some way towards making up for the dearth of readily available confidential information on these countries.

In addition to the material from the archives mentioned above, the book also relies on collections of historical documents published in India and elsewhere. These included the *Selected Works of Jawaharlal Nehru* (*SWJN*), *India-China Relations 1947–2000: A Documentary Study*, the Lok Sabha Parliamentary Debates (LSD), the *Foreign Relations of the United States* (*FRUS*) and the Wilson Center Digital Archives (WCDA). The voluminous *SWJN* series, which contains Nehru's writings, speeches, correspondence and communiqués, as well as memoranda of conversations, helped complement the material found in the Nehru Memorial Library and Museum in New Delhi. The published collection, *India-China Relations 1947–2000: A Documentary Study*, offered a wealth of material on India's relations with China, a significant topic covered in this book. The LSD provided a record of Nehru's parliamentary speeches. As for FRUS, it provided considerable insight into America's regional policy in the 1950s. Finally, the WCDA made available essential Chinese government documents in translation.

The book begins by exploring the global and regional contexts in which post-independence Indian policymakers formulated their nation's foreign policy. More specifically, it identifies the key factors that impacted on the development of India's foreign relations in the early years of the Cold War. Such factors include the rise of the United States as a major catalyst for change, both globally and regionally; the emergence of the Cold War understood as the political, ideological, economic and military rivalry between two opposing blocs vying for global and regional influence; and the resurgence of China as an influential actor in regional affairs. In so doing, Chapter 1 briefly recounts how Nehru's India responded to emerging Cold War tensions between opposing blocs and interacted with the two superpowers and China, the latter which at the time was Moscow's junior partner with the responsibility of promoting communist revolutions in Asia. Chapter 1 also explains why Nehru came to view

American containment, rather than Sino-Soviet communism, as the most significant threat to regional stability. In this context, it assesses the impact on India of the Eisenhower administration's decision to negotiate a bilateral defence agreement with Pakistan, New Delhi's sworn enemy. It shows how Pakistan's emerging alliance with the United States was to harden Nehru's criticism of American policy in Asia while strengthening his opposition to deepening regional Cold War dynamics.

Chapter 2 builds on the preceding one by showing how a spiralling crisis in South-East Asia further hardened Indian opposition to the new Eisenhower administration's policy of containment in Asia. The American response to the collapse of the French military position in Indochina in early 1954 heightened Indian fears that Washington would take precipitous action to prevent Indochina from falling into communist hands, thus triggering a major conflict in Asia. This chapter provides the necessary context to understand the course of Indian foreign policy in the following months. More specifically, it reveals how the Indochina crisis, following hot on the heels of the US-Pakistan defence pact, compelled Nehru to act as a counterbalance to American containment and promote a distinctly different vision of regional order and security, based on his concept of areas of peace and the Five Principles of Peaceful Coexistence.

Nehru's initial steps in this direction were tentative. As Chapter 3 shows, he took advantage of a meeting of Asian leaders convened in Colombo at the end of April 1954 by John Kotelawala, the prime minister of Ceylon, to voice regional concerns about escalating Cold War tensions in Asia and put forward a broad solution to the Indochinese crisis. As a means of defusing tensions and preserving regional stability, he also took the opportunity in Colombo to reaffirm his support for the concept of areas of peace and a neutralised Asia. In this context, Chapter 3 also examines Nehru's approach to Indonesian plans to organise an Asian-African conference, which, according to Jakarta's aims, was meant to foster Afro-Asian coordination on matters of common interest, including the problem of growing competition between the great powers and deepening Cold War tensions. This chapter shows that, contrary to the commonly held view that Nehru was a staunch supporter of Afro-Asian internationalism, he doubted that a large gathering of countries with diverse historical backgrounds and disparate cultural and political traditions could produce significant results. Yet, despite these reservations, Nehru and the other participating Asian prime ministers reluctantly gave Indonesian Prime Minister Ali Sastroamidjojo the go-ahead to begin exploring the idea of an Asian-African conference. In this context, Chapter 3 also sheds light on the perceptions, interests and policies of the so-called Colombo group and its role in setting in motion the diplomatic steps that eventually led to the convening of the Bandung Conference in 1955. However, as the chapter makes it clear, in April 1954, the Indonesian proposal to hold an Asian-African summit was little more than an inchoate idea whose feasibility and purpose were uncertain. Moreover, it was not apparent how such a meeting would fit into Nehru's diplomacy, nor how it would contribute to India's regional policy.

With an Asian-African conference still a long way off, Chapter 4 turns its attention to Chinese Premier Zhou Enlai's visit to India in late June 1954. It does so by detailing Nehru's extensive discussions with his Chinese counterpart and the implications of these discussions for Nehru's regional diplomacy. In this context, Chapter 4 shows how Zhou's brief stop in New Delhi allowed Nehru to advance some major Indian foreign policy goals. Wishing to capitalise on China's moderate turn in foreign policy—a shift that became increasingly evident during 1954—Nehru was eager to improve Sino-Indian relations, defuse domestic and regional concerns regarding China's regional role, enlist Beijing's support for his concept of areas of peace and leverage for closer Sino-Indian cooperation in order to undermine Washington's containment strategy and isolate the United States and its allies in Asia. In addition, Nehru viewed greater Sino-Indian cooperation as an opportunity to ensure that major regional powers like India and China would play a prominent role in defining the region's future. As Chapter 4 evinces, Nehru's first encounter with Zhou turned out to be a success. The two leaders reached significant convergence on several Cold War issues—from their support for the concept of 'areas of peace' to their opposition to what they saw as Washington's aggressive containment in Asia. Zhou was also able to allay Indian fears of Chinese expansionism and reaffirm Beijing's commitment to the Five Principles of Peaceful Coexistence, which the two countries had established as a code of conduct to govern their bilateral relations following the signing of the April 1954 Sino-Indian agreement on Tibet. Although the two leaders did not discuss the potentially contentious border question, the Nehru-Zhou talks paved the way for closer political collaboration between the two countries.

If Zhou's visit to India appeared to mark the beginning of a new era in Sino-Indian relations, there remained much work to be done before China could be considered a credible pillar of Nehru's regional strategy. Nehru's desire to promote greater Chinese engagement with non-communist Asia was unlikely to come true as long as India's neighbours harboured serious misgivings about China's revolutionary role in Asia. As Chapter 5 shows, Burma was one of the countries where these misgivings were felt most acutely. Zhou's brief trip to Rangoon after New Delhi was to provide the litmus test of China's peaceful intentions and the validity of Nehru's own assumptions. Although it was still unclear in late June 1954 whether an Asian-African conference would ever take place, Zhou's talks with U Nu were, in hindsight, an important step in that direction. Not only did Nehru feel more optimistic about Chinese behaviour, but he also came to see China as a stakeholder in, rather than a threat to, regional security. China's constructive role in facilitating an agreement on Indochina at the Geneva Conference (26 April–20 July 1954) further reinforced this perception. As Chapter 5 demonstrates, Nehru's main concern in the late summer of 1954 was not China's regional role but the direction of Western policy in Asia. In the aftermath of the Geneva Conference, Washington's decision to go ahead with the creation of a South-East Asian defence organisation strengthened his conviction that the United States, not China, stood in the way of his efforts to establish a regional area of peace. As Chapter 5 details, he fiercely opposed the creation of SEATO in September 1954 and made every effort to prevent some of India's Colombo partners from joining. It was at this precise juncture that he began to attach greater importance to the notion of an Asian-African summit, viewing it as an opportunity to advance his vision of a neutralised Asia in opposition to the American containment of China.

Chapter 6 delves into Nehru's changing views on the utility of an Asian-African conference in the context of rising regional tensions, prompted by Ali Sastroamidjojo's visit to New Delhi in late September 1954. Despite the Colombo powers' initial tepid response to Jakarta's calls for an Afro-Asian summit, the Indonesian government continued to insist on the necessity of holding such a gathering. By travelling to India, Ali Sastroamidjojo intended to secure a firm Indian commitment to it. Faced with the Indonesian prime minister's determination to get the idea of an Asian-African summit off the ground, Nehru agreed that such a conference should be held at an early date and preceded by a meeting of the five Colombo prime ministers. As Chapter 6 indicates, a variety of factors influenced Nehru's decision, from his perception of Indonesia's increasing importance for India's regional calculations to his emerging realisation that such a conference could provide a platform to promote an alternative approach to regional relations based on areas of peace and peaceful coexistence. Although at this stage he kept silent in public about the possibility of inviting China, Nehru privately recognised the importance of Chinese participation in the future conference, given the role that China could play in furthering his vision of a neutralised Asia.

Nehru's visit to China in October 1954 was crucial in advancing such a vision. As Chapter 7 makes clear, his talks with Mao Zedong and Zhou Enlai in Beijing reassured the Indian prime minister about Chinese professions of peaceful intent. Not only did he gain additional proof of Beijing's commitment to the Five Principles and his concept of 'areas of peace,' but he also witnessed a significant degree of convergence between the two countries on various Cold War issues. As India and China appeared to share similar regional objectives, Nehru saw increased merit in inviting China to a future Asian-African conference, despite remaining non-committal on the matter. He reasoned that a conference that included China would do much to consolidate peaceful coexistence, reassure China's Asian neighbours and overcome Cold War divisions. By the time he left China, he was increasingly persuaded that regional stability depended significantly on Beijing's constructive engagement in international affairs.

In December 1954, as the Colombo powers neared a formal decision on holding an Asian-African conference, Nehru outlined the rationale behind India's support for this initiative. Chapter 8 demonstrates that although he saw the conference as an opportunity to foster Afro-Asian cooperation and discuss shared Afro-Asian concerns, his overriding motivation lay in Cold War considerations. In other words, he primarily intended to use the Afro-Asian gathering to win approval for the Five Principles of Peaceful Coexistence as a means of achieving regional peace and stability, and to promote his vision of a neutralised Asia. In this context, he considered China's participation in the conference essential to achieving India's regional objectives. In addition, Chapter 8 examines Nehru's and the Indian delegation's role in shaping the outcome of the Bogor Conference in late December, where the leaders of the five Colombo powers set the date, agenda and composition of the upcoming Asian-African conference. Finally, this chapter briefly explores Beijing's reasoning for accepting the invitation to the conference.

Chapters 9 and 10 provide an account of the Bandung Conference and its proceedings, and it examines the role played by Nehru and the Indian delegation in it. Finally, Chapter 11 traces the legacy of Bandung on Nehru's foreign policy. As this book contends that he viewed the 1955 Asian-African conference largely as a tool for realising his neutralist vision and securing China's long-term backing of peaceful coexistence, Chapter 11 evaluates whether and to what extent Nehru's grand design was successful. It does so by looking at the evolution of Sino-Indian relations between the late 1950s and early 1960s and by assessing the role of the Afro-Asian caucus in addressing key Indian Cold War concerns. The chapter shows that the post-Bandung years produced mixed results for Nehru's Cold War strategy. However, when it came to forging an enduring Chinese commitment to peaceful coexistence, Bandung and its legacy remain a testament to Nehru's wishful thinking in dealing with China.

1

INDIA AND THE COLD WAR

Indians have in large part failed to appreciate the aggressiveness and imperialistic nature of Stalinism, and as a threat of a world war draws nearer the United States appears to their minds to be ... primarily responsible.

US State Department paper[1]

The genesis of the 1955 Asian-African conference and India's rationale for convening it lie in the climate of the deepening divisions that marked the early Cold War years. The outbreak of the Korean War in June 1950 heightened Soviet-American hostility. Tensions that had previously been confined primarily to Europe now engulfed Asia. North Korea's attack on the South triggered a swift American response. Seeing Stalin's hand in North Korean leader Kim Il Sung's decision to invade, Harry Truman's Democratic administration cast aside its earlier reluctance to intervene in Asian crises and moved to meet the communist challenge in East Asia.[2] Its decision to despatch American forces to Korea under the auspices of the United Nations (UN) was destined to profoundly affect American policy in Asia and the regional balance of power.

In the short term, the war did not immediately shift Washington's strategic priorities towards Asia. On the contrary, it prompted the

United States to reaffirm its commitment to European defence lest Korea be a ploy orchestrated by Moscow to divert the West's attention away from Europe.[3] In the long run, however, it resulted in the growing involvement of the United States in Asia, culminating in the American military intervention in Vietnam a decade later. The early 1950s, therefore, established a significant trend in this regard. Between 1950 and 1953, the Truman administration took various incremental steps to contain regional communism. It adopted an extensive programme of national rearmament, established a network of regional alliances and provided military assistance to non-communist Asian states.[4]

These measures, taken in response to Moscow's and Beijing's efforts to expand communist influence in Asia, only momentarily dampened Sino-Soviet ambitions. In the early 1950s, with the Soviet Union recognising China's leadership of the Asian revolutionary movement, Mao Zedong's radical credentials received a significant boost.[5] Mao saw the promotion of anti-imperialist regional revolutions and the support of local communist parties as 'an ideological and political imperative.'[6] In his view, only the radical transformation of world politics and the establishment of friendly communist regimes on China's periphery would allow it to consolidate its domestic revolution and improve its external security.[7] Mao's willingness to back Kim's adventurism and his decision to economically and militarily aid the Viet Minh in their struggle against French rule in Indochina must be understood in this context.[8] At the same time, his desire to place China at the forefront of the Asian revolution, enhance its standing within the communist bloc and bolster its regional strategic position put him on a collision course with the United States, stoking American anxieties about China's militant regional role. The stage was set for a protracted clash of ideologies and interests between the United States and its communist adversaries.

India and the Early Cold War

Against its will, newly independent India was caught in the crossfire of tensions between opposing ideological blocs. Understandably,

Jawaharlal Nehru, India's first prime minister and foreign minister (he would hold both positions until his death in 1964), reacted with growing unease to these tensions. He had good reasons to dislike what he saw. Strained relations between warring blocs threatened to derail his government's plans to promote domestic economic development and social change by forcing India to divert its limited financial resources towards military spending.[9] He was deeply committed to India's economic and social advancement through democratic means, which he saw as critical to the country's stability and prosperity.[10] As mounting bipolar tensions compelled Asian nations to choose sides, he worried that war between opposing camps would become more likely (and potentially more destructive with the advent of the atomic bomb). Growing instability on its doorstep was the last thing a nation striving to break free from the shackles of poverty and weld a fragmented region into a viable democracy needed.[11] Yet, Nehru was concerned about more than just bipolar tensions. He also feared that superpower competition might have other undesired consequences, such as the continuation of European colonial rule in Asia. America's increasing support for France's military effort in Indochina had alerted him to the danger of Cold War realpolitik giving colonialism a new lease of life. He could see how American aid to non-communist Asian states might turn them into de facto US colonies and give rise to Western neo-colonial domination of Asia.[12]

Since India's independence, Nehru had been firmly opposed to any foreign power exercising covert or neo-imperial control over India.[13] Regarding foreign rule as immoral, exploitative and ultimately harmful,[14] he found it 'intolerable,' as he would put it in 1955, that Afro-Asian nations 'should come out of bondage into freedom only to degrade themselves' by joining military alliances with the West.[15] Accordingly, he had criticised Washington's backing of Taiwan and the establishment of defence pacts with the Philippines (1951) and South Korea (1953).[16] Moreover, he considered American and, more broadly, Western policy in Asia incompatible with his goal of eradicating a Western military presence in Asia.[17] Nehru's regional vision was informed by his belief that Asian powers 'had a role to play in promoting peace in their own region.'[18] By declaring in his inaugural address to the March 1947 Asian Relations Conference in New Delhi that Asians no longer wished to be 'petitioners in Western courts and chancelleries,' Nehru staked his claim for a major role in shaping Asia's future.[19] He viewed India as destined 'to play a very great part in the security problems of Asia and the Indian Ocean.'[20] In brief, Cold War tensions put Nehru's vision of a safer and fairer regional (and global) order at risk. They also went against much of what he stood for: non-alignment, opposition to colonialism and the rejection of power politics, spheres of influence and military power.[21] As a result, he did not shy away from denouncing the intense hostility that marked relations between the two superpowers and their respective blocs.

To escape this unrelenting bipolar logic, Nehru doggedly avoided aligning his country with either of the two contending camps, thus elevating non-alignment to the veritable guiding principle of his foreign policy. Frequently confused with neutrality or equidistance between the two blocs, Nehru's non-alignment entailed neither sitting on the fence nor refraining from choosing sides in international disputes.[22] It meant that India remained 'unaligned,' 'uncommitted to blocs' and eager to 'avoid entanglements,' and did not necessarily rule out some occasional tilting to one side.[23] Nehru's non-alignment resulted from a combination of pragmatic and principled considerations.[24] He once told his sister, Vijaya Lakshmi Pandit, that India had 'to steer a middle course not merely because of expediency but also because we consider it the right course.'[25] According to him, such a middle course would put New Delhi 'in a far better position to cast [its] weight at the right moment in favour of peace,' the preservation of which he and other Congress leaders viewed as a moral imperative.[26] At the same time, it would also allow India to avoid 'put[ting] all [its] eggs in one basket,' both politically and economically.[27] On a political level, India's refusal to join military alliances would allow it to maintain its freedom of manoeuvre in international affairs—a privilege Nehru had no intention of relinquishing now that his nation had attained independence.[28] For him, India's non-alignment was the acid test of its independence.[29] In addition to that, a no-entanglements policy would make it possible for India to 'go farther in gaining security than almost anything else.'[30]

In this respect, Nehru regarded non-alignment as 'the best contribution that a weak, but supposedly powerful, India could make towards maintaining the balance of power between the Soviet and Western blocs.'[31] Moreover, he saw it as a necessary step to avoid giving the two communist land powers a pretext 'to invade India alone or as part of a general attack against the non-communist world.'[32] A factor often forgotten is that, for Nehru, non-alignment was also a means of taking the wind out of the sails of India's homegrown communists through his government's conciliatory approach to the Soviet Union and China.[33] In the economic field, Nehru anticipated that a non-aligned posture would stimulate greater competition between the two blocs, causing them to expand their technical and economic assistance to India.[34] This competition would, in turn, stop the Indian economy from getting increasingly entangled with Western capitalism while forcing the West to pay greater attention to India's needs.[35] Consequently, it would also strengthen India's negotiating position with Western countries.[36]

Nehru's refusal to take sides won him little kudos in Washington and Moscow. Nor did his attempts to act as an intermediary between the Americans and the Chinese in Korea shield him from criticism from either side. These efforts only partially allowed him to defuse tensions between the warring factions. The Americans, Russians and Chinese regarded non-alignment with suspicion, although both the Soviet Union and China would eventually tone down their misgivings towards India.[37] In the Soviet Union, Joseph Stalin's attitude towards India oscillated between coolness and hostility in the immediate post-war years.[38] Although Stalin's negative view of India had softened by the early 1950s, New Delhi's relations with Moscow had failed to gain traction.[39] Stalin deeply mistrusted non-communist nationalist leaders like Nehru, regarding them as reactionaries and agents of the West.[40] In this context, India's decision to remain in the British Commonwealth did little to change Moscow's perception of New Delhi as 'merely a tool of the "Anglo-American imperialists".'[41] In Stalin's eyes, the presence of foreign capital in India provided further 'proof of [India's] vassal status.'[42] Lastly, the fact that in the immediate post-war years, the Governor-General of India, the chiefs of its armed forces, various governors of provinces and high-ranking officials were all Britons 'baffled Soviet leaders.'[43]

India's relations with the People's Republic of China (PRC) were no better than those with the Soviet Union. Despite India's recognition of Mao's regime in December 1949 and its support for the PRC's right to the Chinese seat in the UN Security Council, there was little warmth between New Delhi and Beijing in the early 1950s.[44] Much like their Soviet allies, the Chinese communists initially treated India with contempt.[45] Nehru's outspoken anti-colonial rhetoric and frequent outbursts against the West had not won over Beijing more than they had Moscow.[46] Mao had also condemned India's efforts to cast itself as the 'voice of Asia,' brushing off Indian diplomacy as an instrument of the Americans.[47] Even though, in May 1950, Mao waxed lyrical with K. M. Panikkar, India's first ambassador to the PRC, about the 'warm friendship' and 'deep sympathy' that had 'always existed between the two peoples,' his true feelings were quite different.[48] A few months before, he had written to the Communist Party of India (CPI), expressing hope that it would free India from 'the yoke of imperialism and its collaborators.'[49] In the same year, Liu Shaoqi, Mao's second in command, had described countries like India as semi-colonies that needed to be liberated from the chokehold of European imperialism.[50] Moreover, Beijing-controlled media and Chinese political propaganda had repeatedly hurled crude epithets like 'stooge' or 'running dog of the West' at Nehru.[51] To complicate matters, Chinese Communist Party (CCP) leaders were also suspicious of what they regarded as Indian colonial designs on Tibet, Bhutan and Nepal.[52] In other words, even though Chinese diplomacy towards India displayed, overall, more flexibility than Stalin's, Beijing was reluctant to reciprocate Nehru's efforts to foster closer relations.[53] The following episode, perhaps, captures better than most the nature of India's complex relationship with China in the early 1950s. Writing to Nehru in March 1953 about Beijing's displeasure with India's role in the Korean crisis, the Indian ambassador in Beijing, Nedyam Raghavan, reported that 'Chinese behaviour continue[d] to be cold' despite his best 'efforts to revive friendly relations.' A perplexed Raghavan could not but regret that he did 'not know when and how far [he] shall succeed; with the

Chinese one has to have an infinite capacity for patience. Our files here show that that was our experience even previously.'[54]

In the United States, policymakers were better disposed towards India, viewing it as the symbol of a post-colonial Asia friendly to the West.[55] After its initial neglect of India, the Truman administration came to view it as a possible alternative to the loss of Nationalist China as America's major potential partner in Asia.[56] However, frustration with New Delhi soon set in in Washington. Apart from Nehru's tendency to criticise the United States more readily than the two communist powers, Washington resented his non-alignment and failure to draw any appreciable distinction between a democratic America and totalitarian regimes like the Soviet Union and China.[57] The Truman administration had expected Nehru to share its concerns about the expansionist nature of communism and hoped India could play an important role in containing Soviet and Chinese communism. As a result, the Americans put pressure on him to abandon what they saw as a cavalier attitude to communism and pay more attention to their concerns. To their dismay, Nehru did not share their threat perceptions—at least not to the same extent. Whereas the United States saw itself as the leader of the free world against communist totalitarianism, Nehru's India, 'just emerging from British colonial rule, defined its role as the spokesman of Asia with responsibility to assist smaller countries still struggling against European powers.'[58] The fact that India was a liberal democracy and Nehru was genuinely committed to the democratic method did not necessarily predispose him to follow Washington's lead, as the Americans erroneously thought.

In contrast to the American view that both the Soviet and Chinese brands of communism represented a serious danger to regional security, Nehru concluded that neither posed an imminent threat to India. In early 1951, he told a perplexed Loy Henderson, the American ambassador in New Delhi, that 'he was not convinced of inherent aggressiveness [of] international communism' and that it was India's policy to 'endeavour [to] restore confidence and convince each side [the] other had no aggressive intentions.'[59] In any case, he believed that the best way to prevent the spread of communism was 'to make the newly emerging non-Communist nations economically sound and socially stable.'[60] A few weeks later, talking to the visiting assistant secretary of state of the United States, George McGhee, he conceded that 'Russia had aggressive and expansionist designs.' However, he went on to blame the West for that, arguing that 'Russia is what she is today largely because of the way nations isolated her when young. Same mistake [is] being made today with China.'[61] Nehru, of course, was no communist, despite his admission that Marxism-Leninism had had a profound influence on his thinking and his admiration for Soviet accomplishments in economic planning, education, development and healthcare.[62] A socialist and a firm believer in democracy, he conceptually rejected Soviet totalitarianism.[63] Domestically, his government had firmly clamped down on the activities of the Indian communists.[64] That said, he was not unsympathetic to the Soviet Union. A blend of nationalism and socialism, his worldview 'stemmed from his anticolonial internationalism,' according to which 'anti-imperialists including the Soviet Union and the colonies had collectively sought to challenge imperialism.'[65] In other words, Nehru could simply 'not imagine the country as an imperialist power.'[66]

Nehru's approach to China was equally complex and somewhat ambivalent. Although he reacted with alarm to the arrival of Chinese troops on the Indian-Tibetan border in October 1950, he refused to view the re-imposition of Chinese authority over Tibet as an impending threat to India's national security.[67] With India and China sharing a 2,000-mile frontier, Nehru concluded that the only possible policy was one of accommodation and engagement. In 1952, he told the new American ambassador to India, Chester Bowles, that India had 'only two alternatives' in the long term: either 'to build up a military force which would enable him to speak on terms of equality with China' or 'to seek a *modus vivendi* for co-existence with China.' The first alternative, however, was problematic, as it 'would mean putting a bigger and bigger proportion of the Indian national income into armaments, and that would mean abandoning the Five-Year Plan and the other improvements he has promised to the Indian people.' 'This,' he claimed, was neither 'practical politics' nor 'necessary.' In his view, coexistence with China was 'attainable.'[68] The year before, Nehru had told Bowles that it was 'quite possible the new China [would] develop into [an] explosive dangerous force.' Yet, 'there was at least a good chance that [the] future development of China [could] be guided into different channels' if India, the United States and the free world adopted 'a policy of keeping China's door open.'[69] In other words, Nehru was adamant that if communist China could be brought out of isolation and integrated into the international system, it would be more likely to show moderation.[70] That is why he supported the PRC's entry into the UN and did not brand it as an aggressor in Korea.[71] Similarly, he did not regard China as 'a camp follower of Russia.'[72] In 1953, he said to John Foster Dulles, the US secretary of state, that '[a]lmost assuredly Communist China will divorce itself from Soviet Russia within 15 or 25 years. Already the ties are weakened by the death of Stalin.'[73]

What's more, Nehru appeared to believe that India and China were sister countries and that the Chinese communists were Asian nationalists who shared a similar sense of Asianness and anti-colonialism as India, born out of their encounters with European imperialism.[74] In this respect, his participation as the representative of the Indian National Congress at the 1927 Brussels Congress against Colonial Oppression and Imperialism and for National Independence had a deep and long-lasting impact on his perception of China.[75] Not only did it awaken his interest in the country, but it also led him to believe that what happened there would have significant implications for India 'for reasons to do with geography, ideology and civilizational values.'[76] Furthermore, it persuaded him that India and China were two ancient civilisations and great Asian nations that shared many similarities. As such, they were destined to become natural allies in the struggle to restore Asia to its proper place in international affairs—a belief he maintained even after Mao seized power in 1949.[77]

Unfortunately, as has been noted, Nehru's optimistic predisposition towards China was not 'the product of a clear or profound understanding.'[78] He constantly misjudged the role of ideology in Chinese foreign policymaking, tending to overlook the fact that Chinese leaders were ardent revolutionaries committed to the radical transformation of international politics.[79] Yet, at other times, he could also be pessimistic about China. As he once admitted to B. N. Mullik, the head of India's Intelligence Bureau, 'all through history China had been an aggressive country' and was now 'governed by very aggressive leaders.' He was certain that once it achieved economic and political stability, it would seek to expand its 'influence and leadership, if not political suzerainty, over Asia.'[80] For the time being, however, Nehru was inclined to rule out an outright Chinese assault on India. His rationale was essentially threefold. First, a Chinese military offensive would drag other powers into the conflict.[81] Second, the inhospitable Himalayas would make any large-scale attack all but impossible.[82] Third, he assumed that the Chinese communists 'were full of their own problems, which were terrific' and 'there was no point at all in their indulging in rash adventures.'[83] At any rate, the Secretary-General of the Indian Ministry of External Affairs (MEA), G. S. Bajpai, told the Americans that India would, as a measure of precaution, 'continue to talk softly on [the] subject [of] Communist China.'[84]

India and the First Steps Towards Peaceful Coexistence

Instead of viewing Sino-Soviet communism as incompatible with India's regional interests, Nehru came to the perplexing conclusion that American containment was the primary threat to regional stability. He believed that Washington's expanding military presence in Asia to counter Soviet and Chinese influence would inevitably lead to tensions—so much so that he seemed more anxious to restrain American power than contain regional communism. In September 1953, he criticised Washington's 'strong policy' of 'looking as fierce and ferocious as possible' and 'threatening everybody,' as well as its 'great immaturity in thinking or understanding.'[85] He likened American (and, more broadly, Western) attitudes to communism to the unhealthy passions unleashed by the Crusades of medieval Europe or conflicts such as the Thirty Years War or the Hundred Years War.[86] Moreover, Nehru, like many other Asian nationalists, found it difficult to differentiate between the United States and the European colonial powers—a fact duly noted by a frustrated Dulles in May 1954 when he lamented to the Senate Foreign Relations Committee that the Americans 'were called Europeans in much of the world …

Whenever we go in the world, if we work in cooperation with the British, we are tarred by the same brush.'[87]

Shifting Soviet and Chinese attitudes towards the Cold War reinforced Nehru's pessimistic view of America's regional role. Stalin's death on 5 March 1953 led to a significant reappraisal in Soviet foreign policy. The Kremlin's 'collective leadership,' which succeeded Stalin, gradually shifted emphasis away from Stalin's 'two-camps theory' towards peaceful coexistence, a transition that would be fully accomplished under Nikita Khrushchev.[88] Shortly after Stalin's death, Soviet Prime Minister Georgy Malenkov launched what became known as the 'peace offensive' when he declared, in reference to the United States, that there were no disputes that could not 'be settled peacefully by mutual agreement of the interested countries.'[89] To be sure, early Soviet calls to defuse Cold War tensions did not represent a fundamental shift in Moscow's overall Cold War strategy. The Soviet Union had no intention of abandoning its revolutionary mission or burying its rivalry with the West. Rather, by rejecting the twin Leninist principles of the inevitability of war between capitalism and socialism and violent revolution as a precondition for establishing socialism, Moscow hoped to reduce the risk of nuclear war by confining its rivalry with the West to the political, economic and technological realms. And nowhere was this tactical shift more noticeable than in the Afro-Asian world, where, under Khrushchev, the Soviet Union would embark on a political offensive to win over local national-bourgeois movements.[90] Although Moscow's wooing of the Third World would not begin in earnest until the second half of the 1950s, its early signs were already visible in 1953.[91] In August of that year, Malenkov made Moscow's first truly positive remarks about India, praising its efforts to bring peace to Korea and wishing for its relations with the Soviet Union to 'grow stronger and develop in a spirit of friendly cooperation.'[92] At the same time, the Soviet press ceased its criticism of India and things Indian.[93] That a change of attitude was afoot was not lost on Western observers: in April 1953, the US Department of State called attention to the fact that in New Delhi, the Soviet Ambassador, Kirill Novikov, and his wife 'suddenly evinced a far more amiable attitude toward Indian officials and diplomatic colleagues than they have recently shown.'[94] A year later, a new Soviet ambassador to India, Mikhail Menshikov, would convey to Nehru Moscow's desire for closer political ties.[95]

Given its acceptance of Moscow's ideological leadership, Beijing, too, embraced peaceful coexistence.[96] Bloc loyalty was not its only reason for doing so. In fact, by late 1952, the CCP leadership had already begun calling for a reduction of global tensions, signalling a desire to abandon its earlier revolutionary radicalism in favour of a more accommodating foreign policy stance.[97] Faced with a protracted stalemate in Korea, a war-weary China badly needed peace on its frontiers to improve its economic situation.[98] The PRC had paid a high price in blood and treasure for its Korean military adventure, and its economic reconstruction had lagged behind as a result.[99] To make matters worse, the war had increased Beijing's dependence on Moscow, infuriated Washington and frightened China's Asian neighbours.[100] As a result, Beijing's priorities shifted to economic reconstruction at home and a reduction of hostilities abroad.[101] However, as they focused on rebuilding the economy and promoting revolutionary change at home, Mao and his comrades discovered that lower tensions with the West could bring an additional advantage. Mao and the CCP leaders understood that by allowing China to consolidate its gains in Korea and Indochina, where the Viet Minh had forced the French into the defensive thanks to Chinese military assistance, peaceful coexistence could turn these gains into an effective tool of internal propaganda and mobilisation.[102] Lastly, like Moscow, Beijing came to view peaceful coexistence as a chance to reach out to the developing world and increase its influence and prestige there at the West's expense.[103] It is no coincidence that, by the end of 1952, the CPP leadership had already raised with Stalin the possibility of signing non-aggression treaties with India and Burma and discussed the opportunity posed by Nehru's visit to China with the Indian ambassador in Beijing.[104] In pursuing its engagement with the Afro-Asian world, the CCP leadership would embark on 'united front' tactics to organise an anti-Western movement among sympathetic Afro-Asian nations.[105] To that end, Beijing would work hard in the coming years to portray itself as a friendly developing country that shared with many other Afro-Asian nations not only the 'same experiences with and concerns about Western imperialism' but also similar economic problems.[106] That said, the CCP leaders never saw peaceful coexistence as a rejection of their plans to export revolutions abroad; rather, it was meant 'to create better conditions for China to serve as a supporting base for the world revolution.'[107] In other words, peaceful coexistence was merely a 'tactical tool' to be employed while China was 'readying the world for revolution.'[108]

In India, this emerging shift in Soviet and Chinese foreign policy did not pass unnoticed, but the Indian government chose to move cautiously.[109] In mid-1953, the US Department of State remarked that 'Moscow's new "peace policy" was received with only moderate enthusiasm' in India.[110] The Indian diplomatic establishment was sceptical about the desirability of befriending a communist state committed to world revolution.[111] Yet, for all the Indian government's initial circumspection, Moscow's tentative shift towards peaceful coexistence provided an opportunity to facilitate understanding with India, whose prime minister had repeatedly called for a 'climate of peace' and a reduction in bipolar tensions.[112] Malenkov's statement on 19 September conveying Moscow's wish for the Korean armistice to serve as 'a point of departure for new efforts aimed at lessening international tensions in the entire world, and notably in the Far East' must have pleased Nehru.[113] And so, as 1953 progressed, Soviet-Indian relations gradually thawed.[114] In July, the Soviet Union earmarked 4 million roubles to the UN Expanded Programme of Technical Assistance for projects in developing countries.[115] Five months later, the two nations agreed to a 5-year trade and payments agreement, which promised to increase bilateral trade.[116] No less significant was the fact that as many as fourteen Indian delegations of sportsmen, film artists and industrialists travelled to Moscow in the 18 months following Stalin's death.[117] At about the same time, India's relations with China began to improve noticeably. In April 1953, Beijing sought Indian help to round off the Korean armistice talks.[118] In August, Zhou Enlai indicated to the Indian ambassador in Beijing that Asian nations should resolve their differences if they wanted to stop American penetration in the region.[119] In December, India began negotiations with China to settle 'all matters pending between the two countries with regard to their relations in Tibet,' except for the border question.[120] In Tibet, India still enjoyed rights and privileges inherited from the British Raj, including the right to maintain a small military contingent at Gyantse to protect trade routes between India and Tibet.[121] As we shall see in Chapter 3, these negotiations would result in the signing of the 1954 Agreement on Trade and Intercourse between the Tibet Region of China and India, which would have significant implications for Sino-Indian relations and Nehru's approach to regional security.

The Cold War on India's Doorstep

As the Indian government moved to improve ties with the Soviet Union and China, its relations with the United States experienced significant turbulence. India reacted to the election of a new Republican administration led by Dwight Eisenhower with a mixture of disappointment and concern.[122] The strong anti-communist rhetoric of the Eisenhower campaign and the future president's pledge to pursue Washington's policy of containment more forcefully than his Democrat predecessor struck Indians as both belligerent and dangerous.[123] The appointment of the dour and hawkish John Foster Dulles to the position of secretary of state was especially troubling. As American historian Robert McMahon has noted, Nehru saw Dulles as 'an anti-communist ideologue unsympathetic to the stirrings of Asian nationalism.'[124] Political sympathies also mattered. Despite periodic disagreements with the Truman administration, the Indian government had come to accept that 'a coalition of liberal Democrats in Congress had consistently expressed strong support for India and had worked hard to gain more economic assistance for India.'[125] Dulles, too, considered American economic and financial assistance to India critical to India's domestic stability and survival as a democratic and anti-communist bulwark in Asia.[126] However, the Eisenhower administration was less inclined to defer to Indian sensibilities, as India quickly discovered. Washington would respond 'much more slowly' than Nehru would have desired to Moscow and Beijing's shift towards peaceful coexistence.[127] Moreover, and even more frustratingly, it was committed to fulfilling Eisenhower's campaign pledges and 'was in no mood to be equivocal about American intentions in Asia.'[128] As Dulles made clear in March 1953, it was the duty of the United States to stand firm against communist expansionism and 'hold the vital outpost positions around the periphery of the Soviet bloc,' namely 'Japan, Indo-China, India, Pakistan, Iran and NATO.' Failure to do so would produce a 'chain reaction' that would undermine American strength and influence in these regions. Even though Dulles thought the communist powers would not risk a full-scale war to seize these areas, he still expected them to use subversion to gain control.[129] In this context, two specific actions taken by the United States greatly alarmed Nehru. The first was Washington's decision to begin defence talks with India's sworn enemy, Pakistan. The second, as we shall see in Chapter 2, was Washington's increased military assistance to the French war effort in Indochina—a step that also deeply alarmed Nehru because of its destabilising effects.[130]

Even before the Eisenhower administration took office, the American ambassador in New Delhi, Chester Bowles, had warned Washington that 'if we insist on going ahead willy-nilly with this approach [i.e., the pursuit of a defence relationship with Pakistan], I think I can safely prophesy the future course of events here in India.' 'There is,' he added, 'not the slightest chance that the [Indian] Government will show any increased sympathy for Communism regardless of what we do. This government is sharply and vigorously anti-Communist.'[131] Indeed, in 1952, the Truman administration had begun to view Pakistan as the 'eastern anchor' of a 'northern tier' of anti-communist Middle Eastern and West Asian nations stretching from Pakistan to Turkey.[132] Keen to prevent Soviet penetration in the Middle East, the Truman administration had looked to these states to shore up Western defences in the region.[133] However, given Pakistan's strained relationship with India, the former's participation in any pro-Western defence arrangement was always likely to cause friction with New Delhi. When the Indians learned in late 1953 that the United States intended to negotiate a bilateral defence agreement with Pakistan, they were outraged, as Bowles had predicted. Already in late 1952, India had reacted angrily to rumours of Western plans to include Pakistan in a tentative Middle East defence arrangement.[134]

In the summer of 1953, however, the new Eisenhower administration was confident enough that it would be able to ride out Indian resentment because of New Delhi's desire for substantial American economic aid to fund its ambitious developmental plans.[135] After touring South Asia and the Middle East in the spring of 1953, Dulles urged Washington to go ahead with the formation of a Middle Eastern pact. The US secretary of state, who was 'immensely impressed by the martial and religious characteristics of the Pakistanis,' viewed Pakistan as a potential source of American strength.[136] In June, the National Security Council (NSC) agreed to focus on 'building a defence in the area based on the northern tier, including Pakistan, Iran, Iraq, Syria and Turkey.'[137] A month later, it decided to develop secret plans for the defence of that area and seek, whenever politically possible, the 'participation in such an organization ... of such other Asian and African states, particularly Pakistan, as might contribute to the security and stability of the Near East.' In this context, the United States should offer limited military aid and assist in the development of indigenous forces capable of improving 'political stability, internal security, and the maintenance of pro-Western regimes,' as well as ultimately contributing to the defence of that area.[138] These plans would result in the formation of the Middle East Treaty Organisation, or the Baghdad Pact, two years later. With the (by then lukewarm) blessing of the United States, it brought together Britain, Pakistan, Iran, Iraq and Turkey into a mutual security agreement to prevent Soviet penetration in the Middle East.[139]

By the summer of 1953, negotiations for a bilateral defence agreement with Pakistan were underway. As part of a goodwill trip to the Far East and South Asia, Vice President Richard Nixon flew to Karachi in December 1953 to discuss the details with the Pakistani government led by Mohammed Ali Bogra.[140] During Nixon's stopover in New Delhi, Nehru voiced his 'serious personal concerns' regarding the possibility of American assistance to Pakistan. He warned Nixon that if Washington carried out its plans, 'all the ground gained in developing friendly relations between India and the US would be lost.'[141] Less than a month earlier, Nehru had bitterly complained to U Nu, the Burmese prime minister, that the US government was 'so obsessed with anti-communism' and its policy 'so governed by military factors' that it ignored everything else.[142] According to Nehru, the Eisenhower administration's rigid approach to the Cold War issues had frustrated tentative Soviet and Chinese moves towards peaceful coexistence with the West.[143] India's objections, however, failed to persuade the Americans to change their minds. Also unsuccessful were the warnings sent by George V. Allen, the new US ambassador in New Delhi.[144] In October, the embassy had recommended a 're-examination [of the] method of supplying aid,' informing the State Department that India's response would not only be 'bitter and vigorous' but would also 'color and perhaps change [the] course of United States–India relationship for [a] long time to come.'[145] Rather presciently, Allen warned Washington that American military aid to Pakistan might also 'cause India to lean more towards the Soviet bloc,' a shift that would eventually occur following Nehru's visit to the Soviet Union in June 1955 and Khrushchev's and Nikolai Bulganin's tour of India 5 months later.[146] Indeed, in late 1953, some of Nehru's senior officials had advised him 'to consider entering into non-aggression pacts with the Soviets and the Chinese' while also seeking Soviet assistance to boost India's military capabilities.[147] Dulles was unfazed. He argued that, on balance, the advantages of going ahead with providing military aid to Pakistan outweighed its disadvantages. He believed a defence agreement with Pakistan would benefit regional security no matter what New Delhi said. The fact that Pakistan and Turkey had agreed to a bilateral security arrangement in exchange for Washington's military assistance to Pakistan was thus worth the risk of incurring India's wrath.[148] Both Dulles and the Department of Defence viewed a Turkish-Pakistani defence pact as a necessary first step towards forming a Middle Eastern alliance that would also include Iran and Iraq.[149] As Dulles put it, such a treaty would 'be of military value' and 'provide the framework of collective security which would help to justify extension of aid to Pakistan and minimize adverse repercussions in India and elsewhere.'[150]

In February 1954, the Eisenhower administration publicly announced its decision to go forward with military aid to Pakistan—a move later formalised by the so-called Mutual Defense Assistance Agreement (MDAA) of May 1954. This decision was to turn Pakistan into a linchpin of Washington's regional containment strategy and

'America's most allied ally in Asia,' as a future leader of Pakistan would later put it.[151] The US administration went out of its way to reassure Nehru that closer defence ties between the United States and Pakistan were not directed against India. President Eisenhower told the Indian prime minister that if military aid were 'misused or directed against another in aggression,' the United States would take 'immediate action, both within and without [the] UN, to thwart such aggression.' Eisenhower also assured him that any 'request by India for military aid would receive most sympathetic consideration.'[152] Nehru, however, considered such assurances meaningless. It 'was like promising to scoop up spilt milk,' he complained to the visiting Canadian Prime Minister, Louis St. Laurent.[153] In explaining his opposition to Washington's decision, Nehru emphasised the 'far-reaching' and 'powerful' impact that US plans for 'the building up of Pakistan as a great military centre' would have on India.[154] His concerns were justified. In the decade that followed, the Pakistani Army received substantial military aid, enabling it to equip one armoured division, four infantry divisions and one armoured brigade. The Pakistani Air Force and Navy also secured significant American hardware, with the former receiving jets for six squadrons and the latter getting twelve ships.[155] Nehru had little doubt that Pakistan wanted to increase its military strength, first, to use it 'as a bargaining factor in dealing with India' and, second, to wage 'war on India' if necessary.[156] He feared rearmament might tempt Karachi to seek a military solution to the vexed question of Kashmir.[157]

But Nehru's concerns about American military aid to Pakistan went beyond its harmful repercussions for the balance of power in the Indian subcontinent. The Cold War, he argued, would 'come right up to India's frontiers' if Pakistan became 'a satellite of America with US bases and crowds of Americans all over the place.'[158] He complained that Karachi's alignment with Washington ran against the approach followed by India and other Asian nations of avoiding Cold War entanglements in order to 'preserve an area of peace.' In his view, Cold War alignments were 'most unfortunate.' 'Apart from the danger of extending the sphere of war,' they 'would inevitably bring in powerful outside influences,' limiting the freedom of recently independent Asian nations.[159] His list of grievances did not end there, however. Military assistance to Pakistan, he went on, would entrench the already 'dominating influence' of the Pakistani Army domestically and raise the likelihood of military coups in that country.[160] In India, it would also generate tensions between Hindus and Muslims. Muslim extremists would view the rearmament of Pakistan as an opportunity for the 'renewal of Muslim domination in India,' while Hindu militants would demand 'all sorts of military preparations by India.'[161] Finally, he assumed that by making Pakistan a centrepiece of its Asian strategy, the United States hoped to 'have completely outflanked India's so-called neutralism' and 'thus bring India to her knees.' Yet, '[w]hatever the future may hold,' as he defiantly told K. M. Panikkar, 'this will not happen.'[162] Nehru's prediction proved accurate. Far from forcing India to reconsider its policy of non-alignment, Pakistan's emerging alliance with the United States was to stiffen Nehru's resolve to stick to his guns and harden his criticism of American policy in Asia.

However, as Nehru was still smarting from the news that Washington would move forward with its defence deal with Pakistan, a spiralling crisis in Indochina intervened to heighten Indian fears that anti-communist 'hysteria' might 'cause [the United States] to precipitate [an] all-out holy war or crusade.'[163] As Chapter 2 shows, concerns over France's deteriorating military situation in Indochina spurred the Eisenhower administration to seek ways to alleviate Paris's predicament and stiffen its resolve to fight. In response to the military gains made by the Viet Minh at Dien Bien Phu in the spring of 1954, Dulles proposed the formation of a regional defence grouping to prevent further communist gains in South-East Asia. He also alluded to the possibility of armed intervention alongside America's closest regional allies. Dulles's moves deeply alarmed Nehru and his senior officials. The Indian government concluded that the United States was determined 'to engage in a trial of strength against the Soviet Union and China and make an example of Indochina.'[164] With Dulles clearly in mind, Nehru bitterly complained that '[u]nfortunately, American policy in the East has got tied up with some elements which not only do not inspire respect but are considered completely reactionary.'[165] The combined effect of these two crises—Indochina and the question of US military aid to Pakistan—

would, in due course, compel Nehru to act as a counterbalance to American containment and promote a distinctly different vision of regional order and security, centred on his concept of areas of peace and what became known as the Five Principles of Peaceful Coexistence.[166] However, to appreciate the depth of Nehru's concerns and his disdain for the Eisenhower administration's policy in Asia, it is now necessary to examine in some detail the unfolding of the Indochina crisis and its implications for India's regional policy.

2

THE INDOCHINA CRISIS

The major problem in the world … was the continuing problem of the 'cold war' between two blocs of big and powerful countries.

Jawaharlal Nehru[1]

The world situation is developing very rapidly and in this context our policy is opposed to US policy.

Jawaharlal Nehru[2]

In the spring of 1954, as it moved to secure Pakistan's support for its containment strategy in West Asia, the Eisenhower administration was confronted with the prospect of a French military defeat in Indochina. In mid-March 1954, the French garrison at Dien Bien Phu came under intense attack from overwhelming Viet Minh forces. Surrounded by low mountains, the valley of Dien Bien Phu sat along a route linking North Vietnam to neighbouring Laos, only 20 miles to its east. In 1953, the Commander in Chief of the French Union Forces in Indochina, General Henri Navarre, had chosen this remote location in the highlands of north-west Tonkin to build a heavily fortified garrison to protect Laos from a Viet Minh invasion.[3] By manning the garrison with 12,000 elite troops—supported by artillery, aircraft and an airstrip that would have permitted resupply in case of need—the French High Command also intended to draw the Viet Minh into a major set piece battle in the hope of inflicting significant losses on the enemy.[4] The government of Joseph Laniel was eager to extricate itself from an 8-year-long colonial conflict that had already claimed the lives of thousands of French Union soldiers and depleted French finances. A victory over numerically superior Viet Minh forces could allow France to negotiate an end to the war from a position of strength.[5] In February 1954, at a four-power conference in Berlin, France had secured agreement from the United States, the Soviet Union and Britain to have the question of Indochina placed on the agenda of a forthcoming conference in Geneva at the end of April.[6] The French were reasonably confident of defeating the Viet Minh in open battle and holding Dien Bien Phu despite Navarre harbouring some doubts.[7]

However, when Viet Minh forces opened hostilities on 13 March 1954, the French were in for a rude awakening. Through sheer resolve and a major logistical effort, the Viet Minh were able to transport their artillery up the hills surrounding the valley, from where they began pounding the garrison mercilessly.[8] From that moment on, the French plan unravelled rapidly. Heavy shelling quickly wrecked the airfield, making resupply dependent on parachute drops.[9] Within fewer than 10 days from the outbreak of hostilities, the situation had deteriorated to the point where French General Paul Ely, Chief of Staff of the French Joint Chiefs of Staff, rated French chances of holding out at fifty–fifty.[10] French requests for additional American military aid—only a few weeks before, the administration had agreed to send the French forty bombers and 200 technicians to service them—remained largely unanswered.[11] Ely's visit to Washington on 20–25 April only served to secure a loan of an extra twenty-five bombers.[12] On the battlefield, though, the worst was yet to come. On 30 March, the Viet Minh upped the ante by launching a series of human-wave attacks and subjecting the French garrison to further heavy artillery fire.[13] The French Union forces suffered severe casualties. In France, an increasingly war-weary public and a restless political class renewed pressure on the government to seek a negotiated end to the war or to begin a unilateral withdrawal.[14]

The Eisenhower Administration Steps in

The prospect of a sudden French departure from Indochina deeply troubled the Eisenhower administration. Since assuming office, it had accepted Truman's assessment of Indochina's strategic importance, emphasising the necessity to keep it in anti-communist hands.[15] In the spring of 1953, senior officials had gone as far as to suggest that Indochina was 'in some ways' even 'more important than Korea' because the ripple effect of its loss 'could not be localized' and 'would spread throughout Asia and Europe.'[16] But as Indochina rose in prominence in American strategic calculations, the Eisenhower administration grew increasingly frustrated with the half-hearted way it believed the French were fighting the Viet Minh.[17] Even before Dien Bien Phu came under siege, there had been a growing feeling in Washington that 'the United States could not stand idly by if the threat of a Communist Indo-China became acute.'[18] However, now that the threat was fast materialising, the US administration found itself in a bind. On the one hand, abandoning the French to their fate meant handing over the country to the Viet Minh—no doubt an embarrassing admission of failure after all the military aid the United States had given to France since 1950.[19] On the other hand, rescuing the French would lead to a more direct American military involvement in the conflict—something President Eisenhower was reluctant to do just months after the Korean armistice in July 1953. In the spring of 1954, while ruling out the despatch of ground troops to Indochina, Washington was forced to consider deploying air and naval forces to save the embattled French garrison at Dien Bien Phu. However, such a course of action carried the risk of drawing the Chinese into the conflict on the Viet Minh's side—an event that, if it occurred, would necessitate the deployment of American ground forces.

Caught on the horns of such a dilemma, the Americans devised a compromise, which Dulles outlined in an address to the Overseas Press Club of America in New York on 29 March 1954.[20] In a speech titled 'The Threat of a Red Asia,' Dulles reiterated American support for France's struggle against the Viet Minh, whom he portrayed as an instrument of Sino-Soviet communism. Dulles warned that 'if

Communist forces won uncontested control over Indochina or any substantial part thereof, they would surely resume the same pattern of aggression against other free peoples in the area.' He regarded 'the imposition on Southeast Asia of the political system of Communist Russia and its Chinese Communist ally, by whatever means' as a serious threat to the free world. Faced with such a challenge, the United States should act in concert—or, as he put it, by means of 'united action'—with America's regional allies. While conceding that it was not without dangers, he viewed 'united action' as carrying far fewer risks 'than those that will face us a few years from now if we dare not be resolute today.'[21] Made in the midst of the battle of Dien Bien Phu, Dulles's calls for concerted allied action were intended to strengthen the French resolve to fight while, at the same time, raising the possibility of American intervention alongside its close regional allies. According to Dulles's aide, Robert Bowie, the fact that he deliberately chose his words to sound 'menacing without committing anybody to anything' also indicated his resolve to signal to China that the United States was not prepared to tolerate communist expansion in South-East Asia.[22] In other words, American troop deployments were 'not on the cards.'[23]

Initially, Dulles avoided defining the term 'united action.' In early April, he told the British, French and Australasian ambassadors in Washington that there 'was a gamut of alternative courses of action open. The last and least acceptable was the despatch of American ground forces.' '[M]uch depended,' he said, 'on the view of America's allies and on the degree of support that might be forthcoming from them.' What he had in mind was a 'strong coalition of states' or 'some kind of a collective organization of free world countries' with 'shared interests in Southeast Asia' that would include the United States, Britain, France, Australia, New Zealand, Thailand, the Philippines and the Associated States of Indochina (he deliberately left out the Republic of Korea or the Chinese Nationalist government). This 'ad hoc coalition' ought to be ready 'to protect its interest in the area' and 'fight if necessary.' In any case, such a coalition 'should be formed first in order to permit us to go to Geneva with the required strength' because, if it was prepared to fight, 'there might be successful negotiations at Geneva.' If the United States and its allies, he argued, sent a warning to China that 'they would be prepared to take action against her unless she stopped all help to the rebels in Indo-China,' Beijing would perhaps 'be persuaded to refrain from adventures in that area.' Aware that the creation of 'a formalized treaty system in the Asian area similar to the North Atlantic Treaty' would take time, he later clarified that, for the time being, the US administration was thinking more along the line of 'association' on 'an ad hoc basis' than 'a formula comparable to that of NATO.'[24]

Cleared with the president ahead of his speech,[25] Dulles's 'united action' plan needed some form of congressional support to be viable politically. Mindful that a collective defence arrangement was to provide the legal and diplomatic framework for American intervention in Indochina, both Eisenhower and Dulles agreed to seek the preliminary views of Congressional leaders.[26] On 3 April, when Dulles put to them that 'the President should have Congressional backing so that he could use air and seapower' in South-East Asia if he deemed it necessary to do so, their response was unanimous. Only after the administration had secured a firm commitment from Britain and other allies could Congress pass a resolution authorising the president to commit armed forces in the area. They made it clear that they 'want[ed] no more Koreas with the United States furnishing 90% of the manpower.'[27] Although Dulles concluded from his discussion with congressional leaders that 'Congress would be quite prepared to go along on some vigorous action,' he recognised that the meeting also 'raised some serious problems' for the administration.[28] By urging the government not to shoulder the burden of intervention in South-East Asia alone, congressional leaders complicated the administration's task, for they made Congress's support for American action conditional upon securing allied—mainly British—support. On 6 April, Eisenhower told the NSC that 'there was no possibility whatsoever' of unilateral American intervention in Indochina and that the administration should 'face that fact.' In the ensuing discussion, the NSC agreed to direct American efforts towards, first, 'organising a regional grouping, including initially the U.S., the U.K., France, the Associated States, Australia, New Zealand, Thailand, and the Philippines for the defense of Southeast Asia against Communist efforts by any means to gain control of the countries in this area'; second, securing British support for American goals in the Far East; and, third, urging the French to grant independence to the Associated States.[29]

However, as Dulles discovered over the course of the next 3 weeks, getting allied support for 'united action' was easier said than done. Neither the British nor the French showed much enthusiasm when he visited Europe in mid-April 1954. In London, the Churchill government thought Dulles's initiative was poorly timed. At the Foreign Office (FO), Anthony Eden worried that Washington's plans, if carried through, might spoil any chance of success at Geneva. While he found Dulles's idea of a collective defence arrangement appealing, he thought this could be best explored at a later stage once the Geneva negotiations were over. Believing that Indochina's more immediate problems were political rather than military, Eden was keen to explore a negotiated solution to the conflict. In any case, with the approaching rainy season bound to make large-scale military operations impracticable for months, he did not believe the Indochina situation was as dire as the Americans said. Nor did he think military intervention would be helpful in saving the French garrison at Dien Bien Phu. Moreover, he hesitated to contemplate any move that would increase the likelihood of Chinese intervention in Indochina and, thus, extend the conflict.[30] When he finally met Dulles, Eden sought to buy time. He told the US secretary of state that before considering the allied intervention in South-East Asia, or a warning to China, Britain and the United States should 'at least see what proposals, if any, the Communists had to make in Geneva.' Furthermore, while attracted to the idea of creating some enduring security system for South-East Asia, he cautioned that this would 'take time' and that India and other Asian countries should not be 'deliberately excluded.'[31]

In response, Dulles argued that if 'invitations to join a pact went to India, Pakistan, etc., which were not really a part of Southeast Asia,' this 'would raise the question of also extending invitations to the Chinese Nationalists, the South Koreans and possibly the Japanese.' 'This,' Dulles argued, 'might cause complications in getting ahead with the countries which are primarily threatened.' He pointed out that the battle of Dien Bien Phu had 'reached a crucial phase' and that the garrison 'might fall.' He said that it was precisely to avoid a French collapse that he had devised his 'united action' proposal. He also made it clear that there were two conditions for American intervention in Indochina. First, there should be 'some assurance that the French Government were willing to grant the Associated States real independence within the French Union, so as to provide the necessary political basis.' Second, America's 'allies, especially the United Kingdom, Australia and New Zealand,' shared 'an equally grave view of the situation in Indochina.' Dulles had in mind the 'formation of an "ad hoc" coalition, which might eventually develop into a defence organization for South East Asia on the ANZUS or NATO model.' Such a coalition 'would in itself constitute an effective warning to China and a warning against further Chinese intervention.' He argued that 'only if some action of this kind were taken now, would it be possible to arrest the further deterioration of the situation in Indo-China and thus avoid having to deal with an even more serious situation later on.' He did not think such a course of action would 'provoke further Chinese intervention.'[32] While Dulles and Eden ultimately managed to paper over their differences—the joint communiqué spoke of a shared desire 'to take part, with the other countries principally concerned, in an examination of the possibility of establishing a collective defence' in South-East Asia—there was no doubt that they had very different ideas about the timing of such an initiative.[33]

In Paris, the Laniel government was no more eager to accept the conditions laid out by Dulles for American support under 'united action.' This was hardly surprising considering that Dulles had made 'united action' contingent on France granting independence to the Associated States and accepting a greater allied role in the political and military decision-making in Indochina. Despite the deteriorating military situation in Dien Bien Phu, the French had no intention of budging on this issue. As French Foreign Minister Georges Bidault said to Dulles, why should France continue to fight if the Associated States were no longer tied to France?[34] Like Eden before him, Bidault argued that allied discussions on the formation of an anti-communist coalition as envisaged by Dulles should await the conclusion of the Geneva Conference, set to start on 26 April.[35] If the conference failed, France would be willing to consider 'collective security.'[36] Until then, nothing should be done to undermine Geneva, where the French hoped to negotiate an honourable end to the war and retain some residual influence on the region.[37] In a nutshell, the French government wanted an American air intervention at Dien Bien Phu without giving up political and military control of its Indochina campaign.[38]

Undeterred, Dulles returned to the charge a few days later when he again crossed the Atlantic for a NATO summit in Paris. Although European defence questions took centre stage, Indochina loomed large in the background. As the military situation at Dien Bien Phu became increasingly desperate for the French Union forces, the Laniel government made one last-ditch attempt to secure an American agreement for massive airstrikes against Viet Minh positions in the valley.[39] This time, Bidault was prepared to meet the Americans halfway by suggesting that his government would accept the internationalisation of the war.[40] Dulles urged Eden to 'go along,' but when the British foreign secretary refused, Dulles ruled out unilateral American military action to save Dien Bien Phu, as Bidault had requested.[41] As a result, the inevitable materialised. On 7 May, the French garrison surrendered after 55 days of fierce resistance, thus signalling the beginning of the end for the French in Indochina. As guns fell silent over the valley, international attention shifted from Dien Bien Phu to Geneva, where the representatives of the five big powers were set to begin discussions on the Indochinese (and Korean) question. However, the French defeat and the forthcoming negotiations at Geneva neither killed Dulles's 'united action' initiative nor ended discussions regarding the prospect of American military intervention in Indochina.[42] Quite the contrary, it 'made it more urgent for the United States' to take 'concrete steps' towards its realisation.[43] After the French surrender, Dulles initially kept championing 'united action' in the hope that communist intransigence in Geneva would drive the French to accept US assistance on Washington's terms.[44] However, when the Laniel government was replaced in mid-June by a new administration led by Pierre Mendès France, who was committed to a negotiated solution, Dulles changed his tack somewhat.[45] He kept 'united action' alive, hoping it could serve as a bargaining chip to secure concessions at the negotiating table.[46] With the Soviet Union, China and the Viet Minh all deeply concerned that the United States might use the formation of a regional alliance to undermine their political and strategic interests in South-East Asia, the US secretary of state intended to pressure the three communist delegations to lower their governments' initial demands.[47]

India's Reactions to US Plans

Nehru and his top officials viewed the American response to the Dien Bien Phu crisis and its aftermath with considerable apprehension.[48] With the question of US aid to Pakistan still fresh on their minds, talks of 'united action' in South-East Asia seemed to confirm their worst fears of an Eisenhower administration bent on pursuing an aggressive policy of containment of communism in Asia. Early indications of Indian unease emerged immediately after Dulles's 29 March 'united action' speech. On 31 March, the new MEA Secretary-General, Narayanan Raghavan Pillai, told US Ambassador George Allen that the speech had made some Indian officials believe Washington intended not only to declare a 'Monroe Doctrine for Southeast Asia' with the help of Britain, France, Australia and others but also to 'create [a] second Korea in Indochina if [the] Geneva conference failed.' He 'was afraid,' he went on, that 'these officials would present their interpretation to Nehru,' who might, then, make some 'rash' and 'unhelpful' statements.[49] A few days later, Pillai relayed a similar message to the British high commissioner in New Delhi. The mild-mannered senior Indian official told Alexander Clutterbuck that Dulles 'had caused [the] worst possible impression,' adding that the 'emotional way in which the Americans were approaching the Geneva Conference had given rise to suspicion that they were determined that nothing should come out of it.' He complained that it was very difficult to 'make head or tail of United States policy' and wondered what 'all this talk of "massive retaliation" and "united action" amount[ed] to?' He feared that between two possible alternatives to the Indochinese problem—'settlement by military force' or 'settlement by negotiation'—the Americans would choose the former over the latter. Naturally, Nehru was, Pillai said, 'greatly disturbed.'[50]

As the contours of Dulles's 'united action' initiative became clearer, Indian irritation mounted. In mid-April, Krishna Menon told Clutterbuck that Nehru considered the Western approach 'misconceived'; that collective defence under American leadership would lead to renewed Western intervention in Asia, and this would 'be repugnant' to Asian opinion; that India would regard 'with dismay' any extension of the Franco-Viet Minh conflict.[51] Almost concomitantly, Pillai provided additional insight into Nehru's thinking. After speaking with the prime minister, he informed the British high commissioner that the idea of a South Asian NATO 'appalled' Nehru. The Indian leader felt that '[c]oming on top of [the] United States military aid to Pakistan and the Turkish Pakistan pact it looked as if the United States was more interested in hemming in India than in stopping the spread of communism.'[52] Nehru, therefore, viewed with the 'greatest concern' recent developments regarding Indochina as they affected India's neighbourhood 'very vitally.' He deplored that the Anglo-American plan for a regional defence arrangement had been announced ahead of the Geneva Conference. Such an announcement was unhelpful since it did nothing to foster an atmosphere conducive to successful negotiations. He stressed that the Indochinese problem was, in essence, a question of French colonialism and deprecated Western attempts to deal with it through 'foreign interventions.' He argued that this approach ignored the views and policies of South Asian countries.[53]

In their internal deliberations, Indian policymakers were even blunter in their criticism of American policy. Menon warned Nehru that the Indochina crisis was reaching a climax and that the Americans were preparing to intervene militarily. India, therefore, faced the prospect of a major war close to home, with grave implications for its security. Moreover, Nehru viewed the Indochina imbroglio and the US-Pakistan defence pact not only as part and parcel of an American effort to extend the Monroe Doctrine to Asia but also as a 'pincer action' aimed at 'seeking to neutralise the area's neutralism and pull it or force it the other way.'[54] Nehru, for his part, told India's chief ministers that the United States were 'now definitely trying to function as [the] world leader'; that the old Monroe Doctrine was 'now extended to the entire world except the communist countries'; that Washington's 'policy of all out force and threats'—he expressly referred to Dulles's 'united action' plan and his warnings of nuclear retribution against China if the latter intervened in Indochina—was 'a big and dangerous gamble.' As a result, American actions could result in a catastrophic war that would place Asians at risk of an atomic strike, the second since 1945. Nehru's criticism did not end there. He also feared that American tactics might succeed in sabotaging the Geneva summit. He suspected that this was, in fact, Washington's plan all along so that if the conference failed, the United States could then go ahead with the establishment of a collective defence scheme for South-East Asia.[55]

Reporting back to their respective capitals, Western diplomatic missions in New Delhi ensured that their governments did not underestimate the extent of Indian opposition to such a scheme. In an assessment to the Commonwealth Relations Office that proved both accurate and prescient about India's attitude, Clutterbuck drew attention to the fact that plans for a US-led regional defence arrangement flew in the face of some deeply held Indian notions. As he correctly contended, one such notion was that Western intervention in Asia would amount to a 'reversal of the process of history' and, as such, should be resisted. A second was India's 'utter distrust' of the United States, which it considered an 'ignorant power,' 'drunk and hopelessly unreliable.' Third, creating a South-East Asian NATO hot on the heels of the Pakistani defence deal would be equivalent to the West's 'encirclement' of India—something New Delhi would naturally resist 'at all costs.' Fourth, such a defence organisation was no more than a poorly disguised attempt to perpetuate Western power in the region despite the likely inclusion of Thailand and the Philippines. Fifth, the Indian government feared an escalation in South-East Asia. Since the Chinese would 'never yield to threats,' the West was 'heading for failure at Geneva and thereafter for extension of the conflict' in Indochina. Finally, dismissing the notion that Chinese policy was 'expansionist,' India believed it possible to achieve a reasonable settlement in Indochina that would satisfy local nationalist aspirations while assuaging Western fears of South-East Asia falling under communist control.[56]

Predicting exactly what would happen only a few months later, Clutterbuck confidently ruled out India joining a collective defence arrangement and concluded that all Britain could do was prevent New Delhi from launching another crusade similar to the one against the American military aid to Pakistan.[57] In his report to Ottawa, the Canadian High Commissioner, Escott Reid, covered much of the same ground but added one critical aspect of Indian thinking. Reid emphasised how a US-led military intervention in Indochina would result in the 'shrinkage of the peace area' that Nehru wished to see established in South-East Asia following a successful Geneva settlement.[58] What Nehru meant by 'area of peace' was a non-aligned or neutralised zone in which, as he had told the Lok Sabha (the Indian Parliament's lower house) a few months earlier, there would be no war and nations would 'not want to do anything which helps war.'[59] Since the early 1950s, he had repeatedly alluded to this concept, which he believed offered the best chance of reducing regional tensions.[60] He did not equate the establishment of an area of peace with the formation of a non-aligned bloc.[61] Instead, he viewed it as providing 'an alternative path to security for materially weaker states' and a means of curbing 'great power competition in contested postcolonial areas.'[62] As the following chapters will show, this idea was to become central to his vision of a non-aligned and peaceful Asia.

Given its significance in Nehru's thinking, it is not surprising that the concept of an area of peace made its way into his statement to the Lok Sabha on 24 April, formally outlining India's position on the Indochina crisis. In the statement, Nehru returned to some of the themes mentioned above, laying emphasis, in particular, on the risk that 'repeated references to instant and massive retaliation, to possible attacks on the Chinese mainland and statements about extending the scope and intensity of hostilities in Indochina' might result in a much larger conflagration. These threats, coupled with Western plans for 'united and collective action' in South-East Asia, amounted to a 'lack of faith' in the Geneva negotiations and threatened to undermine them. To make matters worse, the French and the Viet Minh had been receiving increasing military assistance from their backers, which did not bode well for a peaceful resolution of the Indochinese conflict. These developments, Nehru remarked, exacerbated India's misgivings about the future of regional stability.[63] He hoped, therefore, that the Geneva Conference would be successful in bringing peace to Indochina and, in so doing, dispel 'the shadow of war which has far long darkened our proximate regions and threatens to spread and grow darker still.' As far as India was concerned, its role in the unfolding of this complex situation was 'to keep for ourselves and the adherence of others, particularly our neighbours, to a peace area and to a policy of non-alignment and non-commitment to world tensions and wars.' 'This,' Nehru believed, was:

> essential to us for our own sake and can alone enable us to make our contribution to lowering world tensions, to furthering disarmament and to world peace. The present developments, however, cast a deep shadow on our hopes, they impinge on our basic policies and they seek to contain us in alignments. Peace to us is not just a fervent hope; it is an emergent necessity.[64]

India and Indochina

If the emergence of a Western defence arrangement in South-East Asia was to remain a central concern in Nehru's foreign policy in the coming months, the future of Indochina was no less critical. The two issues were closely linked, as the tenor of New Delhi's initial reactions to Western defence plans plainly revealed. Indian policymakers viewed a positive solution to the Franco-Viet Minh war as essential to securing peace and stability beyond Indochina. In their view, Western military intervention, or even the prospect of it, ran counter to such a goal. By preventing a dangerous Cold War flashpoint from spinning out of control into other areas, they hoped peace in Indochina would contribute to enlarging the area of peace in Asia. Nehru, therefore, had not remained indifferent to the unfolding of the Franco-Viet Minh war, nor had he overlooked the war's implications for this part of South-East

Asia.[65] He believed that the stability of this sub-region was at stake, as well as the political and economic future of Vietnam, Laos and Cambodia. Some of the core principles of his foreign policy, such as anti-colonialism and opposition to power politics, also shaped his attitude.[66]

Nehru's approach to the Franco-Viet Minh war was a complex one. Three factors combined to shape his thinking.[67] The first one was realpolitik. Despite India sympathising with the Viet Minh's freedom struggle, the Nehru government had been careful not to antagonise the French, given its aim to persuade Paris to agree to a rapid transfer of power of its remaining settlements on Indian soil.[68] In contrast to his vital role in midwifing Indonesian independence by calling, among other things, an Asian conference on Indonesia in New Delhi in 1949, Nehru never confronted the French in the same manner as he challenged the Dutch.[69] The second factor was the very nature of Vietnamese nationalism. Its political complexion had prevented India from providing anything more than verbal support for the Vietnamese struggle for independence.[70] Even though Indians tended to regard Ho Chi Minh as a nationalist first and a communist second, Nehru was uncomfortable with the Viet Minh coming under growing communist control.[71] At the same time, he regarded non-communist nationalist leaders such as Bao Dai as French puppets without any popular following.[72] Because of this, India had not extended diplomatic recognition to either Ho Chi Minh's or Bao Dai's regime. The third factor shaping Nehru's approach to the Franco-Viet Minh war was geopolitical. The establishment of a communist regime in China in October 1949 had injected an additional note of caution into the Indian government's thinking on the Indochinese problem. Given Beijing's political and military support for the Viet Minh and Indochina's geographical proximity to China, it was anticipated that communist influence would spread across South-East Asia. This prevented India from meddling in China's sphere of influence and ensured that its attitude towards the Viet Minh remained aloof.[73] At the same time, however, India refused to view the conflict in Indochina as an example of communist aggression orchestrated by China.[74] In 1953, Nehru told Dulles that 'the commencement of this trouble in Indo-China had nothing to do with China,' as it predated the establishment of a communist regime in the Chinese mainland. He admitted that the Viet Minh were now receiving 'moral support' and 'possibly some supplies or some training,' but 'there were no Chinese forces' in Indochina. The war, he said, was an 'essentially nationalist' endeavour, albeit 'under communist control.'[75] And so, caught on the horns of a dilemma, the Indian government had chosen to keep out of trouble.[76]

However, the Berlin four-power summit's decision in February 1954 to convene a conference in Geneva to deal with the Korean and Indochinese questions gave Nehru the opportunity to advocate for a negotiated solution to the 8-year-long Franco-Viet Minh war. On 22 February 1954, 3 days after the Berlin conference concluded its deliberations, Nehru called for a ceasefire in Indochina.[77] He made it plain that India had no desire 'to interfere or to shoulder any burden or responsibility in this connection'; yet he seemed eager to put India forward to act as a mediator to end the fighting, as he had done in Korea.[78] He instructed the Indian ambassadors in Moscow and Beijing to seek the views of their communist hosts while Krishna Menon canvassed UN delegations in New York.[79] Both the Soviets and the Chinese were non-committal.[80] The Western response was no more encouraging.[81] The start of the Viet Minh offensive in mid-March 1954 upset Nehru's hopes for an early end to the war and, as mentioned earlier, threatened to derail the upcoming negotiations at Geneva. Moreover, it brought up the possibility of American involvement in the conflict and large-scale retaliation against the Chinese for supporting the Viet Minh. Nehru had already blamed the protraction of the war on increased American financial and military aid, which had allowed the French to carry on fighting.[82] As he told U Nu, France was 'being bled to death,' but the Americans 'would not allow any kind of settlement.'[83] More importantly, Dien Bien Phu solidified his conviction that the United States posed the greatest threat to regional stability and the largest obstacle to his policy for collective peace through coexistence. In other words, American policy threatened to scupper 'the best opportunity India had of extending the area of peace and non-alignment and of stabilizing the relations of South and Southeast Asia with the Communist colossus to its north.'[84]

It is in this context that on 24 April, during a session of the Lok Sabha, Nehru put forward a six-point proposal to end the war in Indochina.[85] India had not been invited to Geneva and its role would be confined to 'informal backdoor contacts,'[86] and Nehru was said to be annoyed at India's exclusion.[87] However, looking to make a virtue out of necessity, he sought to use his proposal to influence the upcoming negotiations and exert pressure on the great powers present in Geneva (the United States, the Soviet Union, China, Britain and France) to break the Indochinese impasse. With such a proposal, Nehru also aspired to create a neutralised area in South-East Asia, the existence of which would be guaranteed by the five powers mentioned above. In detail, Nehru's plan called for the promotion of a climate of peace; ceasefire negotiations between the French and the Viet Minh; independence for the Indochinese states; direct negotiations by the parties involved; a pledge by the Soviet Union, United States, China and Britain not to intervene in Indochina; and the need to seek the UN's assistance to reach a lasting settlement.[88]

Despite being couched in general terms, Nehru's six-point plan sketched out the contours of a prospective settlement and underlined India's desired outcome in Indochina. Nehru regarded these steps as 'both practicable and capable of immediate implementation.'[89] However, whether or not this was the case remained debatable. When the international conference on Korea and Indochina opened on 26 April at the Palais des Nations in Geneva, the prospects for a workable solution were far from encouraging. As the fighting at Dien Bien Phu raged on, it was unclear whether the French government and the Viet Minh would be willing to make peace and on what terms. Washington's desire to avoid Geneva becoming a capitulation to the communists was a further complicating factor, as was Moscow's and Beijing's resolve to take advantage of the Viet Minh's gains on the battlefield to extract concessions from their Western rivals.[90] The Chinese, in particular, wished to turn Indochina into an Asian buffer zone to protect them from the Americans.[91]

In brief, Geneva represented both a source of anxiety and an opportunity for Nehru and his government. It was a concern because, if an agreement could not be reached, hostilities would almost certainly resume, leading to renewed tensions between the two blocs. At the same time, it was an opportunity in that it could result in a much-needed shift towards peaceful coexistence by bringing the 8-year-long Franco-Viet Minh conflict to an end. It was in this unpredictable and high-stakes regional environment that the idea of an Afro-Asian conference began to take shape. As Chapter 3 shows, the seeds of Bandung were planted in Colombo in the spring of 1954. On 28 April, the leaders of Ceylon, India, Indonesia, Burma and Pakistan assembled in the capital of recently independent Ceylon to discuss the most pressing regional security issues of the day, voice their concerns and offer solutions to ease Cold War tensions. During the talks, the Indonesian prime minister urged broadening the discussion to include other Afro-Asian nations and, to this end, advocated for a broader summit to bring them together. Although the other four leaders eventually endorsed the Indonesian proposal, their support was lukewarm. Nehru, for one, remained doubtful about its feasibility and, as we shall see, uncertain how this initiative might fit into India's broader Cold War agenda. In any event, the Colombo meeting, which coincided with the start of the Geneva Conference, provided Nehru with the opportunity to articulate his regional vision and advocate for a reasonable solution in Indochina. And, as his role and advocacy in Colombo indicated, he had no intention of remaining on the sidelines of regional politics while the great powers gathered at Geneva shaped the course of the Asian Cold War.

3

THE COLOMBO CONFERENCE

The Conference has been cast by the Press in the role of an important gathering at which momentous decisions will be taken and also as the beginning, at least, of an Asian or South-East Asian concord bloc!

V. K. Krishna Menon[1]

27 April 1954, Palam Airport, New Delhi. Nehru boarded an Indian Air Force aircraft bound for Colombo. Accompanied by his daughter Indira and a small party of senior officials, including Pillai and his trusted adviser and friend Krishna Menon, the Indian prime minister departed on a mission that the *Times of India* characterised, with some exaggeration, as of 'the greatest importance' and possibly even 'a turning point' in Asian affairs.[2] Awaiting him in the Ceylonese capital were the prime ministers of Burma (U Nu), Indonesia (Ali Sastroamidjojo) and Pakistan (Mohammed Ali Bogra) and the host himself, Sir John Kotelawala, the prime minister of Ceylon. Although no agenda had been agreed upon prior to the gathering, the five Asian leaders were expected to discuss issues of mutual concern, such as security and economic challenges.[3] One of these issues was likely to be the question of hydrogen bomb tests after the 15-megatonne explosion conducted on 1 March 1954 at the Bikini Atoll in the

Marshall Islands.[4] According to two Ceylonese newspapers, the *Ceylon Observer* and *Ceylon Daily News*, other probable discussion topics were communism and the establishment of an Afro-Asian neutralist 'region of peace' or 'third area.'[5] For its part, the *Times of India* speculated that Ceylon would lobby for a joint declaration of non-aggression and non-intervention in each other's affairs.[6] Widely reported were also Indonesian plans for a larger Afro-Asian conference.[7] As the gathering's date drew nearer, press reports also indicated that the worsening situation in Indochina would receive close attention.[8] Lodged at Temple Trees, a charming nineteenth-century colonial building located in central Colombo and the official residence of the Ceylon prime minister, the five Asian leaders aspired to foster greater Asian coordination and play a greater role in shaping the destinies of a region increasingly riven by Cold War tensions and great power rivalry.

John Kotelawala was the meeting's organiser and sponsor. On 25 October 1953, he called for the 'closest possible alliance with our immediate neighbours with whom we have historical, cultural, geographical, religious and linguistic ties.'[9] During a visit to New Delhi earlier that month, he had also declared that 'with the world divided into two camps, the emergence of an Asian bloc which both sides may respect, may be the only means of averting a third world war.'[10] He envisioned a grouping of newly independent South Asian nations, consisting of Ceylon, Burma, Pakistan and India, which he hoped would 'become an effective force in the preservation of world peace.'[11] This group would meet regularly on the model of the meetings of Commonwealth prime ministers in order to develop common policies regarding the 'needs of the region.'[12] By December 1953, he had informally sounded out the other South Asian governments.[13] Indian and Pakistani responses were encouraging.[14] Nehru viewed the idea of regular meetings among South Asian leaders as 'a very good one.' Despite recognising that 'the larger the number, the vaguer the talk,' he encouraged Kotelawala to include Indonesia in the list of possible participants.[15] This the Ceylon prime minister duly did.[16] In January 1954, he cleared the last hurdle after securing Karachi's participation. To do so, he had to reassure Mohammed Ali Bogra that the meeting would not focus on

American military aid to Pakistan.[17] Kotelawala proposed that the summit have no agenda and avoid any topic deemed contentious by the participating nations.[18] He also suggested holding the meeting in Ceylon even though he was open to an alternative location if the other prime ministers objected.[19] In the event, nobody objected to Colombo being chosen as the venue. However, as there was no set agenda, it was unclear what the meeting could accomplish. In mid-April, Pillai told the British and Australian High Commissions in New Delhi that India 'was not taking the conference at all seriously' and that 'nothing but a few platitudes was likely to emerge from it.'[20] According to him, the only factor that could change this assessment was the Geneva Conference, which could allow Nehru to make the Colombo gathering 'an occasion for his own purpose.'[21] As this chapter shows, this is precisely what happened, with Nehru using the Colombo conference as a 'sounding board' for his Indochina peace plan.[22]

The Colombo Conference Begins

The Colombo Conference began on 28 April in the imposing Senate Building, now known as the Republic Building in central Colombo. The five Asian delegations met there twice a day for the first three days before moving to Kandy, a picturesque hill town east of Colombo in Ceylon's central highlands, for two more days of talks.[23] When the five Asian leaders eventually met for its opening, the conference had already attained a level of international notoriety they could not have predicted when they agreed to participate.[24] The escalating international tensions generated by the Indochina crisis, which were causing alarm in more than one Asian nation, were the source of much considerable media attention. This interest, and the fact that the Colombo Conference coincided with the start of the Geneva Conference (which had begun only two days before), gave the five Asian prime ministers the platform and exposure they needed to express their concerns about these tensions and try to affect the course of events in Geneva. The Indian and the Ceylonese press had been highly critical of American calls for 'united action.' They demanded that their prime ministers 'step in either to restore peace themselves in Indo-China or take part at least in the solution of the issue as an Asian affair.'[25]

Unsurprisingly, when the five prime ministers began discussing substantive issues in the afternoon of 28 April, Indochina was uppermost in their minds, taking most of the conference time along with the problem of communism.[26] John Kotelawala argued that the Colombo Conference should attempt to influence the Geneva negotiations by presenting a peace plan agreed upon by the leaders of free Asian countries and that only such a plan—as an expression of Asian will—had a chance of success.[27] Similarly, the Indians felt that 'world opinion would expect some expression of view from the conference.'[28] To this end, Nehru put forward the six-point plan he had outlined to the Indian Parliament a few days earlier. He said his proposal was intended as a set of recommendations to the Geneva Conference—to keep Indochina from becoming 'a focal point for a clash on a larger scale.'[29] However, as the five leaders began to tackle the Indochinese question, Nehru's proposal was slightly altered.[30] Ali Sastroamidjojo demanded that the issue of a ceasefire be linked to China's admission to the UN, believing that doing so would induce the Chinese to exert pressure on the Viet Minh to accept a ceasefire. The discussions, therefore, revolved around the following points: (1) an immediate ceasefire, (2) direct negotiations by the parties concerned, (3) a declaration of independence for Indochina, (4) a non-intervention pledge by outside powers, (5) the need to keep the United Nations (UN) in the picture and (6) the admission of China into the UN. There was general support for the first, third and fifth points.

Some disagreements, however, emerged on this sixth point, with Indonesia standing firm on the need to link China's admission with a ceasefire, while Pakistan believed it should be dropped. Mohammed Ali Bogra stated that while Pakistan supported communist China's admission to the UN, he did not think including this issue in the six points would help the negotiations in Geneva. The Pakistani prime minister also emphasised that the five Asian leaders 'should do nothing to prejudice or anticipate the results of the Geneva Conference,' implying that they should await developments in Switzerland before formulating a proposal. Bogra also contended that while he agreed with the principle of non-intervention by outside powers, he opposed its inclusion in the proposal on Indochina for 'it would embarrass the Geneva Conference.' He said non-intervention was 'likely to be observed by one side only.' He also insisted that negotiations not be restricted to the belligerents (i.e. France and the Associated States of Indochina on the one hand and the Viet Minh on the other).[31] Discussions on the draft resolution on Indochina and the search for an agreed formula continued until the end of the conference.[32] In the end, despite some considerable haggling, the five prime ministers accepted Nehru's proposal with some modifications. In general, during the discussions on Indochina, Kotelawala tended to side with Bogra, while Ali Sastroamidjojo and U Nu supported Nehru.[33] The issue of China's admission to the UN was not included in the final communiqué's section dealing with Indochina but was endorsed separately.[34] With regard to China, the five leaders agreed that China's admission would help 'promote stability in Asia,' 'ease world tensions' and encourage a 'more realistic approach' to world and East Asian problems.[35] As Nehru told his counterparts, China's entry into the UN 'would go a long way towards relieving existing tensions.' The 'history of Korea,' he argued, 'might have been quite different had China been given her seat in the United Nations much earlier.'[36]

The conference's inaugural session also revealed that the relationship between the Indian and Pakistani prime ministers would be far from easy. On the morning of 28 April, Nehru and Mohammed Ali Bogra 'had an initial brush on Kashmir.'[37] Referring to the Kashmir dispute with India, Bogra argued that 'it would be unrealistic for the Conference to consider conflicts in other regions of the world without giving first priority to conflicts and disagreements within the region itself.'[38] Nehru insisted that disputes between members not be discussed 'at this and future Conferences of Asian Prime Ministers.'[39] In the process, they 'both lost their tempers.'[40] Nehru apparently 'banged on the table,' complaining that 'it was no good carrying on the discussion in the presence of America'—a sarcastic remark directed to his Pakistani counterpart. Not to be outdone, Bogra also banged his fist on the table, retorting that there was no point continuing the discussion 'in the presence of Russian and Chinese stooges'—contemptuously referring to Nehru.[41] However, they soon regained composure, and, when he realised that the other leaders supported Nehru's stance, Bogra agreed not to discuss Kashmir.[42] According to the Australians, who had been briefed by the Indonesians, Ali Sastroamidjojo 'spent much of his time making peace between the two.'[43]

Tussling Over Communism

Controversy resurfaced again when the five leaders moved to discuss international communism. On the conference's second day, Kotelawala urged his counterparts to adopt a strongly worded resolution condemning international communism and its attempts to infiltrate non-communist territories.[44] Ahead of the conference, he had instructed one of his closest advisers to inform the press that he 'would enter into league with the Devil to oppose the Communists.'[45] More importantly, he had granted transit clearance (and landing rights at the British Royal Air Force base in Negombo, 19 miles north of Colombo) to seven globe master aeroplanes carrying French troops to Indochina.[46] In what would be a divisive topic at Bandung the following year, the issue of international communism polarised the Colombo proceedings. Whereas Pakistan and Ceylon adopted a robust anti-communist stance, India and Indonesia refused to do so for fear of undermining their non-alignment.[47] The anti-communist Kotelawala argued that 'the gravest danger' to regional security emanated from 'the subversive activities of International Communism.' He called, therefore, on Asian countries to help each other deal with this menace.[48]

Nehru openly disagreed. A member of the Indonesian delegation described his reaction as 'strong' and 'at all times bitter.'[49] He opposed issuing such a categorical statement. He claimed that while colonialism entailed the 'physical conquest and occupation of one country by the other,' communism was essentially an ideology, implying communism posed a lesser threat than colonialism. He conceded that, like other Asian nations, India was 'experiencing difficulties' due to 'the activities of local Communists.' However, he was unable to uncover any subversive Soviet activities in India. In Nehru's view, accepting Kotelawala's resolution would be equivalent to aligning with one of the two Cold War blocs, which was contrary to India's policy of non-alignment. Siding with Kotelawala, Mohammed Ali Bogra argued that if the conference was willing to support a resolution against colonialism, then there was 'no reason why it should not adopt an equally strong resolution condemning the activities of International Communism.' 'If,' he added, 'they could say "hands off Asia" to the Colonial Powers, they could and should say the same thing to the Soviet Union.' Ali Sastroamidjojo backed Nehru, saying that his government was 'non-communist' but not 'anti-communist.' Indonesia, like India, was a non-aligned country, and if it accepted Kotelawala's proposed declaration, it would wind up aligning itself with one bloc. This was not something Indonesia was prepared to do.

When the Ceylon prime minister returned to the charge, insisting that the conference condemn international communism, Nehru responded that he had no problem with countries 'taking all possible steps, either by law or more efficient administrative methods, to stop communist intervention or infiltration into [their] territory.' But the problem, as he saw it, was that communism was an ideology and that, as such, it could only be defeated 'by reason and persuasion' rather than through 'compulsion' or military force. U Nu, who until then had been silent, entered the fray by siding with Bogra and Kotelawala. He said Asian nations should 'be outspoken against the dangers of Communism as they had been against Colonialism.' In the end, Nehru relented, saying he was willing to accept a declaration opposing foreign intervention or external influence without taking sides between the two blocs. However, when the five prime ministers returned to the issue of international communism the next day, Nehru was again at odds with Kotelawala and Bogra. He reiterated that if he were to accept Kotelawala's strong language, he would upset India's policy of non-alignment. He 'had very good reason to believe that the Cominform would cease to exist in the near future' and that 'the whole approach of the Communists towards the rest of the world was undergoing change.' Nehru added that India 'was about to enter into a Treaty of great significance to his country with Communist China' and that 'it would very seriously embarrass him' if he were to accept Kotelawala's and Bogra's views on communism.[50]

Here he was referring to the Sino-Indian agreement on Tibet, which had been signed in Beijing the day before and was now awaiting ratification.[51] In the end, after much deliberation, the five prime ministers reached a compromise.[52] The final communiqué referred to their nations' 'unshakable determination to resist interference in the affairs of their countries by external Communist, anti-Communist and other agencies.'[53]

When the discussion shifted to other topics, such as colonialism and the hydrogen bomb, the five prime ministers were able to reach an agreement more quickly. They regretted that colonialism 'still existed in various parts of the world' and agreed that its continuation violated human rights and threatened world peace. They supported the independence of Tunisia and Morocco. They also agreed on a resolution on Palestine, expressing sympathy for the sufferings of the local Arab population. On the hydrogen bomb, they opposed additional tests and welcomed UN efforts to find an agreed solution to outlaw and abolish such weapons. They also demanded that the world's nuclear powers publish information on the bomb's 'destructive capabilities' so that 'by rousing the conscience of the world' it would be possible to begin finding a solution to 'grave problems that threaten humanity.' Concerning economic cooperation, they agreed that two proposals—one put forward by Burma for the creation of a joint committee to foster cooperation among the five countries and the other sponsored by Indonesia for the establishment of an Afro-Asian Economic Cooperation Organisation to promote economic cooperation among these countries—should be referred to governments of the countries represented in Colombo for further consideration. Finally, they agreed to respect one another's sovereignty and refrain from interfering in each other's domestic affairs.[54]

The Indonesian Proposal for an Asian-African Conference

The five leaders also reached a broad consensus on an Indonesian proposal to hold an Asian-African summit in the near future. Ali Sastroamidjojo briefly explained its rationale in the conference's inaugural session on 28 April. He argued that growing great power competition and deepening world tensions would inevitably drive the two superpowers to drag as many countries as possible into their respective blocs. '[S]uch power politics' would, therefore, 'create the possibility for the recurrence of colonialism, as we know it or in a new form.' This, he added, was a problem 'common' to all Asian and African countries. He, therefore, proposed to organise, 'in due course,' another conference, 'wider in its scope,' which would 'include not only the countries of Asia but the countries of Africa as well.'[55] Returning to his proposal two days later, he noted that while a group of Afro-Asian countries at the UN met to formulate 'common policies on matters of mutual interest,' no such coordination existed outside the UN. The same countries lacked both 'organised contacts with each other' and the 'machinery' to consult 'on matters of common interests.' In putting forward his proposal, Sastroamidjojo said he did not intend to create an Afro-Asian bloc but rather to devise 'occasional meetings of a group of nations with common ideals in order to exchange information and ideas.'[56]

In the ensuing discussion, U Nu agreed 'in principle' with Ali Sastroamidjojo's idea. Nehru's response was more guarded. While he observed that 'there was a great deal of force' in the Indonesian leader's arguments, he 'foresaw several difficulties implementing the Indonesian proposal.' There was, for instance, the risk that in a large conference such as the one proposed there would be significant disagreements among the participating nations, making it difficult to reach a consensus on the topics under discussion. Then, there would be the question of which countries should be invited to such a gathering. Would they, for example, invite the governments of African colonial territories? As for Indochina, would they ask Vietnam or the Viet Minh?[57] Despite these difficulties, Nehru stated that 'he welcomed the proposal made by Indonesia.' He did, however, recall previous failed initiatives to hold an Afro-Asian summit. Consequently, if the five leaders agreed to give Indonesia the green light, it would be critical to ensure that this attempt did not 'fizzle out' like the others. Therefore, a 'great deal of preparation at an official level' would 'be necessary before any conference of the type envisaged could be held.'[58]

Nehru's reaction was not unexpected. He had already put a damper on the Indonesian government's desire to take steps to consolidate the Asian-African group at the UN by hosting a conference to examine issues of mutual interest. In October 1953, he had informed Indonesian Foreign Minister Sunario that previous efforts to develop 'some machinery for cooperation' between Afro-Asian states had not been 'particularly encouraging.'[59] The Asian-African group, Nehru noted, was 'much too amorphous and vague' and 'was pulled in different directions.' Agreement on specific proposals was 'lacking.'[60] Nehru most likely alluded to his stillborn efforts to develop an Asian-African grouping at the time of the New Delhi Asian-African conference on Indonesia in 1949. In January of that year, Nehru had convened a meeting in New Delhi to discuss the Dutch military campaign against the Indonesian Republic and provide help to local nationalists. Even though the conference's focus was on Indonesia, Nehru lobbied for the establishment of a mechanism that would allow its participants to maintain contact.[61] His advocacy fell on deaf ears. Arab countries rejected the idea out of concern that China might join one day.[62] Pakistan, for its part, argued that Nehru's proposal was premature because the conference's participants were far too diverse to form an effective regional organisation.[63]

At any rate, since the late 1940s, some level of cooperation among Asian and Arab countries had emerged in the UN General Assembly on questions such as colonialism and self-determination.[64] In late 1950, following its entry into the UN, Indonesia proposed the creation of an Arab-Asian bloc at the UN, including seven Arab League countries and six Asian countries, to explore collective action on colonial matters and other issues of common interests.[65] Hopes that the Arab-Asian bloc would become an effective group were soon dashed despite some successes in advancing its anti-colonial and human rights views.[66] Not only were its Arab members divided on most questions except Israel,[67] but the group also included countries friendly to, or aligned with, the West that did not agree with India on various issues.[68] To avoid offending his Indonesian counterpart, Nehru told Sunario that he did not rule out the possibility that such a conference might be held 'at a suitable time.' He had, after all, welcomed the creation of such a group and wanted to make it 'firmer.'

At the same time, he warned that a conference of this sort would require significant work.[69] Such misgivings among Indian leaders persisted into 1954. In the run-up to the Colombo Conference, Krishna Menon, at the time also the Indian representative at the UN, warned Nehru that 'such conference would be premature and ill-timed,' given that most of Africa was still under colonial rule and Asian nations were yet to develop some common understanding.[70] However, aware that Indonesia was unlikely to ditch its pet project, Menon advised Nehru to 'offer no frontal opposition' but 'promote more practical ideas.'[71]

When it came Mohammed Ali Bogra's turn to speak, he concurred with Nehru that the Indonesian proposal was 'a desirable one.' Still, he urged the five leaders to carefully consider some of its aspects before endorsing it. Which countries, for example, would be invited to such an Afro-Asian conference? Had Indonesia determined whether they would accept an invitation if extended? What if one of them declined the invitation? For his part, John Kotelawala asked whether the proposed conference would include all Middle Eastern countries and colonial territories in Africa. In response, Ali Sastroamidjojo reiterated that 'to begin with, the conference might include the countries which comprised the Afro-Asian Group at the meetings of the United Nations' and that it 'was not his intention to include colonial territories.' He 'had already informally sounded several Middle Eastern countries regarding this proposal and most of them had reacted favourably.' In any case, he argued, it was unnecessary to go into all the specifics immediately. If the principle of holding such a conference was accepted, then 'the details (such as the countries to be invited and the subjects to be discussed) could be worked out at a later stage.' The Indonesian government, he added, was prepared 'to do all the preparatory work' necessary to organise such a conference. At that point, U Nu chimed in, wondering whether the proposed conference could not be organised on an unofficial level rather than as a government-sponsored event. In that case, political party leaders from the participating nations could attend the meeting as representatives of their respective countries. Ali Sastroamidjojo retorted that 'this suggestion was not practicable.' Indonesia alone had twenty political parties, and it 'would be difficult to decide which parties should attend.' Kotelawala then 'enquired at what level countries would be represented at the proposed conference,' to which Ali Sastroamidjojo replied that he envisaged 'governmental representation at the highest level.' Next, Bogra indicated that he 'welcomed the Indonesian proposal' but added that it would be preferable if they supported it as 'individual governments' rather than as a group.[72]

Confronted with these viewpoints, Ali Sastroamidjojo sensed that none of the other prime ministers shared his enthusiasm for an Afro-Asian conference.[73] As he later recalled in his memoirs, they all lacked faith in Indonesia's ability to host such a large international conference, given the nation's political instability and weak economy.[74] Despite their lack of enthusiasm for the Indonesian proposal, the other four leaders ultimately agreed to it 'with no controversy and little debate,'[75] with Nehru being the one who moved things forward. He reiterated his view that 'in spite of the difficulties, he was attracted to the Indonesia proposal.' He now admitted that he had 'been thinking on similar lines for several years.' He told the other prime ministers that they 'should give Indonesia full moral support in sponsoring an Afro-Asian conference' and 'should refer to this decision in their final communique.'[76] Nehru's closing statement, however, was not exactly the ringing endorsement the Indonesians had looked for.[77] Prior to the conference, they had hoped that 'if things [went] well at Colombo,' it would be possible to establish a 'permanent secretariat,' which might facilitate contacts between Afro-Asian countries.[78] Instead, the Indonesians only got a vague sentence in the final communiqué stating that the 'Prime Minister of Indonesia might explore the possibility of such a [Asian-African] conference.'[79] The British high commissioner in Colombo detected in this wording the intention 'of politely shaving [shelving] what was clearly a half-baked proposal.'[80] In Beijing, the Chinese authorities came to a similar conclusion. The Ministry of Foreign Affairs noted weeks later that Ali Sastroamidjojo 'didn't get definite support or resolution from the [Colombo] conference.'[81] The remarks of Nehru's trusted advisor, Raghavan Pillai, to the British High Commission in New Delhi were also revealing. He conceded that the decision to support the Indonesian proposal was merely a 'sop' to Jakarta, and it was unclear 'whether anything would come of it.'[82]

The Colombo Conference and Its Aftermath

When the conference concluded on 2 May in Kandy, the five leaders expressed satisfaction with their achievements. John Kotelawala praised the decisions they had reached, saying that they 'would be of great value, not only to themselves, but to the world at large.'[83] As did Nehru, Bogra and Ali Sastroamidjojo, he hoped the Colombo conference would pave the way for 'many similar meetings' and 'the closest future contacts and co-operation' between their countries.[84] Nehru described the conference as 'a unique event of historic significance.'[85] The Indian press was equally enthused. It hailed it as a triumph for Nehru, India and Asia.[86] Moreover, the fact that the meeting attracted the attention of both the international media and Western governments 'reinforced the impression that the group was the representative diplomatic force for Asia.'[87] However, for all the hype and the self-congratulatory atmosphere, the conference's achievements appeared mixed at best.[88] Nehru, for sure, performed well. As the Australian high commissioner in New Delhi, Walter Crocker, reported to Canberra, Nehru 'stood head and shoulders above the other Prime Ministers' and 'was the one man at Conference who knew exactly what he wanted.' He got full agreement on the hydrogen bomb and, to a significant extent, on his Indochina proposal.[89] On the other hand, Kotelawala, 'with his blunt and bluff manner,' was criticised for being 'incompetent in his handling of the conference' and, to some extent, 'for the unpleasant atmosphere' that characterised it.[90] U Nu 'kept very much in the background' and 'gave the impression that the discussions were above his head.'[91] Sastroamidjojo 'spoke rarely,' and when he did, 'it was usually either to show concern about West New Guinea as a relic of Colonialism or to minimise the dangers of Communism.'[92]

The Indian delegation left Colombo feeling that 'it was something of an achievement to have held things on a fairly even keel,' given the different ideas and interests of the five countries.[93] Pillai felt that the conference had gone better than he or Nehru had expected.[94] He characterised its approach as 'moderate,' claiming that it had secured 'a wide area of agreement.'[95] Despite this, Pillai did not appear to have enjoyed the event. He admitted that the conference 'suffered badly from lack of preparation and lack of any fixed agenda.' He added that the 'political inexperience of some delegations also caused difficulty at times.'[96] To compound these problems, the 'heavy social programme' to which the five prime ministers were subjected allowed 'little time for Conference discussions,' as the Australian High Commission in Colombo reported to Canberra.[97] If organisational issues and political inexperience did complicate agreement between delegations, the real problem was, as mentioned previously, the inability of the five Asian leaders to reach a consensus on crucial issues like Indochina and communism.[98] The conference's agreed formula on Indochina reflecting Nehru's original six-point plan only sketched the most basic terms of a possible negotiated solution. It did not amount to any detailed or specific plan.[99] India no doubt exploited the Colombo Conference to 'inject its views in the discussions at Geneva,' but, as has been recently noted, 'little thought' seems to have been given in that forum 'to the outcomes and recommendations of the Colombo Conference, and Nehru's proposal on Indochina.'[100] Only Anthony Eden, the British Foreign Secretary and the Geneva Conference chairman, appeared to have paid some attention to the Colombo deliberations. He not only reassured the five Asian leaders that Britain would not take any action in Geneva that 'would conflict with the legitimate desires of Asian nations.' He also asked them if they would consider associating themselves with—and, more importantly, guarantee—a settlement reached in Geneva on Indochina.[101]

Disagreements over the question of communism were especially pronounced. Three of the five nations represented—Pakistan, Ceylon and Burma—expressed serious concerns about it, while India and Indonesia equivocated and did their best to downplay the danger. If Colombo was all about creating a common Asian approach to—or a united front against—deepening Cold War tensions, it did not succeed. Western diplomats in South Asia pointed out, not without some ill-concealed pleasure, that 'India did not speak for South Asia' and the region was not 'unanimous' in its approaches to regional and world affairs.[102] The fact that the final communiqué was 'a patched up compromise' agreed only 'after considerable difficulty,' which contained several 'expressions of hope' but 'added little that was constructive for the area or with respect to international relations,' was evidence of this.[103] News reports on squabbles between leaders and frequent leaks to the media of the confidential proceedings 'did not help to keep the inflated hopes high.'[104] In the end, the Indians blamed the Pakistanis for the disagreements.[105] There was certainly no chemistry between Nehru and Mohammed Ali Bogra. Max Maramis, the Special Assistant to the Indonesian prime minister, spoke of an 'unconcealed animosity' between the two.[106] Pillai revealed the Pakistani leader's 'interest in his new gold cigarette case, his new watch, his new camera and the gadgets in the Super-Constellation plane' that took him to Colombo 'irritated the spartan and puritanical' Nehru.[107] On the other hand, Krishna Menon 'annoyed the Pakistan delegation on several occasions' so much so that Pillai 'himself felt obliged to go along afterwards and apologise for hasty and excitable words shouted out by Mr. Krishna Menon.'[108] The Indonesians were 'distressed by the tense and at times disagreeable atmosphere which permeated the meeting as a result of animosity between Mr. Nehru and Mr. Mohammed Ali [Bogra].'[109] Not only did the heated diatribe on international communism show them that Asian nations remained divided on significant issues such as communism, but they were also disappointed that they did not get a firm commitment to holding an Asian-African meeting in the near future.[110] However, as Chapter 6 will reveal, the Indonesians were not to be so quickly put off by their partners' lukewarm support for such a conference.

In a radio broadcast from the Ceylonese capital before returning to India, Nehru put a nice gloss on the Colombo talks, stating that the 'mere fact of these five Prime Ministers of South Asia meeting together was a unique event of historic significance.' Despite their occasional differences, the five leaders had, by and large, shown a 'common outlook' to Indochina and other 'grave problems' affecting the world, and Asia in particular. Nehru also noted that it remained to be seen whether Indochina would ever achieve peace. Three weeks later, without consulting the other four prime ministers, he would despatch Krishna Menon to Geneva to influence the negotiations from behind the scenes.[111] Between 23 May and early July, Menon flew in and out of Geneva for 6 weeks to lobby for a settlement based on the Colombo declaration and Nehru's six-point plan, which Menon himself had drafted.[112] For the moment, however, Nehru confined himself to calling on countries 'to establish a climate of peace' and accepting peaceful coexistence as the only way to overcome their differing outlooks, objectives and ideologies. By way of example, he mentioned the so-called Agreement on Trade and Intercourse between the Tibet Region of China and India, signed by Indian and Chinese representatives in Beijing just a few days earlier, on 29 April.[113] By removing India's historical rights and privileges from the region, this agreement recognised India's changed position in Tibet and sanctified Chinese sovereignty there.[114] Drawing attention to the Agreement's preamble, Nehru indicated that the two governments had agreed to abide in their relations by the principles of mutual respect for each other's territorial integrity and sovereignty, non-aggression, non-interference in each other's internal affairs, equality and mutual benefit and peaceful coexistence. He welcomed these principles—soon dubbed the 'Five Principles of Peaceful Coexistence'—for placing Sino-Indian relations 'firmly on a peaceful basis' and contributing to peace in Asia. If all nations, he said, recognised these principles in the conduct of their relations, 'there would hardly be any conflict and certainly no war.'[115] As Chapter 4 will show, the visit of Chinese Premier Zhou Enlai to India in late June 1954 presented Nehru with the chance to advance several critical foreign policy objectives—from promoting his regional vision based on the concept of areas of peace and peaceful coexistence to normalising India's relations with China and leveraging closer Sino-Indian cooperation to undermine Washington's containment strategy in Asia. In the spring of 1954, there was still no apparent connection between the Indonesian proposal to organise an Afro-Asian conference, Nehru's regional vision of areas of peace and India's China policy. The Zhou-Nehru talks provided the first necessary step towards establishing that connection.

4

THE NEHRU-ZHOU ENLAI TALKS

The important thing is that India-China relations will now be on a somewhat different and closer basis. This does not mean that we are linking up with China. We retain our position and our policy. It is true, however, that position and policy, in regard to South-East Asia, is nearer to that of China than to that of the U.S.

Jawaharlal Nehru[1]

Nearly 2 months after the conclusion of the Colombo Conference, Zhou Enlai made a surprise trip to New Delhi. In April, the Indian ambassador to China, Nedyam Raghavan, had informally approached the Chinese Ministry of Foreign Affairs to enquire about the possibility of Zhou visiting India.[2] It appeared that Indian *démarche* had got nowhere until, following a meeting with Krishna Menon in Geneva on 21 June, Zhou promptly accepted Nehru's formal invitation to visit India.[3] Zhou's decision to fly to New Delhi only 3 days later took Nehru and his entourage by surprise and threw the Indian government into a frenzy, forcing Nehru to postpone a 10-day trip he had already planned to Shimla, a resort town on the foothills of the Himalayas and the former summer capital of the British Raj.[4] As a result, arrangements for the visit were 'hurriedly put in hand.'[5] Zhou's decision to travel to India on short notice, however rushed it may have been, left nothing to chance. On the contrary, it had been carefully thought through. As Zhou pointed out to Mao and the CCP's Central Committee on the eve of the trip, he was heading to India to carry out the 'centrally approved' instructions on negotiating an Asian peace treaty or treaties. In other words, he hoped the visit would result in the signing of such 'bilateral or multilateral non-aggression treaties with India, Indonesia and Burma.' By doing so, he wished 'to strike a blow at the United States' conspiracy to organize a Southeast Asia invasive bloc.'[6]

On 13 June, while still in Geneva, Zhou received a telegram from Beijing urging him to 'take active actions to win over these Southeast Asian states.' What Mao and the Central Committee had in mind was the negotiation of 'either bilateral or multilateral treaties with India, Indonesia, and Burma, or a collective security pact with them.' China's 'strategic goal,' the telegram stated, was 'to maintain a neutral group in Southeast Asia' and 'to unite Britain and France through these Asian states' to frustrate Washington's containment policy in Asia. If successful, this policy would not only allow China to 'consolidate peace in the Far East and the world,' it would also 'isolate the US and defeat American imperialist aggression policy and frustrate its conspiracy to put together an aggression group in Southeast Asia.' The odds for negotiating such treaties were good, since 'India and Indonesia had already negotiated such a treaty' with each other.[7] Mao and the Central Committee referred to a Treaty of Friendship that New Delhi and Jakarta had signed in March 1951, committing them to 'perpetual peace and unalterable friendship.'[8] Upon receiving the telegram, Zhou immediately consulted Vyacheslav Molotov, the Soviet Minister of Foreign Affairs. After securing Soviet support for these plans, he informed the Central Committee of his preferred course of action. While Zhou was not 'against concluding a multilateral treaty directly' if the circumstances permitted, he would first proceed with the negotiation of bilateral treaties followed by a multilateral pact.[9] He also proposed to extend an invitation to Nehru to visit China in October and accept the concurrent visit of the Indonesian and Burmese prime ministers if the Indian leader raised such a prospect. Lastly, Zhou hoped to persuade India to 'exercise its influence to push for the support of the British Commonwealth for the Indochina ceasefire.'[10]

Zhou Enlai Arrives in New Delhi

With this brief, Zhou flew to New Delhi on a chartered Air India Constellation aeroplane that picked him up in Geneva.[11] The Indian authorities had provided the aircraft for the Chinese premier at his request, given that the Chinese 'had no plane service of their own and faced [the] difficulty of non-recognition by countries en route.'[12] Premier and Foreign Minister of China since 1949, Zhou ranked within the top four of the CCP's hierarchy and was the party's leading negotiator and foreign affairs expert. At one point even more influential than Mao within the CCP ranks, Zhou had been one of his closest associates since 1936. Behind his sophisticated, urbane and even affable demeanour hid a hardened, ruthless and committed communist trained in Japan, France and the Soviet Union.[13]

Nehru had never met Zhou before. During his visit to China in 1939, he had expressed a desire to meet Zhou and other CCP leaders, but the outbreak of the Second World War in September of that year had compelled him to return to India prematurely.[14] Prior to Zhou's arrival in New Delhi, Krishna Menon had portrayed the Chinese premier and foreign minister to Nehru as 'a fine,' 'great and able man,' 'extremely shrewd and observant, very Chinese but modern.' He had also reassured Nehru of Zhou's intentions by noting that he did 'not believe that the Chinese have expansionist ideas.'[15] The Air India jet carrying Zhou landed at New Delhi's Palam airport in the early morning of 25 June 1954. As Zhou descended the gangway dressed in a dark-grey Mao suit and a peaked hat, Nehru stood on the tarmac, ready to greet him. Displaying a red rose in the buttonhole of his white coat, Nehru warmly welcomed Zhou. And so did Nehru's ministers and some members of the ruling Congress party, who were 'delighted' at the importance that Zhou attached to India.[16] As he inspected the guard of honour, cheers of *Zhou Enlai Zindabad* (long live Zhou Enlai) and *Chini-Hindi Bhai Bhai* (Chinese and Indians are brothers) rent New Delhi's early-morning air.[17] On walking across a gathering of the Sino-Indian Friendship Society, he received a garland of scented marigolds and white champa.[18] Once the ceremonial was over, Zhou told reporters that he felt 'much honoured and pleased to have the opportunity of visiting this great neighbour of China' and that his government and the Chinese people 'attached great importance to their friendship with India.' He added, 'May the friendship between China and India develop with each passing day. May the unity of the peoples of all Asian countries become closer daily.'[19] He added that India and China 'constitute[d] an important factor in maintaining the peace of Asia and the world.'[20]

From Palam, Nehru and Zhou travelled to Rashtrapati Bhavan, the imposing former palace of the British Viceroy that was now the official residence of the Indian president. On his way to the presidential palace, where he would be staying as a guest of Rajendra Prasad, Zhou laid a wreath on Mahatma Gandhi's *samadhi* (cremation) site at Raj Ghat.[21] Given that China and the Soviet Union (not to mention the Indian Communist Party) had in the past condemned the reactionary character of the Gandhi phenomenon, it was likely that this gesture was intended to signal a significant shift in attitude towards non-communist India.[22] As the two leaders drove through the city in an open car, thousands of people 'cheered them vociferously and showered flowers on them,' according to the *Hindustan Times*.[23] Western reports, however, revealed a somewhat different story. Despite the government's efforts to encourage people's attendance by providing free transport to the airport and employing paid cheerers from the Public Works Department, the crowds were thin along the route, their demeanour subdued. And they remained small (by Indian standards) and apathetic for the extent of Zhou's visit. As the Australian High Commission reported to Canberra, the visit 'lacked the real fervour as well as the numbers of crowds' that welcomed Pakistani Prime Minister Mohammed Ali Bogra in August 1953.[24] However, the Indian press, under official inspiration, freely indulged in hyperbole and wasted no time in hailing Zhou's 3-day trip as a 'historic event' that symbolised 'the resurgence of Asia' and would usher in a 'new phase of Asian diplomacy.'[25] More improbably, the Indian press claimed that the PRC 'had always been more Asian than Communist.'[26]

Conscious of the importance of Zhou's 3-day visit to India, Nehru spared no effort to make the Chinese premier's stopover 'agreeable,' despite the oppressive heat that would accompany the Chinese leader for the duration of his stay.[27] To ensure that nothing was left to chance, Nehru ended up 'supervis[ing] most functions himself,' directing, for example, 'the band when to stop playing' and 'the people what to do,' or reprimanding the Chief of Protocol 'when a hitch developed in the organisation of the State Banquet.'[28] He also devoted a great deal of time to his guest—13 hours in private conversation plus attendance at various receptions.[29] The Indian leader saw Zhou's visit as key for multiple reasons. On one level, it was an opportunity to take the measure of Zhou and establish a personal rapport with the public face of China's diplomacy—an endeavour that, if successful, could pave the way for normalised relations between India and China. On another level, the visit could serve as a litmus test for communist China's commitment to peaceful coexistence and, more specifically, to the five principles enshrined in the preamble of the Sino-Indian treaty on Tibet, which had been signed 2 months earlier. Moreover, Zhou's presence in the Indian capital made it possible for the two leaders to discuss the most pressing issues affecting peace and stability in Asia and assess the degree to which their respective approaches to regional security were congruent. For Nehru, in particular, the visit presented an opportunity to bring China closer to his regional vision. In brief, the implications of closer Sino-India relations for both Indian security and Asian stability at large were not lost on Nehru, not least because he viewed such rapprochement as a means of placing both India and China back at the centre of Asian politics, even though it 'meant raising the prestige of a potential rival.'[30] This is why, in mid-April 1954, he had instructed Raghavan to press for a speedy conclusion of the negotiations on Tibet, anticipating that a swift agreement between India and China would have a 'salutary effect' on regional politics and would help reduce tensions.[31]

The visit, of course, was important for Zhou Enlai, too. He was expected to sell Nehru on the idea of bilateral or multilateral non-aggression treaties to counter Washington's policy of containment. He also intended to reaffirm China's support for the five principles of peaceful coexistence, which he had proposed in December

1953 as the basis for negotiations of the Sino-Indian agreement on Tibet.[32] By embracing peaceful coexistence, Beijing hoped to break out of isolation, increase its ideological and political influence in the developing world and stir anti-American sentiment there. To this end, the PRC's strategy was to create the impression that the Chinese 'were Asians first and Communists afterwards,' that they did not want to 'convert' other Asians to communism and that non-communist Asian nations should have 'nothing to fear' from Chinese communism as long as they refrained from joining Western defence pacts and remained neutral.[33] In this context, the five principles of peaceful coexistence were intended to serve 'the evolving purposes of Chinese diplomacy brilliantly.'[34] In essence, they amounted to no more than the 'core principles for a world of states, an echo of those underpinned by the UN itself,'[35] but Beijing exploited them to give 'formal expression to some of the CCP's new ideas about diplomacy' and provide 'a unifying concept that the PRC could use to gain support among newly independent countries.'[36]

The five principles of peaceful coexistence were, in other words, 'a convenient peg' on which Zhou could 'hang his Asian policy.'[37] Signs of this new approach had already emerged in Geneva, where the Chinese delegation had been anxious to ensure that its new-found moderation would enhance its peaceful credentials and help end its international isolation.[38] By going to New Delhi, Zhou hoped to reassure a key non-communist Asian nation and enlist its support for China's anti-American agenda. In this context, India could be an essential asset and a tool for advancing China's revolutionary goals.[39] Nehru's role in the struggle for Indian independence, as well as his stature as a politician and diplomat, had made him the veritable voice of the Third World and earned him (and India) significant prestige both within and without the Third World.[40] Not unreasonably, therefore, Beijing viewed New Delhi as wielding 'considerable sway over Asian and African countries due to its neutralist stance'—a factor that placed 'India in a prominent position in Beijing's "united front" orientation.'[41] In comparison, Mao's China 'commanded only a fraction of the international respect enjoyed by Nehru's India.'[42] With this goal in mind, Zhou carefully cultivated his public image and did his best to make a favourable impression on his Indian hosts.

According to the British Deputy high commissioner in New Delhi, George Middleton, in all his public appearances, Zhou 'managed to give the impression of being [a] friendly and disarming visitor with a lively and sympathetic interest in those whom he met and in the sights which they showed to him.'[43] A year later, as we shall see in Chapters 9 and 10, Zhou would deliver a similar performance in front of twenty-eight other Afro-Asian leaders assembled in Bandung.

The Nehru-Zhou Enlai Talks

Thus, determined to impress his hosts, Zhou Enlai struck the right chords from the outset of his discussions with Nehru. In their first meeting on the afternoon of 25 June, the Indian prime minister started off the conversation by seeking Zhou's views on the Geneva talks on Indochina. Zhou informed Nehru that the two agreements had been reached in principle. The first was a military armistice that temporarily created two large regrouping areas for Viet Minh and French troops. The second called for the withdrawal of foreign forces from Laos and Cambodia. Zhou told Nehru that China's position was unequivocal: all foreign troops should be withdrawn, and neither of these two countries should host foreign military bases from where a third country could launch an attack against China or Vietnam. In other words, as he put it, Laos and Cambodia should 'become States of the South-East Asian type,' and this 'would enable the peaceful forces in South-East Asia to strengthen.' After Zhou clarified that the word 'South-East Asian type' meant 'neutral,' Nehru remarked approvingly that he was 'sure that will have a wider influence for peace in South-East Asia and in other countries also, particularly in Burma and Indonesia, the two chief countries in South-East Asia.' When Nehru alluded, somewhat elliptically, to Burmese fears of communist expansion in South-East Asia, Zhou promptly stated that China's 'policy towards South-East Asia is one of peaceful existence.' In order to leave no room for ambiguity, he emphasised that this was 'our policy towards India, Burma, Indonesia and events towards Pakistan and Ceylon, and now towards Laos and Cambodia.' Clearly pleased about what he had heard, Nehru said that 'if as between these countries of South-East Asia and us we can lay down principles like respect for sovereignty and territorial integrity, non-interference in internal affairs, non-aggression, equality and mutual benefit and peaceful coexistence,' this 'would create a large area of peace'—an area, that is, made up of neutral countries that had no foreign bases on their soil and accepted the above principles. The creation of a large area of peace, he added, 'would help peace.' In response, Zhou stated that this was 'also the policy of the Government of China' and that, therefore, China and India were in 'complete agreement' on this point. Despite Nehru complaining about Pakistan's hostility towards India, and Zhou about Ceylon's unfriendliness towards China, the two leaders agreed to 'make efforts' to draw in these two countries 'on the side of peace.'[44]

When the talks resumed after dinner at 10 p.m., Nehru and Zhou returned to the question of Indochina. They discussed the prospect of India's chairmanship of a commission tasked with supervising the armistice. Although Nehru remained non-committal, Zhou praised India's status as a neutral country, adding that everyone involved in the negotiations in Geneva—with the exception, perhaps, of the United States, whose attitude, he said, was 'not very clear'—had 'confidence in India.' A little later, in response to Nehru's comment on Indochina that India was 'prepared to cooperate with any country even though we may not like that country,' Zhou added—no doubt in an attempt to make a good impression on Nehru—that China understood 'the spirit of India.' When, at one point, Nehru returned to the idea of an Asian area of peace in an attempt to probe Zhou's intentions further, the latter again did his best to impress the former, reiterating his support for such a concept and making it clear that the five principles should be extended to other regional states. His response could hardly have been more reassuring to Nehru. As he put it, 'if these principles are applied to all States of Asia, that would be very beneficial,' for 'in this way we can prevent US attempts to organise military blocs in this area.' Zhou did not explain how China proposed to do such a thing. Still, in attempting to draw Nehru out on the question of a non-aggression treaty—and, no doubt, to flatter him—he deferentially sought the Indian leader's view on the matter, claiming that Nehru knew Asian states and governments 'much better' than Zhou himself did. Nehru, however, remained evasive, avoiding all references to a non-aggression pact. During the negotiations on Tibet, the Chinese had already hinted at the desirability of a non-aggression pact with India without receiving any encouragement from the Indians.[45] In line with this approach, Nehru simply indicated that it would be 'better perhaps to have bilateral declarations rather than joint declarations.' He told Zhou that the first step would be for China and Burma to agree to a declaration embodying the above principles 'and then follow it up with Indonesia.' For its part, India would also look to sign a non-aggression pact with Burma and Indonesia. 'Maybe later, it can take some other shape,' added Nehru. In any case, the two leaders agreed to continue these efforts once the Geneva Conference was over.[46]

The following day, Zhou had two more rounds of talks with Nehru sandwiched between an early sightseeing tour of the city, a luncheon with the Indian President Rajendra Prasad and a tea party hosted in his honour by Sarvepalli Radhakrishnan, India's former ambassador to Moscow and its current vice president.[47] During the morning session, Zhou solicited Nehru's views on the current situation in Asia. Nehru obliged, seemingly enjoying playing the role of a senior world statesman.[48] Towards the end of the conversation, Zhou enquired about the Afro-Asian conference that Indonesia planned to organise. Nehru was notably evasive. To Zhou's question about 'the exact state of affairs,' Nehru replied that he could 'not understand it, myself. It is not clear whether it will be at an official or non-official level.' When Zhou probed further, asking whether there had 'been any open contact between the Governments in this matter,' the Indian leader briefly reminded his Chinese guest of the 1947 Asian Conference and the 1949 Asian-African Conference on Indonesia. However, he quickly added that 'nothing much had happened' since then. 'It has been hanging fire' and 'various proposals have been made from time to time.' The problem was: 'suppose we call a conference, whom do we invite?—Governments or the people who are oppressed. There are all kinds of difficulties.'[49]

When Nehru and Zhou Enlai resumed their talks on the afternoon of 26 June, the former tried gently to draw the latter out on the question of international communism. In reiterating the point that 'the more we refer to those [five] principles—and other countries too—the better it is,' Nehru also argued that their mere adoption by India, China and possibly some of their neighbours would not be enough to instil trust among them. There were, Nehru claimed, factors at work that generated fear. Without 'positive steps' to 'get over that fear,' confidence would remain elusive. One such factor was the anxiety with which Asian nations rightly or wrongly perceived India's and China's regional roles. 'We are both big countries,' Nehru said, 'and, to some extent, actually strong or potentially strong. Therefore, there is apprehension in some small countries about us.' In addition, Nehru mentioned regional concerns about the presence of substantial Chinese and Indian minorities throughout Asia. Given their size, population and capabilities, India and China bore substantial responsibility for regional stability. Hence, Nehru argued—and Zhou readily concurred—they should work to ease their neighbours' fears. As he told Zhou, 'of all these people in South-East Asia, the Chinese and Indians are the most mature. So one has to be very careful and friendly with the others so that they may not get any inferiority complex.' But, as Nehru hastened to add, another factor generated fear across the region—international communism. In contrast to the Americans, who believed that communism 'want[ed] to conquer the world,' Nehru did not worry about 'the attitude of great States like Soviet Russia and China.' After all, he said, revolution 'cannot be exported.' What generated anxiety regionally were the activities of regional communist parties who 'rub[bed] up against nationalist feelings' and 'would run down their country and leaders.' Such activity was what stood in the way of good relations with communist countries. While professing to 'not know exactly the activities of the Communist parties in different countries,' Zhou nonetheless argued that 'we must make efforts to remove such entirely groundless, baseless fear which exists in Asia.' He agreed with Nehru that they should include in the final communiqué a statement that South-East Asian nations 'should be independent and should be allowed to develop according to [their] wishes.'[50]

The two leaders met twice on Zhou's last day in New Delhi. In their penultimate meeting on the afternoon of 27 June, Zhou brought up again the issue of bilateral declarations or statements embodying the five principles of peaceful coexistence. He concurred with Nehru that, as a first step, such statements between China and India, Burma and China and China and Indonesia would 'make a great difference in Asia.' However, he added that there might 'be other countries also wishing to make similar statements,' and, if peace could 'be restored in Indo-China,' there would be 'a number of possibilities.' Hence, he argued, it would make sense 'not to restrict the form now.' Despite Zhou's repeated allusions to regional bilateral or multilateral non-aggression treaties, Nehru did not take the bait. In explaining his position, he claimed that his 'mind' was 'not very clear' on how to proceed beyond this point. He stated that 'in increasing the area of peace and strengthening the forces of peace, if we arouse, directly or indirectly, other forces opposed to it, then we create or tend to create obstacles.' As a result, 'the steps' both India and China planned to 'take should strengthen peace without having the other adverse effect.'[51]

Nehru specifically mentioned the United States as an obstacle to peace in Asia.[52] He had already told Zhou that India was 'totally opposed' to American plans for a collective defence organisation in South-East Asia. He had also criticised the Americans for their exaggerated fears of communism and condemned their attempts to build 'hundreds of bases around Russia and China,' which would create 'an impression in the minds of Soviet Russia and China that they will be attacked.' The result, Nehru said, was 'this vicious circle of fear.'[53] As such, he supported British Foreign Secretary Eden's attempts to bring together 'opposing countries to guarantee' the Indochinese settlement.[54] In so doing, Nehru hoped to get the British, the French, the Australians and the New Zealanders to distance themselves from the Americans and support the Indochinese settlement. Zhou, in turn, mentioned a French proposal that 'the States participating in the [Geneva] Conference should jointly guarantee the States of Indochina.' This guarantee could be extended to others and 'include as many States as possible.' 'We should,' Zhou added, 'facilitate collective peace in Asia,' maintaining that if enough countries subscribed to Indian and Chinese plans for collective peace in Asia, the United States would be forced to participate. Nehru, however, remained cautious, explaining that 'some kind of a collective system is good to have, but it must be clear what kind of system it is.' If it meant a system of collective defence, India would be unable to join because it 'was reluctant to commit [itself] to any possible entanglement in war.' Realising that he was not gaining much traction with Nehru on this issue, Zhou limited himself to expressing his desire that India and China 'constantly exchange views in future, as that would be a great force for peace.'[55]

In the following months, however, Zhou would continue to flirt with the idea of negotiating bilateral or multilateral non-aggression pacts with India and other regional powers. In July, for instance, he told the Indonesian ambassador in Beijing that Indonesia and China could indeed agree on 'a mutual non-aggression pact or something along those lines.'[56] In September, he told the Pakistani ambassador that 'there should be a non-aggression treaty between the Colombo Powers and China,' adding that he would 'be prepared to make a declaration with the Prime Minister of Pakistan on the lines of those he had made with the prime ministers of India and Burma, and even to extend its scope.'[57] However, none of these countries except Indonesia seemed willing to negotiate non-aggression treaties with China.[58] In October, the Indian chargé d'affaires in Rangoon told the Australian Legation there that, in Nehru's view, even non-aggression pacts were 'aggressive.'[59] Earlier that October, an official of the Burmese Ministry of Foreign Affairs had let the Australians know that 'no question had arisen regarding non-aggression pacts between countries in [the] area, either on [a] bilateral, or multilateral basis or with or without [the] participation of China.'[60]

The End of the Talks

In the end, Nehru's first encounter with Zhou Enlai was a success. Even though the two leaders appeared to display some 'wariness' towards each other, the talks were friendly.[61] Nehru secured China's commitment to his 'area of peace' idea. He also got Zhou to accept the principle that 'the people of each nation should have the right to choose their own state system and way of life, without interference from other nations. Revolution cannot be exported.' For his part, Zhou did his best to ease Indian anxieties about Chinese expansionism and could realistically claim to have gone some way towards reassuring Nehru of Beijing's intentions.[62] Moreover, his trip to India had a significant symbolic value. Coming in the midst of the Geneva negotiations, where the Chinese delegation's presence had drawn considerable international attention, Zhou's visit no doubt reinforced the impression that China had finally emerged from isolation to reclaim a central role in Asian affairs. As British Deputy High Commissioner Middleton appropriately put it at the time, the visit 'mark[ed] the resumption' of China 'as a respectable great power in the affairs of Asia.'[63] Unsurprisingly, therefore, the Chinese side was said to be delighted at the outcome of his visit.[64] In a statement issued upon his departure from New Delhi, Zhou described the discussions as having produced tangible results.[65]

For his part, Nehru felt that there 'was something historic and far-reaching' about his talks with Zhou.[66] As he wrote to Eden after the visit, Zhou was 'evidently anxious to cultivate friendly and cooperative relations with not only India but other countries of South East Asia.' Nehru saw their discussion as 'helpful in clearing the air and understanding each other.' He believed that Zhou was 'anxious for peaceful conditions and for the countries of Asia to develop and advance.' Nehru also told Eden that, during the talks in New Delhi, Zhou had claimed to be 'impressed by much that he saw' and had drawn attention to 'the economic and industrial backwardness of China compared to India.'[67] Hence, his stated 'desire [was] to concentrate on developing his country.' As Nehru assured the visiting American Supreme Court Justice William O. Douglas after the talks, 'the Chinese Communist will spend [the] next ten or fifteen years in building up their own country.'[68]

In the final communiqué, the two leaders emphasised the importance of the five principles as the overarching paradigm guiding future relations between India and China. More than that, they affirmed that these principles 'should be applied in their relations with other countries in Asia as well as in other parts of the world.' If these principles, the communiqué went on, were 'applied not only between various countries but also in international relations generally,' they 'would form a solid foundation for peace and security and the fears and apprehensions that exist today would give place to a feeling of confidence.' In a point dear to Nehru, the document acknowledged that 'different social and political systems exist in various parts of Asia and the world.' However, it also added that if the five principles were 'accepted and acted upon' and there was 'no interference by any one country with another,' such social and political differences 'should not come in the way of peace or create conflicts.' In fact, '[w]ith the assurance of territorial integrity and sovereignty of each country and of non-aggression, there would be peaceful coexistence and friendly relations between the countries concerned. This would lessen the tensions that exist in the world today and help in creating a climate of peace.'

Rejoicing at the progress being made in Geneva, Nehru and Zhou Enlai expressed hope that the five principles would provide the basis for a political settlement in Indochina centred on the establishment of free and democratic neutral states, which would 'not be used for aggressive purposes' or 'be subjected to foreign intervention.' A settlement informed by these principles would not only 'lead to a growth of self-confidence in these countries' and 'friendly relations between them and their neighbours,' but would also 'help in creating an area of peace which, as circumstances permit, can be enlarged, thus lessening the chances of war and strengthening the cause of peace all over the world.' In any case, the two leaders 'expressed their confidence in the friendship between India and China which would help the cause of world peace and the peaceful development of their respective countries as well as of other countries in Asia.' To this end, they agreed that 'their respective countries should maintain close contacts so that there should continue to be [a] full understanding between them.'[69]

Coming hot on the heels of the successful conclusion of the Sino-Indian agreement on Tibet, Zhou's visit to New Delhi hastened the trend towards a rapprochement between the two Asian giants. Not only did Nehru's extensive discussions with his Chinese counterpart reveal a significant degree of agreement between the two countries on regional Cold War issues, but the cordial atmosphere engendered by the talks appeared to bode well for the future of the bilateral relationship. Although the two leaders did not tackle the question of their ill-demarcated and disputed border—an issue that only a few years later would come back to haunt them and contribute to the dramatic deterioration of their relationship—the visit appeared, for the moment, to lay the groundwork for closer political cooperation between the two countries. For Nehru, in particular, Zhou's brief Indian sojourn provided the opportunity to advance some major foreign policy goals. Enlisting Beijing's support for Nehru's regional vision of areas of peace and committing the PRC to peaceful coexistence was undoubtedly one such goal. But, as he welcomed Zhou to New Delhi, Nehru also had other important objectives in mind, such as defusing domestic concerns about China's regional role and bolstering India's security and geopolitical position in South Asia. In this context, Zhou's claim that China was committed to the five principles and had no intention of exporting communist revolutions across Asia appeared to go some way towards reassuring the Indian government as well as public opinion. Another of Nehru's goals was to leverage closer Sino-Indian cooperation in order to undermine Washington's containment strategy and overcome Cold War divisions. By encouraging China to seek greater engagement with non-communist Asia, Nehru intended to wean China away from the embrace of the Soviet Union and to reassure other regional actors that China posed no threat to them. This, in turn, would hopefully help take the wind out of the sails of American containment. Finally, and perhaps even more importantly, in the long run, such collaboration also offered the possibility of fulfilling Nehru's long-held ambition for major powers such as India and China to have a greater say in determining the region's destiny.

If Zhou's New Delhi visit opened up new possibilities for the future of regional relations, much remained to be done before China could become a credible linchpin of Nehru's regional strategy. Until India's neighbours were completely reassured of China's peaceful intentions, Nehru's plans to promote greater Chinese engagement with non-communist Asia were unlikely to succeed. Although, in Colombo, Nehru and the other Asian leaders had expressed their support for China's UN membership in the belief that Beijing's admission would promote regional stability, non-communist Asian governments still harboured significant misgivings about China's potentially subversive regional role.

Burma was one of the countries where this problem was felt most acutely. Due to its proximity to China, the presence of Kuomintang forces in its territory and the existence of a small Chinese minority inside the country, the Burmese government was exceedingly sensitive to Beijing's opinion and highly apprehensive about its intentions. Unless Zhou could reassure U Nu of Beijing's peaceful intentions, regional fears of China would persist, thus frustrating Nehru's hopes of bringing the PRC out of the cold. In this context, Zhou's brief visit to Rangoon after New Delhi could not have come at a better time. As the next chapter shows, the Indian government was instrumental in making the Chinese premier's visit to Burma possible in the hope that it would help ease Burmese fears of China. Rangoon, therefore, was to provide the litmus test of China's peaceful intentions and the validity of Nehru's assumptions. While the prospect of an Asian-African conference was still very much up in the air, Zhou's arrival in Rangoon would, in hindsight, be an important step in that direction.

5

ENTRENCHING PEACEFUL COEXISTENCE

[The Nehru-Zhou agreement] provides a clear test of Chinese intentions. If the Chinese ... decide temporarily to relax their pressure and consolidate their revolution, India and other free Asian nations will be given a badly needed breathing spell in which to put their own economic and political houses in order. If, as seems more likely, China disregards her new promises and embarks either directly or indirectly on further expansion, the real nature of Chinese Communism will become obvious to many Asians for the first time.

Chester Bowles[1]

From New Delhi, Zhou Enlai flew to Rangoon on the Air India Constellation 'Bengal Princess' for a brief round of talks with U Nu.[2] On Zhou's arrival at Rangoon airport on 28 June, U Nu, the Acting Foreign Minister, U Kyaw Nyein, and other representatives of the Burmese government greeted him warmly.[3] Burma had been among the first non-communist countries to recognise communist China, along with India.[4] Much like New Delhi, Rangoon had also refused to join the United States in condemning China as an aggressor in Korea and supported China's admission to the UN.[5] However, despite Burma's friendly attitude, relations between Rangoon and Beijing had not been all plain sailing, at least at the start.[6] More than one issue had caused concern in Rangoon. In the early 1950s, for instance, China had harshly criticised Burma for its pro-Western attitude and described the U Nu government as a lackey of imperialism. Much to Beijing's annoyance, Rangoon had sought extensive Anglo-American assistance and advocated the establishment of a collective security system in Asia.[7] For their part, the Burmese authorities were highly concerned when, in 1950, Beijing released geographical maps showing parts of north-east Burma as Chinese territory.[8]

This was not the whole story, though. The presence of thousands of Kuomintang troops inside Burma heightened fears in Rangoon that Beijing might one day send the People's Liberation Army (PLA) forces across the border to deal with them. Following the victory of Mao's communist forces in the Chinese Civil War (1945–49), the remnants of the Kuomintang 8th Army, numbering around 12,000 troops, had entered Burma under the command of General Mi Li.[9] Their main goal was to subvert Chinese communist rule in Yunnan (where most of these troops originated from) and establish a foothold from which to facilitate a future nationalist takeover of the mainland.[10] In the past, these troops had launched incursions into Yunnan with the assistance of the United States, which saw them as a means of destabilising communist rule in China and diverting Chinese forces away from Korea to relieve pressure on American troops.[11]

The Burmese government had good reason to feel jittery about the continued presence of Kuomintang forces on Burmese soil. Since 1950, small groups of Chinese communist soldiers had reportedly entered Burma from time to time.[12] In 1953, PLA troops crossed the border into Burma and seized five towns in the Wa States bordering China's Yunnan province.[13] Beijing justified its 'action on the grounds that Burmese forces were incapable of giving adequate protection against the Chinese nationalists.'[14] A few months later, in 1954, the CIA reported that China had established three military posts in the same area.[15] Burma's under-strength armed forces were in no position to repel invading PLA troops, since they were already facing several security challenges from various insurgent groups (ranging from communist rebels to ethnic guerrilla groups like the Karens and the Kachins).[16] Lastly, links between Beijing and the Burmese communists, as well as the presence of 300,000 ethnic Chinese in Burma, exacerbated Burmese fears of China.[17] Like other South-East Asian states, the Burmese government feared that Beijing would exploit the presence of ethnic Chinese in South-East Asia to export communism and subvert its neighbours.[18] Since the establishment of a communist regime in China, the CCP had acted as a protector of overseas Chinese, rejecting any negotiations with its South-East Asian neighbours over this sensitive issue.[19] In a nutshell, confronted with multiple internal security challenges and unable to control many parts of its territory effectively, the Burmese government could not afford to antagonise China. With this in mind, U Nu sought to engage Burma's powerful northern neighbour to secure its commitment to regional peace, stability and good-neighbourly policies.[20]

As a result, in 1953, relations between the two countries began showing signs of improvement. Burma distanced itself from the West in favour of a non-aligned foreign policy, and the CCP leadership adopted a friendlier attitude towards non-communist Asian nations.[21] In late April 1954, Burma and China signed a bilateral trade agreement allowing Burma to sell rice to China for merchandise and technical aid.[22] This agreement was important because Burma, with 70 per cent of its export earnings coming from the sale of rice, had been concerned about American rice outpricing Burmese rice on the international markets.[23] Despite visible progress in Sino-Burmese relations, the Burmese government remained wary of Chinese intentions on the eve of Zhou Enlai's visit to Rangoon. In May, the Burmese had complained to the Indians that 'their experiences with the present Chinese regime have been uniformly discouraging. All efforts at friendly cooperation have been disregarded and Burmese endeavours to get rid of K.M.T. troops have met with [an] entire lack of sympathy or understanding. This has led to serious distrust of Chinese intentions.'[24] Growing concerns over the future of Indochina had revived Rangoon's lingering nervousness about China. The fall of Dien Bien Phu in early May 1954 appeared to have brought home the dangers posed to South-East Asian states by a communist Vietnam increasingly under Moscow's and Beijing's influence.[25] In mid-May, the British embassy in Rangoon had reported to the Foreign Office that Burmese thinking on the communist danger was 'developing fast' and with 'ideal realism.'[26] In early June, U Nu told the American ambassador in Rangoon that he was 'exceedingly concerned over reports that the Chinese Communists have been infiltrating into the northern border areas.' The Burmese government, he said, already had 'some evidence that Chinese Communist agents provocateurs have been sent in,' and that 'when more evidence is at hand,' it would 'make a strong protest to Peiping.'[27] As mentioned above, the Indian government, too, was aware of Burmese discontent to the extent that Nehru feared that Rangoon might be considering abandoning its policy of non-alignment.[28] On 9 May, he instructed Raghavan to tactfully draw Chinese attention to Burmese concerns, hoping that Beijing would 'do something which creates a feeling of assurance and security and friendliness among the Burmese.'[29]

U Nu Meets Zhou Enlai (28–29 June 1954)

It is against this backdrop that Zhou Enlai arrived in Rangoon in the early afternoon of 28 June 1954. Pillai, whom Nehru had instructed to deliver a personal message to U Nu conveying the essence of his discussions with Zhou, accompanied the Chinese premier. By taking this step, Nehru hoped he might persuade his Burmese opposite number to welcome the visiting Zhou. In his message, Nehru emphasised Zhou's desire 'to develop friendly relations with all the South-East Asian countries' and to 'do anything in reason to remove their fears.' He assured U Nu that Zhou was not 'the average Communist leader' and that he had found him 'receptive to ideas' and 'friendly' in his attitude. He welcomed Zhou's continuing support for the Five Principles of Peaceful Coexistence and urged U Nu to embrace them as the guiding principles governing Sino-Burmese relations. Although Zhou 'was thinking of some pact,' Nehru told U Nu that a bilateral Sino-Burmese declaration embodying the above principle would be enough for the time being. It would 'promote friendly relations' between Beijing and Rangoon and help 'advance the cause of peace in Southeast Asia' by opening the door to further bilateral declarations between China, India, Burma and Indonesia. Nehru claimed that these declarations were only a first step, implying that they could be followed by bolder action once a settlement had been reached in Geneva.[30]

Prime minister of Burma since 1947, U Nu enjoyed significant popular support domestically. A former schoolteacher and novelist, he was a devout Buddhist and a man of integrity and modesty. A prominent figure in the nationalist movement that had led Burma to independence in 1948, he succeeded nationalist leader Aung San after the latter was assassinated in 1947. Having inherited a country threatened by ethnic separatism and communist subversion, U Nu needed no reminding of China's potentially destabilising role in the region.[31] And so, when he and Zhou Enlai finally sat down to talk in the late afternoon of 28 June, U Nu wasted no time voicing his anxieties. He told the Chinese premier he was 'very concerned' that some Burmese communists and Kachin insurgents had crossed the border into China and had received political and military training. Burma, he added, had done nothing to 'directly or indirectly assist your enemies.' It hosted no foreign military bases, had 'halted American aid,' and had done its best to crack down on remaining Kuomintang elements in the country. It had also been the first country to recognise China and had supported China's admission to the UN.[32]

When it was his turn to speak, Zhou denied that China posed a threat to Burma, seeking instead to portray the PRC as the target of aggressive American policy in Asia. Reiterating his earlier remarks to Nehru, he said that revolutions could not 'be exported,' that 'Communist parties from various countries must depend on themselves for success' and 'could not expect outside assistance.' He stressed China's commitment to the principles of peaceful coexistence, and he urged U Nu to 'please study the joint statement from China and India,' implying that the two governments of Burma and the PRC could issue a similar one. Such a declaration, Zhou added, would 'be beneficial to improving relations between our two countries.' With regard to U Nu's specific concerns, he dismissed them as mere rumours or misunderstandings, claiming that China did not wish to interfere in Burma's internal affairs. On the contrary, it wanted an independent Burma with the freedom to choose its political system and was ready 'to conduct friendly cooperation' with it. Zhou also stated that the Chinese government appreciated Rangoon's early recognition of China and its support in the UN. Regarding Burma's opposition to American aid and bases on Burmese territory, he affirmed that these decisions were 'all worth commendation.'[33]

When the two leaders reconvened the next day, U Nu reiterated that 'Burma does have some fears towards China.' He hoped China could 'take steps to eliminate our fear' by respecting Burma's territorial integrity. For his part, Zhou repeated that China harboured no territorial ambitions and was 'willing to establish [relations] with our neighbours and get along peacefully with them.' The two leaders then debated the language of the joint statement they intended to issue at the end of the talks. U Nu proposed a number of demanding points, but Zhou's response was somewhat unhelpful. Politely but firmly, the Chinese leader rejected the former's wording and successfully toned it down. He welcomed U Nu's suggestion to include the Five Principles of Peaceful Coexistence in the final text of the joint statement, as well as a written commitment to 'do everything within [their] powers to further peace in the world and especially in South East Asia.' However, he rejected U Nu's request for a mutual pledge not 'to participate in conspiracies to overthrow' each other's governments and a joint appeal to local communists and Kuomintang elements to give up arms. Nor was Zhou more accommodating when it came to the issue of Chinese residents in Burma and the demarcation of the Sino-Burmese frontier. In this regard, U Nu had proposed that the joint statement include a mutual commitment 'to take steps' to demarcate the border, as well as an assurance from China that 'if overseas Chinese have already obtained the citizenship of the host country then China will no longer view them as Chinese citizens.' However, while indicating his willingness to collaborate with Burma to address both challenges, Zhou remained non-committal, stressing that China needed time to prepare. As regards the overseas Chinese in Burma, he told U Nu that China would first settle the question with Indonesia, the country with the most significant Chinese minority in South-East Asia, and then with other countries, including Burma. He announced that China was about to begin negotiations with an Indonesian delegation.[34] In the end, despite his rigidity at times, Zhou did his best to reassure his Burmese hosts during his brief stay in Rangoon. Indeed, his friendliness was said to have surprised his hosts.[35] His visit to the great pagoda Shwe Dagon on 29 June was clearly calculated to impress a profoundly Buddhist nation and its devout prime minister.[36] He also invited U Nu to visit China, promising to take him on a tour of Yunnan so that the Burmese leader might gain a better understanding of Zhou's country.[37]

It is unclear whether Zhou was ultimately successful in easing U Nu's concerns about China. Two weeks after Zhou visited Rangoon, the Burmese chargé d'affaires in New Delhi told the Canadian high commissioner that Zhou 'had not … convinced U Nu of China's peaceful intentions.' U Nu, he added, 'needed deeds to convince him' and '[i]f China, in its dealings with Burma, did not live up to the five principles (panchsheel), one of the first people U Nu would inform would be Nehru.'[38] Be that as it may, neither Nehru's reassurances about Chinese behaviour nor the signs of a developing Sino-Indian rapprochement must have left U Nu indifferent, for, in the end, he agreed to a joint Sino-Burmese declaration embodying the Five Principles. With India and China committing to uphold these principles, U Nu's freedom of action was limited. In any event, he must also have calculated that Burma could benefit from China's commitment to peaceful coexistence in Asia.[39] Thus, on 1 July he informed Nehru that the talks had gone well and he had been impressed by Zhou's 'open countenance and naturalness of manners.' Moreover, he was pleased that Zhou's visit had 'largely contributed to future easier relations between the two countries.'[40]

For Nehru, this was good news on two counts. First, it signalled Burma's increasing political alignment with India, a goal Nehru had long pursued. Not only did Rangoon seem willing to move more closely in step with New Delhi—not entirely a foregone conclusion given Burmese suspicions of India—[41]it also appeared to share a similar approach to China and, more broadly, to regional security. If Nehru's concept of areas of peace were to gain traction regionally, the support of countries like Burma would be necessary, if not crucial. Second, and perhaps more importantly, the U Nu-Zhou talks seemed to provide a further indication of China's desire to reassure its Asian neighbours. As Nehru revealingly remarked to U Nu, Zhou's visit to Rangoon had been 'helpful in carrying matters a little further from what they were after my talks with Chou En-lai.'[42]

Nehru Takes Stock

In the days and weeks that followed, Nehru took advantage of the conclusion of Zhou Enlai's short visits to India and Burma to assess their significance for India's foreign policy. In an open letter issued to the leaders of the State Congress party at the beginning of July, he argued that these visits marked a 'historic change in the relationship of forces in Asia' because they showed that Asian views could no longer be disregarded. If in the past, Nehru wrote, 'Asia's problems were decided chiefly outside Asia,' it was becoming increasingly evident that in the future it would not be viable 'to ignore what countries of Asia think about themselves or their neighbours.' He believed that if Asian nations adopted the Five Principles of Peaceful Coexistence, they would enjoy peace and stability for at least a few years. 'Even a few years gained,' he added, was 'something worth striving for,' since the 'longer this interval of peace' lasted, the less likely future conflict was.[43]

Nehru was aware that some questioned the wisdom of putting faith in declarations of intent, such as the Five Principles. After all, as he wisely observed, in international affairs 'one can never be dead certain that the friends of today might be enemies of tomorrow.' Nonetheless, he felt it was wrong 'to begin with enmity and suspicion and not give any other approach a chance.' 'Surely it is better,' he claimed, 'to hope for and expect the best, but at the same time be prepared for any eventuality.' This attitude, in turn, would generate 'an atmosphere which helps and makes possible a further step in the right direction.' In any case, Nehru added that even if such declarations of intent were 'not sincerely meant, the result will be to create a force in favour of peace and non-interference.' In commending the government's approach to regional security, Nehru argued that 'peace can only be preserved by methods of peace' and that 'peace preserved by threats is unstable.' 'Therefore,' he continued, 'peace as well as security can be best maintained by efforts at collective peace and avoidance of war.' 'If this,' he added, 'cannot be done in the world as a whole, then an attempt should be made to have areas where such peace can be maintained. Gradually that area will spread.'[44]

A few weeks later, on 26 August, Nehru declared before India's upper chamber of parliament, the Rajya Sabha, that the Five Principles represented a 'new approach' to peace and stability 'certainly in South East Asia and, to some extent, elsewhere too.' He had 'little doubt' that other South-East Asian nations 'were entirely agreeable to these five principles.' This was a significant development because it signalled the gradual emergence of an area of peace. Nehru admitted that it was 'true that by some of the countries agreeing to follow this peaceful course we do not guarantee peace in Asia or anywhere else because it is beyond our capacity,' but he was also quick to add that 'we do throw our weight on the side of peace.' He was pleased that India and China found common ground on some critical questions despite their different political and economic systems. In his view, the Chinese government wanted friendly relations with India and was prepared to 'co-operate in as large a measure as possible.' He also argued that India and China were two leading powers in Asia, and it was of 'highest importance' that they should 'understand each other and should, as far as possible, co-operate with each other.'[45]

Nehru returned once more to these themes in a lengthy, 90-minute foreign policy speech to the Lok Sabha at the end of September 1954.[46] Speaking extempore without notes, the Indian leader rejected suggestions that he was being fooled by the communist powers' seemingly friendly attitude. As he told the lower house, he was fully aware of regional worries about the role of communist powers, especially China, in Asia. He emphasised the fear that South-East Asian countries had of China directing and controlling the local Chinese communities. He also mentioned the 'good deal of apprehension and disturbance' generated in countries like Burma and Thailand by the existence of local communist parties. Most South-East Asian countries, he said, were 'afraid, not of what [communist] Governments do officially, but what they might do *sub rosa* through the activities of the Communist Party in those countries.' Since communist parties were 'intellectually, mentally and otherwise tied up with other groups in other countries,' he understood regional worries that the Soviet Union and PRC 'might well utilise' these parties to their advantage.[47] Yet, as he asked rhetorically:

> [i]f you think that Communist countries are up to mischief, what is the best way of dealing with them? It is not by threatening them 'unless you are prepared to go this way'. The best way is ultimately to talk to them, to talk to any opponent of yours, and if it is in the interests of both parties some agreement will be arrived at.[48]

He did not think creating regional alliances was the answer. Doing so would be counterproductive because it would merely frighten the other side, raise the risk of war and generate more insecurity.[49] The proper response was for countries to embrace the Five Principles of Peaceful Coexistence, as India and Burma had done. As he stated in a passage worth citing in full, in dealing with the Soviet Union or China, it was:

> not a question of believing the other party's word; it is a question of creating conditions where the other party cannot break its word, or if I may say so, where it finds it difficult to break its word. … Those conditions are created by the joint statement that was made both in India and in Rangoon and if those five principles are repeated by the various countries of the world in their relations to each other, they do create an atmosphere. That does not mean that all the forces of aggression and interference and mischief in various countries have been ended. Of course not; they are there, but it does mean that you make it slightly more difficult for them to function and you encourage the other forces ….[50]

As Nehru's words indicated, he was not prepared to take Chinese assurances of peaceful coexistence at face value. On the contrary, he intended to hold the Chinese accountable to the Five Principles so that their violation could be properly condemned. He hoped this might serve as a deterrent against any future aggressive communist behaviour. Yet, despite Nehru's compelling logic, it was clear that this strategy had its limitations. How, for instance, would India react if China resorted to aggression or subversion to pursue its regional aims? What measures would it take to stop or limit such behaviour? As eager as he was to bring about a new era in Sino-Indian relations, Nehru never defined what India's backup plan would entail under these circumstances. In the summer of 1954, he was not ready to contemplate alternative scenarios. After all, as has been noted, Nehru's strategy of non-alignment 'was designed to avoid conflict, not to anticipate and prepare for it.'[51] In the coming months, he would concentrate his efforts on obtaining China's repeated affirmations of adherence to the Five Principles in the hope that Beijing would stick to them out of fear of attracting widespread international condemnation.[52]

In this regard, Nehru's attitude resembled that of British Prime Minister Ramsay MacDonald in response to Hitler's early European policy. Faced with the latter's nascent revisionism in 1933, MacDonald assured his French opposite number, Eduard Daladier, that 'if Hitler broke a disarmament agreement ... the strength of world opposition to her [Germany] cannot be exaggerated.'[53] Sadly for MacDonald, subsequent events revealed how mistaken he was in assuming that Germany would feel constrained by its image on the international stage. Like MacDonald, Nehru too would eventually discover how little Mao's China cared about the world's opinion of it. Nehru knew that he was taking a calculated gamble—one premised on the assumption that, its communist ideology notwithstanding, China needed peace and stability to develop its economy and modernise its society. His mistake, however, was that not only did he downplay the revolutionary nature of Mao's communism, but he also overestimated China's commitment to peaceful coexistence, which Beijing saw as a temporary tactical expedient to undermine American containment and expand its influence in the developing world. Worryingly, Nehru did little to bolster India's military capabilities in the event of a conflict with China.[54]

For the time being, however, he had several reasons to be optimistic about Chinese behaviour, as he conceded to British High Commissioner Clutterbuck in August 1954. The first was Zhou's commitment to providing Burma's and China's other neighbours with assurances similar to those embodied by the Sino-Indian agreement on Tibet. The second was Zhou's assurance that China 'wanted to live and let live.' By his admission, China 'desperately needed peace on her border' in order to 'devote all her energies to the huge task of internal reconstruction and development.' In this context, Zhou had made clear that countries in the region 'would have nothing to fear from China' if they 'became part of a no-war area' with no foreign bases or involvement. The third reason was Zhou's intimation of Beijing's new approach to Chinese communities in South-East Asia. This approach was meant to reassure regional countries by requiring overseas Chinese to either acquire the citizenship of their country of residence or keep their Chinese nationality at the expense of being barred from participating in local politics. A fourth factor was China's economic underdevelopment. China, Nehru argued, was 'very backward industrially and economically' and 'had a long way to go even to catch up to Indian standards.' Moreover, while China's 'lack of industries might give her defensive strength' because 'bombing would not paralyse her,' this constituted a significant drawback 'for offensive purposes.' It would be complicated for China 'to engage in an expansionist policy without a firm industrial and supply base to support it.' Lastly, Nehru was impressed by Zhou's 'frankness and sincerity,' and he was heartened by the fact that Zhou was 'feeling his way towards wider contacts with the outside world' and was 'anxious to give weight to Asian opinion.'[55]

Geneva and Its Aftermath

In India, therefore, the signals emanating from Beijing were viewed as encouraging, indicating that Chinese policymakers were genuinely committed to a new course in foreign policy. The conclusion of the Geneva Conference on 21 July 1954 reinforced this perception, raising Nehru's hopes of entrenching peaceful coexistence in Asia. He had appreciated China's constructive role in facilitating an agreement on Indochina—an attitude he interpreted as further evidence of Beijing's restraint and peaceful intentions.[56] Two aspects of China's conduct in Geneva struck him as particularly reassuring. One was the latter's support for the neutralisation of Indochina and the creation of an enlarged area of peace in South-East Asia.[57] The other was Sino-Soviet insistence that the Viet Minh leadership curb their regional ambitions and accept the neutralisation of Laos and Cambodia.[58] China's conciliatory attitude aside, Nehru had two more reasons to welcome the end of the Geneva Conference. To begin with, the final settlement provided the basis for a peaceful solution to a protracted and brutal colonial conflict that had threatened to spiral out of control. Second, the neutralisation of Laos and Cambodia, along with the prohibition for the two provisional Vietnamese states from hosting foreign military facilities and joining military alliances, was entirely in line with Nehru's idea of a regional area of peace. As a sign of the importance it attached to the Geneva settlement, the Indian government agreed to accept the chairmanship of the International Control Commission, whose task was to oversee the implementation of the settlement in Vietnam, Laos and Cambodia. India's chairmanship of the future commission was not only a success for Nehru's neutralist diplomacy (India was the only nation acceptable to both blocs),[59] but it was also seen as a vindication of his advocacy for a peaceful solution in Indochina. More crucially, it allowed India to oversee and play a part in the implementation of the final agreement.[60]

Nehru's hopes that the Geneva Conference would usher in a new phase in regional relations proved unfounded. With little confidence that the communists would stick to the terms of the agreement, the Eisenhower administration concluded that plans for a Western-led regional alliance should be expedited.[61] In late July, Dulles made it clear that it was time for the United States to 'move ahead quickly with those countries in the area who are willing to join in a Southeast Asia Pact.' Washington's chief aim, he explained, was to deter open Chinese aggression and prevent communist subversion and infiltration in the area. This goal was to be achieved by building up local defence forces and providing these countries open to joining the pact with economic assistance and covert intelligence support. From Dulles's standpoint, the pact's primary advantage was that it allowed the United States 'to draw a line which, if crossed, would permit us to retaliate at the source of aggression and do so with the support of other nations.'[62] It was not, he said, that the United States 'expected early overt military aggression.' But they 'must guard against it as the police guard against lawlessness even in an orderly community,' and '[m]ilitary measures were necessary to provide the atmosphere of security indispensable to economic progress.'[63] Under no circumstance, however, should the pact 'require the stationing of large US and other forces in the area' or encourage its members 'to expect large amounts of US military assistance to build up their armed forces.' Nor should it develop into 'a large NATO-type organization.'[64] In practice, this meant that there should be no formal machinery with forces earmarked for the area and no obligation to automatic action in the face of aggression.[65]

The response of Washington's allies was broadly positive. Although they did not all share 'the same level of concern regarding the immediate communist threat to Southeast Asia as the US,' they all wanted to avoid being 'left out of an American-led security framework for the region.'[66] Australia and New Zealand were the keenest supporters of Dulles's initiative. They viewed a political-military guarantee to frontline non-communist South-East Asian states as a crucial step to halt communist expansion. Moreover, with their post-war foreign policy geared toward securing a greater American regional commitment, they welcomed Dulles's plans as a long-awaited opportunity to draw the Americans more firmly into the defence of South-East Asia.[67] Thailand and the Philippines also responded favourably, seeing a collective defence pact as a deterrent against further communist gains in the area and an opportunity to secure much-needed American aid.[68]

More qualified was the support of Washington's key European allies in Asia. While assuring the Americans of their support,[69] the British made it clear that they had no troops to spare and that any British effort in South-East Asia should be confined to Malaya.[70] Eden even tried to emasculate the defence pact by suggesting that such a pact 'might be part of a wider Locarno-like mutual guarantee of the post-Geneva *status quo*.'[71] Eager not to alienate Indian and Asian opinion, the Foreign Office held that Britain should seek 'a loose military link between the Asian countries backed by a more specific form of agreement between the "white powers".'[72] From London's viewpoint, India's inclusion in a Western-led regional defence pact would improve its appeal among the Asian neutrals.[73] Enlisting Indian support, however, also betrayed London's desire to restrain American policy in Asia and ensure that Washington would not make rash decisions.[74] Knowing this, the Eisenhower administration was wary of India's participation in any Western-led collective system in Asia, believing it would hinder Western policy.[75] Although they acquiesced to London's plans to talk to the Colombo powers, Dulles and the State Department remained sceptical about the prospect of India and Indonesia joining the future pact.[76] As for the French, they gave broad support to the idea, but not without expressing some reservations. Prime Minister Pierre Mendès France favoured a 'flexible form' of association, consisting of a simple 'declaration of common intent' in the event of an armed attack. He argued that this approach would provide France with an 'indispensable' American guarantee 'without establishing an alliance system within which most contracting parties would be non-Asian states.'[77]

Nehru's reaction was, predictably, negative. On 2 August, he rejected Eden's suggestion that India and the other Colombo powers join the United States and its allies at their upcoming September summit to discuss the formation of a South-East Asian defence pact.[78] Mincing no words, he told Eden that India's participation in such an arrangement, or even its support, would amount to nothing short of a radical reorientation of its international outlook. It would go against 'the fundamental approach we seek to make to the problem of peace and stability in South East Asia and indeed the world as a whole.' Moreover, it would 'help to extend the area of the cold war with its attendant progressive armed preparedness and the psychosis of hatred and suspicion in this part of the world.' He added that it might even 'result in the formation of a counter-military alliance.' In any case, most Asian governments and peoples would be against it. In his view, peace and stability in South-East Asia could only be achieved if China were given its 'rightful place' in the UN and countries in the region adhered to the Five Principles of Peaceful Coexistence, which India and China had recently adopted and Burma and Indonesia also supported. Nehru noted that these principles were no different from those underpinning the Geneva settlement, of which the British Foreign Secretary had been 'one of the principal architects.' He regretfully observed that the establishment of a military alliance by some of the powers represented in Geneva would do nothing 'to promote the processes of peace and the lowering of tensions which the settlement has happily helped to begin and further.' In fact, it might even 'retard such processes.' In encouraging Eden 'to take a different line,' Nehru reminded him that, irrespective of all the above considerations, India could not support the planned defence scheme because of its role in the international supervisory commissions on Indo-China.[79]

Nehru delivered a similar message to the US Ambassador George Allen a few days later. In reiterating India's firm opposition to a South-East Asian security pact, Nehru claimed that 'anything involving military commitments' would be entirely 'unnecessary since no one threatened this area.' He believed that 'pacts involving military commitments lead to less security because they increased tensions on both sides.' In Nehru's view, the 'best way to reduce chances of war would be for nations outside [the] Communist bloc to accept Peking's assurances of non-aggression as bona fide and to convince Peking that no effort would be made to overthrow [the] regime or invade Chinese mainland.' He claimed that projects like Dulles's 'merely caused Communist bloc to join together more closely.' In response to Allen's objection that 'a policy of no military commitment' would, for instance, give Burma 'no assurance that anyone would come to its aid if its northern border was crossed,' Nehru replied that 'any assurance to Burma would obviously be directed against China and this would increase Peking's feeling of insecurity and consequently its belligerent attitude.' Nehru thought that 'outright Chinese aggression against Burma would in fact lead to World War without any specific commitment and he believed Peking was already well aware of this fact.' He was so impervious to Allen's warnings about Chinese expansionism that the US ambassador concluded that Nehru appeared to have well and truly bought into the view that the PRC had 'no aggressive designs at least for a decade or so.'[80]

With the exception of Pakistan, which expressed interest in Dulles's defence scheme and decided to send a representative to the Manila summit, the responses from the other Colombo powers were, in the end, broadly in line with New Delhi's expectations, despite some hesitation.[81] While Indonesia was firm in its opposition to the scheme, Burma and Ceylon appeared to be less so. In Jakarta, Ali Sastroamidjojo told the British embassy that Indonesia was not keen on 'taking sides' and did not wish to be associated with a West-led alliance. He believed a collective defence organisation 'would be a step towards war.'[82] Moreover, the Indonesian authorities stated that participation in such an organisation 'would be detrimental to the independent foreign policy which has been conducted by Indonesia in and outside the United Nations.'[83] Burma's reply, in comparison, was more cautious. While recognising that sending a 'representative, or even an observer' to the Manila meeting would not be consistent with Burma's non-alignment, U Nu told London that 'it would be most advantageous if the Colombo Powers could meet and seek a solution acceptable to all.'[84] Burmese officials told the US embassy in Rangoon that Burma 'would not be hostile' to collective defence arrangements in South-East Asia. However, despite their government harbouring no illusion about China, 'circumstances would not permit Burma to participate' in such a scheme.[85] According to Ceylon Prime Minister John Kotelawala, however, Burma had not yet entirely made up its mind, but rather was 'leaving the door open for final decision when [the] exact shape of SEATO is known.'[86] As for Ceylon, its attitude was even less firm. C. C. Desai, the Indian high commissioner in Colombo, reported to New Delhi that, with the prevailing opinion in the country against SEATO, Kotelawala seemed 'a little shaky.'[87] The Ceylon prime minister had told the Americans that he supported SEATO in principle but needed to consult the other Colombo powers before making a decision.[88] His rationale for convening a meeting of the Colombo group was, according to the British high commissioner in Colombo, to try and exercise some 'restraining influence' on Nehru. In doing so, he wanted to prevent the Indian leader from publicly denouncing SEATO, 'thus forcing [the] hand of Ceylon and probably Burma.'[89]

However, Kotelawala's efforts to convene another such meeting fell flat. While Burma, Indonesia and Pakistan supported his initiative,[90] Nehru did not. On 31 July, Nehru had already informed his Colombo partners that India firmly opposed SEATO and would not attend any talks to establish such a scheme. All he was prepared to do was convey to the British his ideas for 'a constructive alternative approach to a collective peace system.'[91] Unwilling to fall in with India's uncompromising opposition to SEATO, Kotelawala seized upon Nehru's reference to an alternative approach to collective security to return to the charge. He proposed once more a Colombo powers meeting, ostensibly to discuss such an approach, but in all likelihood to blunt Indian opposition to SEATO.[92] Nehru, however, was immovable. On 7 August, he wrote to Kotelawala that a meeting of the Colombo powers was inopportune. Quite apart from the fact that he would be unable to leave New Delhi until after September, Nehru argued that the Colombo powers, with the exception of Pakistan, had already informed the British government of their refusal to participate. Hence, the convening of a Colombo group meeting at this time might convey the impression that they were reconsidering their stance, thus generating 'misunderstandings about our positions.'[93] Despite Kotelawala's last-ditch efforts to persuade him to reconsider, Nehru reaffirmed his objection to such a gathering.[94] By doing so, Nehru hoped to prevent the fissures already forming behind the group's facade of unity from widening.[95]

As a result, a frustrated Kotelawala was forced to inform London that he 'could not either participate or send [an] observer' to the proposed SEATO conference. As reasons for his being unable to do so, he adduced domestic politics (in particular, the Opposition's attacks on his pro-American stance);his self-appointed role as the convenor of the Colombo group, which demanded 'an appearance of neutrality'; and his belief that he could 'best help by not giving appearance of being committed to either side,' which he suggested might yet allow him 'to influence Mr. Nehru.' In an apparent attempt to demonstrate that he was not personally opposed to SEATO, Kotelawala indicated that 'he was quite willing that [the SEATO] Conference should take place in Ceylon,' provided Britain requested it and his Cabinet authorised it.[96] Furthermore, in a communiqué issued to the press in mid-August, the Ceylon government stated that it was willing 'to maintain an open mind on the subject.'[97] Despite Indian reports that Kotelawala had not given up hope that 'the Colombo powers would meet soon after the SEATO conference ...

to take stock of the situation and take concerted action as far as possible,'[98] Nehru had succeeded in keeping some semblance of group unity and minimising the impact of Pakistan's decision to attend the SEATO talks.[99] Karachi had, in fact, urged Ceylon to follow Pakistan's example.[100]

When, in early September 1954, the foreign ministers of the United States, France, Britain, Australia, New Zealand, the Philippines, Thailand and Pakistan finally signed the treaty establishing SEATO, the military alliance that emerged from the Manila Conference was a far cry from the aggressive manifestation of American containment that many in India had feared it would be. In a brief prepared for Nehru in late September 1954, T. N. Kaul almost conceded as much. In assessing its likely impact on India's regional policy, Kaul, a Joint Secretary in the Ministry of External Affairs, cast doubts on SEATO's effectiveness as a military alliance. He claimed that the participation of Britain and France in SEATO had, to some extent, taken 'the tooth' out of it. There was no provision in the Manila Treaty for the establishment of 'a joint military headquarters' or for 'grouping the armed forces of the signatory powers under one command.' While the United States might provide armaments and equipment to its allies, it was doubtful that it would commit its armed forces to defend the SEATO area. The British had 'their hands full in Malaya' and could 'probably not spare any troops elsewhere.' The Philippines and Thailand were no more likely 'to provide any military strength.' Only Pakistan could provide the required troops for a joint military force, but 'public opposition and sentiment against such a proposal' made it improbable that they would do so.[101]

For all its shortcomings, Kaul still warned Nehru that SEATO threatened India's regional interests and non-alignment policy. If it succeeded 'in attracting other South East Asian powers,' it could significantly hinder Indian efforts to enlarge the area of peace in South-East Asia. It could also exacerbate regional tensions and even prompt China to form a counter-alliance in opposition to SEATO. Finally, it could also allow Pakistan to 'gain military parity with India' and improve its 'bargaining power to settle outstanding disputes, especially that of Kashmir.' For these reasons, Kaul recommended that India direct its efforts towards preventing SEATO's expansion to other Asian countries and 'counteract[ing] the effects' of SEATO 'by offering a bilateral or multilateral declaration based on the Five Principles to all the South East Asian countries, including Pakistan, Thailand and the Philippines.'[102] Moreover, India should attempt to dissuade China from 'adopting an aggressive attitude' and 'forming a counter-alliance,' as this could inflame tensions. Lastly, the Indian government should also encourage Beijing to adopt measures that could help ease its neighbours' suspicions about China's alleged expansionist designs. Kaul suggested that some of these measures could 'be pursued in the Asian-African conference which Indonesia is so anxious to convene.'[103] As will become evident in the following chapters, this is precisely what Nehru would set out to do—at first tentatively, then more assuredly—in the second half of 1954. As he continued to worry about the direction of Western policy in Asia, Nehru began to consider Indonesian calls for an Asian-African conference as an opportunity to widen the area of peace in Asia and pursue his vision of a neutralised Asia in opposition to the US military alliance system. With growing clarity, he also saw how crucial China's attitude would be in achieving such a vision. As Chapter 6 illustrates, the visit of the Indonesian prime minister to New Delhi in late September was to provide Nehru with the opportunity to reassess his approach to Indonesia's Afro-Asian initiative.

6

TOWARDS AN AFRO-ASIAN CONFERENCE

[T]he proposal regarding an Asian-African conference is still in a nebulous state, although we are largely agreed that there should be such a conference ...

Jawaharlal Nehru[1]

Despite the Colombo powers' lukewarm response to Ali Sastroamidjojo's calls for an Asian-African conference, the Indonesians showed no sign of giving up their pet project. 'Imbued with nationalist zeal,' Ali Sastroamidjojo led a coalition government that was 'militantly anticolonial' and eager to play a leading role within the anti-colonialist movement.[2] It was also a government that was well aware of the positive political impact that an Asian-African conference would have on its precarious domestic position.[3] In mid-May, the British embassy in Jakarta informed London that the Indonesian Cabinet had agreed to send invitations to those Afro-Asian nations that were members of the UN.[4] In the same month, Ruslan Abdulgani, the Secretary-General of the Indonesian Foreign Ministry, revealed to the Australian ambassador in Jakarta that 'most of the soundings they [the Indonesians] had made of other countries had so far drawn satisfactory responses' and that 'it might be possible to hold a conference in August.'[5]

However, by late summer, the British and Australian governments were still unsure what the Indonesians were up to, having received conflicting reports that Jakarta had either sent or was going to send early invitations for an Afro-Asian meeting in September or October 1954. Without access to declassified Indonesian papers, tracking the exact actions of the Ali Sastroamidjojo government is impossible. What is certain, though, is that between late July and early August the Indonesian prime minister circulated an *aide-mémoire* outlining Jakarta's plans for such a summit to a selected group of Afro-Asian countries.[6]

India, of course, was foremost on Indonesian minds, as Jakarta considered New Delhi's support for such an initiative critical. In early August, Nehru received the *aide-mémoire* from Lambertus N. Palar, the Indonesian ambassador in New Delhi.[7] In it, the Indonesian government proposed to hold an Asian-African conference in Indonesia in September or October while the UN General Assembly was in session in New York. The conference would last 'about a week' and be an informal gathering of prime ministers, including all members of the Afro-Asian group at the UN plus Ceylon and Jordan. Members of this group were Afghanistan, Burma, Egypt, Ethiopia, India, Indonesia, Iran, Iraq, Lebanon, Liberia, Pakistan, the Philippines, Saudi Arabia, Syria, Thailand and Yemen. According to the *aide-mémoire,* the conference's goals would be to promote world peace 'through constructive ways on moral principles,' foster greater Afro-Asian collaboration and overcome 'common political and economic problems from the Afro-Asian point of view.' In the political field, the Indonesian document envisioned cooperation between Afro-Asian countries in combatting 'colonialism and its vestiges in whatever form it may appear.' At the same time, it could also assist in realising 'the aims envisaged in the words "non-interference" and "peaceful coexistence".' In the economic field, the document conceived Afro-Asian cooperation as a means of helping eradicate poverty and underdevelopment. Last but not least, the *aide-mémoire* made it clear that the proposed conference would not seek to create a 'third bloc.' Instead, it would 'serve as [a] factor of reconciliation to neutralise the causes and power factors which may lead to a world clash.' In short, Afro-Asian nations must play a significant part in helping reduce tensions between the two superpowers and their respective blocs.[8]

Despite his best efforts to establish the Indonesian case for an Afro-Asian summit, Ali Sastroamidjojo continued to struggle to get the idea off the ground. In a reply to his Indonesian opposite number dated 18 August, Nehru reiterated his well-known reservations.[9] He told Ali Sastroamidjojo that while he welcomed the Indonesian idea, such a conference would need to be carefully prepared if it were to produce significant results. He did not think it possible to hold it at such short notice, given that it might take at least 6 months, if not longer, to organise. Besides, the conference's heterogeneous composition deserved careful attention, for he could not 'quite see what a conference made up of these discordant elements is likely to achieve.' He also had qualms about Indonesia's idea of restricting participation to the Afro-Asian group at the UN. In his view, such an approach would pose two types of problems. First, it would 'lead to the exclusion of important countries.' African nations, he noted, 'would hardly be represented.' Second, it would include Arab countries such as Iraq, Syria and Lebanon, which were 'not much interested in South-East Asia or Asian problems as a whole' but were absorbed in 'their own internal problems and more especially that of Palestine.' More problematically, it would also incorporate the Philippines and Thailand, which were 'intimately tied up with the South-East Asia Organisation' that the Americans proposed to set up and 'would probably form part of such an organisation.' These two countries, Nehru went on, 'represent[ed] very much the United States point of view and not so much what might be called the Asian viewpoint.' As a sop to Ali Sastroamidjojo, he proposed that the Colombo powers meet once more to go over the whole idea of an Asian-African summit. However, as he hastened to point out, this meeting could only occur once it became clear what had resulted from the Manila Conference, where, as mentioned in Chapter 5, the United States and its allies were expected to discuss the formation of a South-East Asian alliance. Meanwhile, Nehru invited Ali Sastroamidjojo to New Delhi for informal talks in September before 'any further step is taken in regard to the Afro-Asian Conference.'[10]

Ali Sastroamidjojo Goes to New Delhi

As a result, the Indonesian leader travelled to India for a 4-day visit in late September 1954.[11] Scion of Javanese nobility, conspicuous for his trademark Van Dyke beard, he had been one of the leading personalities of the radical wing of the pre-war Indonesian nationalist movement. Like Nehru, he had served some years in jail for his anti-colonial activities.[12] A close associate of President Sukarno, Ali Sastroamidjojo had held a succession of ministerial posts in the Republican governments that fought for Indonesia's independence from the Dutch between 1945 and 1949.[13] Appointed Indonesia's first ambassador to the United States in 1950, Ali Sastroamidjojo returned to Indonesia in July 1953 to replace Wilopo as prime minister.[14] Calm and untheatrical, he lacked President Sukarno's charisma, penchant for histrionics and excellent oratorical skills. However, once in government, he proved himself 'a skilful tactician' capable of navigating the complexities of Indonesian politics.[15] According to Nehru's sister, Vijaya Lakshmi Pandit, who had got to know Sastroamidjojo well when the two were posted in Washington (she had led the Indian delegation to the UN between 1946–48 and 1952–53), he had 'improved so much since those days as to be anything but a weakling.'[16] Nehru considered him 'an able man with a good grasp of international affairs.'[17] He was also described as a strong believer in Asianism.[18] In foreign policy, he was determined to 'give Indonesia a regional and global presence.'[19] Moreover, following in the footsteps of his predecessor Wilopo, he had sought a 'greater degree of autonomy in foreign affairs.'[20] To this end, he steered Indonesia away from the 'Western-oriented' and 'anti-communist' foreign policy of the early post-independence Indonesian governments.[21] On his journey to New Delhi, Ali Sastroamidjojo was accompanied by a small party, including his wife, Titi Roelia; the head of the Asian Division of the Indonesian Ministry of Foreign Affairs, Soekardjo Wirjopranoto; and the Indonesian ambassador to India, Lambertus Palar, who had returned to Jakarta for consultations.[22] In his 3-year stint as Indonesian ambassador to the UN between 1950–53, Palar had played an essential role in establishing an Afro-Asian group in the General Assembly.[23]

Before Ali Sastroamidjojo's arrival, the Indian ambassador in Jakarta, B. F. H. B. Tyabji, sent a lengthy despatch to the Commonwealth Secretary, Subimal Dutt, urging the Nehru administration to treat the Indonesian leader's upcoming visit as 'one of historic importance.' Mincing no words, Tyabji reminded Dutt that Indonesia was the 'greatest Southeast Asian country' after Pakistan and that this was the first visit by an Indonesian prime minister to India. Ali Sastroamidjojo and his wife, while welcoming 'informality' and 'spontaneous affection,' were 'representatives of a proud and sensitive people,' and 'care must be taken, while preserving a friendly atmosphere, not to overlook the protocol and regular form.' As a result, it was essential that the Indian government carefully plan the visit so as to strengthen 'the old-age ties between our two countries.'[24] Dutt concurred with Tyabji that the Indonesians were 'extremely touchy about their position of independence and strength,' and, in a note to Nehru, he warned the prime minister that 'whatever we do, we must avoid giving them an impression of a big brother attitude.'[25] Heeding his officials' advice, Nehru concluded that India should make every effort to demonstrate that it regarded this visit as 'a very important event.'[26] '[W]e should,' Nehru said, 'keep the importance of Indonesia in mind and fashion our policy accordingly ... We should try our best to be friendly and to cooperate with Indonesia and develop various bonds.'[27] Accordingly, the Indian government drew up an elaborate programme for the Indonesian prime minister, which included an address to parliament, a banquet at the Rashtrapati Bhavan, the residence of the Indian president, and visits to Delhi's most important historical and artistic sites, as well as the Taj Mahal and Fatehpur Sikri in Agra.[28]

On his arrival at Palam Airport on the morning of 22 September, the unassuming Ali Sastroamidjojo was met on the gangway by Nehru and his Cabinet ministers, in addition to members of parliament, the chiefs of the armed forces and the heads of various government departments.[29] As he stepped off the aeroplane, a large crowd cheered him.[30] Despite an indisposition that set him back at the start of his visit and the extensive ceremonial programme arranged for him, Ali Sastroamidjojo was able to see Nehru in the morning and afternoon of each day.[31] In meeting the Indian prime minister, Ali

Sastroamidjojo was determined 'to press in person for a firm date' for his proposed Afro-Asian conference and get the Indians to stop 'hedging.'[32] As he recalled in his memoirs, 'Nehru's opinion was the most important because his influence on the policies of India's neighbours at the time was indeed great. So, it more or less depended on Nehru's attitude whether the other nations would support our government's plans.'[33] Although Nehru's August message had 'disappointed him greatly,' Sastroamidjojo had 'been persistent' in his quest for an Asian-African conference.[34] With a general election scheduled for 1955 to elect a new parliament to replace the existing appointed body and a constituent assembly to draft a permanent constitution, he needed a major international success to boost his standing at home and counter mounting public discontent about his government's increasing ineffectiveness.[35]

Dependent on communist votes to survive in parliament, Sastroamidjojo's Cabinet appeared spectacularly ill-prepared and ultimately unable to address the many problems besetting the young Indonesian democracy.[36] Of particular concern was the deteriorating state of the Indonesian economy, which was plagued by inflation, government deficits, low commodity prices, the worsening balance of payments and corruption.[37] The news of a scandal involving President Sukarno added to Ali Sastroamidjojo's woes. In September, the news broke that, while still married to his third wife Fatmawati, Sukarno was having a secret affair with Mrs Hartini Suwondo, the wife of an oil company official. The revelations of Sukarno's extramarital escapades created a significant stir in Indonesia.[38] As the Indian embassy in Jakarta reported to New Delhi, a 'most serious crisis' was 'developing' in Indonesia—one that 'reek[ed] with palace and political intrigue reminiscent of certain former Indian States.' The position of the prime minister's party was 'obviously threatened,' and it was, therefore, a 'bold act on his part departing for India at this juncture.'[39] The decline of Sukarno's prestige could only reflect poorly on Ali Sastroamidjojo's *Partai Nasional Indonesia* (PNI), given the Indonesian president's close identification with the PNI and strong support for the government despite his supposedly non-partisan constitutional role.[40]

The Nehru-Sastroamidjojo Talks

On arriving in Delhi, Ali Sastroamidjojo found Nehru's attitude still 'hesitant' and 'cool.'[41] Nehru 'again brought up the difficulties he had mentioned at the Colombo Conference and argued that the Asian-African Conference should be postponed.'[42] In reply, Ali Sastroamidjojo 'insisted that nothing less than a full dress Afro-Asian Conference attended by top level Ministers would provide the dramatic appeal necessary to rally opinion in Indonesia and consolidate support for the Government.'[43] Moreover, he argued it was precisely because 'political developments in the world, and especially in Asia, had worsened since the Geneva Agreement' that an Asian-African conference should be held 'as soon as possible.' Such a conference would not only 'contribute towards the lessening of world tensions,' but would also turn Asian-African nations into 'an important bloc which would have to be taken notice of in the game of international politics.' 'If,' he added, 'we allowed this good opportunity to pass by, we would lose momentum in determining the historic role of the Asian and African peoples in world politics.'[44] In an address to the Indian parliament on 23 September, the Indonesian leader issued a clarion call for Afro-Asian unity, arguing that the peoples of Asia had 'friends amongst the nations of the African continent. To a large extent they face the same problems.' Hence, Afro-Asian cooperation was indeed possible and could 'lead to the immense strengthening of the forces marching towards peace.' To this end, he said, 'a conference of Afro-Asian countries could lay down the pattern.'[45] The following day, his proposal for an Afro-Asian conference received an 'enthusiastic reception' during an address to the Indian Council of World Affairs.[46]

That the Indian government was still in two minds about the desirability of an Afro-Asian conference was evident from the advice Nehru received from his closest adviser, Krishna Menon. In the run-up to Ali Sastroamidjojo's visit, Menon had written to Pillai from New York, pointing out that '[e]xcept on racial and colonial questions,' the African-Asian group at the UN 'has rarely moved together or thought the same way and its meetings have mostly been on these questions. Above facts may be placed before the Prime Minister.'[47]

Despite these reservations, Menon ultimately recommended Nehru support the Indonesian proposal if Ali Sastroamidjojo wanted 'a larger conference early next year.' However, he warned the prime minister that the Asian-African group at the UN was 'not a sound or desirable basis.' If such a conference, he said, 'goes beyond South-East Asia, then the exclusion of Japan or China would be most undesirable.' At the same time, he also suggested that an:

> Asian-African Conference much on the basis of [the] Asian Relations Conference of 1946 [sic] providing representation at National but not Governmental levels would perhaps be more practical if Sastroamidjojo is agreeable to it. It will enable an influential gathering to take place in Indonesia. If [this] suggestion ... is not practical or is unacceptable to Sastroamidjojo my feeling is that we should either (a) confine it strictly to South East Asia ... or (b) have a larger all Asia Conference including China and Japan. There is much to be said for the latter if we can get the Chinese to agree to keep it on a general level.[48]

Only after Ali Sastroamidjojo had addressed the Indian parliament did he discern a shift in Nehru's position.[49] In reality, by the time the Indonesian prime minister landed at Palam Airport, Nehru had already concluded that it would 'be difficult to oppose this [conference] or even to ask for a long delay.' Burma and other countries supported it, he said. Indonesia insisted on it. In his view, Indonesia was at present 'facing [a] severe internal crisis due chiefly to private and domestic reasons connected to President [Sukarno]'s private life.'[50] Nehru thought that refusing to give the Indonesians what they wanted would 'create many complications and cause great disappointment.'[51] Throughout 1954, he had come to recognise Jakarta's growing significance in India's regional calculations. Together with India and Burma, Indonesia 'formed the core of the so-called area of peace'—a neutralised buffer zone between Cold War blocs where countries practised non-alignment and peaceful coexistence.[52] Placing a high value on this concept, Nehru was hopeful that if India, Indonesia and Burma '[held] together and [were] firm in their policies,' it might 'not be easy [for the Americans] to change the face of South East Asia,' notwithstanding their efforts to drive non-communist neutrals to take sides in the regional Cold War.[53]

Significantly, Nehru now told Ali Sastroamidjojo that the Indonesian proposal for such a conference had taken on 'an added significance' in light of two critical regional events—the establishment of SEATO and, as will be seen in Chapter 7, the rising tensions in the Taiwan Strait following the PRC's bombing of the Taiwan-controlled Quemoy islands, located a few miles from the Chinese mainland.[54] On 3 September, the PLA pounded Kuomintang defences for 5 hours, killing two American military advisers. On 22 September—the day Ali Sastroamidjojo arrived in New Delhi—the PLA resorted to more shelling in retaliation to Kuomintang air raids on the mainland. The PRC's strong-arm tactics were designed to dissuade the United States from concluding a defence treaty with Taiwan, which, along with SEATO, the Chinese feared would form part of a broader American defence system in East Asia.[55] Concerned that both the creation of SEATO and the Taiwan Strait imbroglio threatened to destabilise an already precarious situation in East Asia, Nehru concluded that these developments 'deserve[d] careful consideration by the countries of Asia, and, more especially, by those of South-East Asia.'[56] He called on India and Indonesia 'to cooperate fully and thereby build up an area of peace which will ever grow.'[57] 'Such a Conference,' he maintained, 'should be held before long.'[58] As he further explained to the Indian ambassador in Colombo, C. C. Desai, the:

> centre of importance for us has shifted from distant countries to South-East Asia. In South-East Asia, the two most important countries, both of which are closely associated with us are Burma and Indonesia. The recent SEATO agreement, as well as the part we are playing in Indochina, have made this South-East Asian corner of the world of extreme importance to us. The attacks and counterattacks on the China coast at Quemoy add to the seriousness of the situation in this large area. Our entire policy of preserving an area of peace depends on the closest cooperation between India, Burma and Indonesia ... There is a possibility of a large-scale Asian Conference being held, probably at Djakarta, and for this to be preceded by a meeting of the

> Colombo Conference countries. All this is in relation to the fast developing situation in South-East Asia.[59]

Although his close advisers appeared to still be divided on the desirability of an Asian-African gathering, Nehru came, in the end, to the conclusion that such a conference might offer India an excellent opportunity to counter Washington's containment policy and its efforts to build a regional defence alliance.[60] In a note to his cousin, Foreign Secretary R. K. Nehru, he denied that his decision had anything to do with the establishment of SEATO, India having accepted the principle of holding an Asian-African conference at the previous April Colombo meeting.[61] Yet, a connection was undoubtedly there, as Nehru realised that such a conference could provide a platform to promote an alternative approach to regional relations. As a result, after months of dithering, Nehru moved a step closer to making the Indonesian-sponsored conference a centrepiece of his regional diplomacy. He suggested to his Indonesian opposite number that the issues to be discussed at the proposed meeting should include 'the promotion of peace' and 'the five principles which have been agreed to as between India, Burma and China.'[62] For the time being, he remained tight-lipped in public about the prospect of inviting China, notwithstanding Ali Sastroamidjojo's remarks that it might be invited and despite sections of the Indian press demanding its participation.[63] In private, however, Nehru indicated that all independent Asian countries should be invited, and 'this would include China, Japan and Turkey at the other end.'[64] 'To exclude,' he added, 'either China or Japan in a conference which is going to deal, to a large extent, with South-East Asian problems would be very odd and liable to much criticism.'[65]

In the end, Ali Sastroamidjojo got what he wanted. The final communiqué stated that both countries 'were anxious to further the cause of peace in the world and more especially in South-east Asia' and were 'in general agreement about the approach to these problems.' More importantly, they agreed that an Afro-Asian conference 'would be desirable and helpful in promoting the cause of peace and a common approach to their problems.' Such a conference 'should be held at an early date' and be preceded by a meeting of the five Colombo prime ministers, preferably in Jakarta.[66] Ali Sastroamidjojo described his visit as 'very fruitful.'[67] He said he was 'much relieved' because Nehru's change of attitude made it simpler for him to gain the backing of Asian and African nations for his initiative.[68] Moreover, he praised the closeness of Indonesia's relations with India, although his ambassador in New Delhi, Palar, appeared to be 'anything but exultant about the achievements of the visit.'[69] The Australian high commissioner in New Delhi, Walter Crocker, reported to Canberra that while '[t]here were courtesy and attention,' 'there was no warmth.' In contrast to 'the interest and the feeling' evident during the earlier visits of Zhou Enlai and the Pakistani prime minister, Mohammed Ali Bogra, the overall Indian reaction was 'cool.' He even noted that Nehru 'at times hardly concealed a look of boredom.'[70] In any case, all that mattered was that Ali Sastroamidjojo had finally secured India's crucial support for a preliminary meeting of the Colombo powers to discuss the convening of an Asian-African conference.[71] After weeks of trying, this was by no means a minor accomplishment.

The Aftermath of Ali Sastroamidjojo's Visit to India

On 26 September, the Indonesian prime minister flew from New Delhi to Rangoon, where he worked 'quite hard' to push the idea of an Afro-Asian conference.[72] Despite the two governments agreeing that such a gathering 'was desirable' and 'should be held at an early date,' Burmese support remained 'lukewarm.'[73] The Burmese authorities still viewed the Indonesian initiative as 'vague and over-ambitious.' They were concerned that it might 'serve as a platform for the ventilation of the various disagreements which exist between the individual Asian and Arab countries.'[74] As a result, they appeared to support it less for its intrinsic merits than to bolster the political position of the Ali Sastroamidjojo government. In any case, with India publicly backing the Indonesian plan, the Burmese had little choice but to go along with it.[75] After Burma gave its approval, Pakistan and Ceylon also gave their (unenthusiastic) go-ahead to the Indonesian proposal.[76] The Ceylonese government still considered it 'a hare-brained scheme' but was unwilling to 'tell the Indonesians to drop it.'[77] As for the Pakistanis, the Secretary of the Ministry of Foreign Affairs, J. A. Rahim, downplayed the importance of the proposed Asian-African conference, pointing out that, if anything, this 'would provide an excellent opportunity for Pakistan to put over a few telling remarks about the domination of unwilling subject peoples in Asia by Asians, and in general to twist Nehru's tail over Kashmir.'[78] After returning to Jakarta from his brief visits to India and Burma, Ali Sastroamidjojo despatched Palar to New York for further consultations with the Afro-Asian group representatives at the UN.[79] The outcome of these soundings was encouraging: only Thailand and the Philippines, out of the fourteen countries consulted, declined to participate.[80] Having secured broad Afro-Asian support and the backing of his Colombo partners, the Indonesian prime minister wasted no time pushing ahead. In October, the Indonesian Acting Minister for Foreign Affairs confirmed to the British embassy in Jakarta that the prime ministers of the five Colombo powers would meet in Indonesia at the end of December and the proposed Asian-African conference would be held the following February or March. Its agenda would focus on reducing world tensions, colonialism and economic cooperation. The Indonesian minister stressed that the conference's tone 'would be kept moderate.'[81]

As the Indonesian prime minister savoured his foreign policy success, Nehru travelled to Beijing in mid-October for the first-ever trip made to China by an Indian prime minister. In late August, he decided to accept Zhou's invitation to visit China, which the Chinese premier had extended to him during his visit to New Delhi.[82] Nehru's 12-day visit was intended to strengthen India's relations with the PRC. On his way to China, he told reporters in Calcutta that he was travelling there with 'no set purpose' other than to promote 'greater understanding' between the two countries. He said it was imperative for India and China to 'understand each other' and develop 'friendly relations' in the interest of regional and world peace. He described the visit as a significant historical moment and an important step towards a greater Asian role in shaping the region's future. He also re-emphasised the importance of the Five Principles of Peaceful Coexistence as a model of diplomatic conduct in Asia. He strongly criticised SEATO but dismissed speculations that India and China were seeking to establish an alternative to it.[83] In this context, it should be noted that, behind the scenes, he had turned down Zhou's suggestion that he travel to China with Burmese Prime Minister U Nu, who was also planning a visit to the country. Eager to avoid giving the impression that the leaders of India, China and Burma were gathering in China to hatch some sort of an anti-SEATO front, Nehru told Zhou that he wished to go to Beijing alone.[84]

In reality, by talking up peaceful coexistence and the role that India and China could play in promoting it, Nehru was plainly championing an alternative approach to regional security centred on close Sino-Indian relations. However, for his vision to become a reality, Nehru required further evidence of Beijing's commitment to peaceful coexistence. He hoped that his trip to China would give him additional assurances of Chinese sincerity, thus allowing India to take its relationship with China to the next level. Auspiciously, the signs appeared to be on Nehru's side. On the eve of his departure for China, India and China signed a bilateral trade agreement—the first of its kind between the two nations.[85] Even though the economic impact of the agreement was expected to be relatively modest, it seemed to represent a step forward in the development of closer relations between the nations.[86] As it turned out, Nehru's visit to China significantly accelerated the process of rapprochement between India and China. As Chapter 7 shows, Nehru's talks in Beijing with Mao Zedong and Zhou Enlai proved to be a success. At least on the surface, they fostered a greater confluence of views between the Indian and Chinese leaders and reassured Nehru of China's motives and support for peaceful coexistence. The fact that he departed Beijing confident that he could work with the Chinese leadership to extend the area of peace in Asia cleared the way for China's invitation to the Asian-African conference.

7

NEHRU'S VISIT TO CHINA

There is a Chinese saying—to 'seize somebody's pigtail'. But China and India do not need to seize each other's pigtail—we are not on alert against each other.

Mao Zedong[1]

Determined to strengthen India's ties with its giant neighbour, Nehru left New Delhi's Palam Airport in the early morning of 15 October on an Indian Air Force Dakota plane. Despite having a slight temperature due to a cold, he was reportedly in a 'very cheerful mood.'[2] Among those who turned out to see him off were the President of India, Rajendra Prasad, Cabinet ministers, chief ministers, service chiefs, members of parliament, government officials, heads of foreign missions, the Chinese vice minister for Foreign Trade and the Chinese chargé d'affairs.[3] The presence of so many notables was no doubt a sign of the importance attributed to the visit. The *Times of India,* the country's largest daily, captured its significance in a brief opinion piece published the following day. Describing the visit as 'a mission on behalf of peace and understanding,' it told its readers that one of its key aims was to probe Chinese sincerity about peaceful coexistence and the concept of a peace area. According to the paper, 'no sentimental or exaggerated concept of Asianism' should conceal the fact that the two nations held different values. India was a democracy, whilst China was a communist state. The former's ideational identification with Western democracy and the latter's ideological closeness with Soviet communism were 'far stronger' factors than 'race and geography.' Hence, the Indian government had every reason to seek specific assurances on Chinese behaviour. Although 'the entire trend of New Delhi's policy towards China has been to reject any presupposition of hostility,' the *Times of India* concluded that India would do well to remember that, 'unless otherwise proved, there can be no friendship.'[4]

At the heart of Nehru's trip to China were his talks with Mao Zedong, Zhou Enlai and other CCP leaders in Beijing. In addition to the capital, he was scheduled to visit Canton (today's Guangzhou), Shanghai, Nanking (Nanjing), Hankow (Hankou), Mukden (Shenyang), Anshan and Dairen (Dailan).[5] His packed programme also included visits to factories, colleges, theatres, museums, department stores, village cooperatives and municipalities.[6] Accompanied by a small party, including his daughter Indira, Pillai and his special assistant, M. O. Mathai, Nehru stopped in Calcutta (as mentioned in Chapter 6), Rangoon and Hanoi before reaching Canton on 18 October.[7] In Rangoon, where he received the 'wildest demonstration of enthusiasm' from local Indians, he found U Nu and his Cabinet still apprehensive about China and its regional role. Mindful that Rangoon's approach to China might influence the attitudes of other Asian governments (and hence affect the pace of China's regional engagement), Nehru sought to ease Burma's concerns. He reminded Burmese ministers that, despite China being a 'communist revolutionary state,' it might still be advantageous 'to talk matters over with the Chinese Government in a friendly way.'[8] In Hanoi, Ho Chi Minh told him he supported the Five Principles and wished to see them applied between Vietnam, Laos, Cambodia and other nations.[9] Incidentally, Nehru's arrival in China was preceded by the visit of a high-powered Soviet delegation led by Nikita Khrushchev. Taking advantage of the celebrations for the fifth anniversary of the establishment of the PRC, the CCP leaders and their Soviet guests pledged to uphold the principles of peaceful coexistence in their relations with other nations.[10] With Beijing fully committed to peaceful coexistence, Nehru's visit could not begin under better auspices, despite India's concerns regarding China's involvement in the Taiwan Strait crisis.[11]

Nehru Arrives in Beijing

On his arrival in Beijing on 19 October, Nehru was received with 'highest honours.'[12] Zhou Enlai and other CCP dignitaries welcomed him.[13] As the two leaders rode from the Hsiyuan Airfield into the imperial city in an open Soviet Zis limousine, they were cheered by an estimated crowd of over 200,000 people lining the road—including a large number of boys and schoolchildren—clapping, cheering and shouting 'long live to peace.'[14] Nehru later wrote to Edwina Mountbatten, a close friend and wife of British India's last viceroy, Louis 'Dickie' Mountbatten, that the welcome he received far surpassed the one given, only a few days earlier, to the Soviet delegation.[15] The British chargé d'Affaires in Beijing, Humphrey Trevelyan, painted a similar picture to his superiors in London. He told the Foreign Office that such a reception was 'in striking contrast' to the one accorded to Khrushchev and his delegation, who 'had travelled behind curtains and were received only by officials.'[16] Similar scenes of excitement were replicated across the country, in Canton, Dairen, Nanking and Shanghai.[17] Wherever Nehru went, Pillai recounted to the British High Commission in Delhi, he received a 'tumultuous reception.'[18] According to Pillai, 'even in India where crowds of 500,000 are not uncommon he had never seen such large gatherings of people' made up mainly of youngsters.[19] While stage-managed, such large, enthusiastic gatherings of people impressed Nehru deeply. He attributed such enthusiasm to 'a sense of Asian cooperation' and spoke of 'an emotional upheaval representing the basic urges of the people for friendship with India' and a welcome that went beyond mere 'political exigency.'[20]

Anxious to project an image of a peaceful, friendly and dynamic China, CCP leaders rolled out the red carpet for the first non-communist leader to visit their country. From the carefully organised tours of Chinese cities, factories and even a farm to the lavish daily banquets, they pulled out all the stops to impress their

Indian guest.[21] In what was soon to become a well-established Chinese practice of giving visiting Afro-Asian dignitaries special treatment, with the view to instilling in them an image of China 'as a peaceful and tolerant nation concerned first and foremost with its own economic development,'[22] Mao and Zhou went out of their way to reassure Nehru of their peaceful intentions. The official CCP line emphasised, among other things, the two countries' '2,000 years of friendship without conflict' and hailed India's peace efforts in Korea and Indochina.[23] In short, Chinese leaders viewed Nehru's visit to China as part and parcel of their charm offensive towards the Third World.

At the same time, however, China had a further motive to keep up its campaign of friendliness with India. The reason was the Republic of China (ROC) or Taiwan. In July 1954, Mao ordered the development of military plans with the ostensible aim of liberating Taiwan.[24] In early September 1954, following a sizeable military build-up along the PRC's coastal areas, Chinese batteries began opening fire against Jinmen (Quemoy), a small Nationalist-controlled island a few miles off the Chinese mainland. This was in response both to Taipei's decision to deploy nearly 60,000 troops there and to ongoing US-ROC talks on a mutual defence pact.[25] Although China's immediate goal was not the takeover of Taiwan, its tactics were nonetheless intended to avoid changes in the regional balance of power that would make this takeover more difficult to achieve in the long term.[26] As Zhou told his advisers in early September 1954, while the takeover remained declared government policy, such an outcome could only be realised through 'a long-term complex struggle.' As a result, unless the United States intervened militarily in the Taiwan Strait, China should stick to 'diplomatic struggle,' which necessitated 'enlarging the international united front and isolating the US aggressive bloc so as to win eventual liberation of Taiwan.'[27] In this context, as Zhou pointed out on the eve of Nehru's arrival in Beijing, his visit and the one planned by U Nu for early December were to provide China with the opportunity to further unite the 'peace-advocating and neutral forces headed by India' in an effort to 'isolate America.'[28] Beijing knew that its bellicose behaviour had raised regional concerns regarding its commitment to peaceful coexistence and that such a perception needed to be rectified.[29]

With this in mind, Mao and Zhou did their best to ensure that the Chinese and Indian governments reached a broad degree of convergence on several regional issues. This task was not beyond their reach, given Nehru's willingness to reciprocate. In his quest for a more stable regional system, the Indian leader had long argued in favour of engaging with China. According to him, there could be no enduring stability if China remained an outcast on the fringes of the international system.[30] The events leading up to and following the Geneva Conference only served to reinforce his belief that neither the containment nor the ostracism of China would provide a solution to regional instability. Consequently, Nehru and his Chinese hosts were ready to forge closer ties between their respective countries. If, during their June talks in New Delhi, Nehru and Zhou had approached each other with a degree of circumspection, now such caution appeared to have given way to a determined effort to take the bilateral relationship to the next level.

Nehru's Talks With Mao Zedong and Zhou Enlai

The first meeting between Nehru and Mao set the tone for the Indian leader's trip to China.[31] Mao told Nehru that he 'had been looking forward to his visit,' while Nehru admitted to being 'overwhelmed' by the 'very warm welcome' he had received in Beijing.[32] More importantly, the two leaders sought to capitalise on their shared experience of Western colonialism to establish a closer rapport and 'lay the philosophical grounds for co-operation,' as historian Sulmaan Wasif Khan noted.[33] Despite their different social systems and political ideologies, said Mao, India and China had a significant 'point in common, that is, all of us have to cope with imperialism.' China had been 'bullied by Western imperialist powers for over one hundred years' whereas India 'was bullied even longer, for more than three hundred years.' Agreeing with Mao that India, China and 'many other countries in Asia ha[d] suffered from the oppression and domination of foreign colonial powers,' Nehru claimed that the ties that bound Asian nations went beyond the shared experience of foreign rule. Despite their different ideologies and conditions, Asian countries had 'many things in common since ancient times, and the problems we are facing now are also commonly shared by us.' Believing that these differences were not important between two friendly countries such as China and India, Nehru also suggested that Beijing and New Delhi should 'play more important roles in Asia.'[34]

To reassure Nehru of China's intentions, and to play down the bellicose rhetoric emanating from Beijing following the escalation of tensions in the Taiwan Strait, Mao and Zhou insisted that China was 'anxious for peace' and 'did not want war.'[35] As Mao told Nehru, the new China was 'truly in need of friends,' for it was still a 'weak' country facing 'a strong opponent, the United States, which is bent on fixing us whenever it has the opportunity.'[36] Mao further argued that, like India, China 'needed peace to reconstruct' its economy as it was 'industrially backward.'[37] Indeed, he added, China needed '[a] peace of at least several decades.'[38] To Nehru's observation that China's regional role aroused 'a certain amount of fear in the minds of the smaller nations in Asia' and that concerns also existed about communist 'interference through local Communist parties,' Mao and Zhou disingenuously replied that it was not China's policy to 'interfere in any way with local affairs.'[39] Zhou, in particular, claimed that these concerns were 'absurd.' He cited the example of the Kuomintang forces inside Burma and said that 'China would have been justified in attacking them as they were creating trouble on the Chinese side.' However, China had refrained from doing so in order to maintain friendly relations with Burma.[40]

While traversing much of the ground he had already covered with Zhou the previous June in New Delhi, Nehru now focused at length on the role of the United States in Asia. Quite predictably, the two Chinese leaders argued that it was Washington's 'aggressive' and 'expansionist' designs in East Asia that 'came in the way of peace' by generating tensions and creating instability.[41] The United States, Mao pointed out to Nehru, had 'advanced its defence lines to South Korea, Taiwan, and Indochina which are so far away from the United States and so close to us. This makes our sleep unsound.' Moreover, he disclosed to Nehru that China was subjected to intrusions into its airspace by American aeroplanes, which included Kuomintang agents (as well as some American ones) and weapons being air-dropped into the interior provinces of Sichuan and Qinghai. For Mao, this was ample evidence that the United States was 'bent on harming us whenever they have the opportunity to do so.'[42] For his part, Zhou attacked the United States for its support of Taiwan, which, he claimed, was intended to 'create a tense situation' and 'make preparations for war.' In his view, the United States did 'not want to instigate a major war now,' but its 'disruptive sabotaging and warfare today' was 'intended for a big war tomorrow.'[43] Nehru acknowledged that the United States had 'no plan for a major war' but also admitted that he had little faith in the current American administration. Although he was less harsh in his condemnation of Washington's Cold War policies than his Chinese hosts, Nehru by no means came across as a friend of the United States. He agreed with Zhou's assessment of the United States as a power that wanted to 'dominate' and 'control the world.'[44] In the Chinese record of the talks, Nehru described the United States as a 'powerful,' 'belligerent' and 'imperialist' nation.[45] He complained to Zhou that Washington exploited the fears that small and weak regional countries harboured towards India and China. Like the Europeans, the Americans were 'jealous of China's power' and did 'not want India to grow stronger.'[46] He also attacked Washington's decision to establish SEATO, which he described as 'America's reaction against the Geneva agreements.'[47] He called US Secretary of State Dulles a 'great menace' and 'narrow-minded and bigoted.' In contrast, President Eisenhower was 'weak' and did 'not understand politics.'[48] Sympathising with China over the issue of Taiwan, Nehru agreed with Zhou's assertion that if Washington were 'unwilling to have peaceful coexistence and wants war instead, then we will isolate America.' 'The question is,' Nehru said, 'at the UN and elsewhere, what steps can be taken to isolate America diplomatically?' A way, he went on, must be found 'to create a situation in which America will feel isolated.' If the United States were isolated, it would 'find it difficult to act.' To this end, Nehru stated that India was 'trying to find ways' to influence Burma, Indonesia and, to a lesser extent, European countries.[49]

Nehru, Mao and Zhou all agreed that to isolate the United States and neutralise its destabilising influence on regional politics, it was essential to win Asian nations over to their cause.[50] Doing so, however, would be easier said than done. As Nehru pointed out with a tinge of condescension, the problem was that, aside from the Soviet Union, there were only two countries in Asia that had 'stable and strong governments' along with 'the support of the people,' and were also 'economically progressing.'[51] These two nations were India and China. The rest of Asia was 'politically and economically weak' and, therefore, 'afraid.'[52] 'On the one hand,' Nehru argued, Asian nations 'do not like imperialism. On the other hand, they fear bigger countries such as China and India.'[53] Because of such 'weakness and fear,' they could 'be won over and made to cooperate with the US.'[54] India and China, he said, must 'keep these nations in the right direction for the peace of Asia and the world.'[55] For Nehru, the key to overcoming the Asian nations' mistrust of India and China lay in the Five Principles of Peaceful Coexistence. If these principles were widely observed, he said, 'tense situations can be greatly reduced and every country will be able to pursue development in accordance with its own wisdom [while maintaining] friendly [relations] with other countries.' In words that could not have failed to please Nehru, Mao replied that 'countries should be committed to [the] Five Principles and assume obligations accordingly. If a country says one thing but acts otherwise, it is justifiable to criticise that country.' Moreover, he was adamant that they 'should be extended to the state-to-state relations among all countries.' He criticised Britain and the United States for not embracing these principles as China and India had.[56]

In his second meeting with Nehru, Zhou made an even stronger commitment, claiming that, in order to allay regional fears of China, the Chinese government was prepared to abide by the Five Principles in its dealings with Asian nations.[57] He pledged that China would 'make greater efforts to implement the Five Principles. We can build greater confidence and show to the world an example that not only can we strictly abide by the principles, but we can do it well.'[58] China wished, Zhou said, 'to cooperate with India in a joint effort for an enhanced regional peace because this is conducive to the elimination of fears.' Revealing his hand, he dropped the hint that the Asian-African conference proposed by Indonesia was 'one of the measures of this purpose.'[59]

Later in the same meeting, Zhou returned to the Indonesian plan to hold an Afro-Asian conference, removing any doubt that China wished to be invited.[60] He told Nehru that 'China supported the convocation of such a Conference' and was 'willing to participate because it is in the interest of peace in Asia and the world and will work towards an area of peace. We want to increase the area of peace.'[61] In the weeks leading up to Nehru's trip to China, the Chinese government had reached an important conclusion in this regard. Recognising the need to 'eagerly work on South East Asian countries, as well as the peaceful and neutral countries of Asia and Africa,' to 'conduct a sharp struggle against imperialism,' China deemed it essential 'to gain participation in the Afro-Asian Conference.'[62] However, despite Zhou's enthusiastic support for the conference, Nehru remained non-committal.[63] Why he did so remains unclear. Two reasons, however, may help explain Nehru's reluctance to be more forthcoming. The first was that the decision to invite China did not lie with India alone but would have to be collectively made by the Colombo group. The second reason was that Nehru might have wished to await further proof of Beijing's commitment to peaceful coexistence. In this respect, U Nu's planned visit to China in December could provide additional clues about Chinese intentions. Because of this, Nehru's October visit to Beijing was neither the time nor the place for him to commit to supporting Chinese participation. Despite his evasiveness, Nehru did, however, say that 'practically every country is being invited.'[64] He also added that India 'welcomed' the conference and that it 'will be held.'[65] However, he also hastened to point out that it 'will not be a united Conference.'[66] The agenda was likely to 'avoid any internal matters of dispute between countries,' and there would 'probably be some such broad questions like peace, colonialism etc.'[67] In any case, Nehru claimed, 'still to have a conference is good and I think, if Asian and African countries can come together, even if they differ, we can still influence them.'[68]

Despite, or perhaps because of, the two governments' strong support for the principles of peaceful coexistence, neither side put forward any proposal for a bilateral or multilateral Asian non-aggression treaty.[69] Unlike during his June visit to New Delhi,

Zhou remained silent on this matter. As for Nehru, after returning home from China he told one of his senior MEA advisers that India did 'not propose to have any such pacts with any country' because 'declarations on the five principles are declarations of non-aggression. That is good enough.' A collective non-aggression pact would 'still be more undesirable.'[70] As the US Central Intelligence Agency (CIA) had correctly predicted in a brief to the Eisenhower administration, Nehru remained hesitant about the need for such a non-aggression pact. He continued to regard the Five Principles as 'an adequate declaration of peaceful intentions of both countries' and 'had no desire'—at least until 'China's intentions in Southeast Asia had been clarified'—'to counter the Manila Pact with a formal association with China and other Asian countries.'[71] Moreover, given his strict adherence to non-alignment, Nehru was unlikely to sign a non-aggression treaty with China that 'could be interpreted as a shift to the left in India's orientation.'[72] For Nehru, in any case, the critical issue was to ensure that China was genuinely committed to the Five Principles. During his second meeting with Zhou, he made the revealing remark that, while the Five Principles could go a long way to ease regional fears and tensions, they must be seen as 'genuine and not fake.'[73] It must not have been lost on Zhou that, without mentioning it directly, Nehru indeed had China in mind.

That Nehru was still fishing for reassurance of China's commitment to peaceful coexistence became evident during his second meeting with Zhou. At one point, he gently sought to draw the Chinese premier out on his country's attitude to the issue of overseas Chinese minorities in South-East Asia, as well as the border question.[74] In order to probe China's intentions, Nehru raised Burma's concerns that some ethnic Chinese, in joining regional communist parties, were doing the CCP's bidding and playing a potentially destabilising role. Given that Beijing still recognised these ethnic Chinese as Chinese nationals, the scope for misunderstanding was significant. However, as he had already done in New Delhi, Zhou reassured Nehru that China was still determined to settle this issue effectively. To 'set the good example,' China would 'first work with Indonesia,' and, to this end, negotiations with Jakarta would start soon, probably by the end of October. What the Chinese government had in mind, he said, was an arrangement whereby overseas Chinese would have to choose which nationality they wished to hold. If they chose the nationality of their country of residence, then, this country could deal with them at its sole discretion, as they were no longer Chinese nationals. If they decided to remain Chinese, they were prohibited from interfering in the internal affairs of their country of residence.[75] In any case, Zhou also pointed out that China had no desire to interfere in the internal affairs of its neighbours. Beijing had, for instance, sought to establish normal relations with the Philippines and Thailand, but the feelers it had put out had thus far produced no result.[76]

With regard to the border question, Nehru once again took Burma as an example. He told Zhou that the Burmese were still very jittery about the fact that Chinese maps showed parts of Burma and India as Chinese territory. While professing not to be worried about this issue because India's boundaries 'were quite clear' and 'not a matter for argument,' Nehru could not fail to note that, if left unresolved, this issue could give rise to suspicions of aggressive intent on the part of the Chinese government. 'Why,' he asked Zhou, 'did not the Chinese government make some clarification?' He also wondered how China would react if Indian maps showed Tibet as part of India.[77] Zhou's response, while not unforthcoming, was not entirely helpful. He told Nehru that these were old maps, implying that his government had not approved them. China, he went on, had 'made no survey of the borders and had not consulted with [its] neighbouring countries'; hence, it had 'no basis for fixing boundary lines' unilaterally. He complained that the 'whole thing' was 'ridiculous'; the border with Burma was 'not settled even in [the] Manchu regime and you will find differences even in our boundaries with the Soviet Union and Mongolia.' China was prepared to further discuss the border question with Burma, but it needed 'time to make preparations.'[78]

Although the border question would later come back to haunt them, the two governments studiously avoided probing their different assumptions. Nehru stuck to his strategy, which was to pretend that the border was settled in the belief (and hope) that the Chinese government's silence would mean acquiescence to India's claims.[79] After all, he had more than once declared in parliament that India considered the McMahon Line its rightful border.[80] For their part, the Chinese leaders must have seen no reason why they should have dealt with such a complex subject at a time when they were seeking Indian collaboration.[81] Other potential differences were glossed over. Although Nehru accepted the legal basis of Beijing's claim to Taiwan, the Indian prime minister must have found it difficult to fully reconcile with his hosts' tough language. China, Zhou told Nehru, would tolerate neither a Taiwan under American influence nor a 'neutralised' Taiwan. 'We want to liberate Taiwan,' he said, but 'we will be very cautious if we were to take any action.'[82] When Nehru suggested the possibility of a UN-brokered armistice to defuse tensions in the Taiwan Strait, Zhou's response was unforthcoming. He pointed out that an armistice would 'mean legalizing America's occupation of our territory,' which was not 'something we can tolerate.'[83]

Similarly, a discussion between Mao and Nehru on 23 October on the consequences of war in the twentieth century revealed important differences in their approach to international relations. While declaring that China wanted peace, Mao nonetheless implied that wars could bring advantages. Drawing upon recent military history, he argued that 'the two world wars had brought benefits to three kinds of countries'—the United States, communist countries like China and those nations led by nationalist parties, as was the case for India, Indonesia, Burma, Syria and Egypt. 'Had it not been for World War II,' Mao added, 'it would have been very difficult [for India and China] to win independence.' In any case, he went on, 'it will not pay for the United States to fight another big war,' because a third world war would 'plunge' the world 'into a state of revolution' and possibly shrink the area under American control.

Thus far unlikely to impress or reassure Nehru, Mao's analysis became even more disconcerting when he raised the issue of nuclear weapons. Arguing that these weapons had brought no fundamental change to the nature of war beyond their capacity to inflict more casualties, Mao was confident that China would survive such a war. As he put it, 'it would be difficult to destroy China completely or sink China to the ocean floor through bombardment'; the Chinese people would 'live on forever.' Unsurprisingly, when his turn to speak came, Nehru politely took exception to various aspects of Mao's analysis, not least the consequences of nuclear war, which he considered simply too awful to contemplate.[84] While Mao's words were intended to signal China's resolve to stand up to the United States in the event of war—and he was probably using the Indian leader to deliver that message to Washington—they should also have served as a warning to Nehru that China's commitment to peaceful coexistence was, at best, uncertain and, at worst, illusory.[85]

For the time being, however, Nehru was bent on securing agreement on broader regional policy aims, and in this respect the Beijing talks did not fail to deliver. The two governments seemed to share a broadly similar approach to what needed to be done to defuse regional tensions, promote regional stability and reassure their neighbours. The key to all of this was, of course, the Five Principles of Peaceful Coexistence, which New Delhi and Beijing saw as the linchpin of their efforts to reshape regional relations and foster a better understanding between China and India. How this could be put into practice remained unclear, even though Zhou, by embracing the idea of the Afro-Asian conference, appeared to grasp its full potential in terms of furthering China's regional vision. In his last meeting with his Chinese hosts, Nehru waxed lyrical on India's rapidly emerging entente with China. He told Mao he had 'made great friendships' in China and felt 'sad' to leave. Not to be outdone, Mao emphasised that China had 'no apprehension that India will harm us' and that 'every piece of good news from India makes us happy. When India gets better, the world benefits.' In any case, he believed India was 'a promising nation, a great nation.'[86] For his part, Zhou expressed hope that 'formalities will be stressed less in our future contacts.'[87] In a message to Zhou before returning to India, Nehru told the Chinese premier that 'our relations have ceased to be purely formal and it is my privilege to claim friendship with you.'[88]

Indian and Western Assessments of Nehru's Visit to China

Nehru and his party judged the talks 'frank,' 'friendly' and 'very promising.'[89] Not generally prone to hyperbole, the Indian ambassador in Beijing, Nedyam Raghavan, went so far as to describe the visit as 'a diplomatic triumph of no mean magnitude'—one that marked 'a definite and important milestone in the history of India-China relations' and 'resulted in a revision by Chinese leaders of many of their erstwhile opinions concerning our country.'[90] Nehru was said to have enjoyed his conversations with Mao despite remarking privately that the chairman 'had tried to lecture him as though he [Nehru] was one of Mao's own ministers.'[91] Pillai, who briefed the British on the talks, also described Mao as a 'dominating figure.' To the MEA Secretary-General, the 'gruff and bluff' 60-year-old Mao also came across as a 'shrewd,' 'forceful' and 'rigid communist' who was nonetheless 'ready to exchange ideas,' not without some 'humour.'[92] In any case, according to Pillai, 'Nehru's personality had made a big impact in Peking.' He had been 'successful in correcting' the Chinese's 'somewhat one-sided version of affairs in the outside world.'[93] There was, Pillai believed, 'a good chance of India being able to exert a moderating influence on China policy,' and there was 'some evidence that she was already doing so.'[94] 'A growing personal friendship,' he said, had developed between Nehru and Zhou, and the two leaders 'had taken greatly to each other.'[95] Optimistically, Pillai told Escott Reid, the Canadian high commissioner in New Delhi, that he had a feeling that Zhou viewed India as 'a useful bridge between China and the West,' given that 'the influence which India exerted was all in the direction of moderation.'[96] Pillai also thought that Zhou's assurances that China would not be interfering in the affairs of its neighbours were 'categorical.'[97] All in all, Nehru returned to India confident that 'China would not undertake any crazy venture. He was absolutely certain about this and nothing would shake him.'[98] In a note summarising the visit's outcomes—a note that the Indians passed to both the British and the Burmese governments—Nehru said that he was convinced that 'the Government and people of China desire peace and want to concentrate on building up their country during the next decade or so.' During its tour of China's major cities, the Indian delegation gained the impression of a communist regime that was here to stay and of 'a country smoothly running with [an] enormous potential strength which was being translated gradually into actual strength.'[99]

Yet, as Western reports following Nehru's return to India outlined, there seemed to be more to Nehru's affirmations of Sino-Indian friendship than met the eye. His sister told Reid that, since his return from China, Nehru 'has been very irritable and worried. Usually … when he returned from a trip abroad … he was full of stories for days about his trip. This time he had nothing to say about the trip to China. Something probably rubbed him the wrong way in China but she did not know what it was.'[100] According to a CIA report, 'China's strength and unity frightened' Nehru and his party, making them realise that 'India would be [the] weaker partner in any firm relationship.'[101] A State Department note claimed that 'Nehru was much impressed by the Chinese Communist economic development, its potential and the likely course of its development.'[102] Unless India sped up 'its own economic and industrial development,' China would 'outstrip it and thus tip the balance of power in Asia, making the Chinese Communists the dominant nation in Asia, with serious and even grave consequences for India and the rest of Southeast Asia.'[103] As the ever-so-cautious and balanced Pillai told the British High Commission in New Delhi, one thing appeared clear:

> namely that India would have to redouble her own development efforts in the light of the Chinese example. It would be fatal if China were to go ahead faster than India since this would spell the doom of democracy here. India had a good start over China which was having to build up from scratch; nevertheless much greater momentum would be needed if she was to keep her lead in the race.[104]

To what extent Nehru was seriously concerned about China's rising strength is hard to say. He told the American ambassador in Phnom Penh during a stopover on his way back from China that 'he was convinced by Mao's assurance that he needed a period of 20 years to consolidate the Chinese socialist revolution.'[105] What is certain, however, is that Nehru's trip to China appeared to have strengthened his belief that Mao and Zhou meant business and that it was indeed possible to establish productive and mutually beneficial relations with India's giant neighbour. He even told Kailas Nath Katju, the Minister for Home Affairs, that 'because of our general policy and various new developments, India is exercising considerable influence on the policy of the Soviet Union and China.'[106] Moreover, Nehru appeared to have concluded that establishing friendly relations with China based on the Five Principles might have the added benefit of lowering 'the danger of internal communism.'[107] Supporting his conclusion was a despatch from the American embassy in New Delhi to the Department of State in Washington, in which the embassy contended that Soviet and Chinese support for peaceful coexistence and united front tactics appeared to have compelled the Communist Party of India to a somewhat moderate stance.[108] In any case, as Nehru told journalists after his return to India, whether China would abide by the principle of non-interference, 'there is nothing to be said except to wait and watch.' He remained 'convinced that China, entirely for its own sake, wanted peace, wanted time to develop its country.'[109]

U Nu Goes to China

In late November, it was U Nu's turn to travel to Beijing for talks with Mao Zedong and Zhou Enlai.[110] U Nu's trip to China was far from insignificant, as China's failure to reassure the Burmese might potentially complicate Beijing's united front strategy towards its Asian neighbours and undermine its quest for a seat at a future Asian-African conference. To ensure this would not happen, the Chinese authorities put a great deal of effort into easing Burmese concerns. The arrangements for U Nu's visit 'followed closely those made for [Nehru],' with a large reception of workers and students awaiting the Burmese prime minister at Beijing Airport upon his arrival.[111] As the Indian ambassador in Beijing reported to Nehru, the Chinese were 'anxious to make him feel that they have not in any way differentiated.'[112] Unfortunately for U Nu, the weather was not as good as it had been when Nehru visited China a few weeks earlier. During U Nu's first week in China, it was 'snowing hard and blowing very often so much so that U Nu and party have had to encounter rather severe cold.' As Raghavan noted, he must have felt it 'all the more so because he [was] sticking to his national dress which [was] hardly suited to North China's wintry conditions.'[113]

As expected, when the talks got underway, U Nu and his hosts reaffirmed their commitment to the Five Principles of Peaceful Coexistence.[114] The Chinese side, in particular, expressed support for the concept of areas of peace, stating that if 'such a Peace Area is expanded,' future wars 'will be delayed or prevented.'[115] The two sides also decided to upgrade their relations by establishing consulates in various cities, opening a Sino-Burmese air service, restoring Sino-Burmese highway traffic and negotiating a post and telegraph agreement.[116] The Chinese delegation also agreed to double the amount of rice imported from Burma in exchange for industrial equipment and consumer goods.[117] Although the Burmese party made no breakthrough on either the demarcation of the Sino-Burmese border or the status of overseas Chinese communities in Burma, the two governments pledged to examine these questions 'through diplomatic channels' in the future.[118] However, on this latter question, Zhou informed U Nu that China and Indonesia had reached an agreement in principle on the status of Indonesia's Chinese minority, implying that the issue of overseas Chinese in Burma might be resolved on the basis of the Sino-Indonesian Agreement on Overseas Chinese.[119]

In his meeting with Mao, U Nu now praised China's 'correct' and 'friendly' attitude towards his country, despite his earlier reservations about Chinese behaviour. The Chinese government, he told Mao, never took advantage of the presence of Kuomintang forces on Burmese soil to destabilise his country or interfere in the latter's internal affairs.[120] If China, he said, 'had not adopted an attitude of sympathy towards us,' this issue 'might have led to a second Korea or a second Indochina.'[121] U Nu went out of 'his way to assure the Chinese of his country's continuing good will,' emphasising Burma's 'inability to interfere in China's affairs since such action would be similar to that of a "small goat wandering aimlessly amidst elephants."'[122] He also reassured the Chinese that Burma would not accept foreign bases in its territory.[123] This, the American embassy in Rangoon observed with concern, went 'far beyond the demands of either courtesy or coexistence.'[124] For his part, Mao sought to ease U Nu's concerns about China.[125] In particular, he reassured his Burmese guest that China would 'never use the Kuomintang troops' presence in Burma as an excuse to undermine the peaceful relations between our two countries.'[126] Zhou praised U Nu's decision to stay out of SEATO.[127] Both Chinese leaders expressed their liking for the idea of an Asian-African conference. 'If we were able to attend,' Mao said, 'we would feel glorious.'[128] More importantly, U Nu told Mao that he and Nehru 'agree[d] to the participation of China, but it is pending a decision by the five prime ministers' conference.'[129] Indeed, upon his return to India from China, Nehru had indicated to one of his senior advisers that China should be invited.[130]

U Nu left Beijing reassured of China's good intentions, so much so that the atmosphere at the Rangoon airport on his arrival was described as 'dazed but triumphant.'[131] A few weeks later, he told the British commissioner general for South-East Asia, Malcolm MacDonald, that 'he was sure that leaders in Peking desired peace' and 'really wanted peaceful coexistence.' U Nu was convinced that communism in China was a 'very different thing from Communism in Russia.' It was 'more democratic,' for one thing.[132] According to U Myint Thein, a former Burmese ambassador to China who had accompanied his prime minister to Beijing, U Nu had concluded that 'the most hopeful way of checking any further Communist advance was to get the Communist leaders bound in an agreement with India, Burma and other non-Communist states to respect the famous Five Principles.'[133] He seemed so reassured about the worth of the five principles that he declared on his return that a pact of non-aggression with China was now 'unnecessary.'[134] U Nu's complete conversion to the rhetoric of peaceful coexistence was met with concern in some Western quarters. As a CIA report observed, it was likely 'to encourage complacency toward the threat of Communist aggression—a complacency which the Burmese had been in the process of shaking off.'[135] Be that as it may, with relations between Beijing and Rangoon thawing, China's participation in the Indonesian-sponsored Asian-African conference appeared increasingly likely.

In late 1954, such a prospect was bolstered by a cautious yet perceptible shift in Indonesia's China policy. As Rangoon moved to improve its relations with its awkward neighbour, Jakarta, too, began the first tentative steps towards a rapprochement with China. Throughout 1954, the Indonesian government had sought to mend fences with Beijing. Not only did it enter into negotiations on a citizenship agreement that would have regularised the position of the large Chinese minority in the country, but it also concluded a trade protocol and a payments agreement with the PRC.[136] What is more, the Indonesians also explored the possibility of a non-aggression pact with China. Having, however, made no progress on this front, they finally abandoned the idea, preferring instead to pursue a declaration similar to the Indian-Chinese and Sino-Burmese joint statements embodying the Five Principles of Peaceful Coexistence.[137]

Despite Zhou being open to the notion of such a declaration (as well as to the idea of a non-aggression pact), two obstacles seemed to stand in the way of the two countries reaching an agreement. According to Indonesian sources, one problem was Jakarta's desire 'first to clear up the problem of double nationality which is concerning them [the Indonesians] in their handling of their large Chinese minority.'[138] The other issue was the Ali Sastroamidjojo government's reluctance to agree that 'such a declaration should be issued without a meeting of the two Prime Ministers.'[139] Given that Zhou had gone to New Delhi and Rangoon but not Jakarta, as the Indonesians desired, no such declaration had yet been signed.[140] As the British chargé d'affaires in Beijing explained to London, 'a question of prestige intervene[d],' as Ali Sastroamidjojo appeared 'reluctant' to go to Beijing after Zhou had already 'paid the initial visits to India and Burma.'[141] However, according to B. F. H. B. Tyabji, the Indian ambassador in Jakarta, there was a further reason why the Indonesians appeared to be treading carefully on the issue of a joint declaration embodying the Five Principles. Tyabji reported to the MEA that the Indonesian government worried that accepting such a declaration might have 'led to [a] more pro-Chinese attitude than acceptable to national sentiments.'[142] In any case, despite the lack of tangible progress on such a declaration, it was clear that even Sino-Indonesian relations were on the mend. More importantly, according to Chinese Ministry of Foreign Affairs (CMFA) sources, the Indonesians too appeared willing to support China's invitation to the Asian-African conference.[143]

As India, Burma and Indonesia normalised or were in the process of normalising their relations with China, doubts remained as to what attitude Ceylon and Pakistan might take with regard to China. In late 1954, Ceylon's prime minister was still inclined to cast serious doubts about the conference's viability and China's participation in it. During a visit to Britain in November, Kotelawala told Eden that he still 'saw many drawbacks and difficulties about this proposal of the Prime Minister of Indonesia,' adding that the 'political situation in Djakarta was so unstable' that 'the proposal might die of a natural death.' In any case, he did not regard 'the matter as finally settled until the Colombo powers meeting [in Bogor at the end of December] had taken place.'[144] On the question of China, he made the startling comment that he and Nehru 'were both definitely agreed that China should not be invited to the Afro-Asian Conference.'[145] This was a somewhat surprising comment, for, as Chapter 8 will reveal, Nehru was indeed in favour of inviting China to the future Asian-African conference. As for Pakistan, the CMFA advised Mao and Zhou that Karachi might oppose China's invitation.[146] Whatever the case, the forthcoming meeting of the five Colombo powers, scheduled for 28–29 December in the Indonesian town of Bogor, would soon reveal where these nations stood on the issue of China.

8

THE BOGOR CONFERENCE

The real point is whether China should be invited ...
China presents some difficulty ...

R. K. Nehru, Foreign Secretary, MEA[1]

In December 1954, as the Colombo powers neared a formal decision on the holding of an Asian-African conference, Nehru and his closest advisers had a further opportunity to mull over the issue. Despite Nehru's support for Ali Sastroamidjojo's idea, some misgivings appeared to linger in New Delhi. According to Krishna Menon, India's ambassador to the UN and Nehru's close associate, the prime minister still 'felt no enthusiasm' for the conference and 'was in some difficulty how to say no.'[2] Menon admitted being 'in some considerable difficulty as to what advise his Government about the Afro-Asian Conference which Indonesia wanted to hold.'[3] Pillai, too, seemed to have a few doubts of his own. According to the British High Commission in New Delhi, Pillai:

> inclines closely to our view about the undesirability of holding an Afro-Asian Conference which may only be designed to bolster up the Indonesian Government and is more likely to cause general embarrassment than to achieve constructive or useful results.[4]

India was not alone in harbouring some lingering reservations. So did the government of Ceylon, as the previous chapter has shown. For their part, the Pakistanis appeared to be no more enthusiastic. The Secretary of the Pakistani Ministry of Foreign Affairs, J. A. Rahim, admitted to the British high commissioner in Karachi that the conference would be a 'waste of time.' The whole idea, he added, 'would probably have died of a natural death if the Indians had not decided it would be of some value to them to try and keep "Jojo" in power.'[5]

These misgivings notwithstanding, the Indian government had no intention of backtracking. Pillai told the British that the conference 'was almost certain to be held.'[6] Therefore, discussion within the Nehru administration centred on its format, agenda and composition, and not on whether India should stand aside. The Indian MEA debated the question of possible attendees thoroughly, but there was little doubt that Nehru would support the inclusion of China among the invited nations.[7] On 19 December, in response to a despatch from Ali Yavar Jung, the Indian ambassador in Cairo, warning that Arab countries were likely to oppose China's participation, Nehru stated that India could 'not leave out China or Japan.'[8] The day before, aware that the British had expressed their misgivings about China being invited, Nehru had told Pillai that

> [f]or us to be told … that the US and the UK will not like the inclusion of China in the Afro-Asian Conference is not very helpful. In fact, it is somewhat irritating. There are many things that the US and the UK have done we do not like at all.[9]

Nehru was not the only member of his government who wished to invite China. Krishna Menon, too, believed that 'any Afro-Asian Conference could not keep out China and Japan.'[10] It would be 'inconceivable,' he argued, to 'subscribe to a conference to cover Asia without the membership of China and Japan.' Excluding China would not only 'weaken the position that we take up in regard to her inclusion in the United Nations and doubt the validity of her position in Asia,' but it would also 'push her further into the Soviet-Chinese bloc and out of the Asian context.'[11] Cautious and level-headed Commonwealth Secretary Subimal Dutt, who the US embassy in

Jakarta described as 'one of the very few Indian officials who has the moral courage to stand up to Nehru,' also supported China's participation.[12] On the other hand, C. S. Jha, former ambassador to Turkey and director of the Middle Eastern and South-East Asian Affairs division in the MEA, was concerned that Pakistan and Ceylon might oppose China's participation and that disagreements on this issue might result in the Afro-Asian conference not taking place at all. Incidentally, Jha also feared that the Indonesians might not be up to the task of organising such a large gathering.[13]

Nehru's and India's Goals at the Bogor Conference

Although in mid-December, Vijaya Lakshmi Pandit still told the Australian high commissioner in New Delhi, Walter Crocker, that his brother was going to Indonesia 'reluctantly' and that he 'would gladly see the Afro-Asian Conference postponed indefinitely,' Nehru had already decided that the Afro-Asian conference would go ahead.[14] On 20 December, he articulated India's reasons for supporting the Indonesian initiative in a lengthy note reportedly sent to the other four prime ministers ahead of the Bogor meeting.[15] These reasons included strengthening cooperation among Afro-Asian nations and discussing issues of common concern, such as mutual trade and the 'removal of colonialism and racialism.' However, as Nehru made clear, 'the maintenance of peace must be in the forefront.' In this context, uppermost in his mind was the inclusion of the Five Principles of Peaceful Coexistence in the future conference's agenda. He stated that India had 'no desire to impose these Five Principles as such on other countries or to consider them unalterable in their present form.' However, they did 'represent a reasonable approach for the problems of today' and 'should govern' relations between the nations of Asia and Africa. For this reason, it was important that they make it to the list of the conference's discussion items.

Mindful that he would have to rely on Chinese cooperation for his vision to work, Nehru made it clear that 'it would be out of the question for us to leave Beijing out.' 'Most of us,' he explained, 'are pressing for the inclusion of China in the UN and for us not to invite China would be opposed to our entire policy. It would also be a little absurd for Asian countries to meet and the biggest Asian country to be left out.' Therefore, he contended, China 'ha[d] to be invited even though this might displease some people.' Referring to Anglo-American misgivings about China's participation, the Indian leader insisted that nobody could accuse India of partiality since, along with China, it supported the invitation of Asian countries allied with the West, such as Japan, Thailand, the Philippines and Turkey. Furthermore, given India's interest in maintaining peace and stability in Indochina, he supported the inclusion of Cambodia, Laos, and North and South Vietnam.

On the issue of Asian attendance, Nehru ruled out the participation of the Soviet Asian republics and the Soviet Union as a unit, given that the latter could 'hardly be described as an Asian Power.'[16] With regard to African participation, he supported the inclusion of Egypt, Ethiopia, Libya and Liberia. He was, in principle, in favour of inviting Israel, but Arab opposition would make it difficult to do so. On balance, he thought it 'better not to include Israel' if that was 'likely to lead to the Arab countries keeping away.' He rejected South African participation on the grounds of Pretoria's racial policies. At the same time, he had no objections to the inclusion of Sudan, Gold Coast and Central African Federation, which were moving rapidly towards independence. According to Nehru, the inclusion of the latter, in particular, would prevent 'drawing racial and colour bars' ahead of the conference. Finally, he made it clear that he did not want the conference to turn into 'a vague and amorphous gathering,' but wished it to be 'businesslike' and 'effective.' To this end, he argued that it should be strictly at the level of prime or foreign ministers. The five sponsoring nations, he concluded, should share the conference's costs equally and 'set up a secretariat to undertake the preliminary work which will be heavy.'[17]

The Bogor Talks

As planned, the five leaders of the Colombo powers travelled to Indonesia at the end of December 1954. Mohammed Ali Bogra was the first to arrive at Jakarta's Kemajoran Airport on the afternoon of 27 December. Cheered by members of the Pakistani community with 'God is great' and 'Long live Pakistan and Indonesia,' Bogra had been delayed because his aircraft had experienced engine trouble en route. He was followed in the late afternoon by Nehru and his party, who had flown to Jakarta via Bangkok and Singapore on an Indian Airforce aircraft. He was accompanied by Menon, Syed Mahmud—the new Muslim member of Nehru's Cabinet and Deputy Minister of External Affairs, a strong supporter of Nehru's policies—and Indira Gandhi.[18] Like Bogra, Nehru was greeted by a large group of his compatriots who were living in Indonesia. U Nu's chartered Union of Burma Airways Dakota aeroplane landed a few minutes after Nehru's. The two leaders had lunched together at the Singapore airport earlier in the day before departing for Jakarta. Prime Minister of Ceylon John Kotelawala would arrive the following day. After arrival, each guest was driven off to call on President Sukarno at the Merdeka Palace and Vice President Hatta at his official residence in Merdeka Selatan—a visit that would be replicated on the day of their departure.[19]

Soon after Kotelawala landed in Jakarta, the five Asian leaders travelled to Bogor to discuss the agenda and the composition of the future Asian-African conference. Known in Java as the city of rain for its copious rainfall, Bogor was a quiet and charming mountain resort town roughly 60 kilometres south of Jakarta.[20] Built in 1756 by the Dutch as the official residence of the East Indies Governor-General and now turned into a presidential palace, the meeting's venue was a stately building located at the edge of Bogor's lush botanical garden, one of the most charming spots in Java.[21] Compared to the first meeting of the five Asian prime ministers in Colombo in the spring of 1954, the Bogor gathering was a friendlier and more cooperative affair.[22] Subjected to a crowded and exacting program of social and ceremonial events, the five leaders had a little more than a day to wrap up the whole proceedings.[23] They were said to be 'rather confused at the outset by the fact that President Soekarno's first wife was located in the central room of the Palace' and 'refused to move out.'[24] With so little time available, the five prime ministers quickly agreed on the shape and membership of the future conference and chose the final week of April as its starting date.[25] In line with Nehru's expectations, they readily accepted the idea of a secretariat and the level of representation at the forthcoming conference (heads of government or foreign ministers).[26]

Most of the time in Bogor was spent discussing which countries should be invited.[27] To Bogra's objections that inviting the Chinese might result in the Arab states, Thailand and the Philippines declining participation, Nehru and U Nu rebutted that China could not be kept out.[28] For the Burmese leader, the conference would be a failure without China, and he threatened not to attend if Beijing were excluded.[29] A Pakistani delegate remarked that he was 'surprised' at U Nu's 'vehemence' in making this point.[30] According to the Chinese mission in Jakarta, U Nu 'said it so sternly that the entire conference became solemnly quiet for a while.'[31] For his part, Nehru sought to reassure his counterparts that China was 'anxious to avoid war, anxious even to avoid friction and possibilities of conflict.' It 'urgently desire[d] peace' to devote its attention to 'the problems of economic uplift.' All Beijing wanted, Nehru said, was 'to be left in peace and to develop relations with other countries. And so, no attack will come from China.' If anything, Beijing feared that the 'neighbouring countries could be used to endanger her security.' He indirectly blamed Western policy towards China for having 'logically and practically thrown [Beijing] in the arms of Russia.' In his estimation, the people in China were 'essentially Chinese,' not communists. Moreover, he did not think China provided direct support to regional communist parties.[32] With no desire to alienate Beijing, Ali Sastroamidjojo backed Nehru and U Nu.[33] Bogra and Kotelawala, who initially resisted sending an invitation to China, eventually gave in.[34] The Pakistani prime minister argued that, given Burma's position, he could not refuse an invitation to China 'without torpedoing altogether the Afro-Asian conference.'[35] Privately, however, the Pakistanis complained that Nehru and U Nu were 'infatuated at present with China.'[36] According to an unconfirmed account from a Ceylonese source, Kotelawala was allegedly swayed by an offer from Zhou Enlai through U Nu whereby Beijing was prepared to consent to terminate the rice-rubber agreement between the two countries.[37] In the end, the five leaders decided to invite China but not Israel in deference to Arab sensitivities.[38] During the discussion, Bogra proposed inviting Formosa, but U Nu forcefully opposed the idea, warning that 'an invitation to Formosa might result in a complete withdrawal of Burma as a co-sponsor.'[39] South African participation was also rejected, and so was that of the two Koreas.[40] Overall, twenty-five Asian and African countries were to be invited to the upcoming Asian-African conference on top of the sponsoring Colombo powers.[41] Of these twenty-five countries, only the Central African Federation (or the Federation of Rhodesia and Nyasaland) would eventually reject the invitation, while Kwame Nkrumah, the prime minister of the Gold Coast, a self-governing territory still under British rule, decided to send two personal observers.[42]

Nehru played a crucial role in shaping the Bogor meeting.[43] As Australian officials observed, 'after his earlier lack of interest,' Nehru now appeared to have become 'wedded to' the idea of an Afro-Asian conference,[44] so much so that, during the conference, Lambertus Palar, the Indonesian ambassador to India and member of the Indonesian delegation, remarked: 'There you have the Indians! Formerly it was they who were the most dubious about the idea of the A-A Conference, and now they want to be the first with formulating the Conference aims!'[45] Nehru and Krishna Menon were said to have made the running and India to be 'the only delegation to have a clear idea of what it wanted.'[46] On his return to New Delhi, Menon told Crocker that Nehru 'went to Bogor with clear ideas, he outlined them to the Conference clearly, and got most of them accepted.' 'The Indian intention,' Menon added, 'was to head off the Indonesians from their plan to turn the Asian-African conference into an anti-colonialist demonstration.' To this end, the Indian delegation worked hard 'to make the [upcoming] Conference constructive.' In this regard, he claimed that 'he pushed the anti-colonial point from the first down into the third paragraph in the communique' and that '[t]he Indonesians were not pleased with this.' Moreover, it was 'due to Indian efforts that colonial liberation movements were debarred from the Conference and that the representation was limited to responsible members of responsible governments, either Prime Ministers or Foreign Ministers.'[47] To facilitate agreement, Menon said, Nehru proposed at the start that 'any proposal which was strongly opposed by the other delegations should be dropped.'[48] Not surprisingly, the final communiqué primarily reflected Indian views and aims.[49] According to the British embassy in Jakarta and the Ceylonese delegation in Bogor, '13 of the communiqué 17 points came straight out of the Indian brief.'[50]

Despite India's skilful diplomacy, Nehru did not get all he wanted. He sought to have the Five Principles included in the communiqué, but, in the end, the latter avoided any explicit mention of them due to Pakistani and Ceylonese opposition.[51] After 40 minutes of intense debate, Nehru had to drop his wording.[52] However, by stating that one of the forthcoming conference's primary aims was to foster goodwill and friendly relations among Asian and African countries and 'to explore and advance' their common interests, the communiqué suggested that the Five Principles would indeed be an item for discussion at the April gathering. Other topics on the agenda included the 'social, economic and cultural problems and relations of the countries represented'; the 'problems of special interest to Asian and African peoples,' especially those 'affecting national sovereignty and of racialism and colonialism'; and 'the position of Asia and Africa and their peoples in the world of today and the contribution they can make to the promotion of world peace and cooperation.'[53] Finally, the five prime ministers agreed that any choice of the conference venue should be left to the Indonesians, who opted for the much cooler and more spacious Bandung over the hot and overcrowded capital, Jakarta, which also lacked adequate accommodation.[54] However, with its goals cast in such vague terms and its membership made up of many diverse countries, the Asian-African conference ran the risk of producing high-sounding platitudes while falling short of practical results. Its chances of success were not enhanced by the five Asian leaders' decision to adopt consensus as a decision-making method. And so, despite the leaders' making clear that they had no intention of seeing Afro-Asian nations 'build themselves into a regional bloc,' the prospect of that happening was minimal.[55] In any event, when the meeting ended on 29 December, as a British official noted, the five Asian prime ministers 'emerged from the Bogor Conference with a greater feeling of solidarity and more enthusiasm for the Afro-Asian Conference than when they arrived.'[56]

On their last day in Indonesia, the five leaders attended a mass meeting at the Ikada Stadium in Jakarta organised by the mayor of

Jakarta, Sudiro. Thousands of people streamed to the stadium despite the rain, with some groups holding officially sanctioned banners exalting peaceful coexistence and condemning colonialism. Taking turns to address the crowd, the five prime ministers touched upon themes such as world peace, cooperation, Afro-Asian solidarity and colonialism. Nehru, in particular, emphasised the need for Asia to be united and work hard—not to 'shout'—if genuine independence and world peace were to be achieved. Ironically enough, when President Sukarno's turn came to speak, 'his final incitement to the crowd,' noted the British ambassador in Jakarta, 'was in flat contradiction to Nehru's call for more work and less shouting.' Sukarno praised the Colombo group for bringing matters of common concern to the fore.[57]

Nehru left Jakarta in the pouring rain on 31 December, sent off by Ali Sastroamidjojo and members of the Indonesian Cabinet.[58] In a press conference he held before departing for India, Nehru told reporters that he was 'completely' satisfied with the results of the Bogor meeting. He emphasised that in organising an Afro-Asian conference, the five Colombo powers had no intention of creating a new bloc. He claimed that, although no mention had been made in the final communiqué of the Five Principles of Peaceful Coexistence, nobody disagreed with them. Regarding doubts about whether these principles could work, he reiterated that 'the mere fact of two or more countries accepting the Five Principles creates an atmosphere in their favour and against anyone breaking them. It is to the disadvantage of the person who wants to break them. It is a bind-up in a moral sense.' Asked whether the Asian-African meeting would become periodic, he remained non-committal, replying that it was 'too early to say how it will develop.' He hoped, however, that the five Colombo powers would continue to meet from time to time. In relation to the Manila Pact, he repeated that it 'was very near reviving the old conception of spheres of influence,' but he counted on the forthcoming Asian-African conference to prevent such spheres of influence from materialising.[59]

During his meeting with the other four prime ministers, Nehru had once again complained that the Manila Treaty had 'brought about quite a new conception,' for its members were 'not only responsible for their own defence but also for that of areas they may designate outside of it if they so agree.' In Nehru's view, this amounted to 'creating a new form of spheres of influence.' He believed that the Manila Treaty 'tend[ed] to increase tension and apprehension in the area and might endanger peace' because it 'could only be directed against China.'[60] For him, the Five Principles remained the only corrective to the rising tension. When questioned, however, how the Colombo powers would react if an Asian country became the object of aggression, Nehru remained vague, saying that the five prime ministers had not discussed this scenario. He expected the reaction to be robust, but he could not say whether India would go to war for it. 'Because war,' he said, 'has become such a dangerous thing, it may not happen; and because aggression may lead to war, we do not expect aggression to happen either.'[61] On his way back to New Delhi, Nehru stopped in Penang, Malaya, on 31 December, where 'he drove past 8 miles of cheering crowds who had waited for many hours along the route from the airport to the British Residence.'[62] On his arrival in India on 3 January, he reiterated to the press that the aim of the forthcoming conference was 'not to create any bloc' but to 'bring countries closer together' and 'strengthen the cause of peace.'[63]

Predictably, the Indian press welcomed the outcome of the Bogor meeting and India's role in it.[64] Agreeing that the Western powers had nothing to fear from it, it emphasised aspects such as the awakening of the East, the need for world peace, colonialism and economic development.[65] *The Statesman* of New Delhi and Calcutta wrote that the forthcoming conference might help reduce tensions, and that China's participation in the upcoming conference would be a 'gain.'[66] The *Times of India*, the country's bestselling daily published in New Delhi and Bombay, described the Bogor meeting as 'a triumph for Nehru.'[67] It welcomed the Bogor meeting's efforts to promote world peace and said that its resolutions were 'no cheap demonstration of the Afro-Asian agitators, but the first signs of political awakening that is destined to play a vital role in world affairs.'[68] Furthermore, it argued that the forthcoming conference would have the same significant political impact as the Geneva Conference from the year before. The *Times of India* also welcomed

China's invitation to the conference as an 'opportunity' as well as a 'challenge' to bring Beijing into closer contact with its neighbours who still 'tend[ed] to regard her as [a] potential danger.'[69] The *Indian Express* in New Delhi wrote that the 'programme drawn up at Bogor points the way to peace and plenty.' Like the *Times of India*, the *Indian Express* denied that the upcoming conference would want to create an Afro-Asian bloc. The *National Herald* in Lucknow welcomed that '[i]n the context of the present day situation, the Afro-Asian Conference in essence means the organisation of an Afro-Asian Front against colonialism and racial discrimination.' The paper also applauded the decision to invite China, arguing that 'China's adherence to the Five Principles of Peaceful Co-Existence is a proof that her policy is one of peace.'[70]

The *Hindustan Times*, India's second-largest daily paper which had close contacts with the government, noted that 'the success of the Bogor talks should provide particular satisfaction to India for, as the decisions show, they embody the aims and principles for which Nehru has been striving in international affairs.'[71] However, while it welcomed the conference as an important step towards the 'emergence of [the] idea that Asia [and] Africa are sooner or later bound to challenge [the] monopoly in world diplomacy exclusively held by some nations of other regions,' it also questioned whether, in the short term, the meeting would produce tangible results, given the different perspectives of the countries invited and their economic or military dependence on Western and other countries.[72] *The Hindu* also praised the five Asian prime ministers' decision to invite China and Japan. For the Madras newspaper, 'history will be made' in Bandung, and 'a permanent settlement in the Far East will be possible only if these two great nations work together as well as in co-operation with the countries of South East Asia and India.' Approvingly quoting Nehru, who had pointed out that 'the purpose of the Conference was more than agitational,' the paper praised the maturity of newly independent Asian and African countries for their moderate approach to colonialism and anti-racialism. The *Free Press Journal* in Bombay, in turn, waxed lyrical on the five leaders' 'unanimity of opinion and identity of approach to world problems,' arguing that Bogor 'mark[ed] the beginning of a new and significant era in world leadership' and 'inaugurate[d] a new chapter of co-prosperity for the east.' It also wrote that '[b]y inviting both China and Japan the Prime Ministers have once again demonstrated that their aim is not to create any new blocs or alliances but merely to raise a new voice for peace.' It concluded that '[b]y their salutary efforts at Bogor the five Prime Ministers have raised themselves from the status of leaders of Asia to that of leaders of men.'[73]

China's Approach to the Asian-African Conference

China's invitation to the first Asian-African conference was, without a doubt, the most consequential decision made by the five Asian leaders at their two-day gathering in Bogor. As the next two chapters show, Beijing's presence in Bandung would help China end its international isolation and usher in a new phase in its regional diplomacy. China's participation in the Geneva Conference had already signalled a significant shift in regional politics. The presence of the Chinese delegation at the Palace of Nations in Geneva alongside the representatives of the major world powers indicated that China had re-entered the great power game and that no enduring peace settlement in Asia would be possible without Beijing's cooperation. While different from the Geneva Conference in scope and membership, the Bandung meeting was to provide China with a further opportunity to engage with the world, and Nehru played an essential role in this. Throughout 1954, as we have seen in earlier chapters, he had taken major steps to normalise relations with Beijing, and in Bogor he had proved to be the most articulate advocate of a policy of constructive engagement with China. With support from U Nu and Ali Sastroamidjojo, Nehru ensured that China would be invited to Bandung. His strong support for China's participation went beyond his desire for good neighbourly relations. It was actually part of a more ambitious plan. As his high-level talks with Chinese leaders had revealed, Nehru considered closer Sino-Indian ties to be fundamental to his vision of a non-aligned Asia centred on areas of peace and the Five Principles of Peaceful Coexistence, which he had come to regard as a model of diplomatic conduct among Asian nations. In New Delhi's view, therefore, Bandung was first and foremost an exercise in regional security—that is, an attempt by India and other like-minded Asian nations to forge a new security approach to regional affairs and manage local Cold War tensions on their own terms.

The Chinese government had followed the lead-up to Bogor and the meeting itself with significant interest.[74] In mid-December, Zhou Enlai told the Indian ambassador in Beijing, Nedyam Raghavan, that 'he would be grateful if, on matters relating to Afro-Asian countries, there would be consultations between himself and the Prime Minister' and if he would be 'kept informed.'[75] Earlier that month, the CMFA had instructed its embassy in Jakarta to monitor Indonesia's attitude towards the Bogor meeting and report back to Beijing. China's policy, the CMFA explained, was to 'conduct a sharp struggle against imperialism, and eagerly work on South East Asian countries, as well as the peaceful and neutral countries of Asia and Africa.' The government was working to gain participation in the Afro-Asian Conference 'in the interest of peace.' If approached by the Indonesians, the embassy was told, it must convey the Chinese government's willingness to participate.[76] Predictably, therefore, when word reached Beijing that the Colombo group had agreed to invite China to Bandung, the Chinese government's reaction was one of satisfaction. In an internal guidance document, the CMFA considered the upcoming Asian-African conference to be 'of historic significance.' There was, it stated, no doubt that China's participation would 'greatly affect the conference.' Hence, China should strive to 'play a positive role' in furthering its goals, which the CMFA described as ranging from the opposition to the formation of Western-led alliances to the promotion of peaceful coexistence and areas of peace. These goals also included condemnation of colonialism and strengthening political, economic and cultural cooperation between Afro-Asian states.[77]

Approved by Zhou Enlai, the CMFA's guidance document set in train the preparatory work needed to formulate a strategy for the conference.[78] To do so, a special task force was set up.[79] In the meantime, the Chinese government formally accepted the invitation to attend on 17 February 1955. In a letter to Ali Sastroamidjojo, Zhou hailed the conference as 'the first of its kind in history convened to promote goodwill and cooperation among the countries of Asia and Africa.' He said its convening reflected 'the great changes which have taken place in recent times in this part of the world' and 'the ever stronger desire of the Asian and African countries to take their destiny into their own hands.' With the Five Principles clearly in mind, Zhou went on to say that the conference would not only help make it 'possible for the Asian and African countries with different social systems to co-exist in peace under the principle that the form of government and the way of life of any one country should in no way be subject to interference by another.' It would also give these countries a chance 'to make contributions towards the promotion of world peace and cooperation.'[80]

In early April, once the task force's preparatory work was completed, the Central Political Bureau of the CCP approved the strategy the Chinese delegation was expected to pursue at the forthcoming conference.[81] Titled 'Draft Plan for attending the Asian African Conference,' the directive stated that Bandung provided a 'favourable' opportunity 'to expand the cause of peace force in the Asian-African region, even in the whole world' at the expense of American imperialism. Consequently, China 'should strive to expand the united front of the world peace force, promote the development of the national independence movement and create conditions for establishing work or diplomatic relations between China and a number of Asian-African countries.' More specifically, this policy should be based on the Five Principles of Peaceful Coexistence. To this end, China should encourage as many countries as possible to accept these principles 'so as to expand the peaceful zone and collective peace.' China should also work 'to establish a permanent institution of the Asian-African Conference and convene a meeting every other year, and suggest to hold the next meeting in India.' Furthermore, it should support a resolution opposing colonialism, racial discrimination and weapons of mass destruction. It should also foster political, economic and cultural links between Afro-Asian nations.[82]

In terms of tactics, the directive divided the participating countries into four major groups: (1) 'Peaceful and neutral' (India, Burma, Indonesia and Afghanistan); (2) 'close to peaceful and neutral' (Egypt, Sudan, Nepal, Syria, Lebanon, Yemen, Saudi Arabia, Jordan, the Gold Coast, Cambodia, Laos and Ceylon); (3) 'close to anti-peaceful and anti-neutral' (Japan, South Vietnam, Libya, Jordan, Liberia, Iran, Iraq, Abyssinia and Pakistan); (4) 'anti-peaceful and anti-neutral' (Thailand, the Philippines and Turkey). To achieve the goal of expanding the 'united front of peace,' the Chinese delegation should first attempt to 'unite the countries of the first category, win over the second, influence the third and isolate the fourth in the conference.' Second, it should work with some of these countries outside the formal conference meeting to address specific issues, such as establishing bilateral diplomatic or economic relations. Third, it should coordinate closely with India, Indonesia and Burma. Finally, it should 'find opportunities' to advocate Taiwan's 'peaceful liberation' and the withdrawal of American forces from the island and Taiwan Strait. If the question of communist subversive activities were brought up at the conference, the delegation ought to reassure its Afro-Asian counterparts by differentiating between interference in the internal affairs of a country and support for communist ideology. In other words, it should emphasise that, while being unable to prevent the 'spread of the Communist ideology,' China had no intention of interfering in the internal affairs of any nation. With CCP leaders unwilling to forgo their support for international communism, it was evident that Beijing felt compelled to provide a reassuringly vague formula to conceal its continuing desire to promote communism through party-to-party contacts. On the issue of the overseas Chinese, China should seek 'an all-round agreement with Indonesia' and then 'seize opportunities' to settle the problem with other Asian nations 'on the basis of this agreement.' With regard to China's border disputes with some of the participating countries, the delegation should 'refute' any accusation of China trafficking in narcotics and detaining prisoners of war.[83]

On the surface, the strategy approved by the politburo appeared not too dissimilar from India's broad approach to Bandung. Like New Delhi, Beijing saw the upcoming Asian-African conference as a means of enlarging the area of peace and converting as many countries as possible to neutralism. Both nations had adopted the Five Principles of Peaceful Coexistence as the basic tenets of their regional policy and were eager to ensure that these principles would gain wide acceptance in Asia. In reality, however, India and China differed fundamentally in their approaches to peaceful coexistence. Whereas India considered peaceful coexistence an instrument to secure long-term peace and stability in Asia, China viewed it as no more than a temporary expedient at the service of its revolutionary aims.[84] As Anton Harder has aptly noted, Nehru saw the Five Principles as a 'grandiose vision' through which India could constrain American power, keep China in check and wean it away from the Soviet Union, while encouraging Sino-Soviet moderation.[85]

Mao had a much 'narrower conception.'[86] Despite their repeated claims during 1954 that China was committed to a 'diplomacy of peace' based on the Five Principles, CCP leaders sang a different tune behind closed doors. In the secrecy of their meetings, they maintained that peaceful coexistence did not require China to cease promoting communist revolutions abroad. On the contrary, all it meant was that it would help 'create better conditions for China to serve as a supporting base for the world revolution.'[87] The Chinese shared the Soviet view that East Asia was 'one of the weakest links in the chain of international imperialism/colonialism' and that, as a result, the two communist powers should strive to keep up the revolutionary 'momentum' there.[88] In this context, Bandung was an opportunity for China to transform Afro-Asian nations into allies in the struggle against American imperialism and, in so doing, to establish a broad 'united front' aimed at isolating and defeating the United States.[89] After all, as Mao claimed in 1948, neutrality was 'merely a camouflage: a third road does not exist.'[90]

Nehru Prepares for the Bandung Conference

Unaware of the Chinese government's inner deliberations, the Nehru administration did not question the basic assumptions underlying its approach to China. Instead, it chose to hold fast to its policy of constructive engagement with its northern neighbour. A month after the Bogor Conference, Nehru travelled to London for a gathering of Commonwealth prime ministers, where he painted the best possible picture of China's intentions. Sticking to his now-familiar arguments, he claimed that the Chinese 'had a strong desire for peace,' were 'primarily concerned' with their economic development and harboured 'no expansionist aims,' apart from Formosa.[91] He contended that the Chinese revolution 'was not due simply to its communist nature' but was 'nationalist in character.' It 'would be a tragedy,' he said, if the West were to antagonise China as it did with Soviet Russia following the Bolshevik revolution. World history, he speculated, might have turned out differently 'if greater efforts had been made to come to terms with Soviet Russia.' He urged, therefore, his Commonwealth opposite numbers to 'accept the success of the Chinese revolution,' for 'continued hostility' to it would 'assist the communist cause' and 'lead to war.' He praised his government's policy of peaceful coexistence and constructive engagement with China. It was primarily thanks to these efforts that India 'had been very successful in meeting the threat of communism' by sapping the Indian Communist Party's 'will to create trouble.' On the question of China's continuing sabre-rattling in the Taiwan Strait in response to the US-ROC mutual defence treaty being signed in December 1954, 'he could easily understand the attitude of the Peking Government' and its 'desire to recover their former territory.'[92] Finally, in a remark clearly directed to the British, Australian and New Zealand prime ministers, Nehru questioned the utility and efficacy of the Manila Treaty, remarking that while its members might view it as 'a purely defensive arrangement,' the Chinese might have a completely different perspective.[93]

In January–March 1955, the deliberations of an interdepartmental working group—tasked with preparing a series of working papers on the political, economic, social and cultural problems of Afro-Asian nations; formulating proposals on political, economic and cultural cooperation; and making suggestions on the organisation of the conference—did not result in any shift of perspective.[94] The paper on China, prepared by T. N. Kaul, reiterated the Indian government's faith in the Five Principles and downplayed the danger represented by China. On the first issue, the paper conceded that the value of these principles could 'only be judged by the passage of time' but went on to say that they 'help[ed] in decreasing tension and creating an atmosphere of peace.' In any event, there was no alternative to them but 'violent co-destruction.' In the case of India and China, the Five Principles showed 'how two great countries, left to themselves, [could] settle problems—left as a legacy by Western imperialism—in a friendly way to their mutual benefit.' On China, the paper asserted that the Chinese were, 'above all, realists.' They had 'everything to gain but nothing to lose by having friendly neighbours like Burma and India, thereby safeguarding [their] Western and South-western borders.' As long as its relations with India and Burma remained friendly, China could focus on strengthening its 'borders elsewhere where [it] may expect threats from outside, especially in the east and south.'[95] For Kaul, therefore, the importance of the Five Principles could scarcely be overstated.

The measure of the importance Nehru attached to the Five Principles and the extent of his commitment to peaceful coexistence emerged in all their intensity in a lengthy speech to the Lok Sabha on 31 March, 3 weeks before the Bandung Conference. Hailing the upcoming Asian-African conference as a historic event symbolising the emergence of Asia on the world stage, Nehru affirmed that all participating nations shared a desire for 'peace and opportunity for progress' despite their 'different policies, different outlooks and sometimes opposing policies.' They were not anti-Europe or anti-America but sought to break free from the destructive logic of blocs. He regretted that after achieving 'a measure of success at Geneva,' the two blocs had 'drifted back to glaring at each other.' He primarily faulted SEATO for this because it ran counter to the entire philosophy 'behind the Geneva Conference which was a conception ... of coexistence.' However, he also blamed US support of the ROC for the Sino-American stand-off in the Taiwan Strait, and the West-sponsored Turkish-Iraqi military pact for dividing the Middle East into hostile camps.[96] In this tense international environment, the Five Principles were the only alternative to military pacts and Cold War logic. Aware of Western criticism of the Five Principles, he denied they were a 'communist trick.' As he had in the past, he acknowledged that some countries might renege on them, but if they did, they would get 'into hot water much more than otherwise.' In any case, the only option available was to accept conflict and devastation or embrace peaceful coexistence. For this reason, he hoped that the forthcoming conference, which he called 'a rather strikingly remarkable example of co-existence,' would firmly stand by the Five Principles.[97] In travelling to Bandung, Nehru was clearly determined to establish these principles as the fundamental pillars of international conduct and the sole feasible basis for world peace.[98]

However, how successful he would be in achieving these objectives remained to be seen. In the weeks preceding the conference, there were indications that it would not all be plain sailing and that Nehru would face some degree of opposition. Following the Bogor meeting, the United States and its principal Western allies, Britain and France, reacted with considerable anxiety to the Colombo group's decision to host an Asian-African conference. In Washington, Dulles feared the Chinese would exploit Bandung to drive a wedge between the West and the other Afro-Asian participants.[99] For the Eisenhower administration, Beijing would, among other things, encourage Indian efforts to win adherents to the Five Principles and the notion of areas of peace in order to boost neutralism and undercut Western influence throughout the Third World.[100] In London, the Foreign Office argued that since anti-colonialism was the only topic on which the participating Afro-Asian nations were likely to agree, the conference would 'do nothing to promote the cause of world peace.' Instead, it would 'strengthen the alignment of the Afro-Asian powers against the West' and 'benefit only the Communist powers.'[101] In Paris, the Mendès France government worried that Beijing would use the conference to spread 'subversive ideas among those who attended it, particularly the Africans.'[102] Consequently, the three Western governments were tempted to pressure friendly pro-Western Afro-Asian nations to postpone the conference.[103]

However, these reservations notwithstanding, they gradually adopted a more constructive approach to the conference.[104] In late January, the US State Department decided to work on friendly Afro-Asian countries to ensure that China would not carry the day in Bandung.[105] It wired US embassies in Asia and Africa, advising that 'it would be preferable for friendly Asian countries to accept [the] invitation to [the] Afro-Asian Conference' despite the risk that China would use the summit as a propaganda tool. On these grounds, the US missions should encourage pro-Western Afro-Asian governments to send their 'ablest possible representation' to Bandung, emphasising that if 'non-Communist delegations cooperate[d] effectively,' the conference 'might conceivably provide [the] opportunity [to] frustrate Communists and achieve constructive results.'[106] A month later, the State Department instructed US missions to urge sympathetic local governments to 'put forward subjects discussion of which would redound benefit [to] free nations and discomfiture Communists.' To this end, it supplied a list of points that non-communist Asian and African delegations at Bandung could use to put communist countries on the defensive.[107]

The French also welcomed the participation of friendly Asian nations to counter the influence of China and other communist countries but continued to oppose the inclusion of African states.[108] Paris worried that 'if a good many African countries attend ... the Conference might prove to be the first step in a longer term attempt on the part of Asia to assume increasing influence over the affairs of Africa with probably unfortunate results.' Recognising that attendance to the conference was outside its control, the French government admitted that it would 'regard it as ideal ... if African attendance could be limited to Egypt.'[109] In any case, it was determined to urge friendly Asian nations to ensure that North African colonial questions be kept off the agenda.[110] In London, the Churchill government decided to 'do nothing to encourage attendance' of friendly Afro-Asian nations but promised 'to give information, help and advice' to those governments wishing to send a delegation to Indonesia.[111] To this end, the British worked with the Americans and French to influence friendly Afro-Asian nations.[112] As the conference approached, the three Western governments began their lobbying campaign and prepared background briefs and other material to send to sympathetic Afro-Asian countries.[113]

The response of many of these nations was forthcoming. Among the conference's organisers, both Ceylon and Pakistan promised to hold China and India in check. Karachi assured Washington it would reject any resolution incorporating the Five Principles and fight Nehru's neutralist efforts. For its part, the government of Ceylon told the Americans that it would do its best to counter the Chinese communists. The Philippines and Turkey appeared no less determined to support the West's anti-communist agenda and combat neutralist tendencies. Other countries, too, made it known that they were prepared to assist.[114] With Afro-Asian nations likely to be at odds over important Cold War issues, Nehru's plans to take advantage of the Bandung Conference to advance India's regional approach to peace and security appeared to be in jeopardy. His vision of a neutralised Asia underpinned by the Five Principles was unlikely to prevail. Indeed, as the next chapter will show, his vision would come under a sustained attack from different quarters during the week-long conference proceedings.

9

THE BANDUNG CONFERENCE

The astonishment caused by the appearance of a domestic cat [Zhou Enlai] instead of a tiger seemed, for a short time, to inhibit proper scepticism.

Berkeley Gage, British ambassador to Thailand, 1954–57[1]

Located at an altitude of 750 metres above sea level in a pleasantly cool mountain resort area beneath one of Java's mostly sleeping volcanos, Bandung was a lovely town of 650,000 inhabitants with a still perceptible European feel. In the 1920s, the Dutch colonial authorities had contemplated making it the new capital of the Dutch East Indies in place of Jakarta (then Batavia). During this period, as Dutch architects competed to give the city a more imposing character, Bandung acquired a series of attractive Art Deco buildings.[2] In the 4 months preceding the Asian-African conference, Bandung received an extensive makeover. The two conference venues, fourteen hotels, the residences for the heads of delegations, the central mosque, the airport and the railway station were all refurbished.[3] Indonesian President Sukarno took a personal interest in some of the renovations.[4] In an attempt to lift its appearance, the conference's precinct was cleared of all street sellers, and the main roads in the town centre were 'literally scrubbed by workers on their hands and knees.'[5] Streets were cleaned, hotels 'tidied up,' houses 'whitewashed,' beggars and prostitutes 'rounded up,' and the street lighting 'much improved,' wrote the Dutch-language Indonesian daily newspaper, *Het Nieuwsblad voor Sumatra*.[6] Bandung was being transformed into a 'super de lux' location, wrote a Chinese-language Indonesian weekly magazine.[7] 'Tidied up,' Bandung 'gives off an air of prosperity,' commented the same Dutch-language daily.[8]

Squeezing a large international conference into Bandung's limited accommodation was no easy task.[9] It was a major logistical headache for the Indonesian government, which had never before organised such a major international event and whose ability to do so was dubious, even among Indonesia's Colombo partners. In the aftermath of the Bogor Conference, Kotelawala had criticised the arrangements made by the Indonesians for the Colombo group meeting, judging them to be inadequate.[10] One of the Burmese delegation members at Bogor also complained about these arrangements, noting that they had been 'far from satisfactory' and that the Indonesians had been 'unable to cope with their responsibilities towards the guests.' 'This was the reason,' he argued, 'for setting up a joint secretariat to organise the Bandung conference.'[11] The Indians were even more scathing in private.[12] Krishna Menon tartly remarked to the British Acting high commissioner in New Delhi that the Indian government did 'not like the Asian-African notions of the Indonesians' and that 'they [the Nehru government] are now trying to control them and they think they can do it.' According to Menon, the Indonesians 'had nothing to contribute except a negative anti-colonialism and their great talents for disorganisation. Their preparations for Bogor had been lamentable.'[13] Nehru's sister, now the Indian high commissioner in London, was equally trenchant in her remarks about the Indonesians. Vijaya Lakshmi Pandit told the British they:

> were completely childish and had no idea how to conduct their affairs. Their great handicap was that they had not the elements of a trained Civil Service such as the British had bequeathed to India and Pakistan and to some extent to Burma. In India and Pakistan, the people at the head of affairs had behind them a solid basis of responsibility and experience which the Dutch had never given to the Indonesians.[14]

Indian Concerns About the Conference's Organisation

In late February, it was the turn of the Indian ambassador to Indonesia, B. F. H. B. Tyabji, to warn Nehru of the 'utter inexperience and incapacity of [the] Indonesian Government to make arrangements for an international conference of this calibre. This extends to all aspects of [the conference].'[15] Since the end of the Bogor meeting, Tyabji had been relaying to New Delhi his serious doubts about the Indonesians' ability and competence to organise such a major event. He had also voiced his significant concerns about their 'happy-go-lucky,' 'egotistical' and 'micawberish-like' attitude, and the slow progress being made in the preparatory work of the conference.[16] Tyabji wrote to Nehru that this made it 'absolutely necessary' that the upcoming conference 'be handled jointly by all sponsoring countries in which undoubtedly, we shall have to play [a] major role.'[17] Nehru, who had spared no criticism of the Indonesians in the past,[18] could not agree more. In his reply to Tyabji, he admitted to being 'rather anxious about this Asian-African Conference and, more especially, about the arrangements.' Given the conference's 'great significance' (it 'might well mould the future of Asia and Africa,' he argued) and its delicate timing (it will probably have to deal with the Taiwan Strait crisis, he added), Nehru feared that the Indonesian government would fall well short of what was expected of it. 'We cannot take the slightest risk of lack of adequate arrangements,' and 'we cannot afford to have everything messed up,' he admonished. 'The whole work of the Conference might go to pieces because of lack of foresight and … proper organisation.' Foreign delegations would 'go back with irritation and, maybe, even ill will.'[19] 'Above all,' he said, 'one fact should be remembered and this is usually forgotten in Indonesia. This fact is an adequate provision of bathrooms and lavatories, etc. People can do without drawing rooms, but they cannot do without bathrooms and lavatories.'[20]

On 20 February 1955, a concerned Nehru wrote to Ali Sastroamidjojo and Sukarno that it was essential to ensure that the forthcoming Asian-African conference be a success 'in every way.'[21] With 'careful and tactful management,' he told Ali Sastroamidjojo, the summit could 'well help in producing a broad common approach in some matters affecting Asia and Africa and throw its weight on the side of the peace.' Clearly referring to the Bogor meeting, he did not want much time taken up with 'protocol routines,' 'banquets and the likes' so that 'the more time we have to have private discussions amongst ourselves, the greater the success of the Conference will be.' He pointed out that the conference was 'unique in many ways' and the 'mere fact of our meeting is of high importance.' On top of that, 'the situation in the Far East' remained 'a very difficult and serious one. Indeed, it might well be called an explosive one,' said Nehru. 'Much,' therefore, 'may happen even before we meet at Bandung.'[22] Here he alluded to the American decision to stand by Taiwan, which he believed could provoke a serious confrontation between the United States and China in the Taiwan Strait.[23]

Indeed, notwithstanding a certain degree of condescension and post-colonial snobbery towards the Indonesians on India's part, the possibility of Jakarta 'messing up' was not far-fetched.[24] In one week, Bandung was expected to cater for and accommodate 'between two and three thousand visitors, representing the twenty-nine delegations, the media, as well as a substantial number of unofficial visitors.'[25] With no fewer than 400 journalists covering the conference, the latter promised to generate significant attention.[26] To make matters worse, Bandung presented a significant security challenge for the Indonesian government. The armed rebels of the *Darul Islam* (Islamic State) movement, which in 1949 had declared the autonomous Islamic State of Indonesia in West Java, were still active in the area.[27] To ensure the delegations were protected, the Indonesian authorities deployed over 2,000 policemen.[28] They also called the army's crack division to erect 'three concentric circles of security around the whole city—the last one of which fenced off the conference buildings and the main hotels.'[29] For the delegates to get through security, 'several passes [had] to be produced.'[30] Delegates also had to be escorted from the airport into town by 'truckloads of white-helmeted military policy with Tommy-guns.'[31] Each delegation was assigned a police commissioner assisted by various police officers.[32]

All in all, contrary to Indian fears, the Indonesian authorities performed well. 'The organization of the conference succeeded beyond expectations,' wrote the British ambassador in Jakarta, Oscar Morland.[33] This was, he claimed, 'mainly due to the stiffening of the joint secretariat by experienced Indian officers.'[34] For Keith Shann of the Australian Department of External Affairs, 'the quality of the Secretariat' was significantly 'enhanced by the experience and capability' of Yunus Khan of India in the protocol section.[35] Tasked with organising the conference—from the provision of lodging and amenities for visitors to the formulation of position papers on topics that would likely be covered during the summit—the Joint Secretariat was made up of the representatives of the five Colombo powers and assisted by an Indonesian government's interdepartmental commission.[36] Despite the inclusion of Indian officers, not all was plain sailing within the Secretariat. The Indonesians 'felt that they were being pushed around by the Indians,' while the Indians were 'impatient of the slowness and "time will fix it" attitude of their Indonesian colleagues.'[37] These misgivings aside, the Joint Secretariat pulled off an organisational feat. It dealt with transport and accommodation 'with great efficiency.'[38] As Tyabji eventually conceded, 'for the Indonesians to have been made to provide accommodation on the scale required' was 'no mean feat.'[39] 'Only those,' he added somewhat condescendingly, 'who have had experience of making things move in this country or making these people [the Indonesians] conform to the standards which are not their own, will appreciate what it means.'[40] A total of 143 cars, thirty taxis and twenty buses were reserved for transporting foreign delegations and journalists.[41] The press was pleased with the facilities provided for their work.[42] A medical centre was also set up, with two ambulances and six motor cars, as well as three doctors and three nurses working there daily.[43] The wealthy residents of Bandung were requested to vacate their residences so that they could be used to host the heads of delegations.[44] The conference's organisers requisitioned some of their cars to drive the delegates around Bandung.[45] Long-term hotel guests were thrown out of their rooms to make way for foreign visitors.[46] For foreign guests, evening performances of Indonesian dancing were organised in local restaurants.[47]

The conference's main attraction was unquestionably Zhou Enlai. The Chinese premier was the last leader to arrive in Bandung.[48] His chartered Indian Skymaster plane had been delayed because of bad weather and forced to make an unexpected landing in Singapore.[49] On his arrival in Indonesia, he received veritable star treatment. In both Jakarta and Bandung, local ethnic Chinese turned out in large numbers to see him and put up thousands of Chinese flags in welcome.[50] Outside the Jakarta airport, the cheering crowd gave him a clenched fist salute.[51] In Bandung, the Indonesian police and army soldiers had to make way for the Chinese leader through applauding crowds both at the airport and along the 3-mile ride into town.[52] Huge crowds also cheered the delegates as they arrived at the Gedung Merdeka building.[53] Together with Zhou and Gamal Abdel Nasser, Nehru was unquestionably 'the biggest crowd-puller and crowd-pleaser.'[54] The fact that he and the other two leaders symbolised the spirit of anti-colonial emancipation and anti-imperialist revolutionary struggle made them especially popular amongst Indonesians.[55] Whenever Nehru saluted the crowds, Indonesians shouted, 'Merdeka, pak!' (Freedom, sir!).[56]

The PRC fielded an impressive delegation at Bandung. Apart from Zhou Enlai, it included the Deputy Premier and former military officer, Chen Yi; the American-educated Deputy Foreign Minister, Chang Han-fu; the Minister for Trade, Yeh Chi-chuang; and the ambassador to Indonesia, Huang Chen.[57] The Indian delegation was no less impressive. Accompanying Nehru were, among others, Krishna Menon, Subimal Dutt (Commonwealth Secretary), Syed Mahmud (Minister of State for External Affairs, MEA), C. S. Jha (Joint Secretary, MEA), B. K. Nehru (Joint Secretary, Economic Affairs, Ministry of Finance) and K. B. Lall (Joint Secretary, Ministry of Commerce and Industry).[58] In addition to China and India, Indonesia, Egypt, Japan, Pakistan, South Vietnam and Burma also fielded large delegations.[59]

The arrival of the Chinese delegation to Jakarta had been preceded by a dramatic accident. An Air India flight from Hong Kong to Jakarta crashed into the sea near Indonesia's Natuna Islands on 11 April 1955 due to an explosion on board caused by a bomb planted by Kuomintang secret agents. The Chinese government had chartered the Indian airliner 'Kashmir Princess' to fly members of its delegation to Indonesia ahead of the conference. The eleven passengers on board, all lesser communist cadres and journalists, died, and only three crew members were found alive. Zhou Enlai was not among the casualties. Aware of a Chinese Nationalist plot to assassinate him, he had secretly changed his travel plans beforehand, although he did not prevent a delegation of lesser communist cadres from boarding the plane in his place.[60] True to its ruthless form, the CCP leadership deliberately refrained from cancelling or diverting the chartered flight. Instead, it exploited the incident to disrupt Taiwan's spy network in Hong Kong and to launch a premeditated propaganda campaign accusing the United States of wanting to sabotage the Bandung Conference.[61] Such was the nature of the Chinese communist regime on which Nehru relied to entrench peaceful coexistence in Asia.

The Bandung Conference Begins

Twenty-nine countries were represented at the conference, making up 60 per cent of the world population but only 15 per cent of the world's income.[62] While they all (apart from Japan) suffered from the ills of economic and social underdevelopment, they differed significantly in their political culture, customs, traditions and religions. And, although they all shared a strong desire to overcome their sense of inferiority vis-à-vis the developed world, often displaying a common resentment towards it, their widely diverging political and economic interests made coordination difficult to achieve. Their economies, for instance, were competitive rather than complementary. They all competed for foreign military and economic aid and displayed significant disparities in terms of political power—a factor that stood in the way of easy collaboration among them.[63] That said, they were aware that—for all their many differences, their distinct national interests, their diverse aims in attending the conference and their reservations that it would ultimately produce tangible results—Bandung provided a platform to develop closer contacts, raise their prestige, voice their concerns and lobby for vital national interests. Even those countries, such as Thailand, which had initially expressed opposition to attending the conference, chose to participate out of a desire not to be excluded from a gathering that might come to represent most of Asia, the Middle East and parts of Africa.

And as to symbolise the potential significance of the Bandung Conference, the Colombo powers had agreed in Bogor that those countries in attendance would be represented at the top level. And so, several delegations were led by their heads of government, a few others by their foreign ministers, other cabinet ministers or, as in Nepal's case, by officials and academics.[64] They fell into three broad clusters, with roughly ten countries (Ceylon, Iran, Iraq, Lebanon, Pakistan, the Philippines, Thailand, South Vietnam and Turkey) demonstrating a friendly attitude towards the West. China and North Vietnam were firmly in the communist camp, while the remaining countries—such as India, Burma and Indonesia—were neutralists.[65] African delegations, with the exception of Egypt, were to play a minimal part in the conference's deliberations. In contrast, a good number of the Arab countries, namely Lebanon and Iraq, took a robust pro-Western stance and were very active throughout the conference.[66]

The Asian-African conference opened on 18 April 1954 with President Sukarno's lengthy opening address, which, apart from dwelling on the evils of colonialism and racialism, also stressed the dangers of war and the climate of fear and suspicion existing in the world.[67] Indonesian Prime Minister Ali Sastroamidjojo followed with a speech emphasising the need for peace, coexistence and economic development.[68] Like Sukarno, he condemned colonialism and racialism. He also singled out underdevelopment and the development of nuclear weapons as sources of world tension. He made the point that world peace could only be preserved by mutual respect for each other's sovereignty and territorial integrity, non-aggression, non-interference in each other's internal affairs, equality and mutual benefit.[69] The conference was held in two large buildings: the Gedung Merdeka (formerly the Concordia Society Club, an elite Dutch social club), which was used for the open general sessions of the conference, and the Dewi-Warna, a large government office building 3 kilometres to the north, for the closed sessions of the committees.[70] Despite the great expectations surrounding this Asian-African meeting, controversy was never far below the surface.

Nehru's attempts, before the conference started, to have copies of the delegations' opening speeches circulated, rather than read aloud, in order to save time and prevent 'the public adoption of hostile attitudes at the outset,' fell flat due to objections from Pakistan, Turkey and some other countries. Mohammed Ali Bogra apparently lost his temper because Nehru didn't consult him.[71]

Unsurprisingly, the first 2 days 'went into speechifying,' with 'most of the Monday and Tuesday open sessions taken up with fairly predictable speeches' and several delegates exceeding the 20 minutes allotted to them.[72] In the end, nineteen delegates delivered their speeches in person, while seven circulated copies.[73] Nehru, U Nu and Saudi Prime Minister and Foreign Minister Faisal Ibn Abdul Aziz chose to do neither.[74] A variety of common themes—from opposition to colonialism to support for the United Nations and the need for economic development—ran through several speeches.[75] According to G. H. Jansen—who, as a member of the Indian embassy in Jakarta, was uniquely well-informed about Bandung's proceedings, Nehru 'sat through the speeches with ill-concealed irritation.'[76] When it was the Arab delegates' time to speak, they attacked Israel as a 'pernicious example of colonialism, and expressed 'support for the claims of the North African peoples under French rule to independence.'[77]

Controversy Over Communism

A number of pro-Western delegates denounced communism as a new type of colonialism, clearly displaying a marked distrust for the idea of peaceful coexistence as espoused by Nehru and Zhou in the Five Principles.[78] On the first day of the conference, the first delegate to refer to the new colonialism of the Soviet Union was the representative from Iran, Jalal Abdoh.[79] He was soon followed by the representative from Iraq, Mohammad Fadhil Jalali, who castigated Soviet communism for being anti-religious and colonialist and argued that the newly independent Afro-Asian nations were in danger of falling prey to it. His speech was loudly applauded.[80] By the second day, 'deep cleavages of view' between the delegations had 'come into the open' on issues such as communism and coexistence,[81] so much so that French observers commented that 'the solidarity displayed by the nations of Asia and Africa is more apparent than real.'[82] The leaders of Pakistan, the Philippines, Thailand, Libya, Turkey and South Vietnam brought their 'outspoken anti-Communist sentiments' into the open.[83] It was, however, Prince Wan Waithayakon of Thailand who, despite his conciliatory tone, dared to openly accuse China of giving shelter to Thai leftist leader Pridi Panomyang and training 'Thai-speaking Chinese and others ... in Yunnan for infiltration and subversion in Siam.' In addition, he asked, what was 'the attitude of the communist Chinese government to the three million Chinese, so-called dual nationals, in Siam?' 'Siam,' he concluded, was 'facing a threat of infiltration and subversion, if not of aggression,' and it was in self-defence that it had decided to join SEATO.[84]

After Prince Wan spoke, it was Turkish Deputy Prime Minister Fatin Rüştü Zorlu's turn to question the communists' commitment to peaceful coexistence. The head of the Turkish delegation compared the attitude of the Western powers, which 'had demobilised [their] armies after the war,' to that of the Soviet Union, which, instead, 'had seized independent countries' and 'threatened Turkish independence and integrity,' thus forcing Zorlu's country to join NATO and other bilateral defensive arrangements in self-defence.[85] During Zorlu's speech, Zhou Enlai was seen busily jotting down some notes and passing them over to his translators, who sat beside him. When his turn to speak came, he made a brief opening remark of greeting in Chinese. He then handed over to an interpreter, who read out not the text in English which had already been circulated—a clarion call for Afro-Asian cooperation, solidarity against colonialism and support for peaceful coexistence—but a hastily translated speech.[86]

In it, Zhou Enlai emphasised 'the need to seek common ground while reserving differences.'[87] He made it clear that China had come to Bandung to 'seek unity and not to quarrel,' 'to seek common ground, not to create divergences.' 'We Asian and African countries,' he said, 'are all backward economically and culturally.' And so, he asked, 'why could not we ourselves understand each other and enter into friendly co-operation?' China believed in such cooperation, and that was why it supported the Five Principles as the basis for establishing friendly relations among Afro-Asian states. Zhou added that it was precisely to foster common ground and avoid unnecessary disagreements among Afro-Asian countries during the conference that the Chinese delegation had decided not to place on the agenda controversial questions such as Taiwan and China's representation at the UN. In a further attempt to reassure his Afro-Asian counterparts, especially those from Muslim nations, Zhou claimed that although the Chinese communists were atheists, they believed in religious tolerance, adding as an example that a member of the Chinese delegation was a respected Muslim imam. Moreover, he claimed that China opposed outside interference and 'had no intention whatsoever to subvert the governments of its neighbouring countries.'[88]

To dispel regional concerns that China might take advantage of the ten million and more overseas Chinese to carry out subversive activities in their countries of residence, Beijing was 'ready to solve the problem of dual-nationality of overseas Chinese with the governments of the countries concerned.' Without referring openly to Prince Wan's accusations, Zhou argued that the creation of an autonomous Thai state in Yunnan did not mean that China harboured hostile intentions against Thailand. 'The national minorities in China,' he said, 'exercise their right of autonomy within China.' Furthermore, he asked, '[h]ow could that be … a threat to our neighbours?' He invited his Afro-Asian counterparts to visit China to see for themselves. 'We have,' he said, 'no bamboo curtain, but some people are spreading a smokescreen between us.' Cleverly, he also brought up the issue of the Kuomintang forces in Burma. The 'problem at the present,' he argued, was 'not that we are carrying out subversive activities' against China's neighbours but that there were 'people who are establishing bases around China in order to carry out subversive activities against the Chinese Government.' Although he only mentioned the United States, it surely was not lost on Prince Wan that Zhou's comments might also have been directed at him, given Thailand's role in helping supply those Kuomintang forces through its territory. In any case, Zhou concluded, 'the 1,600 million people of Asia and Africa wish our conference success' and were 'looking forward to the contribution which the conference will make towards the extension of the area of peace and the establishment of collective peace.'[89] As we shall see in Chapter 10,

Zhou's conciliatory tone paid off. It had 'a very considerable effect on the other delegates who were, possibly without exception, greatly impressed by it.'[90]

With only two days left before the conference closed, the Afro-Asian delegations still had trouble reaching an agreement on issues that went beyond broad resolutions on racialism, human rights, cultural cooperation or economic issues.[91] Reaching a consensus on colonialism, which, as had become apparent during the initial phase of the conference, aroused significant differences between aligned and non-aligned Afro-Asian nations, was a much more difficult task. Countries opposed to communism were still 'insisting on reference in the resolution to all types of imperialism and colonialism.'[92] It was Kotelawala who sparked controversy when he referred to communist colonialism. He argued that colonialism could take many forms, the most obvious of which was its Western brand. However, there was another type of colonialism also existed, such as that of the Soviet Union, which had transformed its Eastern European neighbours into colonies. 'And if we are united in our opposition to colonialism, should it not be our duty openly to declare our opposition to Soviet colonialism as much as to Western imperialism?'[93] In an oblique reference to China, Kotelawala added that Asians must be 'opposed to any form of colonial exploitation by any power in this region, now or in the future.'[94] Kotelawala's remarks led to a 'heated exchange' of words with Zhou, who accused him of wrecking the conference, and which Ali Sastroamidjojo tried to defuse by adjourning the session.[95] Tempers, however, took some time to cool down. After the meeting broke up, Nehru and Kotelawala had a go at each other, with the former accusing the latter of failing to consult him, to which Kotelawala snapped back: 'Do you always tell me, Mr Nehru, what you are going to do?' As the two leaders became increasingly agitated, Indira Gandhi whispered to her father in Hindi to remain calm. At the same time, Zhou tried to placate Kotelawala by telling him in broken English: 'me your friend.'[96]

When the discussion resumed the next day, Zhou sought to quell the idea that communism represented a new type of colonialism.[97] Mohammed Ali Bogra then cut in, saying that while no one was accusing China of being imperialistic, it would be unrealistic for the conference to ignore Soviet imperialism.[98] The representatives from Iraq and Turkey also supported Kotelawala's idea of a new type of colonialism.[99] These two countries joined Libya, Lebanon, Pakistan, the Philippines and Sudan in putting forward a draft declaration condemning colonialism in all its forms.[100] Uncomfortable with how the conversation was going, Nehru sought to move away from this controversial topic by arguing that 'what was happening in Europe was not colonialism.' Eastern European nations such as Poland or Czechoslovakia were sovereign members of the United Nations and it seemed to him 'extraordinary' to refer to them as colonies.[101] His efforts, however, were to little avail. After much wrangling, an agreement was finally reached at the last moment.[102] Colonialism was condemned, but non-communist nations succeeded in having the wording broadened to a condemnation of colonialism 'in all its manifestations' and 'in whatever form it might be.'[103] Zhou, in the end, acquiesced, thus accepting a formula almost identical to the one he had initially rejected.[104]

Disagreements Over the Five Principles and Collective Defence

The conference also reached a last-minute agreement on another controversial agenda item that had exposed significant divisions among the various delegations—that is, the question of 'promotion of world peace and cooperation.'[105] Thanks to Egyptian Prime Minister Gamal Abdel Nasser, who, as Chair of the relevant drafting committee, worked effectively 'to reduce the mass of principles and formulae to their lowest common denominator,' a compromise was struck.[106] Under its terms, cooperation among nations should be conducted according to ten principles: namely, (1) respect for fundamental human rights and the principles of the UN charter; (2) respect for national sovereignty and integrity; (3) recognition of the equality of all races and all nations; (4) abstention from intervention or interference in internal affairs of another country; (5) respect for the right of individual and collective defence in accordance with the UN Charter; (6) abstention from the use by the big powers of collective defence arrangements to further their own interests and from pressure by any other country on others;

(7) abstention from acts or threats of aggression or use of force; (8) settlement of disputes by peaceful means in accordance with the UN Charter; (9) promotion of mutual interests and cooperation; and (10) respect for justice and international obligations.[107]

Only four of these ten principles were enshrined in the 1954 Sino-Indian agreement on Tibet.[108] By Nehru's own admission, the Five Principles of Peaceful Coexistence became a major 'bone of contention,'[109] and so was the issue of collective defence under security pacts such as SEATO.[110] As was to be expected, Nehru made a long and impassioned—and, according to some, intemperate—pitch for his Five Principles and his idea of areas of peace.[111] One delegate caustically referred to his speech as 'the pure theory of neutralism.'[112] In it, Nehru condemned the formation of blocs, which 'could only lead to war.' India was a member of neither of the two blocs and would 'stand alone even if war breaks out.' Nehru supported no ideology, only 'the Gandhi ideology.' Joining a bloc, he said, would mean losing one's own identity. He regretted, therefore, that some Asian countries had joined Western-sponsored pacts. He considered it 'degrading to become camp followers by tagging to one group or the other.' While conceding that every country had the right of self-defence, he said 'he would ask the Conference not to support the idea of forming pacts.' In his view, military pacts only brought insecurity to those countries which had joined them. As the Western powers were 'the protectors of colonialism,' he 'thought it wrong' for Asian nations 'to join them in a pact.'[113] He referred to SEATO as 'an angry reaction to Geneva.'[114] According to British sources, at one point, he thumped the table and castigated Pakistan and Iraq for being lackeys of the West.[115]

Nehru's remarks elicited a strong response from non-communist delegations. Bogra retorted that Pakistan was a sovereign nation and did not have to explain its behaviour to anyone.'[116] Jamali of Iraq, Charles Malik of Lebanon and General Romulo of the Philippines, whom the Indians deeply distrusted for their pro-American attitudes, strongly disputed Nehru's claims. They argued that while India was a big country that could afford to stand alone, their countries were small and felt threatened. As such, it made sense for them to seek the protection of a stronger power. Besides, how could

Nehru be so sure, they questioned, that participating nations would bring insecurity to themselves by joining a pact or an alliance? How could he possibly judge the interests of other countries? Did he know more about their security than they themselves did? If India was in favour of neutralism, why was half its budget allocated to military expenditures?[117]

In an attempt to mediate between these countries and India, Zhou Enlai put forward his own seven principles—territorial integrity, non-aggression, non-intervention, racial equality, equality of nations, the right of people to choose their political and economic systems and abstention from doing damage to each other. In a lengthy speech in which he sought, once more, to dispel regional fears of China, Zhou made it clear that he wished to assure the conference that his country sincerely stood by each of these principles. Concerning territorial integrity, he told U Nu that China was prepared to solve the border question and prevent its people from crossing the border into Burma (and if they did so, to return them to Chinese soil). As for non-aggression, he again invited Prince Wan and Romulo to visit China to see for themselves that Beijing was not carrying out activities threatening their respective countries. With regard to non-interference, Zhou mentioned the assurance he gave Laos and Cambodia during the Geneva Conference as proof that China had 'no intention to interfere in their internal affairs.' 'This was,' he claimed, 'China's policy towards all small countries.' As for the principle of equality of nations, he said that '[i]f any representative of China here did not respect anyone,' the matter should 'be brought up' to him, and 'he assured the conference that he would rectify the mistake.' As for the right of people to choose their way of life, he argued that China 'respected the systems chosen by others including the Americans.' Finally, he called for relations among nations to be guided by 'mutually advantageous' cooperation, especially in trade matters.[118] Only at the eleventh hour on the Saturday afternoon of 24 April did the principle of recognising the right for countries to join defensive alliances—one which 'directly contradicted the neutralist basis of Nehru's diplomacy'—make it into the final communiqué.[119] Putting on a brave face in light of this setback, Nehru argued that the ten principles were no more than 'a reformulation of [the Five

Principles] with some additions which met our purpose.' Still, as Western diplomatic sources pointed out, it was evident that they had 'decreased the moral authority of the five.'[120] However, according to the French ambassador in Jakarta, Nehru was able, with the help of Ali Sastroamidjojo, to prevent the final communiqué from referring to communist 'subversion' and 'infiltration' as a manifestation of colonialism.[121]

The End of the Conference

The Indian press, which had given extensive coverage to the conference, on the whole agreed that the event had successfully reduced world tensions and raised mutual awareness and understanding between African and Asian nations.[122] *The Tribune*, for instance, argued that Bandung represented a 'logical' shift from the logic of 'preparing for war to prevent war' towards 'preparing for peace.' As a result of Bandung, 'a new force has arisen in international politics—a force which constitutes a major factor in the establishment of universal peace and the promotion of general well-being.' *The Tribune* congratulated Zhou for his contribution to the conference's success. Like *The Tribune*, *The Statesman* and the *Hindustan Times* hailed the conference as a success and praised Zhou's role. The *Hindustan Times*, in particular, stressed the conference's contribution to peaceful coexistence. According to the *Times of India*, the conference raised, for the first time in history, the voice of Asia and Africa—a civilised voice that stood for international decency, peace and progress.[123] However, there were also a few dissenting voices among the chorus of approval. *The Pioneer* wrote that India had suffered a diplomatic setback in Bandung because the conference's resolutions on issues such as colonialism, regional defence organisations and peaceful coexistence were weaker than expected. The *Hindustan Standard* claimed that the conference made no progress on the crucial issue of extending a regional area of peace despite admitting that it was moderately successful.[124] Overall, the Indian press praised Nehru's 'self-effacement' because it not only helped him resolve 'differences behind the scenes,' but it also allowed Zhou 'to take the limelight' and 'establish himself among other participants.' Nehru, in brief, was regarded as the conference's 'chief umpire,' with U Nu and Nasser serving as 'his referees.'[125]

As Chapter 10 reveals, several delegations represented in Bandung did not share the same upbeat view of Nehru's role in the first Asian-African conference. Having scrutinised his performance at close range, they found his behaviour and contribution to the conference underwhelming. Instead, they gave high praise to Zhou Enlai. His calm demeanour and consummate ability to reassure other delegations of China's benign intentions greatly impressed Nehru and his Afro-Asian peers, as well as Western diplomats and government officials. However, as the chapter further emphasises, Zhou's bonhomie was part of a calculated strategy designed to boost China's influence in the Afro-Asian world so as to turn it into a support base for Beijing's revolutionary aims. Although the fundamental differences between the Indian and Chinese approaches to regional affairs remained buried beneath the high-minded and intoxicating rhetoric of Afro-Asian solidarity and peaceful coexistence, some differences did emerge between Nehru and Zhou Enlai in Bandung. As we will see, these differences centred on whether some Afro-Asian machinery should be established to promote deeper Afro-Asian cooperation and if Afro-Asian conferences should become a regular feature of international life. Unlike Zhou, who was enthusiastic about it, Nehru baulked at the idea of more Afro-Asian jamborees. Having secured a Chinese commitment to peaceful coexistence and facilitated Chinese peaceful engagement with the rest of the Third World—or so he thought—Nehru may have felt that a Bandung-style conference was not the most effective way of pursuing his goal of a neutralised and peaceful Asia.

10

BANDUNG'S AFTERMATH

Jawaharlal [Nehru] brought Chou to the Conference as his godson; Chou left the Conference as everyone's godfather, including Jawaharlal's. China, not India, is now uncontestably the leading power in Asia.

C. Khaliquzzaman, Pakistan's ambassador to Indonesia[1]

As soon as the inaugural Asian-African conference drew to a close and the hustle and bustle of its proceedings settled down, participants and interested observers began to assess the summit's accomplishments and dissect the role played by its protagonists. As the conference's most prominent organiser and probably the best-known Third World leader, Nehru's performance received considerable scrutiny and generated much commentary. In the West, opinion was divided on his accomplishments in Bandung. Some officials remarked, for instance, that Nehru's neutralist vision for Asia did not come to pass, with several non-communist governments speaking out against communism and in support of defence pacts.[2] To Roderick Parkes, Counsellor at the British embassy in Jakarta, Nehru 'failed to sell his brand of neutralism' to his Asian-African counterparts. Instead, he 'accepted the principle of the right of self-defence, singly or collectively.' As a result, Parkes surmised, 'the setback suffered by

Gandhian neutralism may well oblige Nehru to recast his cherished philosophy; and that the recognition of defence pacts ... could have far-reaching results.'[3] For the Office of Commissioner-General for the United Kingdom in South-East Asia in Singapore, Nehru 'played throughout a surprisingly undistinguished part.' He was not only 'overshadowed' by Zhou Enlai but was also 'forced into a defensive role' due to the tactics of anti-communist delegations.[4] Some Americans were also critical of Nehru despite acknowledging his merits. According to Hugh S. Cumming, the US ambassador in Jakarta, Bandung 'witnessed the eclipse of Nehru' and the 'growing dislike of India.'[5] While recognising that Nehru 'had played an important part in discussions outside the conference proper, particularly in regard to Indo-China,' State Department sources concluded that Nehru 'had lost prestige, and the Japanese and Turks, as well as smaller nations had been resentful of Nehru's attempts to control proceedings.'[6]

Other Western assessments of Nehru's performance were more sympathetic. A despatch from the US embassy in Jakarta to the Department of State noted that the Indian prime minister had successfully brought 'the Communist and non-Communist delegates together under friendly and relaxed circumstances.'[7] A State Department intelligence report conceded that Nehru sometimes seemed to lose 'his temper when the majority of newly-independent states demonstrated their independence' and, as a result, his reputation was 'somewhat diminished.' However, the report also noted that with the help of U Nu, Ali Sastroamidjojo and Nasser, Nehru had successfully created an 'atmosphere in which peaceful settlement would become easier' and had basically achieved what he had set out to accomplish.[8] According to Keith Shann, unofficial observer for the Australian Department of External Affairs (ADEA) at the conference, 'while he did not play a spectacular public part in the Conference,' Nehru was 'tireless in entertaining various delegations and bringing together people who might not otherwise have made contact.'[9] Through moderation, he and Zhou Enlai 'accomplished a considerable amount in increasing their prestige in Asia, without making obvious, and thus counter-productive, attempts to do so.'[10] Shann reported to Canberra that 'Nehru always appeared to be a dominating figure to whom everyone listened with respect.'[11] He annoyed some with 'his egotism and his assumption of being right, most notably the representatives of Iran and Lebanon, who did not conceal their pleasure at the fact that Mr. Nehru had been unable to show the contenders in the Cold War that he was the leader of a large and influential neutralist group.'[12] However, for Walter Crocker, now Australian ambassador in Jakarta, the idea of Nehru's 'decline in prestige' vis-à-vis Zhou Enlai was 'wishful' thinking. He argued that it 'was, after all, Nehru who insisted on Chou's being invited, who indoctrinated him carefully before the Conference, and who sponsored him in the difficult opening days at Bandung. Mr. Nehru did not strike me as feeling that he had been supplanted by Chou.'[13]

Afro-Asian views on Nehru's demeanour and accomplishments in Bandung were also far from unanimous. Unbeknownst to Nehru, Zhou Enlai disliked his big brother attitude. He would later tell a Ceylonese diplomat: 'I have met Chiang Kai-shek, I have met American generals, but I have never met a more arrogant man than Mr. Nehru.'[14] Other Afro-Asian delegations were similarly critical of him. In the conference's aftermath, John Kotelawala told the British that 'Nehru had been angered by the way the smaller nations had declined to recognise his leadership' and that he 'had also made up to Chou En-lai to an excessive extent.' The prime minister of Ceylon added that many delegates 'had been annoyed at the elaborate build-up of Nehru as "the great statesman of Asia" which Krishna Menon and [the] Indian Ambassador at Djakarta had attempted.' According to him, Nehru 'had not gained ground at Bandung.'[15] The Lebanese delegation was 'completely disillusioned' by Nehru, and his 'neutralism' elicited 'a shocked reaction' from them. They were said to be 'très deçu' (i.e. very disappointed) by him and considered his reputation to 'far transcend his merits.'[16] According to a Turkish delegate, Nehru's 'patronising attitude' had, at times, been 'widely resented' by other delegations, as was Krishna Menon's behaviour.[17] Ahmed Shuqairi, the Palestinian Assistant Secretary of the Arab League and Syrian ambassador to Cairo, was 'very annoyed' with Nehru's attitude and claimed that other Arabs were 'now similarly ill-disposed towards him.' Shuqairi said they 'resented Pandit Nehru's assumption that the Conference would follow the lines he thought good' and 'commented that he lost his grip when he could not get his way, becoming irritable and rude.'[18] The Indonesians appeared to be equally dissatisfied with the Indian leader's performance. Ali Sastroamidjojo's wife told the US ambassador that Nehru had 'got in his [her husband's] hair. Instead of treating him as a Prime Minister he treated him as someone without experience who didn't know how to run a conference.'[19]

If Nehru did not shine as brightly as anticipated, Zhou Enlai far surpassed all expectations. By Nehru's own admission, Zhou was a 'star performer.'[20] Nehru recalled that Zhou 'did not speak much, but what he said was to the point and authoritative.'[21] He was, Nehru added, 'quiet and restrained and obviously determined to do everything in his power to make the Conference a success.'[22] He 'spent long hours in subcommittees' and 'turned down no invitations to parties or meals, however boring or difficult.'[23] 'Accessible' and 'always courteous,' Zhou lost his temper on only one occasion but soon regained composure.[24] In his efforts to charm all and sundry, he even gave Nasser a Chinese edition of the Koran.[25] His performance, Nehru believed, 'was all the more remarkable' because he 'was not very well,' as he was 'convalescing from an operation.'[26]

Nehru no doubt played a significant role in easing Zhou's way into the conference. As an Australian reporter told his readers, Nehru 'shepherded' Zhou through the conference's complexities with 'the care of a mother with a debutante daughter,' 'arrang[ing] dinners and luncheons' and '[seeking] out those who fear Communism to bring them together with' him.[27] It clearly worked. In a private conversation with the prime ministers of Ceylon, Pakistan, Indonesia and Burma, and the foreign ministers of Thailand and the Philippines, the Chinese leader further reassured them of his government's peaceful intentions.[28] Indeed, Zhou went to great lengths to do so. During the conference, the Chinese delegation invited more than twenty delegations to its receptions and parties, whereby Zhou projected an image of a friendly and reassuring China while also attempting to establish contacts with countries that did not recognise the PRC.[29] In his talks with Mohammed Ali Bogra, Zhou invited the Pakistani prime minister to visit China—an invitation Bogra promptly accepted.[30] Significantly, Bogra told Zhou that Pakistan neither opposed nor feared China, adding that, despite its close relations with Washington, Karachi would not join the United States in a war against China.[31] During a dinner at Nehru's residence in Bandung, Zhou followed the same script, telling Romulo: 'Come to China ... see the good and the bad we will show you both. We are neighbours and must know each other better.'[32]

The signing on 22 April of the dual nationality agreement between the PRC and Indonesia appeared to be a good starting point to allay Indonesian fears of communist subversion.[33] More broadly, it also allowed the PRC to demonstrate to its South-East Asian neighbours that it did not intend to meddle in their internal affairs. In the end, as Nehru recognised, '[e]ven his [Zhou's] opponents melted somewhat and agreed that he was an attractive person.'[34] According to a Turkish delegate, Zhou 'had astonished the Turks by asking whether there were any Chinese in Turkey about whom the Turks would like him to make an arrangement as he had done in the case of the overseas Chinese in Indonesia.'[35] For the Lebanese delegation, Zhou was 'head and shoulders above everybody else at the conference' and was 'assisted by a small team of first-class young officials, men who had graduated in Western universities, linguists, and willing helpers.' While Nehru 'was unhelpful and surrounded by sycophantic admirers,' Zhou was 'all sweetness and light, moderation itself.' The Lebanese found him 'très fin' (i.e. very subtle, shrewd).[36]

Western assessments of Zhou's performance were equally glowing. According to the Australian ambassador in Jakarta, the 'rise in the personal prestige of Chou En-lai, and through him of China (at least to some extent) struck everybody at Bandung.'[37] 'There was,' Crocker reported to Canberra, 'no doubt whatever as to the effect he created even on delegates who had come prepared to fight him, such as Romulo or Mohammed Ali [Bogra].'[38] Shann told the ADEA that Zhou's tactics had produced 'a significant weakening in the sentiment against the Chinese Communists on the part of a number of otherwise pro-Western delegates, which could result in a dangerous relaxation of alertness to the Communist menace.'[39] According to the French ambassador in Jakarta, Renaud Sivan, Zhou turned out to be the playmaker at Bandung, and 'China played a leading role—a role commensurate to its specific weight, to its recent successes and its traditions.'[40] As for the Americans, they were 'concerned at the considerably enhanced prestige' with which Zhou had 'emerged from Bandung' and expected the Chinese communists to 'succeed in making a good deal of capital out of it.' In their view, Bandung was 'a great personal triumph' for Zhou. His 'considerable personal charm' had 'deeply impressed' many influential people at the conference.[41] The British were on the same wavelength. For the Foreign Office, Zhou had 'emerged as the most striking figure of the Conference, eclipsing Mr Nehru, who might have been expected to dominate the occasion.' 'In general,' the Foreign Office argued that

> greater respect for and sympathy with Communist China were gained, China's influence in Asia was much augmented, and anti-Communism was proportionately diminished. In consequence, any hope that might have existed that additional states could be attracted to SEATO has now vanished, and a growing tendency towards a neutralist attitude in line with India's position is to be expected.[42]

For the Foreign Office, Zhou 'made an excellent impression' by making it clear that China 'had no desire to subvert neighbouring countries or to force their views on others'; that it 'wanted only peaceful co-existence on the basis of the five principles already agreed with India'; that it was prepared 'to settle the problem of the Overseas Chinese in a friendly manner'; and that it was also willing 'to enter into discussions' with the Americans on the issue of Formosa. The reality was, the Foreign Office concluded, that the 'widespread fear of war' pushed 'Asians as much as others to grasp at any hope of peace.' Hence, Zhou's proclamations of China's peaceful intentions inevitably 'commanded more respect and carried more conviction than on any objective view they were entitled to.'[43]

Nehru's Assessment of the Bandung Conference

Nehru considered the conference 'exciting' and the coming together of delegates from Asia and Africa 'fascinating.'[44] Given the several countries represented and their diverse political and cultural makeup, he felt it had been an 'outstanding success' and 'productive of more good to our common cause than perhaps we dared to anticipate.'[45] The impression made on him 'was a very great one.'[46] Nehru graciously congratulated the Indonesians for what, in the end, turned out to be a well-organised conference. He said that they had discharged their task 'remarkably well,' adding that he doubted New Delhi could have provided the same level of amenities.[47] He told one of his ministers that the arrangements were 'excellent and on a large scale.'[48] Much less complimentary was India's ambassador in Jakarta, B. F. H. B. Tyabji. Ever critical of the Indonesians, Tyabji complained that the Ali Sastroamidjojo government still 'refused to give any credit' to the other Colombo countries for their help in organising the conference and that the Indonesians had 'gone out their way' to belittle India—'the very country which has given them the greatest help.'[49]

However, the final communiqué, Nehru claimed, was a 'good' one.[50] While admitting that 'some of us would have liked [it] to be somewhat different,' he conceded that 'we were anxious to succeed and agreed to many things.'[51] In any case, what he found particularly remarkable about the conference was 'the sense of community which it engendered amongst the delegates. They felt more and more that they belonged to something, that something had value, and that they and it counted in the world.'[52] In his view, the conference generated 'a pro-Asian, a pro-African' sentiment and a 'feeling of Asia standing on its own feet and not being pushed this way or that by Europe or America.'[53] The conference, he argued, 'opened a new chapter not only in Asia and Africa, but in the world.'[54] It was, in other words, 'the first clear enunciation by the countries of Asia especially that they have an individuality and viewpoint which they are not prepared to give up because of the views of or pressures from other countries.'[55] Furthermore, Nehru praised the quiet role India had played behind the scenes. While, he said, it 'was not India's purpose to play any aggressive role or, indeed, to seek the limelight,' the fact remained that India, together with China, had been the most influential country present at Bandung. He agreed with U Nu that 'without India and China the Conference would not have had much significance.'[56]

Moreover, Nehru felt vindicated in his decision to invite China to the conference. He liked much of what the Chinese leader had said during the conference: that China wanted to reach 'a common understanding' with its neighbours; that it 'desired no expansion or internal subversion in any country'; that it believed that 'each country must respect the way of life and economic system chosen by another country'; that it had no wish to establish a communist regime in Tibet; that it 'asked for no special privileges or special status in dealings with other countries' and was 'prepared to settle international disputes by peaceful means'; that it 'wanted a peaceful settlement' to the Taiwan question,' 'was prepared to have direct talks with the United States' and, in any case, 'had no desire to punish in any way Chiang Kai-shek's officers and army'; that it 'entirely agreed' with the Five Principles and that, despite not 'press[ing] for the exact language of these five principles,' China 'wanted the substance with a view to establishing collective peace.'[57] In brief, Nehru was reassured that Zhou meant 'what he says—he wants peace with America and with the world.'[58] His strategy to bring China out of isolation, push it to commit to peaceful coexistence and reassure its neighbours of its peaceful intentions appeared, therefore, to be crowned with success.

Nehru also welcomed the agreement reached on the conference's various resolutions—from economic and cultural cooperation to human rights and colonialism. Yet, he regarded the principles contained in the communiqué's 'Declaration on World Peace and Co-operation' as the conference's most significant outcome. These principles, he claimed, were both of universal application and historical significance and should 'govern the relations of the nations of the world if world peace and co-operation are to be achieved.' Despite only four of the Five Principles enshrined in the 1954 Sino-Indian agreement on Tibet making it into the declaration, Nehru fully supported it and was prepared to honour it. He said India had never put forward the Five Principles of Peaceful Coexistence 'as though they were divine commandments' or 'as though there was a particular sanctity about their formulation.' 'The essence of them is the substance,' he claimed, 'and this has been embodied in the Bandung Declaration.' That said, Nehru had to grin and bear the fact that the declaration recognised the right of individual and collective self-defence under the UN Charter—a principle strongly advocated by several pro-Western Afro-Asian nations. After speaking forcefully against military pacts during the conference proceedings, Nehru had no option but to accept the principle of self-defence. In doing so, however, he drew attention to the fact that the declaration also included an important caveat—namely, that no country should be pressured to join collective defence arrangements and that the world's great powers should not use them to serve their particular interests.[59] From Nehru's standpoint, such formulation more than met India's interests.

Disagreements on the Prospect of a Second Asian-African Conference

That Nehru regarded Bandung primarily as an opportunity to fulfil his Cold War vision and advance India's politico-strategic objectives in Asia also became clear from his opposition to a second Afro-Asian conference. Despite waxing lyrical about Afro-Asian solidarity at the conference's end, he appeared extremely reluctant to give in to calls to turn Bandung's incipient Afro-Asianism into a long-term political phenomenon. According to two Turkish and Syrian delegations members, Nehru obstructed Arab attempts to lobby for another similar conference.[60] Australian sources revealed that some countries, such as Indonesia and Egypt, had 'wanted the Asian-African Conference to become a permanent group with permanent machinery both in the political and economic fields,' but Nehru and U Nu had 'resolutely opposed' the idea.[61] No more encouraging had been those Middle Eastern nations friendly to the West.[62]

Meeting Zhou and U Nu on 16 April before the start of the conference proceedings, Nehru had already put a dampener on the idea of a 'permanent political institution' tasked with promoting the principles espoused by the conference. As mentioned in Chapter 8, one of China's key goals for Bandung was the creation of a permanent Afro-Asian organisation. According to Chinese plans, this organisation should meet every two years and commit to the Five Principles of Peaceful Coexistence, which would, in turn, help establish a zone of peace in Asia.[63] In contrast to Zhou, Nehru argued that it was difficult to imagine 'how this institution would effectively perform its function' with so many different countries.[64] U Nu held the same view. Noting that the conference could not agree on important issues, the Burmese leader concluded that, even if a permanent institution were established, it would have no effective means of implementing its recommendations.[65] Despite Zhou's urging, Nehru remained steadfast in his opposition to the concept, arguing that it would not be prudent for a formal Afro-Asian caucus to compete with the United Nations.

In his memoirs, Tyabji claimed that Krishna Menon was 'staunchly opposed to the idea' and 'succeeded in carrying Panditji [Nehru] along with him.' Menon worried that the creation of such a permanent secretariat would drag India into the internal 'rivalries of comparatively small and underdeveloped countries' and divert its attention from the much weightier task of mediating between the two superpowers.[66] In reality, the Indian government had already made up its mind before the conference started. In March, Commonwealth Secretary Subimal Dutt had ruled out the prospect of 'setting up a permanent machinery or Secretariat for the Conference' because it 'would unduly interfere with the freedom of action by individual countries in dealing with urgent issues.'[67] Moreover, in a statement made upon his arrival in Bandung, Nehru poured cold water on the notion that the present conference would establish a permanent Afro-Asian secretariat.[68] In the end, U Nu, too, refused to budge. He reiterated the view that 'even if an institution could be set up after the conference, it could not win respect from the world due to its ineffectiveness.' It would, he added, be 'much better to form a small but effective institution later.'[69] However, he did not specify what he had in mind.

Undaunted, Zhou made one last attempt a few days later. While acknowledging that India and Burma 'were not very enthusiastic,' he was encouraged by the fact that 'the Philippines, Thailand, Turkey, and some other nations [had] immediately expressed consent.'[70] Hoping to win Nehru over, he once more proposed establishing a liaison office or a joint secretariat in preparation for a possible future Asian-African conference in Egypt. Before Nehru could even say a word, U Nu interjected, saying, 'his mind was quite clear that there should be no kind of organisation or liaison office.' He warned that 'if another session of the Conference was held,' he would send no representatives, adding that he 'was firm about it.'[71] As he would indicate to the British ambassador in Rangoon a few weeks later, U Nu had not enjoyed the conference. He had welcomed the informal encounters between leaders outside the formal sessions but felt that the conference 'resulted in the necessity for accepting compromises of a kind which nobody liked.'[72]

U Nu ought not to have worried, as Nehru remained opposed to the idea of another Asian-African conference. At the same time, however, the Indian leader recognised that despite all the 'difficulties and differences of opinion, the net result of this Conference was very good'—'perhaps not so much' in terms of 'the resolutions passed' but because of 'the effect it produced in Asia and the world.' When Zhou concurred with Nehru, U Nu would have none of it, claiming that the conference had 'only brought out differences of opinion and even the resolutions passed indicated that. What was the good of repeating platitudes, etc.' Faced with the Burmese leader's refusal to budge, Nehru, too, reiterated his opposition to the idea of a joint secretariat, adding that it was 'unwise to fix the place and time of the next conference.'[73] Indian hostility to establishing a permanent Asian-African machinery would persist well after the conference, as the next chapter will clearly show.[74] Although, in the end, the final communiqué recommended that the five Colombo powers 'consider the convening of the next meeting of the Conference, in consultation with the participating countries,' no steps were taken to make such a meeting a reality.[75] As Nehru told Crocker, the conference had 'broken up without any commitments as regards a further meeting, in Cairo or anywhere else.'[76] Western fears that Nehru might exploit the Bandung conference to create an Afro-Asian grouping proved unwarranted.

China's Post-Bandung Moment

Zhou departed Indonesia on 28 April. Exhausted after days of intense diplomatic and social activity, he flew to Kunming for some rest. From the capital of China's southern Yunnan province, he despatched to Mao and the CCP a series of reports on the conference and its outcomes.[77] In them, the Chinese premier praised China's consensus-seeking role in the conference and welcomed its results. In his report on political questions, Zhou characterised the Bandung meeting as a contest 'between two different lines.' On one side, he said, were the friends of the United States who tried to 'use anti-Soviet and anti-communist slogans to bog the conference down in a debate on ideology, to prevent the conference from achieving anything.' 'On the other side,' he went on, stood countries seeking to reach consensus on 'the basis of opposition to colonialism and maintenance of world peace and cooperation in order to enable the conference to reflect the common wishes of African and Asian people as much as possible.' 'The results of the conference,' Zhou concluded, 'proved that the second line was largely successful.'[78]

In Zhou's report on cultural cooperation, he welcomed the successful conclusion of the dual citizenship agreement with Indonesia—an agreement that finally ended a controversial issue that had been a source of fear amongst China's South-East Asian neighbours. In his view, it was 'a timely and important step' towards enhancing China's regional reputation.[79] In his report on economic cooperation, Zhou wrote that he shared the other delegations' desire for greater economic cooperation among Afro-Asian nations and greater intra-regional trade. That said, he stressed the need for such cooperation to be based on 'technologies and experiences obtained by Asian and African people' because these technologies and practices 'were more suitable' to developing nations. He also insisted that their economic development be based primarily on 'self-reliance with some international assistance,' provided the latter would not come with 'unfavourable political and economic conditions for the recipient nations.' In any case, China was willing to 'provide some industrial equipment and experts, and exchange technologies and training experts within our power,' which he said drew 'the attention of many delegates.' Despite saying that the final communiqué 'did not completely match our expectation,' Zhou was pleased that China had helped forge 'an ideological foundation for the promotion of the economic independence of Asian and African regions.' During his talks with various delegations outside the conference, he detected a strong interest by countries such as Egypt, Syria, Ceylon, India, Burma and Pakistan to foster trade with China.[80]

A few weeks later, the CMFA released a report that communicated this same sense of achievement, praising the 'extremely important role' played by the Chinese delegation at the conference—in particular, in its efforts to seek 'common ground while reserving differences' and encourage 'friendly consultation.' This, the CMFA claimed, demonstrated two things: first, that 'the cooperation between the Communists and nationalists in the struggle against colonialism and for peaceful co-existence' was not only 'possible' but 'necessary'; second, that the very existence of the Soviet Union, China and other communist nations had 'restrained the enemy of the national liberation movement and promoted the struggle of the Asian-African people for peace, freedom and independence.' According to the report, Bandung had 'reflected the profound change of the political situation in the Asian-African region.' Its key achievements included 'the relaxation of international tension and the maintenance of world peace.' In this context, the CMFA hailed 'the Bandung Spirit' as the attitude of 'seeking common ground' between nations with different political systems and views. Finally, the CMFA declared that the Asian-African conference had 'made a great contribution to the strengthening of the national consciousness of the Asian-African countries.' Seen from Beijing, therefore, the Bandung Conference was an unmitigated success. Not only had China managed to break free from its isolation, but it was now in a position to exploit the political and reputational 'Bandung dividend' to make diplomatic inroads into the Afro-Asian world.[81]

Therefore, in the years following the Bandung Conference, Chinese leaders strove to promote an image of China as 'a strong, independent Asian country committed to peace and development' and to fully engage with the Afro-Asian world.[82] As the CMFA outlined in a draft paper dated July 1955, the Asian-African conference had demonstrated that China 'enjoyed a great prestige among the Asian-African countries' and that its policy of 'seeking common ground' with them 'while reserving differences' had turned out to be 'correct.' The paper welcomed the fact that 'more and more people [were] in favor of peaceful co-existence' and that the Five Principles had 'become the banner of the peace-loving people in the world.' 'Such development,' the CMFA pointed out, was 'conducive to the relaxation of the international tensions.' In this context, China should take full advantage of the situation to develop friendly relations with other Asian-African countries. The CMFA acknowledged that China had not done enough in this area. As the paper put it, China's:

> past understanding of the united front of international peace was rather narrow ... our attitude was not very active, and our understanding of the specific conditions of the Asian-African countries ... was not in depth enough ... and at the same time, we didn't know the ins and outs of the imperialist conspiratorial activities in Asia and Africa.[83]

Warning that imperialist powers had 'been increasingly intensifying their conspiratorial activities in Asia and Africa,' the CMFA stated that China must redouble its efforts 'to carry out energetic work towards the Asian-African countries in order to promote the continuous relaxation of the international tensions.'[84]

In outlining a comprehensive strategy to deal with the Afro-Asian world, the CMFA indicated a number of important steps necessary to increase Chinese presence there. First, China should 'continue to exchange visits of high-leveled governmental delegations' (on the model of those visits already undertaken with India, Burma and Indonesia) and do its best 'to establish diplomatic relations with more Asian and African countries.'[85] With countries with which it had no diplomatic relations, China ought to maintain and develop existing contacts.[86] Second, it should 'consolidate and develop economic and cultural relations,' since it was 'easier to open a channel for exchanging visits by trade delegations or art and cultural delegations.' In this context, it should also encourage 'the exchange of visits by specialized delegations (such as educational, agricultural, medical, etc.)' and 'consider inviting more guests with social or academic status to visit China.' The international liaison departments of the Chinese trade unions and the women's and youth federations had an important role in implementing this strategy. By inviting their guests, they would not only help expand China's contacts with the Asian-African world, but they would do so without raising the alarm from Afro-Asian governments. Finally, religion, too, had a part to play in the unfolding of this strategy. In this area, the CMFA recommended that China take no 'antagonistic attitude towards many religious countries in Asia and Africa' but rather try 'to promote friendly relations between China and Asian-African countries through religions.' What CMFA officials had in mind was, for instance, the setting up of Buddhist and Islamic associations. Beijing should also make it easier for Chinese Muslims to travel to Mecca.[87]

Apart from expanding and deepening contacts with Afro-Asian countries, the CMFA paper also stressed the need to strengthen propaganda work in the developing world. As CMFA officials put it, this would help counter Western propaganda by exposing the activities of the imperialist powers and expressing China's attitude towards major Afro-Asian developments. Furthermore, it would assist in reducing the impact of the West's vilification of China by making known the 'foreign affairs, economy, culture, ethnic groups, religions, etc of the New China in a planned and systematic way to the Asian-African countries.'[88] In this respect, the CMFA proposed to improve the distribution of written and visual materials such as movies (regarded as 'the most convenient and effective tools for propaganda to foreign countries') and magazines.[89] Last but not least, the paper also recommended that the Chinese government make serious efforts to promote a better understanding of the political, economic, social and historical conditions of various Afro-Asian countries, as well as to properly train 'the cadres needed for [the] development of the work towards the Asian and African countries.'[90]

Predictably, Beijing followed up words with deeds.[91] Before Bandung, only seven of the twenty-nine countries represented at the conference had diplomatic relations with Beijing. Several of them had formal ties to Formosa.[92] This situation, however, was destined to change, as Beijing was determined to make up for the lost ground. Unsurprisingly, therefore, in the wake of Bandung, China launched an unrelenting charm offensive in the Afro-Asian world to achieve these objectives.[93] It did so by hosting foreign leaders, sending high-ranking officials abroad, providing economic aid and sponsoring delegations of all sorts—from cultural and economic to religious and educational.[94] Immediately after Bandung, China and Egypt concluded a bilateral trade agreement, followed in 1956 by the establishment of diplomatic relations and the signing of a cultural agreement.[95] In the 5 years following the Bandung Conference, China established diplomatic relations with seven more African countries—Morocco, Ghana, Mali, Guinea, Sudan, Somalia and the Provisional Government of the Republic of Algeria.[96] Moreover, between 1957 and 1959, numerous African delegations travelled to China.[97] In the first half of 1960 alone, Mao welcomed 111 African representatives—a major increase, considering that he had only met 163 of them throughout the preceding decade.[98] In line with China's growing interest in the African continent, the CMFA also started to post some of its most skilled and seasoned diplomats to African capitals.[99] Asia, too, witnessed China's charm offensive. Between 1955 and 1957, China established formal diplomatic relations with Afghanistan, Nepal, Syria, Yemen and Ceylon.[100]

These efforts did not go unrewarded: the post-Bandung years witnessed a growing tendency among Asian countries to give China the benefit of the doubt.[101] However, as China made diplomatic inroads into the Third World, Nehru's India grew increasingly wary of Chinese intentions. As Chapter 11 makes clear, instead of being the catalyst for stronger Sino-Indian relations, Bandung came to represent the fleeting heyday of Sino-Indian rapprochement. Far from embracing Nehru's vision of collective peace, China was soon to embark on a renewed revolutionary phase of its foreign policy, thus demonstrating that its verbal support for the Five Principles and Nehru's areas of peace was not a repudiation of the 'revolutionary foreign policy that they had adopted in the first five years of the People's Republic.'[102] Where Nehru dreamed of a tension-free region, and 'an Asia shared with China,'[103] Mao and his comrades remained committed to revolutionary change domestically and internationally.

11

EPILOGUE

We were always against repeating 'Bandung' in a hurry as some wanted because we were afraid we would undo the good done there. It was the high point of Asian unity.

Krishna Menon[1]

The Bandung Conference represented the high point of Nehru's policy of peaceful coexistence—an approach centred on areas of peace, the Five Principles of Peaceful Coexistence and India's rapprochement with China. Although the final communiqué did not incorporate these Five Principles—it endorsed, instead, a broader set of principles (the 'ten principles'), which included the right of countries to join defensive alliances—Nehru appeared successful in securing two key objectives: first, ensuring that the 'ten principles' were 'in general conformity with the Five Principles';[2] and second, committing the Chinese to his vision of collective peace and socialising them into what he regarded as the norms and values of acceptable international behaviour.[3] Nehru drew reassurance from the fact that Zhou Enlai publicly supported peaceful coexistence and went out of his way to convince all and sundry of Beijing's peaceful intentions. Nehru assumed that Beijing would not renege on its promises, since doing so would expose China to widespread international condemnation. Regrettably for him, subsequent events would reveal how wrong he was in expecting the weight of world opinion to act as a constraint on Mao Zedong's China. Far from recruiting India's northern neighbour to his vision of peace and non-alignment, Nehru soon found himself confronted with an increasingly militant China bent on exploiting Afro-Asian solidarity to advance its revolutionary goals.

For all the talk of Sino-Indian brotherhood and lofty declarations of support for the Five Principles and areas of peace, the harsh reality was that India and China had very different understandings of peaceful coexistence. Whereas the Indians saw the Five Principles as a means of overcoming Cold War tensions, the Chinese continued to regard them as a tactical adjustment to the international realities of the moment—in other words, no more than a mere concession to the necessities of fighting the Cold War. As one historian has perceptively noted, China saw Afro-Asian neutralism as a convenient tool for furthering its strategic objectives, initially centred on halting American penetration in Asia.[4] But as its foreign policy shifted from advocating peaceful coexistence to promoting violent national liberation struggles throughout the Afro-Asian world, the latter became an area of increasing Chinese revolutionary activity.[5] Predictably enough, China's radical brand of Afro-Asianism would put it on a collision course with India. Unlike Mao's China, Nehru's India advocated a peaceful path to colonial emancipation. Unlike its northern neighbour, India continued to view Afro-Asian cooperation as a mechanism to create neutralised areas of peace and avoid Cold War conflict. With such diverging goals and different strategic visions, it is no coincidence that the two Asian giants grew increasingly estranged within a few years of Bandung. To compound the growing chasm between China's and India's approaches to regional security, serious misunderstandings began to emerge on the issue of Tibet and the still un-demarcated Himalayan border.[6] However, the relationship between India and China was already built on shaky ground, given the different premiums they placed on peace and stability, and their clashing visions for the postcolonial Afro-Asian world; the border question would then undoubtedly provide the catalyst for the rapid and dramatic unravelling of Sino-Indian ties.[7]

India's Opposition to a Second Asian-African Conference

Some differences, albeit seemingly minor ones, began to emerge even before Bandung concluded. Zhou's proposal that the Colombo powers organise another Asian-African conference in 1956 went unheeded.[8] The only thing the various delegations in Bandung could agree on was the vague formula committing no one to anything. As seen in the previous chapter, neither Nehru nor U Nu showed any enthusiasm for a second conference. Nehru's lack of enthusiasm remained palpable even after the conference ended. According to his chief of security, K. F. Rustamji, Nehru 'never liked talking about the conference' after he returned to India from Indonesia. 'Whenever I spoke about Bandung,' Rustamji recalled, 'a cloud gathered over his face.'[9] As the events of the following autumn revealed, Nehru remained averse to another Asian-African conference.

In September 1955, John Kotelawala, in his capacity as the original convenor of the Colombo group, contacted Nasser about the possibility of holding a new Afro-Asian meeting in Cairo in June 1956.[10] Nasser responded that he welcomed the idea, but in private the Egyptians expressed reservations about holding a new conference so soon.[11] A few weeks later, in November 1955, Indonesia's new Masyumi government led by Burhanuddin Harahap wrote to Kotelawala proposing an early meeting of the five Colombo powers 'to review the international situation affecting South and South East Asia and to settle an Agenda for the next Asian African Conference.'[12] The Harahap government justified its request by citing concerns over political tensions in the Middle East and Indochina, as well as relations between the five Colombo powers. It also communicated its wish to capitalise on a new Asian-African summit to press for the implementation of the resolutions adopted in Bandung.[13] However, according to Pakistani sources, other factors were driving the Indonesians' sense of urgency: namely, their eagerness to mobilise Afro-Asian support in order to pressure the Dutch government to relinquish sovereignty over West New Guinea.[14]

When Kotelawala replied, agreeing to a meeting of the Colombo powers and suggesting they meet Rangoon in January 1956,[15] India's reaction was negative. Nehru rejected the notion of both an early meeting of the Colombo powers and an Asian-African conference. In his opinion, there was a danger that a new Asian-African gathering 'might not result in general agreement,' thus eroding the 'very good effect' generated by the Bandung Conference in Asia and around the world. Nehru did not believe such a meeting would be appropriate, given the current acute tensions between Israel, Egypt and other Arab nations, especially if it were held in Cairo. He also indicated that considerable time would be needed to prepare for the conference, and he was unwilling to rush this matter.[16] Pakistan's reaction was also unfavourable.[17] The Pakistani Ministry of Foreign Affairs told the Australian High Commission in Karachi that the government would be '"throwing all the cold water" it could on the idea of an Asian-African Conference in 1956.'[18] Pakistan's main objection was that 'all the subjects on which such a Conference could agree had been agreed last year and there was no point in further discussion of them.'[19] As for Burma, U Nu told Kotelawala that 'the Asian-African Conference need not to be an annual affair' and he 'was in favour of postponing [it].'[20] As Mynt Thein, one of Nu's closest advisers, put it to the British, it 'might be better to rest on the laurels of Bandung and not try to hurry the next Conference.'[21] In the face of such a reaction, the Ceylonese government desisted.[22]

When the Colombo prime ministers, with the exception of Pakistan's H. S. Suhrawardy, finally gathered in New Delhi in mid-November 1956 to discuss the group's attitude towards the Suez and Hungarian crises, they expressed hope that a second Asian-African conference could be held in the second half of 1957.[23] Yet, at the same time, Nehru, Ba Swe (Burma), S. W. R. D. Bandaranaike (Ceylon) and Ali Sastroamidjojo (Indonesia), who had returned to power the previous March, were forced to recognise that such a meeting 'might not be feasible' in the current complex international situation.[24] The venue and date, therefore, were left undecided, but the four prime ministers agreed to set up a consultative committee to facilitate discussion of current economic problems, especially those generated by the Suez Canal crisis.[25] Proposed by Bandaranaike, this economic consultative committee met once in Colombo in June 1957, but no further discussions occurred afterwards.[26]

Incidentally, the New Delhi meeting proved to be the last hurrah for the Colombo powers, who from then on 'ceased to operate as a group.'[27] According to G. H. Jansen, the 'acrimonious debates' and the 'firm positions' adopted during the Bandung Conference undermined them as a group.[28] In any case, India's coolness towards a second Asian-African conference remained tangible despite signs that China, Egypt, Ceylon and Indonesia all favoured one.[29] In January 1957, Nehru told visiting Syrian President Shukri al-Quwatli that, given the current international context, the time was 'not yet ripe' for a second Afro-Asian conference.[30] A few weeks later, he returned to the issue, writing in an internal note that, although Bandung had been a success, 'even there it was clear that there were rifts,' and that 'these cleavages have widened.' As such, holding a second Bandung would not 'be suitable at this stage.'[31]

While India continued to resist calls for a second Bandung, China was eager to make it happen. During a visit to Colombo in February 1957, Zhou Enlai issued a joint communiqué with Bandaranaike calling for a second Asian-African conference to secure the implementation of the Five Principles.[32] China was keen to ensure that 'all the countries that participated in the first conference can make it; and there must be even more countries. For example, countries like Morocco, Tunisia, etc.'[33] However, as Zhou made clear to the Indonesian ambassador in Beijing a month later, his government 'would rather wait for a bit' if the number of interested countries turned out to be 'very small.' The other caveat he introduced was the need for the new Asian-African conference to avoid disagreements and bolster solidarity. '[W]e do not want,' he said, 'the conference to become a place for arguments.'[34]

Incidentally, Zhou's visit to Colombo was one of the stops on a tour of eight Asian (North Vietnam, Cambodia, India, Pakistan, Burma, Afghanistan, Nepal and Ceylon) and three Eastern European (Poland, Hungary and the Soviet Union) nations that the Chinese premier undertook between November 1956 and February 1957. Considered 'the most extensive trip abroad ever made by a CCP official,' Zhou's tour took place in the wake of the Polish and Hungarian crises in October 1956.[35] While the European leg of his tour sought to help restore the unity of the communist camp, the Asian one was conceived as 'an extensive diplomatic campaign' intended 'to reaffirm the importance of the Five Principles' and reassure China's neighbours of its peaceful intentions.[36] As Gregg Brazinsky noted, it was no coincidence that 'seven of the eight Asian countries that Zhou visited bordered directly on the PRC. Having watched the Soviet Union invade Hungary with China's tacit consent, these neighbors were now anxious that Beijing might one day use similar means to settle its differences with them.'[37] Mindful of such views, Zhou considered the chief aim of his Asian tour 'to seek friendship, peace and knowledge.'[38] By demonstrating generosity as well as respect for neighbouring nations' culture and history, Zhou hoped to 'build on what he had done to improve China's image at Bandung.'[39] He wanted the PRC to 'be admired for its commitment to peace' and 'seen as a sympathetic friend to other Asian nations with which it shared not only a continent but also a history of anticolonial struggle.'[40]

Despite Zhou's and Bandaranaike's support for a second Bandung, in November 1957, the Ceylonese leader concurred with Nehru that 'the difference of opinion on important matters of principle between Powers that might attend are so great that it is not yet profitable to hold [a] further meeting.'[41] As Nehru's private secretary C. R. Srinivasan bluntly stated to James Plimsoll of the Australian Department of External Affairs, there would be no second Bandung anytime soon 'if India can help it.'[42] According to the Indian official, 'the various members of the Afro-Asian group had too many private axes to grind.'[43] The Indian view was that 'if a meeting were held it would be used by member countries as an occasion for rallying support for their own private interests.'[44]

In April 1958, Hirendranath Mukerji, a member of the Indian Communist Party, told the Lok Sabha that India ought to take steps to convene another Bandung Conference, since 'a follow up' to Bandung was needed to meet the 'conspiracy of diehard imperialism rampant all over the world from Indonesia to Algeria.'[45] Nehru would have none of it. In his reply, he argued that 'a second Afro-Asian Conference at [the] Governmental level would not be possible at the present state owing to the situation in the Middle East and Indonesia.'[46] This time, he was referring to a rebellion launched in February 1958 by some elements of the Indonesian army against

President Sukarno in the islands of Sumatra and Sulawesi, and the serious political unrest pitting Lebanon's Christian and Muslim communities against one another over the succession of President Camille Chamoun.[47] That same April, he poured cold water on the idea of an 'economic Bandung' aimed at fostering greater economic cooperation among Afro-Asian countries, arguing, among other things, that such a conference would neither be easy to organise nor would it provide the best format to achieve that cooperation.[48] A few months later, in December 1959, Nehru turned down suggestions from Cambodian Prime Minister Norodom Sihanouk to hold another fully fledged Afro-Asian conference.[49] He said a Bandung-type conference 'could never consider such questions as the Sino-Indian border.'[50] Nor was Nehru better disposed towards 'a meeting of the uncommitted and non-aligned nations so as to reduce world tensions'—an idea that Nehru believed Sihanouk 'had been put up to' by Egyptian President Gamal Abdel Nasser who, together with Yugoslav President Josip Broz Tito, had 'pedalled the idea on a number of occasions.'[51] Tito, in particular, had been keen on such an idea for a while, believing that the principles of non-alignment and peaceful coexistence transcended strict Afro-Asian boundaries and that a future event similar to Bandung should also include European and Latin American countries.[52] His diplomatic overtures, however, had received short shrift from Nehru.[53] The Yugoslav leader attributed Nehru's reluctance to India's position of pre-eminence among non-aligned countries and his eagerness to deal directly with the United States and Soviet Union.[54] Despite Tito's best efforts to garner support for his idea among Afro-Asian nations to force India's hand, his lobbying produced no results.[55] Yugoslavia's ideological conflict with Moscow and Beijing at the end of the 1950s threw a further spanner into Tito's works by forcing him to focus on this problem.[56]

Although, as seen above, Nehru cited a variety of reasons for rejecting calls for a second Bandung, it was first and foremost his sense of disillusionment with Afro-Asian solidarity that fed his aversion to a new Asian-African conference. The fear that a new conference might do more harm than good to Afro-Asian unity by publicly exposing differences and tensions weighed heavily on his mind.[57] As he pointed out to his closest advisers in November 1959, 'most of the Asian and African countries are at sixes and sevens and I am not clear in my mind as to what we should achieve by such conference at this stage.'[58] That same month, Nehru told the Yugoslav ambassador in New Delhi, Dušan Kveder, that such meetings would only 'demonstrate disunity' among these countries.[59] He suggested, instead, that the consultations between him, Tito, Nasser and Sukarno be intensified.[60] By 1960, however, another issue arose that made Nehru reluctant to agree to a new Asian-African conference. That issue was China. In 1959, as relations between the two Asian giants took a definite turn for the worse following clashes between Indian and Chinese patrols on the Himalayas, New Delhi came to view a summit involving both India and China as being likely to 'damage the dormant Asian-African Movement beyond repair.'[61] In early 1960, Nasser and Sukarno attempted to get Nehru to agree to a second Bandung with the view to urging Beijing to adopt a less aggressive stance towards India in the name of the Bandung spirit.[62] Nehru's response, however, was no more encouraging. He believed such a conference would fail.[63]

There is, however, a further aspect that must be considered in assessing Nehru's negative attitude towards a second Bandung. By the end of the 1950s, as shall be seen in the next section, China's approach to peaceful coexistence and the Afro-Asian world had changed substantially as a result of Mao's return to a more radical approach to international affairs. In a climate of increasing political and ideological tensions between Beijing and New Delhi, it is no coincidence that Nehru judged that a re-run of the Bandung conference would be unhelpful, if not outright self-defeating. After all, Bandung had served a specific purpose in his regional policy: it had secured Beijing's commitment to peaceful coexistence and the notion of areas of peace, thus making it harder for China to violate these principles. With New Delhi now perceiving Beijing as bent on pursuing an aggressive policy in the Himalayas and the Third World, it was clear that Nehru's strategy of containing China by lofty principles or grand diplomatic schemes was showing its limitations. Nehru knew a second Bandung would not turn the clock back to 1955 and might even provoke a break among Afro-Asian countries. In this context, it was not surprising that when Nasser and Sukarno visited New Delhi in 1960 to seek Nehru's support for a new Afro-Asian conference, Nehru reacted coolly. Although they tried to persuade him that 'the convening of a second Asian African Conference could result, inter alia, in an accession of "moral force" to India which would be helpful to him in resisting Chinese aggression,' Nehru could not be swayed.[64]

That, of course, did not mean that as relations with China worsened, Nehru refrained from seeking support from other Asian-African nations.[65] According to Jovan Čavoški, India was aware that conflict with China 'required a new approach to Afro-Asian nations'—one that centred on 'world opinion' rather than 'borderlines.'[66] Consequently, India opted to engage with these nations bilaterally, eschewing multilateral initiatives.[67] Such a strategy, however, presented problems of its own. In 1961, Nasser and Tito managed to get the first conference of non-aligned nations off the ground in Belgrade.[68] From 1–6 September, twenty-five delegations converged on the Yugoslav capital to discuss the current international situation, the promotion of world peace and security and the problem of unequal economic development.[69] The criteria for participation comprised, among other things, an independent foreign policy premised on the principles of peaceful coexistence and non-alignment, the refusal to host foreign military bases on national soil and the support for national liberation movements.[70] Although its membership was largely Afro-Asian, Europe (with Yugoslavia and Cyprus) and Latin America (with Cuba) were also represented, while Brazil, Ecuador and Bolivia sent observers.[71] Only fifteen of the twenty-nine countries attending the Bandung Conference were represented in Belgrade. Given the focus on non-alignment, countries such as China, Pakistan, Turkey, Thailand, Japan and the Philippines were excluded. Although the Belgrade gathering endorsed some of the principles established in Bandung, it kicked off a political movement that was to become distinct from, and alternative to, Afro-Asianism.[72]

Despite Nehru's attempts to forestall the conference—he not only quibbled about the meaning of non-alignment, but he also took issue with the proposed list of invited nations—he eventually relented.[73] Given the large number of countries that had accepted

Tito and Nasser's invitation, he was forced to go along with the fait accompli.[74] He told John Kenneth Galbraith, the US ambassador in New Delhi, that he was unenthusiastic about it. Still, he would go to Belgrade in the hope of keeping the conference 'as sensible as possible.'[75] His hopes, however, were never realised. The Indian government 'overestimated its strength, respect, influence, and role' among its Afro-Asian peers.[76] As Kveder, the Yugoslav ambassador to India, noted in the aftermath of the Belgrade conference, India had 'lost touch with the Afro-Asian world and sensibility for its aspirations.'[77] Although Nehru was, in the end, able to prevent countries such as Ghana, Guinea, Mali, Cuba and Indonesia from 'turn[ing] the Conference into an "anti-colonialist" forum dictating a "bloc" approach on all colonial issues,'[78] some Indians were dissatisfied with Belgrade. Whereas R. K. Nehru, the MEA's Secretary-General (and Nehru's cousin), played down differences between India and the other conference members, stating that relations were 'harmonious' and press reports 'greatly exaggerated,' India's Foreign Secretary, M. J. Desai, told the Australian High Commission in New Delhi that 'some of the African delegates were ignorant, immature and living on nothing except anti-colonialist slogans and were hard to pull back to reason and realities.'[79]

Desai's scorn, however, was explicitly directed at Sukarno and the Indonesians.[80] G. H. Jansen, a former Indian diplomat turned correspondent for the Calcutta newspaper *The Statesman*, confirmed to the Australians that India 'became highly unpopular' at the conference and that 'Sukarno set out from the beginning to sabotage India's standing largely by a whispering campaign to the effect that Nehru had come to the Conference only to sabotage it just as he was trying to sabotage plans for a second Bandung.' Jansen claimed that the result was 'a diminution in India's standing in the Afro-Asian group,' adding that 'Krishna Menon's impatience in general and scarcely concealed contempt for certain delegates did not help.'[81]

Divergences between India and its Afro-Asian and non-aligned partners would have important implications for India's foreign policy. When, in 1962, at a time of grave tensions with China, Nehru badly needed support from several of these countries, some of them were at first hesitant to help India, a country they perceived as having pursued 'a policy of "nonalignment towards the nonaligned".'[82] Significantly, such divergences also forced India to fight a rear-guard battle for the hearts and minds of the Afro-Asian neutralists when China, with the help of Indonesia, redoubled its efforts in the early 1960s to sway many of these countries towards its radical vision of Afro-Asian solidarity. It is to India's China challenge that the next three sections will now turn.

Mao Zedong's Radical Turn in Domestic and Foreign Policy

In the second half of the 1950s, Mao gradually turned his back on peaceful coexistence and returned to a more radical vision of international politics based on class struggle.[83] As recent historical scholarship on China's foreign relations shows, Beijing's support for peaceful coexistence was both conditional and short-lived.[84] After Khrushchev denounced Stalin's crimes at the Twentieth Party Congress on 25 February 1956, Mao and CCP leadership began casting doubts on his leadership, displaying an increasing readiness (albeit still behind closed doors) to criticise the Soviet premier's support for peaceful coexistence.[85] For instance, at an international gathering of communist and workers' parties in Moscow in November 1957, the Chinese delegation, led by Mao, handed their Soviet counterparts a secret memorandum detailing Beijing's disagreements with the doctrine of peaceful coexistence.[86] Despite refraining from launching a frontal attack on Khrushchev, Mao told him that the communist movement should no longer fear confrontation with the West.[87] Believing that 'the forces of socialism [were] overwhelmingly superior to the forces of imperialism' and that 'the east wind [was] prevailing over the west wind,' Mao professed to be upbeat about the future of the international communist movement's struggle with the capitalist West.[88] On his return to Beijing, he also contended that respect for the principles of peaceful coexistence should not inhibit the communist bloc's support for national liberation movements and revolutions in the Third World.[89]

By 1958, however, the Chinese leader had well and truly put peaceful coexistence behind him, choosing instead to 'persist in a struggle with the United States' and abandon Beijing's 'smile diplomacy' in favour of a more militant foreign policy.[90] By then, he had also embarked on the Great Leap Forward, a radical attempt to fast-forward China's socialist transformation. No longer willing to conform to the Soviet industrialisation model, which centred on prioritising heavy industry, Mao dispensed with Moscow's economic leadership to experiment with an alternative, albeit flawed, path to socialism.[91] In early 1958, Zhou, China's public face of peaceful coexistence, stepped down as the PRC's foreign minister following Mao's stinging attack on his supposedly rightist-leaning tendencies.[92] Although he remained premier, Zhou was careful not to challenge Mao's growing radicalism in domestic and international affairs.[93] 'Mao and his comrades,' Chen Jian argues, 'were eager to reclaim China's central position in the world by promoting an Eastern, or even global, revolution.'[94] The catastrophic failure of the Great Leap Forward in the early 1960s temporarily stalled Mao's efforts to fast-track China's transformation into a communist society, thus resulting in a less strident foreign policy.[95] With Mao adopting a lower profile and pulling back from the day-to-day running of government after 1960–61, leaders such as Liu Shaoqi and Deng Xiaoping stepped in to reverse Mao's ruinous Great Leap policies.[96] However, as soon as the economic emergency was over, Mao moved to reaffirm his commitment to class struggle. By 1962, he was again pressing for a more radical approach to domestic and foreign affairs, which eventually led to the Cultural Revolution.[97]

As a result, pronouncements coming out of Beijing increasingly focused on China's role in promoting revolutionary change in the developing world.[98] At the same time, he 'came to see India as a major ideological rival in both Asia and the Third World.'[99] If, in 1956, Beijing still viewed India as its 'best non-communist friend,' praised its anti-imperialist stance and accepted its neutralist orientation as the best that could be hoped for from a non-communist Afro-Asian nation, that perception was soon to change.[100] As Chinese historian Xiaoyuan Liu notes, within less than 3 years, 'the image of Nehru and the meaning of India to the PRC went through a sea change in Beijing's foreign policy analyses.'[101] Beijing's generally positive view of India gave way to a much more critical assessment of its internal and external policies—a shift in perception largely attributable to Mao's return to a more openly revolutionary course in domestic politics and international affairs.[102] In other words, Mao ceased to depict Nehru's India as 'an oppressed nation and a state led by patriotic groups or parties,' as he briefly had during the mid-1950s, and returned to a class-based understanding of India as a 'reactionary nationalist state.'[103] For instance, not only did Beijing criticise Nehru's alleged growing collaboration with the American imperialists and his more moderate approach to colonial issues,[104] it also found faults with India's economic policies.[105] In this context of shifting perceptions, Mao and other CCP leaders began questioning India's utility to the cause of the communist camp, and to China, in particular.[106] By 1962, Mao's view of India had become 'a casualty of an aggressive Chinese turn in Chinese foreign policy.'[107] As we shall see in the next section, Beijing's increasingly shrill support for Third World liberation movements was to heighten the competition between China and India for leadership of the Third World, thus driving New Delhi and Beijing further apart.[108]

Sino-Indian Relations Worsen

As Mao put China through a new revolutionary phase, policymakers in New Delhi gradually took stock of the changed circumstances. It is true that as late as 1958 Nehru was still prepared to consider Zhou an 'honourable man' he could trust.[109] But Zhou's four visits to India between November 1956 and January 1957 had revealed disagreements between the two leaders on matters such as Tibetan autonomy and Soviet behaviour in Hungary.[110] According to American sources, 'with Chou unwilling to include Sino-Indian differences in a communique and Nehru unwilling to settle for platitudes alone,' no final joint statement was issued.[111] On the subject of Tibet, Zhou warned Nehru that Indian cooperation was critical if Tibetan autonomy was to be maintained.[112] 1956 saw a wave of unrest engulf Inner (eastern) Tibet in response to Beijing's attempts to tighten its grip on the region and transform it into a communist society through the implementation of so-called 'democratic reforms.' As such, the CCP leadership was extremely sensitive to further instability in Tibet and feared interference from India.[113] As Zhou put it bluntly, espionage activities 'were carried out in the open in Kalimpong.' Hence, the Indian government 'should intervene because these activities will interfere with religious contacts and exchange.'[114] For his part, Nehru sought to reassure Zhou that India had no intention of interfering.[115] However, he somewhat acerbically noted that 'if an assurance [from China] was given that Tibet would have full internal autonomy, then there was no reason why there should be any trouble.'[116]

On the Hungarian issue, Nehru strongly criticised Soviet behaviour, saying that he was 'very much distressed' and found it 'difficult to justify what has happened' there. According to him, it was 'mainly a national uprising of the workers, students and the youth … to get rid of foreign domination, namely, that of the Soviet Union.'[117] For his part, Zhou stood firmly behind the Soviet intervention, arguing that Moscow 'had no choice but to send troops at the Kádár government's request to save Hungary's socialist system' against 'Hungarian reactionary forces aided by West countries.'[118] In his view, 'there were only two roads for Hungary: either the West would take it, or the Soviet Union would send troops [in] … There was no other way.'[119] Although, at the end of his second visit to India, Zhou reiterated the Chinese view that the Five Principles (as well as Bandung's Ten Principles) continued to govern relations between socialist and non-aligned countries, Nehru must, nonetheless, have felt perplexed by Zhou's full support for the Soviet invasion, which he regarded as 'opposed to the Five Principles.'[120] Nehru's and Zhou's rapport had 'remained largely intact,' but these disagreements had taken some shine off their relationship.[121] In the summer of 1957, the Indian ambassador in Beijing and the consul-general in Shanghai alerted New Delhi that 'a coolness was growing on the part of the Chinese authorities' in relation to India.[122] At the same time, the Indian government was becoming increasingly uneasy about Chinese activity near the India-Tibet frontier, involving the construction of a truck road connecting Kashgar in western Xinjiang to Lhasa in Tibet. The road—which was intended to provide all-year-round access to Tibet and thus held significant strategic value for China—ran through Aksai Chin, a remote, barren, uninhabited high plateau at the junction of Kashmiri Ladakh, Tibet and Xinjiang, which India claimed as its own.[123]

By 1958, the writing was definitely on the wall for Nehru and Zhou's relationship. In the spring of that year, Beijing's propaganda attacks against India's close non-aligned partner, Yugoslavia, rubbed Nehru the wrong way, for he saw them as incompatible with the Five Principles and the logic of peaceful coexistence.[124] In June, a concerned Nehru wrote to his Foreign Secretary, Subimal Dutt, that what the CCP was:

> doing in regard to Yugoslavia is clearly ideological interference and, in fact, something more than that. Therefore, the Five Principles have gone by the board. If the Soviet Union or China can do this in regard to Yugoslavia, there is no particular reason to imagine that they cannot or will not do so in the case of India.[125]

In the same note, Nehru observed that whatever the internal reasons for Chinese behaviour might be, Beijing's attitude had 'stiffened somewhat even in regard to India.' 'I am thinking,' he added, 'of the long discussions about our frontier with Tibet.'[126] In April–May, the long-awaited negotiations on Bara Hoti, a small contested grazing area along the Tibet-Uttar Pradesh border, had failed to make any headway due to Chinese intransigence.[127] Meanwhile, Beijing's decision to publish—for the sake of sustaining domestic mobilisation during the Great Leap Forward—new maps showing a large part of the North-East Frontier Agency (NEFA), Ladakh and some parts of Uttar Pradesh as falling under Chinese jurisdiction had raised fresh concerns in New Delhi.[128] Beijing's growing assertiveness on the border question, coupled with New Delhi's realisation of China's road building in Aksai Chin, drove the Indian government to deploy troops forward in the border areas claimed by India.[129] The fact that both the Indian and Chinese governments had, up until now, deliberately refrained from discussing the possible contours of a mutually agreed border added a further complication and threatened to destabilise the bilateral relationship.[130] The 1954 Sino-Indian agreement on Tibet had not dealt with the border question, and Nehru and Zhou had only cursorily referred to it during their talks in 1954 and 1956.[131] Unwilling to jeopardise their budding rapprochement, the Chinese and Indian governments had placed the whole question on the back burner.[132] Unsurprisingly, in September 1958, the Australian High Commission in New Delhi detected among Indian leaders a growing sense of disillusionment and nervousness towards China.[133]

The worst, however, was yet to come. One of the consequences of Mao's Great Leap Forward was the roll-out of a new wave of 'democratic reforms' in the Tibetan-inhabited regions of Sichuan, Yunnan and Qinghai. Predictably, the imposition of yet more radical reforms generated further local opposition, which, in turn, was met with more repression from the PLA. Upheaval in Inner Tibet could not spare Outer (western) Tibet, which had until then enjoyed a significant degree of internal autonomy and where communist reforms had not yet been introduced. The PLA's repression produced an influx of refugees and rebels into Lhasa. As a result, tensions grew between Lhasa and Beijing as the latter accused the former of tolerating the activities of these rebels.

In early March 1959, increasing anti-CCP sentiment turned into a large-scale popular uprising in Lhasa. In response, Beijing moved to quell the revolt, which led to the Dalai Lama's—the spiritual leader of Tibet—decision to flee to India. To top it all off, Beijing also used the rebellion to revoke Outer Tibet's autonomous status and set about introducing long-delayed communist reforms.[134] As Beijing clamped down on Tibetan autonomy, relations between India and China began to unravel. Developments in Tibet produced a significant change in the CCP leaders' approach to Nehru's India, thus signalling a major turning point in Sino-Indian relations.[135] Nehru's decision to grant asylum to the fleeing Dalai Lama and a large number of his followers provoked an angry Chinese reaction. In April, Mao instigated a polemic against Nehru, accusing him of being behind the troubles and harbouring expansionist designs to overthrow China's sovereignty in Tibet.[136] The fact that the US CIA had begun a limited covert assistance program in support of the Tibetan insurgency in 1957, with American secret agents active in northern Indian towns with a significant Tibetan population (such as Darjeeling, Kalimpong and Gangtok), made the Chinese fearful of Indo-American collusion.[137] However, these accusations were so exaggerated, given that the Nehru government offered no armed support to the Tibetan rebels,[138] that Nehru complained privately about the Chinese authorities having 'lost all balance.'[139] The uprising in Tibet soon had a knock-on effect on the unresolved border question. With Beijing deploying troops along Tibet's eastern border with India in an attempt to quash the rebellion, and with India reinforcing its positions there, military clashes between the two countries became a distinct possibility.[140] In August 1959, Chinese and Indian patrols clashed near Longju in the eastern sector.[141] In late October, a second clash occurred at the Kongka Pass in the western sector.[142] Rising Sino-Indian hostility along the border prompted Nehru to conclude that India and China had 'fallen out and, even though relative peace may continue at the frontier, it is some kind of an armed peace and the future appears to be one of continuing tensions.'[143]

Zhou Enlai's trip to India in late April 1960 to defuse the border dispute produced no breakthrough, thus killing any prospect of salvaging the bilateral relationship.[144] With China dealing with the severe economic fallout of the Great Leap Forward, Zhou appeared eager to find a compromise.[145] He hinted at the possibility of Beijing accepting the McMahon Line (a boundary between Tibet and India negotiated by Britain in 1914 but never accepted by China) in the eastern sector as the official boundary between the two countries in exchange for New Delhi's acceptance of Chinese control over Aksai Chin.[146] However, no longer trusting the Chinese and under pressure from the press, parliament and public opinion, Nehru did not accept Zhou's deal.[147] In late 1961, he started reinforcing India's defences along the disputed border by establishing armed posts where New Delhi claimed the boundary ran.[148] Initially, the intention of the Indian government was not to forcibly dislodge the Chinese from those frontier areas India regarded as its own, but to prevent further Chinese incursions and bolster its border claims by establishing an Indian presence there.[149] In 1962, New Delhi adopted a more vigorous posture by seeking to drive back Chinese patrols from the post they already held.[150] In response, Mao instructed the PLA to pursue more assertive tactics to stop what Beijing viewed as Indian attempts to nibble away at Chinese territory.[151] At the same time, Beijing accused India of behaving recklessly, warning that China would be ready to retaliate unless India desisted from its forward policy.[152] India's 'forward policy' and Chinese counter-moves provoked minor armed clashes between Indian and Chinese patrols.[153]

In October 1962, deeply distrustful of Indian motives and frustrated with Nehru's insistence on carrying out his 'forward policy,' Mao and the CCP leadership decided the time had come to teach Nehru a lesson.[154] They unleashed a full-scale military attack on Indian positions and infrastructure south of the McMahon Line and in Aksai Chin. Poorly equipped and outgunned, Indian forces were overwhelmed in both the western and eastern sectors of the border. In the east, PLA troops almost reached the northern Indian plains in Assam when, on 21 November 1962, the Chinese government suddenly declared a unilateral ceasefire and began pulling its troops back 20 kilometres behind the line of actual control.[155] For Nehru, the 1962 border war was a major foreign policy disaster. Having invested significant political capital in a rapprochement with China, he ended up empty-handed and dejected. Far from being his crowning success, Nehru hopes for enduring Sino-Indian amity and long-term regional stability, built upon a Sino-Indian entente, remained just that—lofty hopes.

For India, the 1962 war was also a major strategic watershed, the consequences of which are still felt today, as both Delhi and Beijing continue to look askance at each other. At the time, it was as if, all of a sudden, there were two worlds: one before 1962 and one after. The one that emerged from the ashes of Nehru's China policy was a much less benign one, with India now having to contend not only with New Delhi's historical foe, Pakistan, but also an assertive and markedly hostile China. The latter's growing friendship with Pakistan in the 1960s would also heighten India's security concerns by raising the spectre of Islamabad and Beijing fighting side by side against India.[156] Although this much-feared war scenario never materialised, Indian policymakers could never rule it out altogether.

The Struggle for Afro-Asia

The 1962 war was also to have flow-on effects in other areas—namely, the direction of Third World internationalism and the role of

India and China in it. China's attack on India spurred efforts by non-aligned Asian-African nations to intercede between the two Asian giants.[157] On the day the war broke out, Nasser offered Egypt's good offices to the two warring sides but received no favourable response from Beijing.[158] When, at the initiative of Ceylon's Prime Minister Sirimavo Bandaranaike, a summit of non-aligned African-Asian nations met in Colombo in mid-December 1962 to put forward a mediation plan, the participating delegations were divided between those more sympathetic to China (Indonesia and Cambodia) and those closer to India (Egypt).[159] However, the summit's compromise solution on the Sino-Indian dispute failed to secure Chinese support,[160] which created a major rift between those Third World nations who pushed for a radical redefinition of Afro-Asian solidarity and those who prioritised non-alignment, coexistence and disarmament over revolutionary anti-imperialist struggle.[161] These divisions rapidly developed into a fierce political contest between two ideological models (the radical and more geographically confined Afro-Asianism and the somewhat more moderate and globalist non-alignment) and two conference formats (Bandung and Belgrade), with each of the two camps forcefully claiming to represent the Third World.[162] The first group included, above all, China and Indonesia, but also Ghana, Pakistan and Algeria. The second group consisted of India, Egypt and Yugoslavia.[163]

Far from sharing the latter group's vision of a non-alignment as a mediating caucus between the two blocs, Jakarta and Beijing called for a renewed effort in the revolutionary struggle against imperialism. Not only did they intend to transform international politics in the wake of decolonisation. They also sought to 'reshape the face of Afro-Asian politics along more confrontationist lines.'[164] In the early 1960s, Sukarno's Indonesia quickly became one of the most vocal advocates of revolutionary Afro-Asianism.[165] By peddling the cause of anti-imperialism among Afro-Asian nations, Sukarno aspired to weaken the West's political and economic ascendancy in international affairs and thus reduce the vast gap between the affluent West and poor Third World nations. Furthermore, he was determined to boost his international reputation 'by finding a new arena to demonstrate his international importance.'[166] In his address to the United Nations in

1960, and then to the Belgrade conference in 1961, Sukarno urged these nations to join Indonesia in a momentous fight between the 'new, emergent forces for freedom and justice' and 'the old forces of domination.'[167] In Belgrade, incidentally, Sukarno had apparently refused to greet Nehru, and the two had engaged in a verbal duel over the priorities of the non-aligned caucus: imperialism and anti-colonialism for the Indonesian president, and peace and non-aligned mediation for the Indian prime minister.[168]

Although he was a keen proponent of an anti-imperialist second Bandung, Sukarno had decided to go to Belgrade not only because the non-aligned conference would take place regardless, but also because he hoped that it would speed up the convening of the Afro-Asian meeting later on.[169] Ahead of the non-aligned summit, Mao had encouraged him to travel to Belgrade to promote Indonesia's and China's brand of Third World internationalism.[170] The Chinese leader told the Indonesian president that Nehru wanted to 'snatch the leadership of the world anti-imperialist movement' away from him.[171] The Belgrade meeting, therefore, provided Sukarno with the opportunity to articulate his vision of radical and anti-imperialist Afro-Asian solidarity. As it turned out, he was not the only one seeking to turn the conference into an anti-imperialist platform. Other Afro-Asian nations—such as Mali, Ghana and Guinea—were keen to launch a crusade against the evils of imperialism, colonialism and neocolonialism.[172] At the same time, as Indonesian foreign policy came to display an increasingly intense and ideologically driven animosity towards Western colonialism, neo-colonialism and imperialism, Sukarno's Indonesia moved closer to China.[173] In August 1965, Jakarta's growing tilt towards Beijing reached its climax when Sukarno spoke of a Jakarta-Phnom Penh-Hanoi-Beijing-Pyongyang axis.[174]

Like Jakarta, Beijing also advocated revolutionary change in the Third World. By the early 1960s, in addition to hurling its familiar anti-imperialist barbs at the West, Beijing had grown increasingly restless at Moscow's lack of revolutionary fervour in the Third World.[175] It considered Soviet efforts at détente with the West to be at odds with the revolutionary radicalism emerging from the Afro-Asian world. It accused Moscow of underestimating the anti-imperialist potential of several Afro-Asian independence movements.[176] In contrast to the Soviet approach to the Third World, which prioritised a gradual transition to socialism through non-violent and parliamentary means, Beijing embraced anti-imperialism as a means of ridding the Third World of Western influence.[177] Aware that some Afro-Asian leaders were attracted to China's uncompromising revolutionary message and frustrated with Moscow's moderatism, Beijing was determined to exploit this and aimed to project itself as the champion of the underdeveloped and oppressed Third World.[178] In the words of Taomo Zhou, it 'aimed to organize a bloc of Afro-Asian countries that opposed both superpowers instead of carefully maneuvering between the two camps.'[179]

In any case, Chinese hostility was not directed solely towards the Soviet Union and the West. Moderate Third World nations, like India, also became the target of Beijing's ideological animosity. Beijing wanted to hinder the likes of India and Yugoslavia from 'tying the hands and feet of the Afro-Asian people' with slogans like 'peace' and 'disarmament,'[180] and had, for instance, criticised Yugoslavia for its 'false anti-imperialist and anti-colonial credentials.'[181] Thus, sharing a common desire to overcome the established order,[182] Jakarta and Beijing sought to turn Afro-Asian solidarity against their enemies—the West for Indonesia and the United States, the Soviet Union and India in China's case. To achieve their goal, both China and Indonesia renewed calls for the convening of a second Bandung.[183] As Zhou told Indonesian Foreign Minister Subandrio in 1965, the 'emphasis of the first Afro-Asian Conference was on the struggle for national independence; the emphasis of the second Afro-Asian Conference will be a full realization of that independence. Today, the world should not be divided into Communist versus non-Communist camps, but into imperialist and anti-imperialist countries.'[184]

Chinese and Indonesian efforts to convene a second Bandung conference in 1963–64 spurred a reaction from Tito, Nasser and Bandaranaike, who convened a non-aligned preparatory meeting in Colombo in late March 1964 to foil Beijing's and Jakarta's radical plans.[185] By then, two different 'ideological conference models,' targeting a similar audience, had clearly emerged.[186] In contrast to his past behaviour, Nehru wholeheartedly supported India's participation in a second non-aligned conference in Cairo in October 1964.[187] Since the 1962 war with China, India had manifested a less passive and more energetic preference for the non-aligned caucus.[188] However, a little more than 2 weeks later, China and Indonesia succeeded in holding a preparatory meeting in Jakarta for a second Bandung conference.[189] At the Jakarta meeting, the Chinese and Indonesian delegations insisted on an early date for the conference and pushed for adopting a radical anti-imperialist agenda.[190]

For its part, India fought a rear-guard battle, seeking to delay a second Bandung and throwing a spanner into Jakarta's and Beijing's works by proposing to extend an invitation to the Soviet Union on the grounds that a significant part of its territory and population were located in Asia.[191] In the end, the meeting reached no agreement on the issue of Soviet participation, but the conference's date was set for 10 March 1965. To this end, the meeting formed a standing committee of ambassadors to continue preparations.[192] By the time the second non-aligned conference was held in Cairo in October 1964, it had become evident that significant divisions also existed within the non-aligned camp, with the more anti-Western and radical delegations gaining ascendancy over the more moderate participants such as India.[193] As Robert Rakove has pointed out, '[w]ith a larger and more African pool of attendees, and the general absence of Cold War tensions, the anti-colonial imperative was free to dominate the agenda.'[194] Despite China's exclusion, radicals like Sukarno ensured that the 'anti-colonial imperative' remained alive even within self-proclaimed non-aligned countries.[195]

In the end, disagreements within the non-aligned caucus not only undermined its effectiveness, but also weakened its core message based on non-alignment, coexistence and disarmament, thus blurring the difference with the competing Afro-Asian project espoused by Indonesia and China. It would not be until 1970 that a new non-aligned summit would be held in the Zambian capital, Lusaka. But if the non-aligned caucus came out weakened from its internal divisions, Beijing's and Jakarta's radical brand of Afro-Asianism, centred on a more geographically restricted membership and revolutionary anti-imperialism, fared even worse. The second Bandung conference, scheduled for March 1965 in Algiers, was postponed to the end of June due to the delays faced by the Algerian authorities in completing the conference facilities on time.[196] Then, a few days before the conference was supposed to start, a military coup against Algerian President Ben Bella led to the conference being further postponed and ultimately cancelled in November.[197] No second Bandung would ever take place. In any case, with Sukarno also removed from power following an army coup on 30 September, and with China's declining influence in the Afro-Asian world due to its growing radicalism, Afro-Asianism had already run out of steam.

China's failure to impose its brand of radical Afro-Asian solidarity was no doubt good news for India. Although Jawaharlal Nehru was no longer alive in 1965 to witness Beijing's political and diplomatic setback (he had passed away in April 1964), he could nonetheless take some credit for limiting Chinese inroads into the Third World. He had, after all, often taken positions contrary to China's goals and interests in the Afro-Asian world. At the same time, however, the India that emerged after nearly two decades of Nehru's rule was a less influential country in the Third World. Nehru's refusal to jump on the Afro-Asian bandwagon in the aftermath of the 1955 Bandung Conference, his aversion to the radical brand of Afro-Asianism favoured by the likes of China and Indonesia and his lukewarm support for Tito and Nasser's non-aligned initiative did not raise India's stocks among Afro-Asian nations. Incidentally, his support for peaceful coexistence and direct dialogue between the superpowers during the 1961 non-aligned summit in Belgrade almost suggested a lack of ambition on his part when compared to his Bandung grand vision.[198] Furthermore, growing divisions over the direction of Third World internationalism further compounded India's difficulty in playing a leading role among its Third World peers. Yet, while this was certainly the case, it should not be forgotten that, as Nehru intended it, Bandung was first and foremost an exercise in peaceful coexistence. It was a further step, albeit an important one, to entrench his vision of neutralised areas of peace and seek Beijing's continuing commitment to it. It was also an attempt to get China and its neighbours to establish closer and more fruitful contacts. Nehru hoped that bringing China out of the cold would enhance regional security. As we have seen in this chapter, that strategy ran into trouble well before the battles for the hearts and minds of the Afro-Asian world and, more broadly, the Third World. If, as Eric Getting claims, 'the collapse of Bandung II did mark the end of the "Bandung era" in the international history of the Third World,' for Nehru, that era ended well before its final denouement.[199] It ended as Sino-Indian tensions rose over the border question. When China launched a blitzkrieg against India in 1962, the 'Bandung era' had already, for all intent and purpose, come to an end.

CONCLUSIONS

We were getting out of touch with the realities of the modern world. We were living in an artificial atmosphere of our own creation and we have been shocked out of it.

Jawaharlal Nehru[1]

This book has examined India's role in organising the first Asian-African conference in Bandung. It has done so by highlighting the foreign policy concerns, goals and calculations that prompted the Nehru government to lend its support to what was, in origin, an Indonesian idea. As the book has shown, Nehru initially did not set great store by Ali Sastroamidjojo's calls for an Asian-African conference. He judged the Indonesian idea premature and ill-defined, and it was not until the second half of 1954 that he changed his mind. Three major factors made him reconsider. One was the direction American policy in Asia was taking, particularly Washington's desire to form a regional alliance led by the United States to contain communism in South-East Asia. Nehru considered the new Eisenhower administration's regional strategy to be dangerous and misguided. In his opinion, it threatened to pull apart the fragile Indo-Chinese settlement that had been painstakingly negotiated in Geneva, and it risked derailing Sino-Soviet support for peaceful coexistence. The second factor that influenced Nehru's change of attitude towards the conference was China's embrace of peaceful coexistence. Nehru perceived this shift in Chinese foreign policy as an excellent opportunity to accomplish vital foreign policy objectives, such as securing Beijing's long-term commitment to regional stability and preventing the rise of a potentially hostile power on India's frontiers. The third factor was Nehru's reluctance to do anything that would weaken a struggling Ali Sastroamidjojo government in Indonesia. As both New Delhi and Jakarta professed themselves to be fiercely non-aligned, Nehru saw Indonesia as a critical ally in his efforts to obstruct American plans in Asia.

By the time Nehru travelled to Indonesia in December 1954 for a meeting of the Colombo group, his mind was made up. The Asian-African conference, he concluded, should go ahead, and his government should give it its full support. In Bogor, he and Krishna Menon played a crucial role in defining the rationale and identifying the priorities for the upcoming Bandung summit. They also had a considerable say in selecting which countries to invite. In the 4 months between the Bogor meeting and the Bandung conference, the Indian government did its best to ensure that the impending Asian-African summit mirrored India's regional vision and goals. Bandung, in other words, was to be the crowning achievement of India's efforts to reduce Cold War tensions and entrench peaceful coexistence in Asia. As this book has detailed, Nehru believed that, to achieve regional stability, states must embrace peaceful coexistence and refrain from joining adversarial blocs. Following the Sino-Indian agreement on Tibet in April 1954, he made the Five Principles of Peaceful Coexistence the focal point of his diplomacy, promoting them as the cornerstone of a new approach to international affairs and a new code of conduct for states. In this context, he also argued that, if regional governments based their diplomacy on these principles, they would be able to establish 'areas of peace' and achieve 'collective peace' in Asia. For a nation like India, which, in Nehru's words, required 'at least twenty years of peaceful progress' to 'build up the economy' and 'make [its] people prosperous,'[2] the concept of an Asian area (or areas) of peace was of vital importance.

As this study has indicated, Nehru's vision of 'areas of peace' and 'collective peace,' underpinned by the Five Principles, received a boost in June 1954 when Zhou Enlai briefly travelled to New Delhi and Rangoon to confer with both Nehru and U Nu. His polished demeanour and studied air of reasonableness assuaged Indian and Burmese concerns about China's regional role. In New Delhi, Nehru and Zhou reaffirmed their commitment to the Five Principles and the idea of a neutralised Asia. Their agreement on this point was so comprehensive that the Five Principles became, for all intents and purposes, a Sino-Indian 'co-sponsored project' in the following months.[3] It is against this backdrop that Nehru's attitude to Indonesian calls for an Asian-African conference began to shift. To be sure, it would have been difficult for Nehru to temporise for much longer without angering Indonesia and weakening the Ali Sastroamidjojo government, whose support was important for his achieving an area of peace in Asia. Yet, as this book's central chapters have suggested, the interplay of Chinese and American Cold War policies in Asia hastened Nehru's decision to back the Indonesian proposal. As China embraced peaceful coexistence, the decision by the United States to establish SEATO in the autumn of 1954 in order to deter further communist gains in South-East Asia convinced Nehru to get behind the Indonesian proposal. It also reinforced his belief that China had an important role to play in his quest for a neutralised Asia.

As a result, Beijing came to hold a special place in Nehru's regional strategy. The Indian leader was well aware of lingering Asian concerns about China's potentially disruptive influence in regional politics, and he was not immune to them. Indeed, his desire for a Sino-Indian reconciliation was not unrelated to his underlying fear of Chinese power. Yet, he chose to downplay these concerns, and, in pressing Beijing to adhere to the Five Principles, he genuinely hoped to 'create an environment,' as he put it, 'wherein it becomes a little more dangerous to the other party to break away from the pledges given.'[4] He regarded these principles not as a 'permanent guarantee' but as 'one major step to help us in the present and in the foreseeable future.'[5] Idealistic and naïve as this may sound, it was not entirely implausible. Moreover, by supporting Beijing's participation in the Bandung conference, Nehru hoped to end China's isolation and bring it back into the international fold, thus making a crucial contribution to regional stability. He had viewed such isolation as 'the root cause of all troubles and crises in East and Southeast Asia.'[6] In any event, he argued, countries had few options. They could either aggressively contain China at their peril or they could seek closer relations with it, hoping that constructive engagement would induce Beijing to adopt more moderate policies.[7] Hence, by inviting China to Bandung, India hoped to encourage moderation on China's part.[8]

Given these considerations, it is not difficult to understand why Nehru considered the Bandung Conference more of an exercise in regional diplomacy than an expression of Afro-Asian solidarity. Even though Nehru waxed lyrical on the awakening of Asia and Africa before and during the conference,[9] he did not support the idea of such a gathering out of any strong feeling of Afro-Asian solidarity. Rather, what drove him was his desire to see the Five Principles widely accepted and the area of peace in Asia extended. Put another way, he saw Bandung through the lens of his Cold War strategy rather than Afro-Asian internationalism. In brief, Bandung served to give expression to his vision of an Asian area of peace underpinned by the Five Principles. From his perspective, it also served to cement—or so he hoped—China's commitment to peaceful coexistence and an area of peace in Asia. With China on board, Nehru's vision appeared to have a greater chance of becoming a reality.

However, as the book's final chapters have demonstrated, the Bandung Conference produced mixed results for Nehru. Contrary to his expectations, his vision of a neutralised Asia did not come to pass. Non-communist delegations spoke out against communism, questioned Nehru's neutralism and voiced their support for defensive alliances. In these circumstances, no agreement could be reached on the Five Principles, which became a bone of contention during the conference's deliberations. Despite Nehru's advocacy, only four of the Five Principles made it into the final communiqué, which, much to his distaste, recognised the right for countries to join such alliances when their security interests were at stake. In short, the existence of differing views on crucial Cold War issues among the conference's attendees underscored the difficulty for India in leading an Afro-Asian grouping between superpower blocs.[10] On the other hand, Nehru's efforts to engage China and push it to commit unequivocally to peaceful coexistence appeared to bear fruit. Not only did Zhou's calm demeanour impress him, but so, too, did Zhou's proclamations that China desired peace, sought no expansion and had no intention of subverting its neighbours.

Unfortunately for the Indian prime minister, the years following the Bandung summit delivered no less equivocal results. On the plus side, SEATO never became the aggressive tool of US containment strategy that Nehru had envisaged, nor did it serve as a platform to promote military intervention in Asia.[11] As Pillai frankly admitted to Malcolm MacDonald, the British high commissioner to India, in late 1955, the Indian government's 'dislike' of SEATO 'had cooled' considerably in recent months, given that it had not been as 'provocative as they originally feared.'[12] Pillai had, of course, more than one good reason to say so. In February 1955, the eight founding members of SEATO had gathered in Bangkok to add flesh to the bones of their fledgling alliance. Despite agreeing to build a formal administrative structure and undertake joint military planning, they were unable to make much headway in the months that followed.[13] Progress was so slow that, in September 1955, the CIA felt compelled to alert Dulles to the 'rapidly deteriorating morale' of SEATO's Asian members 'due to an utter lack of accomplishment of the organisation and the highhanded manner in which the U.S. military are running it.'[14] Some progress was eventually made as the Eisenhower administration moved to revitalise SEATO. Forces were earmarked to it, its administrative machinery further developed and a permanent military planning structure established.[15] These improvements notwithstanding, SEATO was never able to establish itself as an effective politico-military alliance.[16] The misalignment of national goals, priorities and means, as well as persisting disagreements among its Western members over strategic policy, hampered SEATO's ability to intervene effectively in regional crises.[17] In other words, despite Nehru's vehement initial opposition to it, 'the "real" SEATO never quite matched up with the "imaginary" SEATO of India's political lore.'[18]

On the upside, Nehru could also take heart from the fact that his vision of a non-aligned Asia appeared ultimately validated. In 1960, a British Foreign Office paper perceptively remarked how enthusiastically neutralism had 'been adopted in much of Asia' and how it expressed 'a very real sentiment held by millions of people.'

Since Bandung, 'no neutralist state ha[d] committed itself to the West, but one formerly committed State, Ceylon, ha[d] turned to neutralism.' Moreover, whereas the 'attachment of the neutralists to their neutralism' was 'strong,' the 'alignment of committed [pro-West Asian] states' was not always 'altogether dependable.'[19] In the late 1950s, significant support for neutralism existed even in those Asian countries that had chosen to align themselves with the West, notably Pakistan, the Philippines, Thailand and South Vietnam.[20] Meanwhile, peaceful coexistence became the catchphrase for all diplomatic exchanges between Afro-Asian states, whether they were non-aligned or sympathetic to one of the two blocs.[21]

On the minus side, however, it was evident that proclamations of neutralist intent and adherence to the Five Principles were no indication that Asia had become, or was ever likely to become, an 'area of peace' shorn of Cold War tensions, as Nehru had envisioned. Nor did they provide the kind of defence guarantee against regional security threats that Nehru had hoped they would. What these proclamations often concealed was that the proponents of a neutralist 'third way' were a heterogeneous bunch, which, despite harbouring a common desire for peace, had adopted neutralism for a variety of complex (and different) reasons, rarely shared identical national interests and, at times, even held significant misgivings towards each other.[22] Furthermore, while many Asian neutralists held out hope that as long as a non-aligned 'third force' existed, the divide between the two blocs could 'be bridged' and Cold War tensions contained, they remained unclear as to how this could be achieved in practice, either individually or collectively. In this respect, behind their professed support for peaceful coexistence and a neutralised Asia, some non-aligned Asian governments privately continued to welcome a Western politico-military presence in the region as a counterbalance to Chinese power.[23] In short, for all his tireless efforts to promote his vision of a neutralised Asia, Nehru was unsuccessful in creating an effective area of peace that would help India protect itself against external dangers.

Indeed, as this book has demonstrated, one crucial component of Nehru's neutralist Asian vision—namely, China's commitment to peaceful coexistence and a close relationship with India—

evaporated in October 1962 when China launched a swift military attack across the disputed Sino-Indian border. In India's darkest hour, Nehru tragically discovered how shaky the foundations of his vision were and how professions of neutralism and peaceful coexistence proved to be no insurance against the threat posed by China to Indian security. As A. Appadorai and M. S. Rajan aptly put it, all the 'limitations of *Panchsheel* [Five Principles], which provided the pedestal for a sort of non-military defence system for India as well as the countries of Southeast Asia,' were 'exposed,' and Nehru 'was dismayed to find that India was living in a world of make-belief.'[24] Moreover, he realised how much he had misread the nature of Mao's regime and misjudged its intentions. For the Chinese leadership, peaceful coexistence had been nothing more than a pragmatic and opportunistic response to the domestic and international conditions of the mid-1950s. When Mao reverted to a more radical vision of international politics based on class struggle, it was only a question of time before Nehru's assumptions would be tested. And when they were, he sadly concluded that Beijing's pledges were not worth the paper they were written on.

Lastly, the breakdown of the Sino-Indian *entente cordiale* in the early 1960s had another unwelcome consequence. By promoting China's participation in the Bandung Conference, Nehru opened the way for Beijing's growing engagement with the Afro-Asian world. Although Beijing's invitation to the Asian-African summit was a calculated attempt to turn China into a responsible stakeholder in regional security, Nehru's plans did not work out as he had intended. Between the late 1950s and mid-1960s, Beijing exploited the Afro-Asian movement to promote its revolutionary gospel while trying to seize its leadership and weaken Indian influence in the Third World. To be sure, in the years following Bandung, Nehru no longer set much store by Afro-Asian solidarity to advance India's national interests, given the diverse agendas and persistent disagreements among Afro-Asian nations. Nor did he show much enthusiasm for Tito's and Nasser's non-aligned initiative in view of his reservations about the nature and membership of the proposed non-aligned conference. As a result, as this book has documented, India's star lost some of its shine (and influence) within the Afro-Asian and neutralist galaxy. Yet, despite Nehru's disenchantment with his Afro-Asian partners, there is no denying that China did its best to undermine India's ascendancy in the Third World and that India grew all the more resentful with its northern neighbour because of New Delhi's role in helping Beijing develop its links with other Afro-Asian nations. For Nehru, in other words, China came to represent a failed gamble in more ways than one.

NOTES

INTRODUCTION

1. Prime Ministers Museum and Library, New Delhi [henceforth PMML], Jawaharlal Nehru Papers [henceforth JN], file 306 part I, Note on Proposed Afro-Asian Conference (by Nehru), 19 December 1954.
2. Sarvepalli Gopal, *Jawaharlal Nehru: A Biography. Volume Two: 1947–1956* (London: Vintage Digital, 2014), Kindle edition, ch. 9; National Archives of Australia, Canberra [henceforth NAA], A1838, 169/1/3 part 1, Walter Crocker (Australian High Commissioner to India) to Richard Casey (Australian Minister of External Affairs), despatch 21, 2 December 1954.
3. Judith M. Brown, *Nehru: A Political Life* (New Haven, CT and London: Yale University Press, 2003), p. 270.
4. Benjamin Zachariah, *Nehru* (London: Taylor & Francis, 2004), p. xxi.
5. Ibid.
6. Ibid.; Judith M. Brown, 'Jawaharlal Nehru,' in Steven Casey and Jonathan Wright (eds), *Mental Maps in the Early Cold War Era, 1945–68* (London: Palgrave Macmillan, 2011), p. 213.
7. Zachariah, *Nehru*, p. xxi; Michael Dillon, *Zhou Enlai: The Enigma Behind Chairman Mao* (London: I. B. Tauris, 2019), p. 180; C. L. M. Penders (ed.), *Milestones on My Journey: The Memoirs of Ali Sastroamijoyo, Indonesian Patriot and Leader* (St. Lucia, Australia: University of Queensland Press, 1979), p. 278.
8. PMML, V. K. Krishna Menon Papers, subject file 868, Joint Communiqué by the Prime Ministers of Burma, Ceylon, India, Indonesia and Pakistan, 29 December 1954.
9. M. S. Rajan, *India in World Affairs, 1954–56* (London: Asia Publishing House, 1964), p. 185.
10. Ibid.
11. On this point, see Cheng Guan Ang, 'The Bandung Conference and the Cold War International History of Southeast Asia,' in See Seng Tan and Amitav Acharya (eds), *Bandung Revisited: The Legacy of the 1955 Asian-African Conference*

for International Order (Singapore: National University of Singapore Press, 2008), p. 27; see also Amitav Acharya and See Seng Tan, 'The Normative Relevance of the Bandung Conference for Contemporary Asian and International Order,' in ibid., p. 1.

12. G. H. Jansen, *Afro-Asia and Non-Alignment* (London: Faber and Faber, 1966), p. 182. At the time of writing, Jansen was working for *The Statesman* of Calcutta and New Delhi.
13. See e.g. A. Appadorai and M. S. Rajan, *India's Foreign Policy and Relations* (New Delhi: South Asian Publishers, 1985); Charles Heimsath and Surjit Mansingh, *A Diplomatic History of Modern India* (New Delhi: Allied Publishers, 1971); Jayanta Kumar Ray, *India's Foreign Relations, 1947–2007* (New Delhi: Routledge, 2011).
14. Jansen, *Afro-Asia*, pp. 143–67 and 168–80.
15. NAA, A1838, 3034/11/147 part 1, Crocker to ADEA, cablegram 497, 16 September 1961.
16. Lucy Mair, 'The Third World,' *New Statesman*, 19 July 1966, p. 171; Rudolf Schlesinger, 'Review of G. H. Jansen, *Non-Alignment and the Afro-Asian States* (Faber and Faber, 1966),' in *Journal of Asian and African Studies*, 3:1 (1968), p. 140.
17. He did, however, have some access to confidential information.
18. See e.g. Rajan, *India in World Affairs*, pp. 201–3; George McTurnan Kahin, *The Asian-African Conference, Bandung, Indonesia, April 1955* (Port Washington, NY: Kennikat Press, 1972); David Kimche, *The Afro-Asian Movement: Ideology and Foreign Policy of the Third World* (Jerusalem: Israel Universities Press, 1973); Vijay Prashad, *The Darker Nations: A People's History of the Third World* (New York: New Press, 2007); A. Appadorai, 'The Bandung Conference,' *India Quarterly*, 11:3 (1955), pp. 207–35; Jamie Mackie, *Bandung 1955: Non-Alignment and Afro-Asian Solidarity* (Singapore: Editions Didier Millet, 2005); Sisir Gupta, *India and Regional Integration in Asia* (Bombay: Asian Publishing House, 1964), pp. 63–8.
19. Nicholas Tarling, '"Ah-Ah": Britain and the Bandung Conference of 1955,' *Journal of Southeast Asian Studies*, 23:1 (1999), pp. 74–111; Lorenz Lüthi, *Cold Wars: Asia, the Middle East, Europe* (Cambridge, UK: Cambridge University Press, 2020), Kindle edition, ch. 11; Amit Das Gupta, *Serving India: A Political Biography of Subimal Dutt (1903–1992), India's Longest Serving Foreign Secretary* (New Delhi: Manhoar, 2017), pp. 214–19; H. W. Brands, *The Specter of Neutralism: The United States and the Emergence of the Third World, 1947–1960* (New York: Columbia University Press, 1989), ch. 3; Amitav Acharya, *East of India, South of China: Sino-Indian Encounters in Southeast Asia* (New Delhi: Oxford Academic: 2017), online edition, ch. 3.
20. Cindy Ewing, 'The Colombo Powers: Crafting Diplomacy in the Third World and Launching Afro-Asia at Bandung,' *Cold War History*, 19:1 (2019), pp. 1–19.
21. Andrea Benvenuti, 'Nehru's Bandung Moment: India and the Convening of the 1955 Asian-African Conference,' *India Review*, 21:2 (2022), pp. 153–80.
22. In a recent work on the Indian civil service and Indian foreign policy, Amit Das Gupta correctly observes that no country's foreign policy is ever a 'one-man show' and that Nehru's foreign policy was no exception, being 'the outcome of the interaction of several actors with diverse ideas and attitudes.' See Amit

Das Gupta, *The Indian Civil Service and Indian Foreign Policy, 1923–1961* (London: Routledge, 2021), p. 1. Nonetheless, the fact remains that Nehru's imprint on India's approach to the Bandung Conference (as on many other foreign policy matters) was profound, even when one considers the valuable contribution made to policy formulation by advisers such as V. K. Krishna Menon. His decision to hold the external affairs portfolio in addition to his prime ministerial responsibilities, combined with his political prestige, charisma and knowledge of world politics (Nehru was by far the Congress leader with the greatest experience and interest in foreign affairs), made it difficult for anyone in New Delhi to challenge him on foreign policy issues. In any event, other Congress leaders showed limited interest in international affairs, thus giving Nehru practically free rein in formulating India's foreign policy. On this point, see B. R. Nanda, *Jawaharlal Nehru: Rebel and Statesman* (New Delhi: Oxford University Press, 1998), p. 224.

23. C. S. Jha, *From Bandung to Tashkent: Glimpses of India's Foreign Policy* (Madras and Hyderabad, India; London: Sangam Books, 1983), p. 62.
24. See also National Archives of the United Kingdom, Kew, [henceforth NAUK], DO 35/6095, Extract of a letter to Sir S. Garner (CRO) from G. H. Middleton (British High Commissioner to India), 23 December 1954.
25. Nehru cited in R. SarDesai, *Indian Foreign Policy in Cambodia, Laos and Vietnam 1947–1964* (Berkeley and Los Angeles, CA: University of California Press, 1968), p. 30.
26. NAA, A1838, 169/11/87 part 4, Commonwealth Prime Ministers' Conference 1955. Volume II – Agenda Papers, Part A: Relations between India and China, undated. On the Five Principles as a Chinese idea, see Zhou Enlai, *Selected Works of Zhou Enlai, Volume II* (Beijing: Foreign Languages Press, 1988), p. 128; Xiaoyuan Liu, 'Friend or Foe: India as Perceived by Beijing's Foreign Policy Analysts in the 1950s,' *China Review*, 15:1 (2015), pp. 121–2. See also NAUK, FO 371/112196, DL1022/2, India's North-East Frontier Policy, 2 June 1954; Gopal, *1947–1956*, ch. 9; Anton Harder, 'Defining Independence in Cold War Asia: Sino-Indian Relations, 1949–1962' (PhD thesis, London School of Economics, 2015), p. 129; Kuisong Yang, 'The Theory and Implementation of the People's Republic of China's Revolutionary Diplomacy,' *Journal of Modern Chinese History*, 3:2 (2009), p. 137.
27. Harder, 'Defining Independence,' p. 131; see also Sulmaan Wasif Khan, 'Cold War Cooperation: New Chinese Evidence on Jawaharlal Nehru's 1954 Visit to Beijing,' *Cold War History*, 11:2 (2011), pp. 211–12.
28. For the 'de-centring' of Cold War history and the historiography focusing on the role of Third World countries in shaping the course of Cold War, see e.g. Robert J. McMahon, 'Introduction' in id. (ed.), *The Cold War in the Third World* (Oxford: Oxford University Press, 2012), Kindle edition; Odd Arne Westad, *The Global Cold War: Third World Interventions and the Making of our Times* (Cambridge, UK: Cambridge University Press, 2005), pp. 2–5.
29. On this point, see Andrea Benvenuti, 'Frustrating the Americans and Befriending the Communists: Nehru's Policy in the Early Asian Cold War, 1947–54,' in Brian

P. Farrell, S. R. Joey Long and David J. Ulbrich (eds), *From Far East to Asia Pacific: Great Powers and Grand Strategy 1900–1954* (Berlin: De Gruyter Oldenbourg, 2022), pp. 251–79.

30. Some excellent examples are Srinath Raghavan, *War and Peace in Modern India* (London: Palgrave Macmillan, 2010); Zorawar Daulet Singh, *Power and Diplomacy: India's Foreign Policies During the Cold War* (New Delhi: Oxford University Press, 2019), Kindle edition; Manu Bhagavan, *India and the Quest for One World: The Peacemakers* (London: Palgrave Macmillan, 2013); Tanvi Madan, *Fateful Triangle: How China Shaped U.S.-India Relations During the Cold War* (Washington, DC: Brookings Institution Press, 2020), Kindle edition; Francine Frankel, *When Nehru Looked East: Origins of India-US Suspicion and India-China Rivalry* (Oxford: Oxford University Press, 2020), Kindle edition; Das Gupta, *Serving India*; Harder, 'Defining Independence.'
31. Odd Arne Westad, 'The Cold War: A World History,' *LSE Podcasts* [podcast], 9 February 2018, https://soundcloud.com/lsepodcasts/the-cold-war-a-world-history, accessed 5 July 2023; see also Vojtech Mastny, 'The Soviet Union Partnership With India,' *Journal of Cold War Studies*, 12:3 (2010), p. 89.
32. On this point, see Benvenuti, 'Nehru's Bandung Moment,' p. 172, fn 10.
33. On this point, see e.g. Gheng Guan Ang, *Southeast Asia and the Vietnam War* (Abingdon, UK, and New York: Routledge, 2010), pp. 1–4.

1. INDIA AND THE COLD WAR

1. National Archives and Records Administration, College Park, MD [henceforth NARA], RG 59, Lot file 57 D462, box 4, Examination of Tendencies towards anti-Westernism, 22 January 1951.
2. On American perceptions of Soviet involvement in Korea, see Geir Lundestad, *The United States and Western Europe Since 1945: From 'Empire' by Invitation to Transatlantic Drift* (Oxford: Oxford University Press, 2003), pp. 148–9.
3. Ibid.; Saki Dockrill, *Eisenhower's New-Look National Security Policy, 1953–61* (New York: St. Martin's Press, 1996), p. 14; William Keylor, *The Twentieth Century World and Beyond: An International History Since 1900* (Oxford: Oxford University Press, 2006), pp. 256–7.
4. Andrea Benvenuti, 'US Diplomacy in Asia,' in Andrew T. H. Tan (ed.), *Handbook on the United States in Asia: Managing Hegemonic Decline, Retaining Influence in the Trump Era* (Cheltenham, UK: Edward Elgar Publishing, 2018), pp. 163–4.
5. Zhihua Shen and Yafeng Xia, 'Leadership Transfer in the Asian Revolution: Mao Zedong and the Asian Cominform,' *Cold War History*, 14:2 (2014), pp. 212–13.
6. Andrea Benvenuti, 'US Relations With the PRC During the Cold War,' in Andrew T. H. Tan (ed.), *Handbook of US-China Relations* (Cheltenham, UK: Edward Elgar Publishing, 2017), p. 48; Qiang Zhai, *China and the Vietnam Wars, 1950–1975* (Chapel Hill, NC: University of North Carolina Press, 2000), p. 4; Jian Chen, *Mao's China and the Cold War* (Chapel Hill, NC: University of North Carolina Press, 2010), Kindle edition, ch. 3.

7. Benvenuti, 'US Relations With the PRC,' p. 48; Zhai, *China and the Vietnam Wars*, p. 4.
8. Benvenuti, 'US Relations With the PRC,' p. 48; Fredrik Logevall, 'The Indochina Wars and the Cold War, 1945–1975,' in Melvyn Leffler and Odd Arne Westad (eds), *The Cambridge History of the Cold War. Volume 2* (Cambridge, UK: Cambridge University Press, 2010), p. 120.
9. See e.g. Sisir Gupta, *India and Regional Integration in Asia* (Bombay: Asian Publishing House, 1964), p. 10; Ashoka Mody, *India Is Broken: And Why It's Hard to Fix It* (New Delhi: Juggernaut, 2023), ch. 3.
10. Judith M. Brown, 'Jawaharlal Nehru,' in Steven Casey and Jonathan Wright (eds), *Mental Maps in the Early Cold War Era, 1945–68* (London: Palgrave Macmillan, 2011), pp. 206–7; Judith M. Brown, *Nehru: A Political Life* (New Haven, CT, and London: Yale University Press, 2003), p. 342.
11. For a brief account of India's challenges in the early years of independence, see D. R. SarDesai, *Indian Foreign Policy in Cambodia, Laos and Vietnam, 1947–1964* (Berkeley and Los Angeles, CA: University of California Press, 1968), pp. 28–30.
12. For instance, this is precisely how Nehru viewed American plans to provide military aid to Pakistan. See A. Martin Wainwright, *Inheritance of Empire: Britain, India and the Balance of Power in Asia, 1938–55* (Westport, CT: Praeger, 1994), pp. 156–7.
13. Brown, 'Jawaharlal Nehru,' p. 208.
14. Ibid.
15. Nehru cited in Amitav Acharya, *Whose Ideas Matter? Agency and Power in Asian Regionalism* (New York: Cornell University Press, 2009), p. 58.
16. Charles Heimsath and Surjit Mansingh, *A Diplomatic History of Modern India* (New Delhi: Allied Publishers, 1971), pp. 352–3.
17. Ibid.
18. Brian Tsui, 'Coming to Terms With the People's Republic of China: Jawaharlal Nehru in the Early 1950s,' in Young-Chan Kim (ed.), *China-India Relations: Geo-Political Competition, Economic Cooperation, Cultural Exchange and Business Ties* (Cham, Germany: Springer Publishing, 2020), p. 22.
19. Nehru cited in NAUK, FO 371/116987, D2232/3, 'Asian Conferences 1947–1955,' Foreign Office draft paper, 2 December 1955. See also Vineet Thakur, 'An Asian Drama: The Asian Relations Conference, 1947,' *International History Review*, 41:3 (2019), p. 679. For Nehru's Asian vision, see e.g. Giri Deshingkar, 'The Construction of Asia in India,' *Asian Studies Review*, 23:2 (1999), p. 177.
20. *Selected Works of Jawaharlal Nehru* [henceforth *SWJN*], Second Series [henceforth II], Volume 1 (New Delhi: Jawaharlal Nehru Memorial Fund, 1984–2015), p. 451.
21. For Nehru's dislike of colonialism and power politics, see A. Appadorai and M. S. Rajan, *India's Foreign Policy and Relations* (New Delhi: South Asian Publishers, 1985), pp. 34, 36, 44–6 and 51.
22. Far from it. Nehru's non-alignment was in no way intended to be 'a passive, inactive retreat from political involvement' in international questions. See

Heimsath and Mansingh, *Diplomatic History*, p. 61; see also B. R. Nanda, *Jawaharlal Nehru: Rebel and Statesman* (New Delhi: Oxford University Press, 1998), p. 228. On the contrary, as G. L. Metha, India's Ambassador to Washington from 1952 to 1958, once noted, it was intended to empower India to 'exercise discrimination in judging international issues without preconceived notions or ideological obsessions.' See G. L. Metha cited in SarDesai, *Indian Foreign Policy*, p. 28.

23. Nehru cited in Appadorai and Rajan, *India's Foreign Policy*, p. 86; *SWJN*, II/1, p. 539; Benjamin Zachariah, *Nehru* (London: Taylor & Francis, 2004), p. 157.
24. Zachariah, *Nehru*, p. 156. According to Walter Crocker, who knew him well, Nehru's non-alignment stemmed, in part, from his 'own predisposition to avoid all emotional involvement with others.' See Walter Crocker, *Nehru: A Contemporary Estimate* (New Delhi: Penguin Random House India, 2016), Kindle edition, ch. 3. At the same time, it was also rooted in the worldview of India's nationalist leaders, who had envisaged independent India as a prominent force for peace. See Heimsath and Mansingh, *Diplomatic History*, pp. 55–7.
25. *SWJN*, II/1, p. 539.
26. A. Appadorai, *Select Documents on India's Foreign Policy and Relations, 1947–1972, Volume I* (New Delhi: Oxford University Press, 1982), p. 14.
27. Jawaharlal Nehru, *India's Foreign Policy: Selected Speeches, September 1946–April 1961* (New Delhi: Government of India, 1961), p. 35.
28. Andrew B. Kennedy, 'Nehru's Foreign Policy: Realism and Idealism Conjoined,' in David M. Malone, C. Raja Mohan and Srinath Raghavan (eds), *The Oxford Handbook of Indian Foreign Policy* (Oxford: Oxford University Press, 2015), pp. 96–97. According to one of his biographers, B. R. Nanda, Nehru's aversion to military alliances also appears to have stemmed from his understanding of the origin of World War I and the role that such alliances played in the outbreak of the conflict. See Nanda, *Jawaharlal Nehru*, p. 224.
29. Heimsath and Mansingh, *Diplomatic History*, p. 58.
30. Appadorai, *Documents on India's Foreign Policy*, p. 16.
31. Lorne J. Kavic, *India's Quest for Security: Defence Policies, 1947–1965* (Berkeley and Los Angeles, CA: University of California Press: 1969), p. 208.
32. Ibid., p. 40.
33. B. N. Mullik, *My Years with Nehru, 1948–1964* (Bombay: Allied Publishers, 1972), p. 177; Heimsath and Mansingh, *Diplomatic History*, p. 404.
34. Andreas Hilger, 'Socialist Internationalism, World Capitalism, and the Global South: Soviet Foreign Economic Policy and India in Times of Cold War and Decolonization, 1950s–1960s,' *Journal of World History*, 32:3 (2021), p. 454.
35. Paul McGarr, *The Cold War in South Asia. Britain, the United States and the Indian Subcontinent, 1945–1965* (Cambridge, UK: Cambridge University Press, 2013), p. 35.
36. Hilger, 'Socialist Internationalism, World Capitalism, and the Global South,' p. 454; McGarr, *Cold War in South Asia*, p. 34.
37. Robert Barnes, 'Between the Blocs: India, the United Nations and Ending the Korean War,' *Journal of Korean Studies*, 18:2 (2013), pp. 263–86; Heimsath and

Mansingh, *Diplomatic History*, pp. 70–3; Tanvi Madan, *Fateful Triangle: How China Shaped US-India Relations During the Cold War* (Washington, DC: Brookings Institution Press, 2020), Kindle edition, ch. 1. On Moscow and Beijing toning down their misgivings, see SarDesai, *Indian Foreign Policy*, p. 29.

38. On early Indian-Soviet relations, see e.g. Swapna Kona Nayudu, 'The Soviet Peace Offensive and Nehru's India, 1953–1956,' in Manu Baghavan (ed.), *India and the Cold War* (Gurgaon, India: Penguin, 2019), pp. 38–40; Rakesh Ankit, 'India-USSR, 1946–1949: A False Start?,' in Madhavan K. Palat (ed.), *India and the World in the First Half of the Twentieth Century* (New York: Routledge, 2018), pp. 160–88; Davendra Kaushik, *Soviet Relations With India and Pakistan* (Delhi: Vikas Publications, 1971).
39. See Andrea Benvenuti, 'Frustrating the Americans and Befriending the Communists: Nehru's Policy in the Early Asian Cold War, 1947–54,' in Brian P. Farrell, S. R. Joey Long and David J. Ulbrich (eds), *From Far East to Asia Pacific: Great Powers and Grand Strategy 1900–1954* (Berlin: De Gruyter Oldenbourg, 2022), pp. 268–9. For Stalin's reassessing his view of India, see Record of a conversation between Stalin and representatives of the Indian Communist Party, 9 February 1951, Wilson Center Digital Archive [henceforth WCDA], https://digitalarchive.wilsoncenter.org/document/113938, accessed 5 March 2021; see also Nayudu, 'Soviet Peace Offensive,' pp. 38–9.
40. Ted Hopf, *Reconstructing the Cold War: The Early Years, 1945–1958* (New York: Oxford University Press, 2012), p. 131; Vladimir Pechatnov, 'Reflections on Soviet Foreign Policy, 1953–1964,' in Helene Carlbäck, Alexey Komarov and Karl Molin (eds), *Peaceful Coexistence? Soviet Union and Sweden in the Khrushchev Era* (Moscow: Centre for Baltic and East European Studies Södertörn University, 2010), p. 27; Vojtech Mastny, 'The Soviet Union Partnership With India,' *Journal of Cold War Studies*, 12:3 (2010), p. 52.
41. Heimsath and Mansingh, *Diplomatic History,* p. 400; NAUK, FO 371/116667, NS10385/3, Indo-Soviet Relations, 1947–1957, 15 April 1955. For India's decision to stay in the Commonwealth, see Michael Brecher, 'India's Decision to Remain in the Commonwealth,' *Journal of Commonwealth and Comparative Politics*, 12:1 (1974), pp. 62–90.
42. Kaushik, *Soviet Relations*, p. 28.
43. Ibid.
44. François Joyaux, *La Chine et le Règlement du Premier Conflict d'Indochine: Genève 1954* (Paris: Publications de la Sorbonne, 1979), Kobo edition, ch. 8; Anton Harder, 'Defining Independence in Cold War Asia: Sino-Indian Relations, 1949–62' (PhD thesis, London School of Economics, 2015), ch. 2. Nehru also declined American overtures to India to take the Chinese seat at the UN in 1950. See Nabarun Roy, 'In the Shadow of Great Power Politics: Why Nehru Supported PRC's Admission to the Security Council,' *International History Review*, 40:2 (2018), pp. 376–96; Anton Harder, 'Not at the Cost of China: New Evidence Regarding US Proposals to the for Joining the United Nations Security Council,' *Cold War International History Project, Working Paper 76* (Washington, DC: Woodrow Wilson Centre for Scholars, 2002), pp. 1–16, https://www.wilsoncenter.org/sites/default/files/

media/documents/publication/cwihp_working_paper_76_not_at_the_cost_of_china.pdf, accessed 1 February 2020.

45. SarDesai, *Indian Foreign Policy*, pp. 22–3.
46. Ibid., p. 23.
47. Madan, *Fateful Triangle*, ch. 1.
48. Indembassy Peking to Foreign New Delhi, telegram 95 and 96, 20 and 21 May 1950, docs. 0172 and 0172, Avtar Singh Bhasin (ed.), *India-China Relations 1947–2000: A Documentary Study, Volume 2* (New Delhi: Geetika Publishers, 2018).
49. SarDesai, *Indian Foreign Policy*, p. 23.
50. Ibid.
51. Ibid.; Joyaux, *La Chine et le Règlement du Premier Conflit d'Indochine*, ch. 8; Jian Chen, 'Bridging Revolution and Decolonisation: The "Bandung Discourse" in China's Early Cold War Experience,' *The Chinese Historical Review*, 15:2 (2008), p. 207 fn2; Qiang Zhai, 'Road to Bandung: China's Evolving Approach to De-Colonization,' in Tomohiko Umaya (ed.), *Comparing Modern Empires: Imperial Rule and Decolonization in the Changing World Order* (Hokkaido, Japan: Slavic-Eurasian Research Centre, Hokkaido University, 2018), pp. 187–8.
52. Nirupama Rao, *Fractured Himalaya: India Tibet China 1949–1962* (n. p.: Penguin Books, 2021), Kindle edition, ch. 1.
53. Harder, 'Defining Independence,' p. 96.
54. Nedyam Raghavan (Beijing) to Nehru, 17 March 1953, doc. 0563, Bhasin (ed.), *India-China Relations, vol. 2*. For some background on India's mediating role with regard to the question of the prisoners of war and New Delhi's UN resolution of November 1952, which upset the Chinese, see Barnes, 'Between the Blocs,' pp. 274–6; Harder, 'Defining Independence,' pp. 104–5. For Beijing's displeasure, see Chang Han-fu (Chinese Vice Foreign Minister) to Raghavan, 8 March 1953, doc. 0562, Bhasin (ed.), *India-China Relations, vol. 2*.
55. Benvenuti, 'Frustrating the Americans,' p. 260. On such expectations, see Robert J. McMahon, *The Cold War on the Periphery: The United States, India and Pakistan* (New York: Columbia University Press, 1994), pp. 43–5, 50–2 and 54–55; Srinath Raghavan, *Fierce Enigmas: A History of the United States in South Asia* (New York: Basic Books, 2018), Kindle edition, ch. 4.
56. Heimsath and Mansingh, Diplomatic History, pp. 352–3. On Truman's initial neglect of India, see Benvenuti, 'US Diplomacy in Asia,' p. 165; Madan, *Fateful Triangle*, ch. 1. On the Administration's reassessment of India's importance in its strategic calculus, see H. W. Brands, The Specter of Neutralism: The United States and the Emergence of the Third World (New York: Columbia University Press, 1989), p. 14 and Report to the National Security Council by the Executive Secretary (Lay), 17 May 1951, doc. 12, Foreign Relations of the United States (FRUS), 1951, *Asia and the Pacific, Volume VI, Part 1* (Washington, DC: GPO, 1977), https://history.state.gov/historicaldocuments/frus1951v06p1/d12
57. Benvenuti, 'Frustrating the Americans,' p. 269.
58. Francine Frankel, *When Nehru Looked East: Origins of India-US Suspicion and India-China Rivalry* (Oxford: Oxford University Press, 2020), Kindle edition, ch. 1.

59. NARA, RG59, Central Decimal Files [henceforth CDF] 1950–54, box 2858, 611.91/76-7, Loy Henderson (US ambassador to India) to Secretary of State, telegram 2191, 21 February 1951.
60. SarDesai, *Indian Foreign Policy*, p. 34.
61. NARA, RG59, CDF 1950–54, box 2858, 611.91/3–1051, Henderson to Secretary of State, telegram 2374, 10 March 1951. On the Soviet threat, see also Benvenuti, 'Frustrating the Americans,' pp. 264–5.
62. Michele Louro, *Comrades Against Imperialism: Nehru, India and Interwar Internationalism. Global and International History* (Cambridge, UK: Cambridge University Press, 2018), p. 278; McGarr, *Cold War in South Asia*, p. 31; Brown, 'Jawaharlal Nehru,' p. 208. Moreover, he viewed the Soviet Union 'as a font of lessons for promoting rapid, state-led industrialisation.' See Rajan Menon, 'India and Russia: The Anatomy and Evolution of a Relationship,' in David M. Malone, C. Raja Mohan and Srinath Raghavan (eds), *The Oxford Handbook of Indian Foreign Policy* (Oxford: Oxford University Press, 2015), pp. 509–10.
63. Frankel, *When Nehru Looked East*, preface; Brown, *Nehru*, p. 342. For Nehru's socialism, see Nanda, *Jawaharlal Nehru*, pp. 185–93.
64. Benvenuti, 'Frustrating the Americans,' p. 260; SarDesai, *India Foreign Policy*, p. 23.
65. Louro, *Comrades Against Imperialism*, p. 279; Tsui, 'Coming to Terms,' pp. 117 and 119–20.
66. Louro, *Comrades Against Imperialism*, pp. 273 and 278.
67. *Jawaharlal Nehru Letters to Chief Ministers, 1947–64 (JNLCM), volume 2 (1950–52)*, pp. 238–9; Extract from the Note by Prime Minister on policy towards East and South Asia, 8 November 1950, doc. 0266, Bhasin (ed.), *India-China Relations, vol. 1*; NAA, A1838, 3107/40/147 part 1A, AHC New Delhi to ADEA, cablegram 311, 31 October 1950. He did, however, seek to strengthen India's geopolitical position along the Sino-Indian border by signing treaties with Bhutan, Nepal and Sikkim in 1949–50—treaties that allowed New Delhi to have a say in the foreign and security policies of these countries. See Madan, *Fateful Triangle*, ch. 1.
68. NAA, A1838, 169/11/87 part 2, 'India Foreign Policy and Mr. Nehru,' ministerial despatch 47, 16 August 1952. Nehru's remarks were conveyed by Bowles to the Australian High Commissioner to India, Walter Crocker.
69. The US ambassador to India (Bowles) to the Secretary of State, 7 November 1951, doc. 488, *FRUS*, *1951*, *Asia and the Pacific, Volume VI, Part 2* (Washington, DC: GPO, 1977), https://history.state.gov/historicaldocuments/frus1951v06p2/d488, accessed 11 October 2019.
70. On this point, see e.g. Harder, 'Defining Independence,' ch. 2.
71. Giri Deshingkar, 'India-China Relations: The Nehru Years,' *China Report*, 27:2 (1991), p. 93.
72. Nehru cited in Tsui, 'Coming to Terms,' p. 19.
73. Memorandum of Conversation by the Secretary of State, 21 May 1953, doc. 39, *FRUS, 1952–1954, The Near and Middle East, Volume IX, Part 1* (Washington, DC: GPO, 1986), https://history.state.gov/historicaldocuments/frus1952-54v09p1/d39, accessed 10 April 2020.

74. Deshingkar, 'India-China Relations,' p. 88; Tsui, 'Coming to Terms,' pp. 19–21; Frankel, *When Nehru Looked East*, preface.
75. For Nehru's role at the 1927 Brussels Congress, see Louro, *Comrades Against Imperialism*, pp. 65–102.
76. Brown, 'Jawaharlal Nehru,' pp. 203–5.
77. Ibid., p. 235; Heimsath and Mansingh, *Diplomatic History*, p. 56.
78. Rao, *Fractured Himalaya*, ch. 1; see also Harder, 'Defining Independence,' p. 69; Deshingkar, 'India-China Relations,' p. 92.
79. Madan, *Fateful Triangle*, ch. 1; Harder, 'Defining Independence,' p. 69.
80. Mullik, *My Years With Nehru,* p. 78.
81. *SWJN*, II/15, pp. 342–7.
82. *SWJN*, II/26, p. 315; NAUK, FO 371/112196, DL1022/2, India's North-East Frontier Policy, 2 June 1954; McGarr, *Cold War in South Asia*, p. 39; Lorenz M. Lüthi, 'India's Relations With China, 1945–74,' in Amit Das Gupta and Lorenz Lüthi (eds), *The Sino-Indian War of 1962: New Perspectives* (London: Taylor & Francis, 2016), p. 31.
83. *SWJN*, II/22, p. 511.
84. Lüthi, 'India's Relations with China, 1945–74,' p. 31.
85. Heimsath and Mansingh, *Diplomatic History*, p. 355; Lok Sabha Debates (LSD), Session VI, 17 September 1953, cols. 3976, https://eparlib.nic.in/bitstream/123456789/55611/1/lsd_01_04_17-09-1953.pdf, accessed 11 November 2021.
86. LSD, Session VII, 30 September 1954, col. 3884, https://eparlib.nic.in/bitstream/123456789/55721/1/lsd_01_07_30-09-1954.pdf, accessed 11 November 2021.
87. Dulles cited in Ronald W. Pruessen, 'John Foster Dulles and Decolonization of Southeast Asia' in Marc Frey, Ronald W. Pruessen and Tan Tai Yong (eds), *The Transformation of Southeast Asia: International Perspectives on Decolonisation* (Singapore: Singapore University Press, 2003), p. 228.
88. A. A. Fursenko and Timothy J. Naftali, *Khrushchev's Cold War: The Inside Story of an American Adversary* (New York: W. W. Norton & Company 2010), Kindle edition, ch. 1; Vladislav Zubok and Constantine Pleshakov, *Inside the Kremlin's Cold War: From Stalin to Khrushchev* (Cambridge, MA: Harvard University Press, 1996), p. 184.
89. Jeffrey Brooks, 'When the Cold War Did Not End: The Soviet Peace Offensive of 1953 and the American Response,' https://www.files.ethz.ch/isn/19774/OP278.pdf, accessed 20 March 2020. For the 'Peace Offensive,' see also Vojtech Mastny, 'The Elusive Détente: Stalin's Successors and the West,' in Klaus Larres and Kenneth Osgood (eds), *The Cold War After Stalin's Death: A Missed Opportunity for Peace* (Lanham, MD: Rowman & Littlefield Publishers, 2006), pp. 3–26.
90. Odd Arne Westad, *The Global Cold War: Third World Interventions and the Making of Our Times* (Cambridge, UK: Cambridge University Press, 2005), p. 67; Robert J. McMahon, '"The Illusion of Vulnerability": American Reassessments of the Soviet Threat, 1955–1956,' *International History Review*, 18:3 (1996), p. 601.

91. On Nikita Khrushchev's wooing of Afro-Asian nations and how this played out in India, see Hilger, 'Socialist Internationalism, World Capitalism, and the Global South,' pp. 439–64.
92. Heimsath and Mansingh, *Diplomatic History*, p. 407; Kaushik, *Soviet Relations*, p. 45.
93. Appadorai and Rajan, *India's Foreign Policy*, p. 264.
94. NARA, RG 59, CDF 1950–54, box 2858, 611.91/4-1553, State Department to US Embassy New Delhi and US consulates Calcutta, Bombay and Madras, circular airgram 2112, 15 April 1953.
95. *SWJN*, II/26, pp. 516–17 and 520–1.
96. Jeremy Friedman, *Shadow Cold War: The Sino-Soviet Competition for the Third World* (Chapel Hill, NC: University of North Carolina Press, 2015), p. 25.
97. Gregg Brazinsky, *Winning the Third World: Sino-American Rivalry During the Cold War* (Chapel Hill, NC: University of North Carolina Press, 2017), pp. 76–7.
98. Kuisong Yang, 'Changes in Mao Zedong's Attitude Toward the Indochina War, 1949–1973,' *Cold War International History Project Working Paper 34* (Washington, DC: Woodrow Wilson Centre for Scholars, 2002), p. 11, https://www.wilsoncenter.org/sites/default/files/media/documents/publication/ACFB04.pdf
99. Chen, 'Bridging Revolution,' p. 218; John W. Garver, *China's Quest: The History of the Foreign Relations of the People's Republic* (Oxford: Oxford University Press, 2016), Kindle edition, ch. 4.
100. Garver, *China's Quest*, ch. 4; Chen, 'Bridging Revolution,' p. 218.
101. Guang Shu Zhang, 'Constructing "Peaceful Coexistence": China's Diplomacy Toward the Geneva and Bandung Conferences, 1954–55,' *Cold War History*, 7:4 (2007), p. 510; Yang, *Mao Zedong's Attitude*, pp. 11–12.
102. Chen, 'Bridging Revolution,' p. 220.
103. Brazinsky, *Winning the Third World*, pp. 76–8; Nicholas Tarling, *Britain and the Neutralisation of Laos* (Singapore: National University of Singapore Press, 2011), p. 16; Zhai, 'Road to Bandung,' pp. 195 and 205–6; Kuo-kang Shao, 'Chou En-lai's Diplomatic Approach to Non-Aligned States in Asia: 1953–60,' *China Quarterly*, 78 (1979), pp. 324–5 and 326–7; Ronald C. Keith, *The Diplomacy of Zhou Enlai* (London: Macmillan, 1989), p. 69.
104. Hand-delivered note, Zhou Enlai to Stalin, conveying telegram from Mao Zedong to Zhou Enlai, 16 September 1952, WCDA, http://digitalarchive.wilsoncenter.org/document/113030, accessed 15 November 2020; Brazinsky, *Winning the Third World*, p. 77.
105. Zhang, 'Peaceful Coexistence,' p. 525; Keith, *Zhou Enlai*, p. 119.
106. Zhang, 'Peaceful Coexistence,' p. 513; see also General CIA Records [henceforth CIA], Communist China's Role in Non-Communist Asia, NIE 13-2-57, 3 December 1957, https://www.cia.gov/readingroom/docs/CIA-RDP98-00979R000400480001-5.pdf, accessed 5 May 2018.
107. Chen, 'Bridging Revolution,' p. 221.
108. Odd Arne Westad, *Restless Empire: China and the World Since 1750* (London: Vintage Books, 2013), p. 321.

109. Nayudu, 'Soviet Peace Offensive,' p. 40.
110. NARA, RG 59, CDF 1950–54, box 2858, 611.91/7-1553, John Foster Dulles (US Secretary of State) to US Embassy New Delhi and US consulates Calcutta, Bombay and Madras, circular airgram 1657, 15 July 1953.
111. Nayudu, 'Soviet Peace Offensive,' p. 40.
112. Heimsath and Mansingh, *Diplomatic History*, p. 407.
113. Malenkov cited in SarDesai, *Indian Foreign Policy*, p. 31.
114. Nayudu, 'Soviet Peace Offensive,' p. 38.
115. Kaushik, *Soviet Relations*, pp. 48–9.
116. NAUK, FO 371/116667, NS10385/3, Indo-Soviet Relations, 1947–1957, 15 April 1955; Hilger, 'Socialist Internationalism, World Capitalism and the Global South,' p. 450.
117. Kaushik, *Soviet Relations*, pp. 48–9; see also Appadorai and Rajan, *India's Foreign Policy*, p. 264.
118. Anton Harder, 'Compradors, Neo-Colonialism, and Transnational Class Struggle: PRC Relations With Algeria and India, 1953–1965,' *Modern Asian Studies*, 55:4 (2021), p. 1240.
119. Ibid.
120. Foreign New Delhi to Indembassy Peking, telegram 5025, 29 September 1953, document 0585 and Foreign New Delhi to Indembassy Peking, telegram 21925, 1 September 1953, document 0580, Bhasin (ed.), *India-China Relations, vol. 2*.
121. K. Gupta, 'Sino-Indian Agreement on Tibetan Trade and Intercourse: Its Origin and Significance,' *Economic and Political Weekly*, 13:16 (1978), pp. 696–702.
122. McMahon, *Cold War*, p. 156; Brands, *Specter of Neutralism*, p. 85.
123. McMahon, *Cold War*, p. 156; Brands, *Specter of Neutralism*, p. 85. For a brief examination of the Eisenhower campaign's anti-communist rhetoric, see Chris Tudda, '"Reenacting the Story of Tantalus": Eisenhower, Dulles, and the Failed Rhetoric of Liberation,' *Journal of Cold War Studies*, 7:4 (2005), pp. 8–11; Dockrill, *Eisenhower's New-Look*, p. 20; John Lewis Gaddis, *Strategies of Containment: A Critical Appraisal of Postwar American National Security Policy* (Oxford and New York: Oxford University Press, 1982), pp. 127–8.
124. McMahon, *Cold War*, p. 156; see also Brands, *Specter of Neutralism*, p. 85.
125. McMahon, *Cold War*, p. 155. For a brief description of such disagreements, see Heimsath and Mansingh, *Diplomatic History*, pp. 352–4.
126. Brands, *Specter of Neutralism*, pp. 81–3.
127. NAUK, FO 371/123587, L10338/3, Escott Reid (Canadian High Commissioner to India) to Lester B. Pearson (Canadian Secretary of State for External Affairs), telegram 817, 3 December 1955.
128. S. R. Joey Long, 'Adversaries, Allies and the Shaping of US Grand Strategy: The Eisenhower Administration and the 1954 Geneva Conference,' Brian P. Farrell, S. R. Joey Long and David J. Ulbrich (eds), *From Far East to Asia Pacific: Great Powers and Grand Strategy 1900–1954* (Berlin: De Gruyter Oldenbourg, 2022), p. 314.
129. Dulles cited in Memorandum of Discussion at a Special Meeting of the National Security Council, 31 March 1953, doc. 553, *FRUS 1952–1954, II/1*, https://

history.state.gov/historicaldocuments/frus1952-54v02p1/d53, accessed 3 June 2019; Long, 'Adversaries, Allies and the Shaping of US Grand Strategy,' p. 314.

130. Gilles Boquérat, 'India's Commitment to Peaceful Coexistence and the Settlement of the Indochina War,' *Cold War History*, 5:2 (2005), pp. 215–17.
131. NARA, RG59, CDF 1950–54, box 2858, 611.91/1-1553, Chester Bowles (US ambassador to India) to General Walter Bedell Smith (Director of Central Intelligence), 15 January 1953.
132. H. W. Brands, 'India and Pakistan in American Strategic Planning, 1947–54: The Commonwealth as Collaborator,' *Journal of Imperial and Commonwealth History*, 15:1 (1986), pp. 49–50.
133. Robert J. McMahon, 'United States Cold War Strategy in South Asia: Making a Military Commitment to Pakistan, 1947–1954,' *Journal of American History*, 75:3 (1988), pp. 822–30.
134. Ibid., p. 829.
135. Brands, *Specter of Neutralism*, p. 86.
136. Memorandum of Discussion at the 147th Meeting of the National Security Council, 1 June 1953, doc. 137, FRUS, 1952–1954, IX/1, https://history.state.gov/historicaldocuments/frus1952-54v09p1/d137, accessed 5 July 2018; see also Brands, *Specter of Neutralism*, p. 86.
137. Memorandum of Discussion at the 147th Meeting of the National Security Council, 1 June 1953, doc. 137, *FRUS, 1952–1954, IX/1,* https://history.state.gov/historicaldocuments/frus1952-54v09p1/d137, accessed 5 July 2018.
138. Memorandum of Discussion at the 153rd Meeting of the National Security Council, doc. 144, FRUS, 1952–1954, IX/1, https://history.state.gov/historicaldocuments/frus1952-54v09p1/d144, accessed 5 July 2018; Statement of Policy by the National Security Council, 14 July 1953, doc. 145, FRUS, 1952–1954, IX/1, https://history.state.gov/historicaldocuments/frus1952-54v09p1/d145, accessed 5 July 2018; see also Brands, 'India and Pakistan in American Strategic Planning,' p. 50.
139. McGarr, *The Cold War in South Asia*, p. 21. On the troubled genesis and life of the Baghdad Pact, see Nigel John Ashton, 'The Hijacking of a Pact: The Formation of the Baghdad Pact and Anglo-American Tensions in the Middle East, 1955–1958,' *Review of International Studies,* 19:2 (1993), pp. 123–37. After Iraq's withdrawal in 1959, the Middle East Treaty Organisation or Baghdad Pact was renamed the Central Treaty Organization (CENTO) and the United States became an associate member. CENTO was disbanded in 1979 as a result of Iran's departure in the wake of the fall of the Shah.
140. Brands, *Specter of Neutralism*, pp. 89–90. Karachi was the first capital of independent Pakistan until 1959, when President Ayub Khan designated Rawalpindi as the provisional seat of government while a new capital was being constructed nearby. Islamabad became the capital of Pakistan in 1967.
141. NARA, RG 59, CDF 1950–54, box 2858, 611.91/12-353, George V. Allen (US ambassador to India) to Dulles, telegram 872, 3 December 1953.
142. *SWJN*, II/24, pp. 420–2. For a full discussion of early Indian reactions to American plans to enlist Pakistan's support, see Zorawar Daulet Singh, *Power*

and Diplomacy: India's Foreign Policies During the Cold War (New Delhi: Oxford University Press, 2019), ch. 3.

143. *SWJN*, II/24, pp. 417–18.
144. On Allen's objections, see McMahon, 'United States Cold War Strategy,' pp. 836–7.
145. The Charge in India (Mills) to the Department of State, 19 October 1953, doc. 156, *FRUS, 1952–1954, IX/1*, https://history.state.gov/historicaldocuments/frus1952-54v09p1/d156, accessed 5 July 2018.
146. NARA, RG 59, CDF 1950–54, box 2858, 611.91/12-353, Allen to Dulles, telegram 872, 3 December 1953.
147. Singh, *Power and Diplomacy*, ch. 3.
148. Brands, *Specter of Neutralism*, p. 91.
149. Ibid., pp. 91–2.
150. Dulles cited in ibid., p. 91.
151. McMahon, 'United States Cold War Strategy,' pp. 812 and 838.
152. The US ambassador to India (Allen) to Department of State, 24 February 1954, doc. 1077, *FRUS, 1952–1954, Africa and South Asia, Volume XI, Part 2* (Washington, DC: GPO, 1983), https://history.state.gov/historicaldocuments/frus1952-54v11p2/d1077, accessed 5 July 2018.
153. Canadian High Commissioner in India (Escott Reid) to Secretary of State for External Affairs (Lester B. Pearson), telegram 96, 3 March 1954, doc. 438, *Documents on Canadian External Relations, Volume 20 (1954)* (Ottawa: Department of Foreign Affairs and International Trade, 1997), https://epe.lac-bac.gc.ca/100/206/301/faitc-aecic/history/2013-05-03/www.international.gc.ca/department/history-histoire/dcer/details-en.asp@intRefid=611, accessed 10 March 2018.
154. *SWJN*, II/24, pp. 421 and 434.
155. Frankel, *When Nehru Looked East*, ch. 6.
156. *SWJN*, II/24, p. 432.
157. Ibid., p. 437.
158. Ibid., p. 421; see also Sarvepalli Gopal, *Jawaharlal Nehru: A Biography. Volume Two 1947–1956* (London: Vintage Digital, 2014), Kindle edition, ch. 9.
159. *SWJN*, II/24, p. 436.
160. Ibid., p. 421.
161. Ibid., p. 442; The US ambassador to India (Allen) to Department of State, 24 February 1954, doc. 1077, *FRUS*, *1952–1954, XI/2*, https://history.state.gov/historicaldocuments/frus1952-54v11p2/d1077, accessed 5 July 2018.
162. Raghavan, *Fierce Enemies*, ch. 5; see also *SWJN*, II/24, p. 424.
163. For this perception, see NARA, RG 59, CDF 1950–54, box 2858, 611.91/9-1053, Allen to Dulles, telegram 472, 10 September 1953.
164. Boquérat, 'Peaceful Coexistence,' p. 216.
165. *SWJN*, II/26, p. 514.
166. On this point, see also Singh, *Power and Diplomacy*, ch. 3.

2. THE INDOCHINA CRISIS

1. PMML, JN, file 250, APM(54), 1st meeting, 28 April 1954, 10 am.
2. Jawaharlal Nehru, cited in *SWJN*, Second Series [henceforth II], Volume 26 (New Delhi: Jawaharlal Nehru Memorial Fund, 1984–2015), p. 513.
3. George C. Herring and Richard H. Immerman, 'Eisenhower, Dulles, and Dienbienphu: "The Day We Didn't Go to War" Revisited,' *Journal of American History*, 71:2 (1984), p. 345.
4. Ibid.; Fredrik Logevall, *Embers of War: The Fall of an Empire and the Making of America's Vietnam* (New York: Random House, 2012), Kindle book, ch. 16 and 17; Central Intelligence Agency (CIA), Information Report: Indochina. Preparations for a Showdown at Dien Bien Phu, 3 March 1954, CIA Historical Collections, https://www.cia.gov/readingroom/docs/CIA-RDP81-01036R000100140053-8.pdf, accessed 5 September 2018; NSC Briefing: Indochina, 8 January 1954, CIA Historical Collections, https://www.cia.gov/readingroom/docs/CIA-RDP80R01443R000200090003-9.pdf, accessed 10 October 2018.
5. David Mark Thompson, 'Delusions of *Grandeur*: French Global Ambitions and the Problem of Revival of Military Power, 1950–1954' (PhD Dissertation, University of Toronto, 2007), pp. 277–8 and 299–300; Laurent Cesari, *Le Problème Diplomatique de l'Indochine, 1945–1957* (Paris: Les Indes savantes, 2013), p. 168.
6. NAUK, FO 371/112051, DF1071/172, Washington to FO, telegram 691, 10 April 1954; James Cable, *The Geneva Conference of 1954 on Indochina* (New York: St. Martin's Press, 1986), pp. 23–4 and 42–3; Pierre Grosser, 'La France et l'Indochine (1953–1956): Une "Carte de Visite en Peau de Chagrin"' (PhD thesis, Institut d'Études Politiques de Paris, 2002), p. 32.
7. NAUK, FO 371/112047, DF1071/74, The Situation in Indo-China: Malcolm MacDonald's report to FO, 12 March 1954; The Ambassador at Saigon (Heath) to Department of State, 3 January 1954, doc. 491, *FRUS, 1952–1954, Indochina, Volume XIII, Part 1* (Washington, DC: GPO, 1982), https://history.state.gov/historicaldocuments/frus1952-54v13p1/d491, accessed 15 April 2018.
8. Herring and Immerman, 'Eisenhower, Dulles, and Dienbienphu,' p. 346; Logevall, *Embers of War*, chs. 16–17.
9. NSC Briefing: Conditions at Dien Bien Phu, 18 March 1954, CIA Historical Collections, https://www.cia.gov/readingroom/docs/CIA-RDP79R00890A000200050018-1.pdf, accessed 5 January 2018; Herring and Immerman, 'Eisenhower, Dulles, and Dienbienphu,' p. 346.
10. Memorandum for the Record by Captain G. W. Anderson, Assistant to the Chairman of the Joint Chiefs of Staff (Radford), 21 March 1954, doc. 626, *FRUS, 1952–1954, XIII*/1, https://history.state.gov/historicaldocuments/frus1952-54v13p1/d626, accessed 15 April 2018.
11. Herring and Immerman, 'Eisenhower, Dulles, and Dienbienphu,' p. 346.
12. Ibid., pp. 346–7.
13. Ibid., p. 359.
14. NAUK, FO 371/112049, DF1071/103/G, Policy towards Indochina, 31 March 1954; DF1077/97, Keith Officer's Views on French Attitude to Indo-China, 22 March 1954.

15. George C. Herring, '"A Good Stout Effort": John Foster Dulles and the Indochina Crisis, 1954–1955,' in Richard H. Immerman (ed.), *John Foster Dulles and the Diplomacy of the Cold War* (Princeton, NJ: Princeton University Press, 1990), p. 214.
16. Ibid.
17. Ibid., pp. 214–15.
18. NAUK, FO 371/112047, DF1071/25, Roger Makins (British ambassador to the United States) to FO, telegram 288, 17 February 1954.
19. In September 1953, the Eisenhower administration had announced the contribution of US$385 million to the French military effort in Indochina for 1954 (equivalent to two-thirds of French defence spending in Indochina in 1954). See Cable, *Geneva Conference*, p. 25. According to British sources, in 1954 the United States was paying 78 per cent of the cost of the war. See NAUK, FO371/112050, F1071140/D, J. G. Tahourdin's note, 9 April 1954.
20. Memorandum of Conversation by the Deputy Assistant Secretary of State for Foreign Affairs (Drumright), 2 April 1954, doc. 679, *FRUS*, *1952–1954, XIII/1*, https://history.state.gov/historicaldocuments/frus1952-54v13p1/d679, accessed 15 April 2018.
21. Editorial note, doc. 141, *FRUS*, *1952–1954, East Asia and the Pacific, Volume XII, Part 1* (Washington, DC: GPO, 1984), https://history.state.gov/historicaldocuments/frus1952-54v12p1/d141, accessed 2 February 2018; see also 'Action Against Red Threat in S.-E. Asia,' *Times of India*, 31 March 1954.
22. Robert Bowie cited in Herring and Immerman, 'Eisenhower, Dulles, and Dienbienphu,' p. 351.
23. Cheng Guan Ang, *The Southeast Treaty Organisation* (New York: Routledge, 2022), p. 27.
24. NAUK, FO 371, 112049, DF1071/134/G, Dulles and Makins, 2 April 1954; Memorandum of Conversation by the Deputy Assistant Secretary of State for Foreign Affairs (Drumright), 2 April 1954, doc. 679, *FRUS*, *1952–1954, XIII/1*, https://history.state.gov/historicaldocuments/frus1952-54v13p1/d679, accessed 15 February 2018; Memorandum of Conversation by the Deputy Assistant Secretary of State for European Affairs (Bonbright), 3 April 1954, doc. 687, *FRUS*, *1952–1954, XIII/1*, https://history.state.gov/historicaldocuments/frus1952-54v13p1/d687, accessed 15 February 2018; Memorandum of Conversation by the Deputy Assistant Secretary of State for European Affairs (Bonbright), 4 April 1954, doc. 689, *FRUS*, *1952–1954, XIII/1*, https://history.state.gov/historicaldocuments/frus1952-54v13p1/d689, accessed 15 February 2018; The First Secretary of Embassy in France (Godley) to Department of State, 21 April 1954, doc. 747, *FRUS*, *1952–1954, XIII/1*, https://history.state.gov/historicaldocuments/frus1952-54v13p1/d747, accessed 15 February 2018; NAUK, FO 371/112051, DF1071/173/G, Makins to FO, telegram 679, 10 April 1954; DF1071/174/G, Makins to FO, telegram 680, 10 April 1954; DF1071/176, Makins to FO, telegram 688, 10 April 1954.
25. Kevin Ruane and Matthew Jones, *Anthony Eden, Anglo-American Relations and the 1954 Indochina Crisis* (London: Bloomsbury, 2019), pp. 95–6.

26. The issue of Congressional support is discussed in Herring and Immerman, 'Eisenhower, Dulles, and Dienbienphu,' pp. 351–2.
27. Memorandum for the file of the Secretary of State, 5 April 1954, doc. 686, *FRUS, 1952–1954, XIII/1*, https://history.state.gov/historicaldocuments/frus1952-54v13p1/d686, accessed 15 February 2018.
28. Memorandum of telephone conversation between the President and the Secretary of State, 3 April 1954, doc. 688, *FRUS, 1952–1954, XIII/1*, https://history.state.gov/historicaldocuments/frus1952-54v13p1/d688, accessed 15 February 2018.
29. Memorandum of Discussion at the 192d Meeting of the National Security Council, 6 April 1954, doc. 705, *FRUS, 1952–1954, XIII/1*, https://history.state.gov/historicaldocuments/frus1952-54v13p1/d705, accessed 15 February 2018.
30. NAUK, CAB129/67, C(54)134, 7 April 1954; FO371/112052, DF1071/202/G, Indo-China: Brief for Discussion with Mr Dulles, 9 April 1954.
31. Memorandum of Conversation, by the Counselor (MacArthur), 11 April 1954, doc. 736, *FRUS, 1952–1954, XIII/1*, https://history.state.gov/historicaldocuments/frus1952-54v13p1/d736, accessed 3 February 2018; NAUK, FO 371/112054, DF1071/267/G, Memcon, Anthony Eden (British Secretary of State for Foreign Affairs) and John Foster Dulles (US Secretary of State), 11 April 1954.
32. Memorandum of Conversation, by the Counselor (MacArthur), 11 April 1954, doc. 736, *FRUS, 1952–1954, XIII/1*, https://history.state.gov/historicaldocuments/frus1952-54v13p1/d736, accessed 3 February 2018; NAUK, FO 371/112054, DF1071/267/G, Memcon, Eden and Dulles, 11 April 1954. Established in 1949, the Associated States of Vietnam, Laos and Cambodia enjoyed a certain degree of self-government within the French Union and were even allowed to establish diplomatic relations with a handful of countries. However, they remained subject to France (through the ministry responsible for relations with the Associated States), which retained control over their finances, external defence and foreign relations. In 1953, the Laniel government promised to grant the three Associated States full independence and began devolving some additional powers to them. See Christopher E. Goscha, *Historical Dictionary of the Indochina War (1945–1954): An International and Interdisciplinary Approach* (Copenhagen: Nordic Institute of Asian Studies Press, 2011), p. 44.
33. Gary R. Hess, 'Redefining the American Position in Southeast Asia: The United States and the Geneva and Manila Conferences,' in Lawrence S. Kaplan, Denise Artaud and Mark R. Rubin (eds), *Dien Bien Phu and the Crisis in Franco-American Relations, 1954–1955* (Wilmington, DE: Scholarly Resources, Inc., 1990), p. 128.
34. Logevall, *Embers of War*, ch. 19.
35. The First Secretary of Embassy in France (Godley) to the Department of State, 21 April 1954, doc. 747, *FRUS, 1952–1954, XIII/1*, https://history.state.gov/historicaldocuments/frus1952-54v13p1/d747, accessed 3 February 2018.
36. Ibid.

37. Ibid.
38. George C. Herring, 'Franco-American Conflict in Indochina, 1950–1954,' in Kaplan, Artaud and Rubin (eds), *Dien Bien Phu*, pp. 29–48.
39. Logevall, *Embers of War*, ch. 20.
40. Ibid.
41. Memorandum of Conversation, by the Assistant Secretary of State for European Affairs (Merchant), 26 April 1945, doc. 788, *FRUS*, *1952–1954, XIII/1*, https://history.state.gov/historicaldocuments/frus1952-54v13p1/d788, accessed 3 February 2018.
42. Herring and Immerman, 'Eisenhower, Dulles, and Dienbienphu,' p. 362.
43. Ang, *Southeast Asia Treaty Organisation*, p. 28.
44. Herring and Immerman, 'Eisenhower, Dulles, and Dienbienphu,' p. 362.
45. Ibid.
46. Roger Dingman, 'John Foster Dulles and the Creation of the South-East Asia Treaty Organization in 1954,' *International History Review*, 11:3 (1989), p. 459; Ang, *Southeast Asia Treaty Organisation*, p. 28.
47. Ang, *Southeast Asia Treaty Organisation*, p. 29. See also Tao Wang, 'Neutralizing Indochina: The 1954 Geneva Conference and China's Efforts to Isolate the United States,' *Journal of Cold War Studies*, 19:2 (2017), pp. 3–42; Cheng Guan Ang, 'China's Influence Over Vietnam in War and Peace,' in Evelyn Goh (ed.), *Rising China's Influence in Developing Asia* (Oxford: Oxford University Press, 2016), Kindle book.
48. Lakshmana A. Chetty, 'India and Southeast Asia Treaty Organization (S.E.A.T.O.), *Proceedings of the Indian History Congress*, 42 (1981), p. 617.
49. The US ambassador to India (Allen) to the Department of State, 31 March 1954, doc. 663, *FRUS*, *1952–1954, XIII/1*, https://history.state.gov/historicaldocuments/frus1952-54v13p1/d663, accessed 20 February 2018.
50. NAUK, FO 371/112051, DF1071/181, Alexander Clutterbuck (British High Commissioner to India) to CRO, telegram 348, 9 April 1954.
51. NAUK, FO 371/112053, DF1071/229, Clutterbuck to CRO, telegram 366, 14 April 1954.
52. Ibid.
53. NAUK, FO 371/112053, DF1071/242, Clutterbuck to CRO, telegram 374, 16 April 1954.
54. Zorawar Daulet Singh, *Power and Diplomacy: India's Foreign Policies during the Cold War* (New Delhi: Oxford University Press, 2019), pp. 116–67.
55. *SWJN*, II/25, pp. 553–4. In India, a Chief Minister is the elected head of government for each of the Union's states and territories.
56. NAUK, FO 371/112053, DF1071/229, Clutterbuck to CRO, telegram 376, 17 April 1954.
57. Ibid.
58. Escott Reid, *Envoy to Nehru* (Delhi: Oxford University Press, 1981), p. 73.
59. LSD, Session V, 23 December 1953, cols. 2979–81, https://eparlib.nic.in/bitstream/123456789/55592/1/lsd_01_05_23-12-1953.pdf, accessed 15 July 2022.

60. Singh, *Power and Diplomacy*.
61. *SWJN*, II/24, p. 565.
62. Singh, *Power and Diplomacy*.
63. Lok Sabha, *Parliamentary Debates*, I/II, cols. 5581–82, https://eparlib.nic.in/bitstream/123456789/55922/1/lsd_01_06_24-04-1954, accessed 15 July 2022.
64. Ibid.
65. Gilles Boquérat, 'India's Commitment to Peaceful Coexistence and the Settlement of the Indochina War,' *Cold War History*, 5:2 (2005), p. 212.
66. Ibid.; Marek W. Rutkowski, 'Expanding the Area of Peace: India, Colombo Powers and the Geneva Conference of 1954,' in Brian P. Farrell, S. R. Joey Long and David J. Ulbrich (eds), *From Far East to Asia Pacific: Great Powers and Grand Strategy 1900–1954* (Berlin: De Gruyter Oldenbourg, 2022), pp. 344–5.
67. A. Appadorai and M. S. Rajan, *India's Foreign Policy and Relations* (New Delhi: South Asian Publishers, 1985), p. 352.
68. Boquérat, 'Peaceful Coexistence,' pp. 212–13; D. R. SarDesai, *Indian Foreign Policy in Cambodia, Laos and Vietnam, 1947–1964* (Berkeley and Los Angeles, CA: University of California Press, 1968), pp. 11–15 and 18–20. Between 1947 and 1954, France retained control of five small settlements (Pondicherry, Chandernagore, Kerikal, Mahé and Yanam). See Akhila Yechury, 'Imaging India, Decolonizing l'Inde Française, c. 1947–1954,' *The Historical Journal*, 58:4 (2015), pp. 1141–65.
69. SarDesai, *Indian Foreign Policy*, pp. 14–15.
70. Ibid., p. 16; Rutkowski, 'Expanding the Area of Peace,' p. 345.
71. SarDesai, *Indian Foreign Policy*, pp. 16 and 20–1; Boquérat, 'India's Commitment,' pp. 213–14.
72. SarDesai, *Indian Foreign Policy*, pp. 24–5.
73. Ibid., pp. 23–4; Boquérat, 'Peaceful Coexistence,' p. 214.
74. Ibid.
75. *SWJN*, II/22, p. 511.
76. SarDesai, *India Foreign Policy*, pp. 26–7.
77. LSD, Session VI, 22 February 1954, cols. 415–16, https://eparlib.nic.in/handle/123456789/55729?view_type=browse, accessed 15 July 2022.
78. Ibid.; Rutkowski, 'Expanding the Area of Peace,' p. 346.
79. Rutkowski, 'Expanding the Area of Peace,' p. 346; Boquérat, 'Peaceful Coexistence,' p. 215.
80. Boquérat, 'Peaceful Coexistence,' p. 215; Rutkowski, 'Expanding the Area of Peace,' p. 346; Singh, *Power and Diplomacy*, p. 115.
81. Singh, *Power and Diplomacy*; Rutkowski, 'Expanding the Area of Peace,' pp. 346–7; Boquérat, 'Peaceful Coexistence,' p. 215.
82. Boquérat, 'Peaceful Coexistence,' pp. 215–16.
83. *SWJN*, II/24, p. 422.
84. SarDesai, *India Foreign Policy*, p. 35.
85. The six-point proposal on Indochina was included in the above-mentioned statement he made to the Lok Sabha regarding the Indochinese crisis.

86. Francine Frankel, *When Nehru Looked East: Origins of India-US Suspicion and India-China Rivalry* (Oxford: Oxford University Press, 2020), Kindle edition, preface.
87. Cindy Ewing, 'The Colombo Powers: Crafting Diplomacy in the Third World and Launching Afro-Asia at Bandung,' *Cold War History*, 19:1 (2019), pp. 7–8.
88. Lok Sabha, *Parliamentary Debates*, I/II, cols. 5581–82, https://eparlib.nic.in/bitstream/123456789/55922/1/lsd_01_06_24-04-1954, accessed 15 July 2022.
89. Ibid.
90. S. R. Joey Long, 'Adversaries, Allies and the Shaping of US Grand Strategy: The Eisenhower Administration and the 1954 Geneva Conference,' in Farrell, Long and Ulbrich (eds), *From Far East to Asia Pacific*, pp. 315–16 and 324–6.
91. Ibid., p. 316.

3. THE COLOMBO CONFERENCE

1. PMML, JN, file 250, Note on Colombo (by V. K. Krishna Menon), undated (circa April 1954).
2. 'Premier's Vital Mission,' *Times of India*, 27 April 1954; NAUK, CO 936/347, BHC New Delhi to CRO, telegram 421, 27 April 1954.
3. See for instance 'Communism to Be Main Topic at Asian Talks,' *Times of India*, 19 March 1954; 'Future of H-Bomb Will Figure at Asian Premiers' Conference,' *Times of India*, 11 April 1954; 'Mr. Nehru to Propose Plan for Indo-China,' *Times of India*, 21 April 1954; 'Future of H-Bomb Will Figure at Asian Premiers' Conference,' *Times of India*, 11 April 1954.
4. 'Call off H-Bomb Experiments,' *Times of India*, 5 April 1954.
5. NAUK, CO 936/347, Extract from Telegram from UK High Commissioner in Ceylon to CRO, saving 41 part II, 19 March 1954; Extract from Ceylon fortnightly summary for the period 12 to 26 March 1954.
6. 'Non-Aggression Pact Between Asians,' *Times of India*, 12 April 1954.
7. See, for instance, NAUK, CO 936/347, Extract from telegram from UK High Commissioner in Ceylon to CRO, saving 41 part II, 19 March 1954; 'Communism to Be Main Topic at Asian Talks,' *Times of India*, 19 March 1954; 'Non-Aggression Pact Between Asians,' *Times of India*, 12 April 1954; 'Permanent Body to Deal With Asian Affairs,' *Times of India*, 17 April 1954.
8. 'Mr. Nehru to Propose Plan for Indo-China,' *Times of India*, 21 April 1954.
9. NAUK, DO 201/4, Extract from 'Ceylon Observer,' 25 October 1953 and N. E. Costar (BHC Colombo) to Captain Crookshank, telegram 70, 31 October 1953; see also CO 936/347, Cecil Syers (British High Commissioner to Ceylon) to CRO, 23 June 1954; Cindy Ewing, 'The Colombo Powers: Crafting Diplomacy in the Third World and Launching Afro-Asia at Bandung,' *Cold War History*, 19:1 (2019), p. 6.
10. *SWJN*, Second Series [henceforth II], Volume 24 (New Delhi: Jawaharlal Nehru Memorial Fund, 1984–2015), p. 443, fn. 2. On Kotelawala's role in organising the Colombo summit, see Ewin, 'Colombo Powers,' pp. 6–7.

11. NAA, A5954, 1412/2, Australian Embassy Jakarta to ADEA, cablegram 13, 13 January 1954; NAUK, DO 201/4, Costar to Crookshank, telegram 70, 31 October 1953.
12. NAUK, DO 201/4, Costar to Crookshank, telegram 70, 31 October 1953; Ewing, 'Colombo Powers,' p. 6.
13. NAUK, DO 201/4, Costar to Crookshank, telegram 70, 31 October 1953; FO 371/111930, D2231/39, Syers to Viscount Swinton (British Secretary of State for Commonwealth Relations), telegram 35, 2 June 1954.
14. NAA, A5954, 1412/2, 'A proposed conference of Asian Prime Ministers,' Colombo Ministerial Despatch 1, 13 January 1954.
15. *SWJN*, II/24, pp. 443–44.
16. NAA, A5954, 1412/2, 'A proposed conference of Asian Prime Ministers,' Colombo Ministerial Despatch 1, 13 January 1954; A5954, 1412/2, Australian Embassy Jakarta to ADEA, cablegram 13, 13 January 1954.
17. NAUK, DO 35/6096, BHC New Delhi to CRO, telegram 445, 6 May 1954; CO 936/347, Extract from telegram from acting British High Commissioner in Ceylon to CRO, saving 7, 23 January 1954.
18. NAA, A5954, 1412/2, 'A proposed conference of Asian Prime Ministers,' Colombo ministerial despatch 1, 13 January 1954.
19. Ibid.
20. NAA, A5954, 1412/2, AHC New Delhi to ADEA, cablegram 90, 14 April 1954; NAUK, CO 936/347, BHC New Delhi to CRO, telegram 346, 14 April 1954. The conference's agenda was agreed in the opening session on the morning of 28 April.
21. NAA, A5954, 1412/2, AHC New Delhi to ADEA, cablegram 90, 14 April 1954.
22. D. R. SarDesai, *Indian Foreign Policy in Cambodia, Laos and Vietnam, 1947–1964* (Berkeley and Los Angeles, CA: University of California Press, 1968), p. 40.
23. Ewing, 'Colombo Powers,' p. 7.
24. NAUK, FO 371/111930, D2231/39, Syers to Viscount Swinton, telegram 35, 2 June 1954.
25. The US ambassador in Ceylon (Crowe) to Department of State, telegram 540, 6 May 1954, doc. 627, *FRUS, Africa and South Asia, Volume XI Part 2* (Washington, DC: GPO, 1983), https://history.state.gov/historicaldocuments/frus1952-54v11p2/d627, accessed 15 November 2019.
26. NAUK, DO 35/6096, BHC New Delhi to CRO, telegram 445, 6 May 1954; NAA, A5954, 1412/2, Memcon, C. Lee (Australian Embassy Jakarta) and Max Maramis (Special Advisor to the Indonesian Prime Minister and Foreign Minister), 11 May 1954.
27. Ewing, 'Colombo Powers,' p. 8.
28. NAUK, DO 35/6096, BHC New Delhi to CRO, telegram 445, 6 May 1954.
29. PMML, JN, file 250, APM (54) 2nd meeting, 28 April 1954, 2:30 p.m.; The US ambassador in Ceylon (Crowe) to Department of State, telegram 540, 6 May 1954, doc. 627, *FRUS, 1952–1954, XI/2,* https://history.state.gov/historicaldocuments/frus1952-54v11p2/d627, accessed 15 November 2019. For Nehru's original six-point proposal, see LSD, Session VI, 24 April 1954, cols.

5581–82 available at https://eparlib.nic.in/bitstream/123456789/55922/1/lsd_01_06_24-04-1954.pdf#search=null%20[1952%20TO%201959]%20 1954, accessed 5 May 2019. For the six-point plan he had outlined to the Lok Sabha on 24 April, see Chapter 2.

30. NAA, A5954, 1412/2, AHC Colombo to ADEA, cablegram 104, 29 April 1954.
31. PMML, JN, file 250, APM (54) 2nd meeting, 28 April 1954, 2:30 p.m. and APM (54) 3rd meeting, 29 April 1954, 10 a.m.; NAUK, FO 371/111930, D2231/43, APM (54) 7th meeting, 1 May 1954, 5:15 p.m.; DO 35/6096, BHC New Delhi to CRO, telegram 445, 6 May 1954; FO 371/111930, D2231/39, Syers to Viscount Swinton, telegram 35, 2 June 1954; CO 936/347, BHC Colombo to CRO, telegram 153, 3 May 1954.
32. NAUK, CO 936/347, BHC Colombo to CRO, telegram 149, 1 May 1954.
33. NAUK, FO 371/111930, D2231/39, Syers to Viscount Swinton, telegram 35, 2 June 1954.
34. NAUK, FO 371/111930, D2231/43, APM (54) 7th meeting, 1 May 1954, 5:15 p.m.; FO 371/111930, D2231/43, Final Communiqué issued by the Right Honourable Sir John Kotelawala, Chairman, Conference of South-East Asian Prime Ministers, 2 May 1954.
35. NAUK, FO 371/111930, D2231/43, Final Communiqué issued by the Right Honourable Sir John Kotelawala, Chairman, Conference of South-East Asian Prime Ministers, 2 May 1954.
36. PMML, JN, file 250, APM (54) 2nd meeting, 28 April 1954, 2:30 p.m.
37. NAUK, DO 35/6096, BHC New Delhi to CRO, telegram 445, 6 May 1954; NAA, A5954, 1412/2, Walter Crocker (Australian High Commissioner to India) to Richard Casey (Australian Minister of External Affairs), despatch 9, 9 May 1954.
38. PMML, JN, file 250, APM (54) 1st meeting, 28 April 1954, 10 a.m.
39. Ibid.
40. NAUK, DO 35/6096, BHC New Delhi to CRO, telegram 445, 6 May 1954.
41. NAUK, FO 371/111930, D2231/35, BHC Karachi to CRO, telegram 605, 5 May 1954; PMML, JN, file 250, APM (54) 4th meeting, 29 April 1954, 3:30 p.m.
42. NAUK, DO 35/6096, BHC New Delhi to CRO, telegram 445, 6 May 1954; PMML, JN, file 250, APM (54) 1st meeting, 28 April 1954, 10 a.m.
43. NAA, A5954, 1412/2, J. C. G. Kevin (Australian Minister and Chargé d'Affaires to Indonesia) to Casey, ministerial despatch 9/1954, 14 May 1954.
44. PMML, JN, file 250, APM (54) 4th meeting, 29 April 1954, 3:30 p.m.
45. NAA, A5954, 1412/2, AHC Colombo to ADEA, cablegram 99, 24 April 1954.
46. Ibid.
47. NAUK, FO 371/116987, D2232/3, 'Asian Conferences 1947–1955,' FO draft paper, 2 December 1955; NAA, A5954, 1412/2, Memcon, Lee and Maramis, 11 May 1954.
48. PMML, JN, file 250, APM (54) 4th meeting, 29 April 1954, 3:30 p.m.
49. NAA, A5954, 1412/2, Memcon, Lee and Maramis, 11 May 1954.

50. PMML, JN, file 250, APM (54) 4th meeting, 29 April 1954, 3:30 p.m. and NAUK, FO 371/111930, D2231/43, APM (54) 5th meeting, 30 April 1954, 10 a.m.; FO 371/111930, D2231/39, Syers to Viscount Swinton, telegram 35, 2 June 1954.
51. See Announcement regarding Signing of the Agreement on Tibet, 29 April 1954, doc. 0673, Avtar Singh Bhasin (ed.), *India-China Relations 1947–2000: A Documentary Study, Volume 2* (New Delhi: Geetika Publishers, 2018).
52. NAUK, FO 371/111930, D2231/43, APM (54) 7th meeting, 1 May 1954, 5:15 p.m.; FO 371/111930, D2231/43, Final Communiqué issued by the Right Honourable Sir John Kotelawala, Chairman, Conference of South-East Asian Prime Ministers, 2 May 1954.
53. NAUK, FO 371/111930, D2231/43, Final Communiqué issued by the Right Honourable Sir John Kotelawala, Chairman, Conference of South-East Asian Prime Ministers, 2 May 1954.
54. PMML, JN, file 250, APM (54) 3rd meeting, 29 April 1954, 10 a.m.; APM (54) 4th meeting, 29 April 1954, 3:00 p.m.; NAUK, FO 371/111930, D2231/43, APM (54) 6th meeting, 30 April 1954, 3:00 p.m.; NAUK, FO 371/111930, D2231/43, Final Communiqué issued by the Right Honourable Sir John Kotelawala, Chairman, Conference of South-East Asian Prime Ministers, 2 May 1954. On the Indonesian and Burmese proposals on economic cooperation, see NAUK, FO 371/111930, D2231/43, South-East Asian Prime Minister's Conference, April 1954. Draft Proposals APM (54) 6(1) and APM (54) 6(2).
55. PMML, JN, file 250, APM (54) 1st meeting, 28 April 1954, 10:00 a.m. See also NAUK, FO 371/111930, D2231/43, South-East Asian Prime Minister's Conference. Appendix 1: Opening Addresses; C. L. M. Penders (ed.), *Milestones on My Journey: The Memoirs of Ali Sastroamijoyo, Indonesian Patriot and Leader* (St. Lucia, Australia: University of Queensland Press, 1979), p. 275.
56. NAUK, FO 371/111930, D2231/43, APM (54) 6th meeting, 30 April 1954, 3:00 p.m.
57. Ibid. By Vietnam, Nehru meant the Associated State of Vietnam, and by the Viet Minh, the Democratic Republic of Vietnam.
58. Ibid.
59. *SWJN*, II/24, pp. 553–4.
60. Ibid.
61. Lorenz Lüthi, *Cold Wars: Asia, the Middle East, Europe* (Cambridge, UK: Cambridge University Press, 2020), Kindle edition, ch. 11; NAUK, FO 371/116987, D2232/3, 'Asian conferences 1947–1955,' FO draft paper, 2 December 1955. Predominantly Asian (Afghanistan, Burma, Ceylon, India, Pakistan, the Philippines and Iran), the conference's membership also included Australia and a few Arab and African nations (Egypt, Saudi Arabia, Lebanon, Iraq, Syria, Yemen and Ethiopia). Chiang Kai-shek's Republic of China (ROC), as well as Nepal, New Zealand and Thailand sent observers.
62. Lüthi, *Cold Wars*, ch. 11.
63. Ibid. In fact, Pakistan was working to create a different kind of organisation, the Muslim World Congress.

64. NAUK, FO 371/116987, D2232/3, 'Asian conferences 1947–1955,' FO draft paper, 2 December 1955; Lüthi, *Cold Wars*, ch. 11; Cindy Ewing, '"With a Minimum of Bitterness": Decolonization, the Right to Self-Determination, and the Arab-Asian Group,' *Journal of Global History*, 17:2 (2022), p. 256.
65. Lüthi, *Cold Wars*, ch. 11. The seven Arab League nations were Egypt, Transjordan, Iraq, Lebanon, Saudi Arabia, Syria and Yemen, while the six Asian countries were Afghanistan, Burma, India, Indonesia, Pakistan and the Philippines.
66. Ibid. PMML, JN, file 249, 'Other proposals probably from Indonesia,' note by V. K. Krishna Menon, undated (circa April 1954). On the group's achievements, see Ewing, '"With a Minimum of Bitterness,"' pp. 254–71.
67. PMML, JN, file 249, 'Other proposals probably from Indonesia,' note by V. K. Krishna Menon, undated (circa April 1954).
68. Ibid. For a more positive assessment of the Arab-Asian group's achievements at the UN, see Ewing, '"With a Minimum of Bitterness,"' pp. 254–71.
69. *SWJN*, II/24, pp. 553–4.
70. PMML, JN, file 249, 'Other proposals From Indonesia,' note by V. K. Krishna Menon, undated (circa April 1954).
71. PMML, JN, file 250, Note on Colombo (by V. K. Krishna Menon), undated (circa April 1954).
72. NAUK, FO 371/111930, D2231/43, APM (54) 6th meeting, 30 April 1954, 3:00 p.m.
73. Penders, *Milestones*, p. 277.
74. Ibid., p. 278.
75. G. H. Jansen, *Afro-Asia and Non-Alignment* (London: Faber and Faber, 1966), pp. 161–64.
76. NAUK, FO 371/111930, D2231/43, APM (54) 6th meeting, 30 April 1954, 3:00 p.m.
77. At the very end of the conference, Nehru told the other four leaders that he 'looked forward to the Afro-Asian Conference envisaged by Indonesia.' He 'was sure,' he said, that it 'would open up vistas of fruitful co-operation between the countries of Asia and Africa.' See NAUK, FO 371/111930, D2231/43, APM (54) 7th meeting, 1 May 1954. However, speaking to the Indian ambassador in Jakarta, Nehru sounded a much more cautious note. He told B. F. H. B. Tyabji that '[o]ur first instinct is, of course, to accept this proposal, but the more we discuss it, the more different it appears. Even with the five P.M.s here there were difficulties enough. If there is a crowd, it may well happen that nothing effective may be done by the [Afro-Asian] Conference.' See PMML, JN, file 251 part 1, Nehru to B. F. H. B. Tyabji (Indian High Commissioner to Indonesia), 2 May 1955.
78. NAA, A5954, 1412/2, AHC New Delhi to ADEA, cablegram 90, 14 April 1954.
79. NAUK, FO 371/111930, D2231/43, Final Communiqué issued by the Right Honourable Sir John Kotelawala, Chairman, Conference of South-East Asian Prime Ministers, 2 May 1954.
80. NAUK, CO 936/347, Syers to CRO, 23 June 1954.

81. Chinese Foreign Ministry Intelligence Department Report of the Asian-African Conference, 4 September 1954, WCDA, https://digitalarchive.wilsoncenter.org/document/112440, accessed 10 October 2019.
82. NAUK, CO 936/347, BHC New Delhi to CRO, telegram 444, 6 May 1954.
83. NAUK, FO 371/111930, D2231/43, APM (54) 7th meeting, 1 May 1954, 5:15 p.m.
84. Ibid.
85. Nehru cited in Ewing, 'Colombo Powers,' p. 10.
86. NAA, A5954, 1412/2, Crocker to Casey, despatch 9, 9 May 1954.
87. Ewing, 'Colombo Powers,' p. 10.
88. NAUK, CO 936/347, Syers to CRO, 23 June 1954; The Ambassador in Ceylon (Crowe) to Department of State, telegram 540, 6 May 1954, doc. 627, *FRUS, 1952–1954, XI/2,* https://history.state.gov/historicaldocuments/frus1952-54v11p2/d627, accessed 15 November 2019; Jansen, *Afro-Asia*, pp. 148 and 150. For a divergent view, see M. S. Rajan, *India in World Affairs, 1954–56* (London: Asia Publishing House, 1964, pp. 197–8.
89. NAA, A5954, 1412/2, Crocker to Casey, despatch 9, 9 May 1954.
90. NAA, A5954, 1412/2, Memcon, Lee and Maramis, 11 May 1954. On Kotelawala's demeanour, see NAUK, CO 936/347, Extract from Acting UK High Commissioner in Ceylon to S/S CRO, saving 20, 11 March 1954.
91. NAA, A5954, 1412/2, Memcon, Lee and Maramis, 11 May 1954; A5954, 1412/2, Kevin to Casey, ministerial despatch 9/1954, 14 May 1954.
92. NAA, A5954, 1412/2, Crocker to Casey, despatch 9, 9 May 1954.
93. NAUK, DO 35/6096, BHC New Delhi to CRO, telegram 445, 6 May 1954.
94. NAA, A5954, 1412/2, Crocker to Casey, despatch 9, 9 May 1954.
95. Ibid.
96. NAUK, DO 35/6096, BHC New Delhi to CRO, telegram 445, 6 May 1954; NAA, A5954, 1412/2, Crocker to Casey, despatch 9, 9 May 1954.
97. NAA, A5954, 1412/2, Cutler (Colombo) to Casey, cablegram 107, 30 April 1954.
98. Jansen, *Afro-Asia*, pp. 148 and 151–6; NAUK, CO 936/347, BHC Colombo to CRO, telegram 143, 29 April 1954; Syers to CRO, 23 June 1954.
99. Marek W. Rutkowski, 'Expanding the Area of Peace: India, Colombo Powers and the Geneva Conference of 1954,' in Brian P. Farrell, S. R. Joey Long and David J. Ulbrich (eds), *From Far East to Asia Pacific: Great Powers and Grand Strategy 1900–1954* (Berlin: De Gruyter Oldenbourg, 2022), p. 349.
100. Ibid., p. 350. With regard to India exploiting the Colombo Conference, see Francine Frankel, *When Nehru Looked East: Origins of India-US Suspicion and India-China Rivalry* (Oxford: Oxford University Press, 2020), Kindle edition, ch. 6.
101. Eden cited in Rutkowski, 'Expanding the Area of Peace,' p. 350. Nehru responded positively, stating that 'within the limits of [India's] policy of non-alignment and [its] resources,' India would be prepared to 'assist in promoting and maintaining a settlement in Indo-China.' See *SWJN*, II/25, p. 436.
102. The US ambassador in Ceylon (Crowe) to Department of State, telegram 540, 6 May 1954, doc. 627, *FRUS, 1952–1954, XI/2*, https://history.state.gov/

historicaldocuments/frus1952-54v11p2/d627, accessed 15 November 2019; see also NAA, A5954, 1412/2, Crocker to Casey, despatch 9, 9 May 1954.

103. The US ambassador in Ceylon (Crowe) to Department of State, telegram 540, 6 May 1954, doc. 627, *FRUS, 1952–1954, XI/2*, https://history.state.gov/historicaldocuments/frus1952-54v11p2/d627, accessed 15 November 2019.
104. Rutkowski, 'Expanding the Area of Peace,' p. 349.
105. PMML, JN, file 251 part 2, Colombo Conference, Draft Report by the Prime Minister to Cabinet, 5 May 1954.
106. NAA, A5954, 1412/2, Memcon, Lee and Maramis, 11 May 1954.
107. NAA, A5954, 1412/2, Crocker to Casey, despatch 9, 9 May 1954.
108. Ibid.
109. NAA, A5954, 1412/2, Kevin to Casey, ministerial despatch 9/1954, 14 May 1954.
110. NAA, A5954, 1412/2, Memcon, Lee and Maramis, 11 May 1954. Nor did they succeed in getting the question of West New Guinea included in the final communiqué.
111. Ewing, 'Colombo Powers,' 11; Rutkowski, 'Expanding the Area of Peace,' p. 355.
112. Jairam Ramesh, *A Chequered Brilliance: The Many Lives of V. K. Krishna Menon* (New Delhi: Penguin Random House India, 2019), Kindle edition, ch. 13.
113. *Jawaharlal Nehru's Speeches, Volume 3, March 1953–August 1957* (New Delhi: Government of India, 1970), pp. 251–53. For the genesis of the Sino-Indian agreement on Tibet, see Chapter 1 in this book.
114. The agreement contemplated, among other things, the removal of a small Indian military contingent and the transfer to China of the Indian government-owned rest-houses and post and telegraph installations that the government of British India had operated since 1904. See Lorenz M. Lüthi, 'Sino-Indian Relations, 1954–1962,' *Eurasia Border Review*, 3 (2012), pp. 96–7; Rajan, *India in World Affairs*, p. 218; K. Gupta, 'Sino-Indian Agreement on Tibetan Trade and Intercourse: Its Origin and Significance,' *Economic and Political Weekly*, 13:16 (1978), p. 701; Avtar Singh Bhasin, *Nehru, Tibet and China* (New Delhi: India Viking, 2021), Kindle edition, ch. 7; Bertil Lintner, *China's India War: Collision Course on the Roof of the World* (New Delhi: Oxford University Press, 2018), Kindle edition, ch. 1. For the full text of the agreement, see PMML, JN, file 250, Agreement between the Republic of India and the People's Republic of China on Trade and Intercourse Between the Tibet Region of China and India, 26 April 1954.
115. *Jawaharlal Nehru's Speeches, Volume 3*, pp. 251–3.

4. THE NEHRU-ZHOU ENLAI TALKS

1. Nehru to N. Raghavan, 29 June 1954, document 0716, Avtar Singh Bhasin (ed.), *India-China Relations 1947–2000: A Documentary Study, Volume 2* (New Delhi: Geetika Publishers, 2018).
2. Indembassy Peking to Foreign New Delhi, telegram 227, 23 June 1954, document 0703, ibid.
3. Indembassy Peking to Foreign New Delhi, telegram 24245, 21 June 1954, document 0701, ibid.

4. NAUK, FO 371/112210, DL10310/8, G. H. Middleton (British Deputy High Commissioner to India) to CRO, despatch 56, 1 July 1954; L10310/6, Press Round-Up on Mr Chou En-Lai's Visit, 30 June 1954; NAA, A1209, 5454, Walter Crocker (Australian High Commissioner to India) to Richard Casey (Australian Minister of External Affairs), despatch 12, 30 June 1954; *SWJN*, II, Volume 25 (New Delhi: Jawaharlal Nehru Memorial Fund, 1984–2015), p. 470; NAA, A1838, 3017/40/147 part 2, AHC New Delhi to ADEA, cablegram 135, 22 June 1954.
5. NAUK, FO 371/112210, DL10310/8, Middleton to CRO, despatch 56, 1 July 1954.
6. PRC FMA 203-00005-01, 3–4, Premier's Intentions and Plans to Visit India, 22 June 1954, WCDA, http://digitalarchive.wilsoncenter.org/document/112437, accessed 10 October 2018.
7. PRC FMA, 203-00005-06, 58–60, Opinion About Concluding a Mutual Non-Aggression Treaty with Southeast Asian States, June 17 1954, cited in Tao Wang, *Isolating the Enemy: Diplomatic Strategy in China and the United States, 1953–1956* (New York: Columbia University Press, 2021), Kindle edition, ch. 5.
8. L. P. Singh, 'Dynamics of Indian-Indonesian Relations,' *Asian Survey*, 7:9 (1967), p. 656.
9. PRC FMA, 203-00005-06, 58–60, Opinion About Concluding a Mutual Non-Aggression Treaty With Southeast Asian States, June 17 1954, cited in Wang, *Isolating the Enemy*.
10. PRC FMA 203-00005-01, 3–4, Premier's Intentions and Plans to Visit India, 22 June 1954, WCDA, http://digitalarchive.wilsoncenter.org/document/112437, accessed 5 October 2018.
11. NAA, A1209, 5454, Crocker to Casey, despatch 12, 30 June 1954.
12. PMML, JN, 281 part I, Foreign New Delhi to Indembassy Jakarta, telegram 27086, 19 August 1954.
13. National Archives and Records Administration, College Park, RG59, Central Decimal Files 1950–54, box 2668, 670.901/2-555, State Department to American Embassy Jakarta, telegram A-145, 11 March 1955; Bertil Lintner, *China's India War: Collision Course on the Roof of the World* (New Delhi: Oxford University Press, 2018), Kindle edition, ch. 1.
14. Avtar Sigh Bhasin, *Nehru, Tibet and China* (New Delhi: Penguin, 2021), Kindle edition, ch. 3.
15. Bashin, *India-China Relations, Volume 2*, footnote to doc. 0700, p. 1168.
16. NAUK, FO 371/ 112210, DL10310/8, Middleton to CRO, despatch 56, 1 July 1954; NAA, A4231, 1954/New Delhi, Crocker to Casey, despatch 12, 30 June 1954; 'Chou En-Lai in Delhi for Talks with Nehru,' *Canberra Times*, 26 June 1954; 'Indians Cheer, Fete Chinese President,' *Daily Telegraph*, 26 June 1954.
17. 'Early Cease-Fire in Indo-China Looms Large in Delhi Parleys,' *Times of India*, 26 June 1954.
18. 'Indians Cheer, Fete Chinese President,' *Daily Telegraph*, 26 June 1954.
19. 'Early Cease-Fire in Indo-China Looms Large in Delhi Parleys,' *Times of India*, 26 June 1954.

20. 'Indians Cheer, Fete Chinese President,' *Daily Telegraph*, 26 June 1954.
21. Ibid.; NAA, A1838, 3017/40/147 part 2, Survey of China Mainland Press, American Consulate General Hong Kong, 26–28 June 1954; 'Rousing Reception to Mr. Chou Planned,' *Times of India*, 25 June 1954; François, Joyaux, *La Chine et le Règlement du Premier Conflit d'Indochine: Genève 1954* (Paris: Publications de la Sorbonne, 1979), Kobo edition, ch. 8.
22. Joyaux, *La Chine et le Règlement du Premier Conflit d'Indochine*, ch. 8.
23. 'Civic Reception to Chou at Red Fort,' *Hindustan Times*, 28 June 1954.
24. NAA, A4231, 1954/New Delhi, Crocker to Casey, despatch 12, 30 June 1954.
25. NAUK, FO 371/ 1122010, DL10310/8, Middleton to CRO, despatch 56, 1 July 1954.
26. NAA, A4231, 1954/New Delhi, Crocker to Casey, despatch 12, 30 June 1954.
27. Ibid.
28. NAUK, FO 371/112210, DL10310/8, Middleton to CRO, despatch 56, 1 July 1954.
29. Ibid.
30. Gregg Brazinsky, *Winning the Third World: Sino-American Rivalry During the Cold War* (Chapel Hill, NC: University of North Carolina Press, 2017), p. 78.
31. *SWJN*, II/25, pp. 467–8.
32. Xiaoyuan Liu, 'Friend or Foe: India as Perceived by Beijing's Foreign Policy Analysts in the 1950s,' *China Review*, 15:1 (2015), pp. 121–2. See also this book's Introduction.
33. Humphrey Trevelyan, *Worlds Apart: My Experiences in China (1953–5) and the Soviet Union (1962–5)* (n. p.: Lume Books, 2019), Kindle edition, ch. 5.
34. Brazinsky, *Third World*, p. 78; see also Anton Harder, 'Defining Independence in Cold War Asia: Sino-Indian Relations, 1949–1962' (PhD thesis, London School of Economics, 2015), p. 129.
35. Nicholas Tarling, *Britain and the Neutralisation of Laos* (Singapore: National University of Singapore Press, 2011), p. 16.
36. Brazinsky, *Third World*, p. 78.
37. Trevelyan, *Worlds Apart*, ch. 5.
38. Tarling, *Britain and the Neutralisation of Laos*, p. 16.
39. Liu, 'Friend or Foe,' p. 118.
40. Lorenz M. Lüthi, 'Sino-Indian Relations, 1954–1962,' *Eurasia Border Review*, 3 (2012), p. 96.
41. Liu, 'Friend or Foe,' p. 118.
42. Lüthi, 'Sino-Indian Relations, 1954–1962,' p. 96.
43. NAUK, FO 371/112210, DL10310/8, Middleton to CRO, despatch 56, 1 July 1954.
44. PMML, JN, file 264 part 1, Record of Conversation Between Zhou Enlai and Jawaharlal Nehru. First session, 3:30 p.m. to 6:15 p.m., 25 June 1954.
45. *SWJN*, II/25, p. 470.
46. PMML, JN, file 264 part 1, Record of Conversation Between Zhou Enlai and Jawaharlal Nehru. Second session, 10:00 p.m. to midnight, 25 June 1954.

47. NAA, A1838, 3107/40/147 part 2, Chou En-Lai's Visit to India, 26–28 June 1954.
48. Nehru tended to regard himself as 'a senior mentor to other Third World leaders.' See Judith M. Brown, 'Jawaharlal Nehru,' in Steven Casey and Jonathan Wright (eds), *Mental Maps in the Early Cold War Era, 1945–68* (London: Palgrave Macmillan, 2011), p. 210.
49. PMML, JN, file 264 part 1, Record of Conversation Between Zhou Enlai and Jawaharlal Nehru. Third session, 10:45 a.m. to 12:15 p.m., 26 June 1954.
50. PMML, JN, file 264 part 1, Record of Conversation Between Zhou Enlai and Jawaharlal Nehru. Fourth session, 3:00 p.m. to 5:00 p.m., 26 June 1954.
51. PMML, JN, file 264 part 1, Record of Conversation Between Zhou Enlai and Jawaharlal Nehru. Fifth session, 3:00 p.m. to 5:15 p.m., 27 June 1954.
52. Ibid.
53. PMML, JN, file 264 part 1, Record of Conversation Between Zhou Enlai and Jawaharlal Nehru. Second session, 10:00 p.m. to midnight, 25 June 1954; fourth session, 3:00 p.m. to 5:00 p.m., 26 June 1954.
54. PMML, JN, file 264 part 1, Record of Conversation Between Zhou Enlai and Jawaharlal Nehru. Fifth session, 3:00 p.m. to 5:15 p.m., 27 June 1954. On 23 June, British Foreign Secretary Anthony Eden publicly proposed a Locarno-type arrangement committing its participating countries to take action against any violation of a future Indochina settlement. It was to be jointly underwritten by both Western and communist powers, as well as Asian neutrals. Its aim was to guarantee the terms of the Indochina settlement that would result from the Geneva Conference. See e.g. '"Locarno Pact" for S.-E. Asia Proposed by Eden,' *Sydney Morning Herald*, 24 June 1954; see also Marek W. Rutkowski, 'Expanding the Area of Peace: India, Colombo Powers and the Geneva Conference of 1954,' in Brian P. Farrell, S. R. Joey Long and David J. Ulbrich (eds), *From Far East to Asia Pacific: Great Powers and Grand Strategy 1900–1954* (Berlin: De Gruyter Oldenbourg, 2022), p. 352; Kevin Ruane and Matthew Jones, *Anthony Eden, Anglo-American Relations and the 1954 Indochina Crisis* (London: Bloomsbury Academic, 2019), pp. 197–8. By Locarno, Eden referred to the Locarno Pact of 1925, which, among other things, included undertakings by Germany, France and Belgium not to resort to war and respect their common borders. At the same time, Britain and Italy agreed to guarantee these undertakings by pledging to assist in the event of a violation of the foregoing obligations. See Henry Kissinger, *Diplomacy* (New York: Touchstone, 1994), p. 274.
55. PMML, JN, file 264 part 1, Record of Conversation Between Zhou Enlai and Jawaharlal Nehru. Fifth session, 3:00 p.m. to 5:15 p.m., 27 June 1954.
56. PRC FMA 105-00042-03, 78–79, Zhou Enlai's Conversations With the Ambassadors of India, Indonesia, and Burma, 10 July 1954, WCDA, http://digitalarchive.wilsoncenter.org/document/112439, accessed 20 October 2018.
57. NAUK, FO 371/110251, FC1072/4, Humphrey Trevelyan (Chargés d'Affaires to China) to Foreign Office, telegram 722, 13 September 1954 and Trevelyan to W. D. Allen (FO), 23 September 1954.
58. NAUK, FO 371/110251, FC1072/4, Trevelyan to Allen, 23 September 1954.

59. NAA, A1838, 3006/9/5, Australian Legation Rangoon to ADEA, cablegram 187, 20 October 1954.
60. NAA, A1838, 3002/1 part 1, Australian Embassy Jakarta to ADEA, savingram 33, 4 October 1954.
61. NAUK, FO 371/ 112210, DL10310/8, Middleton to CRO, despatch 56, 1 July 1954.
62. NAUK, FO 371/110226, FC10385/5, Replies given by Mr Chou En-lai at a Press Conference on 27 June 1954.
63. NAUK, FO 371/ 112210, DL10310/8, Middleton to CRO, despatch 56, 1 July 1954.
64. Raghavan to Nehru, telegram 241, 1 July 1954, doc. 0718 and Raghavan to Nehru, telegram 252, 8 July 1954, doc. 0722, Bhasin, *India-China Relations, vol. 2;* Reception of Chinese ambassador to the Soviet Union Zhang Wentian, 1 July 1954,' 1 July 1954, WCDA, http://digitalarchive.wilsoncenter.org/document/111362, accessed 10 October 2018.
65. NAUK, FO 371/112210, DL10310/8, Statement by Chou En-Lai, Premier of the People's Republic of China Upon Departure from Delhi, 28 June 1954.
66. Nehru to Raghavan, 29 June 1954, doc. 0716, Bhasin, *India-China Relations, Volume 2*.
67. NAUK, FO 371/112210, DL10310/4, BHC New Delhi to CRO, telegram 619, 28 June 1954.
68. The US ambassador in India (Allen) to the Department of State, 17 July 1954, doc. 233, *FRUS*, *1952–1954, China and Japan, Volume XIV, part I* (Washington, DC: GPO, 1985), https://history.state.gov/historicaldocuments/frus1952-54v14p1/d233, accessed 1 November 2018.
69. NAUK, FO 371/112210, DL 10310/8, Joint Statement of Prime Ministers of India and China, 28 June 1954.

5. ENTRENCHING PEACEFUL COEXISTENCE

1. Chester Bowles, 'A Fresh Look at Free Asia,' *Foreign Affairs*, 1 October 1954, https://www.foreignaffairs.com/articles/asia/1954-10-01/fresh-look-free-asia, accessed 15 April 2021.
2. 'Mr Chou arrives in Rangoon,' *Times of India*, 29 June 1954.
3. Ibid.; NAUK, DO 35/5945, Paul Gore-Booth (British Ambassador to Burma) to FO, despatch 145, 7 July 1954.
4. Burma announced its decision to recognise China on 16 December 1949, 2 weeks ahead of India. The latter, however, formally established diplomatic relations in April 1950, nearly 2 months ahead of Burma. See NAUK, FO 371/110251, FC1072/3, FO to British Embassy Beijing, 5 October 1954; Liang Zhi, 'Heading Toward Peaceful Coexistence: The Effects of the Improvement in Sino-Burmese Relations from 1953 to 1955,' *Asian Perspective*, 42 (2018), p. 529.
5. Tao Wang, *Isolating the Enemy: Diplomatic Strategy in China and the United States, 1953–1956* (New York: Columbia University Press, 2021), Kindle edition, ch. 5.

6. Zhi, 'Heading Toward Peaceful Coexistence,' p. 529; Ralph Pettman, *China in Burma's Foreign Policy* (Canberra, Australia: Australian National University Press, 1973), pp. 5–8; Shen-Yu Dai, 'Peking and Rangoon,' *China Quarterly*, 5 (1961), p. 131–4.
7. Liang Zhi, 'Rethinking Sino-Burmese Relations, 1949–1954,' *Social Sciences in China*, 39:2 (2018), pp. 155, 157 and 165; Zhi, 'Heading Toward Peaceful Coexistence,' pp. 532–3. For Burma's friendly attitude to the West, see Peter Lowe, *Contending With Nationalism and Communism: British Policy Towards Southeast Asia, 1945–65* (London: Palgrave, 2009), pp. 98–9. See also Nabarun Roy, 'Assuaging Cold War Anxieties: India and the Failure of SEATO,' *Diplomacy & Statecraft*, 26:2 (2015), pp. 327–30.
8. Zhi, 'Rethinking Sino-Burmese Relations, 1949–1954,' p. 158.
9. In 1953–54, 7,000 of them were repatriated to Taiwan, whilst another 3,000 men were resettled in Thailand following an agreement between the United States and its two Asian allies. In 1956, 3,000 Chinese nationalist irregulars were estimated to be still in the country. See National Intelligence Estimate (NIE) 61-56, Probable Developments in Burma, 10 April 1956, CIA Historical Collections, https://www.cia.gov/readingroom/document/cia-rdp79r01012a008000030001-1, accessed 5 April 2020; Pettman, *China in Burma's Foreign Policy*, p. 11. For somewhat slightly different figures, see NAA, A1838, TS383/2/1 part 1, T. K. Critchley (Australian Commission for Malaya, Singapore) to Alan Watt (Secretary, ADEA), memo 694, 11 September 1951; A1838, TS383/2/1 part 1, Political Appreciation – Burma, Annexure C to Appendix A, Revised JIC Appreciation 6/1949, April 1952. For the question of KMT troops in Burma, see also Keynton Clymer, 'The United States and the Guomindang (KMT) Forces in Burma, 1949–1954: A Diplomatic Disaster,' *The Chinese Historical Review*, 21:1 (2014), pp. 24–44.
10. Jovan Čavoški, 'Arming Nonalignment: Yugoslavia's Relations With Burma and the Cold War in Asia (1950–1955),' *Cold War International History Project Working Paper 61*, April 2010, https://www.wilsoncenter.org/publication/arming-nonalignment-yugoslavias-relations-burma-and-the-cold-war-asia-1950-1955, 17–18, accessed 20 July 2020.
11. Ibid., p. 18; NIE-74, Probable Developments in Burma Through 1953, 20 February 1953, CIA Historical Collections, https://www.cia.gov/readingroom/docs/CIA-RDP79R01012A002500020001-3.pdf, accessed 5 April 2020.
12. The Burma-China Border, CIA/RR-GR-53, July 1954, CIA Historical Collections, https://www.cia.gov/readingroom/docs/CIA-RDP79-01009A000700010010-3.pdf, accessed 10 April 2020.
13. Ibid.; Chinese Communist Forces reportedly Enter Northeast Burma, 11 July 1953, CIA Historical Collections, https://www.cia.gov/readingroom/docs/CIA-RDP91T01172R000200320011-4.pdf, accessed 10 April 2020.
14. Chinese Communist Forces Reportedly Enter Northeast Burma, 11 July 1953, CIA Historical Collections, https://www.cia.gov/readingroom/docs/CIA-RDP91T01172R000200320011-4.pdf, accessed 10 April 2020; The Burma-China Border, CIA/RR-GR-53, July 1954, CIA Historical Collections, https://

www.cia.gov/readingroom/docs/CIA-RDP79-01009A000700010010-3.pdf, accessed 10 April 2020.

15. Current Intelligence Bulletin, 16 June 1954, CIA Historical Collections, https://www.cia.gov/readingroom/docs/CURRENT%20INTELLIGENCE%20BULL%5B15689558%5D.pdf, accessed 10 April 2020.
16. National Intelligence Estimate (NIE) 61-56, Probable Developments in Burma, 10 April 1956, https://www.cia.gov/readingroom/document/cia-rdp79r01012a008000030001-1, accessed 5 April 2020. For Burma's understrength army, see Jovan Čavoški, 'Arming Nonalignment,' p. 16.
17. François Joyaux, *La Chine et le Règlement du Premier Conflit d'Indochine: Genève 1954* (Paris: Publications de la Sorbonne, 1979), Kobo edition, ch. 8. In the mid-1950s, the British and Americans estimated the size of the Chinese community in Burma to be at 300,000, while the Burmese authorities placed it at half a million. See NAUK, FO 371/111963, DB1022/8, Roderick Serell (British Embassy Rangoon) to J. G. Tahourdin (FO), 28 April 1954; National Intelligence Estimate (NIE) 61-56, Probable Developments in Burma, 10 April 1956, CIA Historical Collections, https://www.cia.gov/readingroom/document/cia-rdp79r01012a008000030001-1, accessed 5 April 2020. According to American intelligence sources, communist rebels had not received significant help from Beijing. Kachin insurgents, however, had received guerrilla training in Yunnan. See NIE-74, Probable Developments in Burma Through 1953, 20 February 1953, CIA Historical Collections, https://www.cia.gov/readingroom/docs/CIA-RDP79R01012A002500020001-3.pdf, accessed 5 April 2020.
18. Tao, *Isolating the Enemy*. In general, South-East Asian nations followed the *jus soli* (citizenship by birthright), whereas China observed the *jus sanguinis* (citizenship by right of blood). As a result, a significant number of these ethnic Chinese had dual citizenship.
19. Wang, *Isolating the Enemy*, ch. 5.
20. Čavoški, 'Arming Nonalignment,' p. 16.
21. Zhi, 'Rethinking Sino-Burmese Relations,' pp. 161–5; NIE-74, Probable Developments in Burma Through 1953, 20 February 1953, CIA Historical Collections, https://www.cia.gov/readingroom/docs/CIA-RDP79R01012A002500020001-3.pdf, accessed 5 April 2020.
22. Zhi, 'Rethinking Sino-Burmese Relations,' p. 164; National Intelligence Estimate (NIE) 61-56, Probable Developments in Burma, 10 April 1956, CIA Historical Collections, https://www.cia.gov/readingroom/document/cia-rdp79r01012a008000030001-1, accessed 5 April 2020. Beginning in late 1954, Burma also negotiated a number of barter agreements with other communist countries, namely the Soviet Union, East Germany, Czechoslovakia, Poland and Hungary. By 1956, according to American intelligence sources, Burma's exports to communist countries were estimated to account for between a quarter to one-third of Burma's total exports.
23. Wang, *Isolating the Enemy*, ch. 5.
24. NAUK, FO 371/111963, DB1022/10, BHC New Delhi to CRO, telegram 451, 8 May 1954.

25. NAUK, FO 371/111963, DB1022/8, Serell to Tahourdin, 28 April 1954 and DB1022/10, BHC New Delhi to CRO, telegram 451, 8 May 1954.
26. NAUK, FO 371/111963, DB1022/12, Gore-Booth to FO, telegram 243, 12 May 1954.
27. Memorandum by the Assistant Secretary of State for Far Eastern Affairs (Robertson) to the Secretary of State, 28 June 1954, doc. 170, *FRUS*, *1952–1954, East Asia and the Pacific, Volume XII, part 2* (Washington, DC: GPO, 1987), https://history.state.gov/historicaldocuments/frus1952-54v12p2/d170, accessed 10 May 2020.
28. Nehru to Indian ambassador in Burma, K. K. Chettur, 9 May 1954, doc. 0686, Avtar Singh Bhasin (ed.), *India-China Relations 1947–2000: A Documentary Study, Volume 2* (New Delhi: Geetika Publishers, 2018). However, in a 2-hour-long conversation with the US ambassador on 1 June, U Nu had told William J. Sebald that he had no plans to align Burma with the West, arguing that neutrality remained 'the best course for Burma to follow in view of Burma's internal difficulties' and 'divisions of opinion within his own Cabinet.' See Memorandum by the Assistant Secretary of State for Far Eastern Affairs (Robertson) to the Secretary of State, 28 June 1954, doc. 170, *FRUS*, *1952–1954, XII/2*, https://history.state.gov/historicaldocuments/frus1952-54v12p2/d170, accessed 10 May 2020.
29. Nehru to Raghavan, 9 May 1954, doc. 0687, Bhasin, *India-China Relations, Volume 2*.
30. *SWJN*, II, Volume 26 (New Delhi: Jawaharlal Nehru Memorial Fund, 1984–2015), pp. 407–10.
31. National Archives and Records Administration, College Park, RG59, Central Decimal Files, box 2668, 670.901/2-555, State Department to US Embassy Jakarta, telegram A-145, 11 March 1955; 'U Nu, First Premier of Independent Burma and Democracy Advocate, Dies at 87,' *New York Times*, 15 February 1995.
32. U Nu and Zhou Enlai (first meeting), 28 June 1954, Wilson Center Digital Archive [henceforth WCDA], http://digitalarchive.wilsoncenter.org/document/112438, accessed 5 April 2020; see also Zhi, 'Heading Toward Peaceful Coexistence,' pp. 535–6; NAUK, DO 35/5945, Gore-Booth to FO, despatch 145, 7 July 1954.
33. U Nu and Zhou Enlai (first meeting), 28 June 1954, Wilson Center Digital Archive [henceforth WCDA], http://digitalarchive.wilsoncenter.org/document/112438, accessed 5 April 2020; see also Zhi, 'Heading Toward Peaceful Coexistence,' pp. 535–6; NAUK, DO 35/5945, Gore-Booth to FO, despatch 145, 7 July 1954.
34. U Nu and Zhou Enlai (second meeting), 29 June 1954, WCDA, http://digitalarchive.wilsoncenter.org/document/120364, accessed 5 April 2020; PRC FMA 105-00042-03, 78-79, Zhou Enlai's Conversations With the Ambassadors of India, Indonesia, and Burma, Cable From the Chinese Foreign Ministry, 10 July 1954, WCDA, http://digitalarchive.wilsoncenter.org/document/112439, accessed 5 April 2020; Current Intelligence Bulletin, 6 July 1954, CIA Historical Collections, https://www.cia.gov/readingroom/docs/

CURRENT%20INTELLIGENCE%20BULL%5B15706797%5D.pdf, accessed 10 April 2020.

35. NAUK, DO 35/5945, Gore-Booth to FO, despatch 145, 7 July 1954.
35. Joyaux, *La Chine et le Règlement du Premier Conflit d'Indochine.*
37. Zhi, 'Heading Toward Peaceful Coexistence,' p. 536.
38. Escott Reid, *Envoy to Nehru* (New Delhi: Oxford University Press, 1981), pp. 55–6.
39. NAUK, DO 35/5945, Gore-Booth to FO, despatch 145, 7 July 1954.
40. *SWJN*, II/26, p. 412, fn 2.
41. On India's relations with Burma, see Roy, 'Assuaging Cold War Anxieties,' pp. 327–32.
42. *SWJN*, II/26, p. 412.
43. "Significance of Talks with Chou En-lai: Nehru's letter to P.C.C. Presidents," Hindustan Times, 8 July 1954; see also NAUK, DO 35/5945, D. Cole (BHC New Delhi) to A. Golds (CRO), 8 July 1954.
44. 'Significance of Talks with Chou En-lai: Nehru's letter to P.C.C. Presidents,' *Hindustan Times*, 8 July 1954; see also NAUK, DO 35/5945, D. Cole (BHC New Delhi) to A. Golds (CRO), 8 July 1954.
45. NAUK, FO 371/112197, DL1022/18, Rajya Sabha: Prime Minister's Speech in Foreign Affairs Debate, 26 August 1954.
46. NAUK, FO 371/112197, DL1022/28, Escott Reid (Canadian High Commissioner to India) to Lester B. Pearson (Canadian Secretary of State for External Affairs), telegram 1134, 5 October 1954; LSD, Volume VII, part II, 29 September 1954, cols. 3672–97, https://eparlib.nic.in/bitstream/123456789/55720/1/lsd_01_07_29-09-1954.pdf, accessed on 5 March 2020.
47. Ibid., cols. 3691–3.
48. Ibid., col. 3686.
49. Ibid., cols. 3683–6.
50. Ibid., col. 3687.
51. Stephen P. Cohen, *India: Emerging Power* (Washington, DC: Brookings Institution Press, 2001), p. 130.
52. On this point, see also Rosemary Brissenden, 'India's Opposition to SEATO: A Case Study in Neutralist Diplomacy,' *Australian Journal of Politics and History*, 6:2 (1960), pp. 228–9.
53. MacDonald cited in Henry Kissinger, *Diplomacy* (New York: Touchstone, 1994), p. 291.
54. For a brief analysis on this issue, see e.g. Cohen, *India*, pp. 127–30; Yaacov Vertzberger, 'India's Strategic Posture and the Border War Defeat of 1962: A Case Study in Miscalculation,' *Journal of Strategic Studies*, 5:3 (1982), p. 381.
55. NAUK, PREM 11/651, Alexander Clutterbuck (British High Commissioner to India) to CRO, telegrams 798 and 799, 16 August 1954.
56. Marek W. Rutkowski, 'Expanding the Area of Peace: India, Colombo Powers and the Geneva Conference of 1954,' in Brian P. Farrell, S. R. Joey Long and David J. Ulbrich (eds), *From Far East to Asia Pacific: Great Powers and Grand Strategy 1900–1954* (Berlin: De Gruyter Oldenbourg, 2022), pp. 352–3. For China's

role at Geneva, see Qiang Zhai, 'China and the Geneva Conference of 1954,' *China Quarterly*, 129 (1992), pp. 103–22.

57. Rutkowski, 'Expanding the Area of Peace,' pp. 352–3.
58. Fredrik Logevall, *Embers of War: The Fall of an Empire and the Making of America's Vietnam* (New York: Random House, 2012), Kindle edition, ch. 24.
59. Rutkowski, 'Expanding the Area of Peace,' p. 354.
60. Ibid.
61. Damien Fenton, *To Cage the Red Dragon: SEATO and the Defence of Southeast Asia, 1955–1965* (Singapore: National University of Singapore Press, 2012), p. 25.
62. Minutes of a Meeting on Southeast Asia, 24 July 1954, doc. 267, *FRUS, 1952–1954, East Asia and the Pacific Volume XII, Part 1* (Washington, DC: GPO, 1984), https://www.history.state.gov/historicaldocuments/frus1952-54v12p1/d267, accessed 10 May 2020.
63. Memorandum of Conversation, by the Director of the Office of Chinese Affairs (McConaughy), 26 July 1954, doc. 270, *FRUS*, *1952–1954, XII/1*, https://www.history.state.gov/historicaldocuments/frus1952-54v12p1/d270, accessed 10 May 2020.
64. Minutes of a Meeting on Southeast Asia, 24 July 1954, doc. 267, *FRUS, 1952–1954, XII/1*, https://www.history.state.gov/historicaldocuments/frus1952-54v12p1/d267, accessed 10 May 2020.
65. Kevin Ruane and Matthew Jones, *Anthony Eden, Anglo-American Relations and the 1954 Indochina Crisis* (London: Bloomsbury Academic, 2019), p. 223; NAUK, FO 371/111874, D1074/283, British Embassy Washington to FO, telegram 1645, 30 July 1954.
66. Fenton, *To Cage the Red Dragon*, p. 26.
67. Andrea Benvenuti, 'The British Military Withdrawal From Southeast Asia and Its Impact on Australia's Cold War Strategic Interests,' *Cold War History*, 5:2 (2205), p. 191; Cheng Guan Ang, *The Southeast Treaty Organisation* (New York: Routledge, 2022), pp. 29–30.
68. Ang, *The Southeast Asia Treaty Organisation*, p. 32; Ruane and Jones, *Anthony Eden, Anglo-American Relations*, p. 96; Donald E. Nuechterlein, 'Thailand and Seato: A Ten-Year Appraisal,' *Asian Survey*, 4:12 (1964), p. 1174; Cheng Guan Ang, 'Southeast Asian Perceptions of the Domino Theory,' in Christopher E. Goscha and Christian F. Ostermann (eds), *Connecting Histories: Decolonization and the Cold War in Southeast Asia, 1945–1962* (Washington, DC: Woodrow Wilson Center Press, 2009), pp. 312–13 and 321–3; Brian P. Farrell, 'Alphabet Soup and Nuclear War: China and the Cold War in Southeast Asia,' in Malcolm H. Murfett (eds), *Cold War: Southeast Asia* (Singapore: Marshall Cavendish, 2012), pp. 131–2.
69. In April 1954, Foreign Secretary Eden had conveyed to Dulles Britain's 'real willingness to consider defence arrangements in SE Asia on the basis of united action,' despite hastening to clarify that he was 'against implementation of any coalition prior to Geneva.' On Eden's remarks to Dulles, see The Ambassador of the United Kingdom (Aldrich) to the Department of State, 12 April 1954, doc. 435, *FRUS, 1952–1954, Western Europe and Canada, Volume VI, Part 1* (Washington,

DC: GPO, 1986), https://history.state.gov/historicaldocuments/frus1952-54v06p1/d435, accessed 10 May 2020.

70. Prime Minister Churchill to President Eisenhower, 21 June 1954, doc. 460, *FRUS, 1952–1954, VI/1,* https://history.state.gov/historicaldocuments/frus1952-54v06p1/d460, accessed 10 May 2020.
71. Roger Dingman, 'John Foster Dulles and the Creation of the South-East Asia Treaty Organisation in 1954,' *The International History Review*, 11:3 (1989), p. 460. For Eden's idea of a Locarno-type pact, see Chapter 4 in this book.
72. NAUK, FO 371/111874, D1074/283, FO to British Embassy Washington, telegram 3825, 31 July 1954; FO 371/111875, D1074/313, Joint United Kingdom – United States Study Group on South-East Asia. Minute by J. G. Tahourdin, 30 July 1954.
73. Kevin Ruane, 'SEATO, MEDO, and the Baghdad Pact: Anthony Eden, British Foreign Policy and the Collective Defense of Southeast Asia and the Middle East, 1952–1955,' *Diplomacy & Statecraft*, 16:1 (2005), p. 178.
74. Ruane and Jones, *Anthony Eden, Anglo-American Relations*, p. 132.
75. Ibid., p. 121.
76. Dingman, 'Dulles and the South-East Asia Treaty Organisation,' pp. 460–1.
77. Pierre Mendès France (French Prime Minister and Minister of Foreign Affairs) to René Massigli (French ambassador to the UK), telegram 11699–11704, 13 August 1954, doc. 60, *Documents Diplomatiques Français* (*DDF*), *1954, 21 July–31 December* (Paris: Imprimerie Nationale, 1987). For the French approach, see also Pierre Journoud, 'La France et l'Asie du Sud-Est, de l'Indochine à l'Asean,' in Pierre Journoud (ed.), *L'Évolution du Débat Stratégique en Asie du Sud-Est depuis 1945* (Paris: IRSEM, 2012), pp. 34–5; Laurent Cesari, *Le Problème Diplomatique de l'Indochine 1945–1957* (Paris: Les Indes Savantes, 2013), pp. 273–4.
78. NAUK, PREM 11/651, BHC New Delhi to CRO, telegram 739, 2 August 1954 and FO to British Embassy Jakarta, telegrams 273 and 274, 30 July 1954; FO 371/111875, D1704/302A, CRO to BHC New Delhi, BHC Karachi and BHC Colombo, telegram Y 335, 30 July 1954.
79. NAUK, PREM 11/651, BHC New Delhi to CRO, telegram 739, 2 August 1954.
80. The US ambassador in India (Allen) to the Department of State, 9 August 1954, doc. 291, *FRUS, 1952–1954, XII/1*, https://history.state.gov/historicaldocuments/frus1952-54v12p1/d291, accessed 10 May 2020.
81. For Prime Minister Bogra's response to Eden, see NAUK, PREM 11/651, BHC Karachi to CRO, telegram 1084, 4 August 1954.
82. NAUK, FO 371/111875, D1074/295, Oscar Morland (British Embassy Jakarta) to FO, telegram 211, 2 August 1954.
83. NAUK, FO 371/111875, D1074/295, British Embassy Jakarta to FO, telegram 319, 13 August 1954.
84. NAUK, FO 371/111875, D1074/308 (A), Gore-Booth to FO, telegram 369, 2 August 1954; PMML, JN, file 271 part II, Nehru to U Nu, 4 August 1954.
85. Chargé in Burma (Acly) to Department of State, 26 July 1954, doc. 271, *FRUS, 1952–1954, XII/1,* https://history.state.gov/historicaldocuments/frus1952-54v12p1/d271, accessed 10 May 2020.

86. PMML, JN, file 271 part II, Hicomind Colombo (Desai) to Foreign New Delhi (Pillai), telegram 136 D, 5 August 1954.
87. PMML, JN, file 271 part I, Hicomind Colombo (Desai) to Foreign New Delhi (Pillai), telegram 133 D, 2 August 1954.
88. Ambassador in Ceylon (Crowe) to Department of State, 29 July 1954, doc. 277, *FRUS, 1952–1954, XII/1,* https://history.state.gov/historicaldocuments/frus1952-54v12p1/d277, accessed 10 May 2020.
89. NAUK, PREM 11/651, Cecil Syers (British High Commissioner to Ceylon) to CRO telegram 287, 3 August 1954
90. PMML, JN, file 271, part II, U Nu to Nehru, 4 August 1954; Hicomind Colombo (Desai) to Foreign New Delhi (Pillai), telegram 136 D, 5 August 1954; JN, file 273 part I, Externsec Colombo to Foreign New Delhi, telegram 7, 10 August 1954.
91. PMML, JN, file 270, part II, Foreign New Delhi (Nehru) to Hicomind Colombo (Desai for Kotelawala) and Hicomind Karachi (Metha for Ali), primin 22374, 31 July 1954 and Foreign New Delhi to Indembassy Rangoon (Chettur for Nu), Indembassy Jakarta (Tyabji for Ali Sastroadmidjojo), primin 22373, 31 July 1954.
92. PMML, JN, file 271, part II, Externsec Colombo to Foreign New Delhi, telegram 4, 3 August 1954; NAUK, PREM 11/651, BHC Colombo to CRO, telegram 287, 3 August 1954. The Indian High Commissioner to Ceylon, C. C. Desai, told his American counterpart in Colombo, Philip Crowe, that Nehru was 'planning to submit [a] regional alliance to [the] Colombo powers as [an] alternative to SEATO.' See footnote 4 to Ambassador in Pakistan (Hildreth) to Department of State, 4 August 1954, doc. 284, *FRUS, 1952–1954, XII/1*, https://www.history.state.gov/historicaldocuments/frus1952-54v12p1/d284, accessed 10 May 2020; see also NAUK, PREM 11/651, BHC Colombo to CRO, telegram 286, 2 August 1954. On 4 August, in a brief to the NSC, the CIA mentioned an 'Indian proposal for a regional alliance, including military clauses and allegedly conferring most of the benefits of SEATO without Western participation.' See NSC Briefing. Background – Colombo Powers and SEATO, CIA Historical Collections, https://www.cia.gov/library/readingroom/docs/CIA-RDP79R00890A000300050007-2.pdf, 15 August 2019. In reality, Nehru's 'constructive alternative' amounted to no more than an approach to regional security based on the Five Principles of Peaceful Coexistence. See PMML, JN, file 270, part II, Foreign New Delhi (Nehru) to Indembassy Rangoon (Chettur) and Indembassy Jakarta (Tyabji), primin 22373, 31 July 1954.
93. PMML, JN, file 272 part I, Foreign New Delhi (Nehru) To Hicomind Colombo (Desai), primin 22380, 7 August 1954.
94. PMML, JN, file 273 part I, Externsec Colombo to Foreign New Delhi, telegram 7, 10 August 1954; Foreign New Delhi to Hicomind Colombo (Desai), primin 22389, 11 August 1954.
95. Brissenden, 'India's Opposition to SEATO,' pp. 220–1.
96. NAUK, PREM 11/651, BHC Colombo to CRO, telegram 302, 9 August 1954; see also BHC Colombo to CRO, telegram 303, 10 August 1954.

97. NAUK, FO 371/111879, D1074/405, BHC Colombo to CRO, telegram 312, 14 August 1954.
98. PMML, JN, file 274, part II, C. C. Desai (Indian High Commissioner to Ceylon) to M. O. Mathai (Special Assistant to the Prime Minister), 19 August 1954. Desai also reported to Delhi that while it would 'not participate in the conference held in the Philippines,' Ceylon would judge its outcome 'on its merits and take a final decision at a later date.'
99. On this point, see also Roy, 'Assuaging Cold War Anxieties,' p. 327–37. Interestingly, some Burmese ministers revealed to the British that the Burmese Cabinet 'would have taken a more friendly line' towards SEATO had 'Nehru's critical attitude' not 'made that impossible.' NAUK, DO 35/5977, Malcolm MacDonald (British High Commissioner to India) to Earl of Home (Secretary of State for Commonwealth Relations), 1 May 1957.
100. NAUK, FO 371/111880, D1074/415, BHC Karachi to CRO, telegram 1159, 17 August 1954; PMML, JN, file 274, part II, Desai to Mathai, 19 August 1954.
101. PMML, JN, file 285 part 1, T. N. Kaul to Prime Minister, 23 August 1954.
102. According to Kaul, if Pakistan, the Philippines and Thailand refused 'to sign such declaration,' it would expose SEATO as 'an offensive and not a defensive alliance.' Ibid.
103. Ibid.

6. TOWARDS AN AFRO-ASIAN CONFERENCE

1. PMML, JN, file 287, Nehru to T. N. Kaul (Joint Secretary, MEA), 30 September 1954.
2. Herbert Feith, *The Decline of Constitutional Democracy in Indonesia* (Singapore: Equinox, 2006), p. 385; Badr-ud-din Tyabji, *Memoirs of an Egoist. Volume I: 1907 to 1956* (New Delhi: Roli Books, 1988), p. 305.
3. Feith, *The Decline of Constitutional Democracy in Indonesia*, p. 385.
4. NAUK, DO 35/6096, British Embassy Jakarta to FO, 14 May 1954.
5. NAA, A11604, 604/5, Conversation With the Secretary-General of the Foreign Ministry (Mr. Ruslan Abdulgani), 20 May 1954; see also Roeslan Abdulgani, *The Bandung Connection: The Asia-Africa Conference in Bandung in 1955* (Singapore: Gunung Agung, 1981), p. 20.
6. PMML, JN, file 275, part I, Ali Sastroamidjojo to Kotelawala, 21 July 1954; NAUK, DO 35/6096, BHC Karachi to CRO, savingram 89, 6 August 1955; British Embassy Bangkok to FO, telegram 260, 13 August 1954; 'Proposed Afro-Asian conference to be held at Djakarta about February/March 1955,' factual note, 17 November 1954; FO to British Embassy Addis Ababa, savingram 12, 21 October 1954; NAA, A1838, 3002/1 part 1, 'Africa-Asian Conference': minute by Walter Crocker (Australian ambassador to India), 2 September 1954; AHC Karachi to Arthur Tange (Secretary, ADEA), memorandum 502/54, 7 August 1954; Charles Lee (Australian Embassy Jakarta) to Tange, memorandum 829, 2 July 1954; G. H. Jansen, *Afro-Asia and Non-Alignment* (London: Faber and Faber, 1966), p. 170.

7. PMML, JN, file 274, part II, Foreign New Delhi (Nehru) to Indembassy Jakarta (Tyabji), Primin 22401, 18 August 1954.
8. PMML, JN, file 275, part I, [Indonesian] Aide-Memoire, 23 July 1954.
9. PMML, JN, file 275, part I, Nehru to Ali Sastroamidjojo, 18 August 1954. In a message to U Nu dated 19 August, Nehru told his Burmese counterpart that he 'like[d] this idea' and hoped that 'such a conference [would] be held some time or other.' However, he was also quick to note that much preparatory work was needed before it could take place. See PMML, JN, file 275, part I, Nehru to U Nu, 19 August 1954 and New Delhi (Nehru) to Indembassy Rangoon (Chettur for U Nu), primin 22405, 20 August 1954. A few weeks later, Nehru told the Indian ambassador in Cairo, Ali Yavar Jung, that while he was 'more and more inclined to think that such a conference might do some good,' he did not see how it could be held 'without the fullest preparation.' See PMML, JN, file 280, part II, Nehru to Ali Yavar Jung (Indian ambassador to Egypt), no. 1157-PMH/54, 8 September 1954.
10. PMML, JN, file 275, part I, Nehru to Ali Sastroamidjojo, 18 August 1954.
11. 'Indonesian Premier Will Visit Delhi on Sept. 22,' *Times of India*, 21 September 1954.
12. 'Dr. Ali Sastroamidjojo is Dead; Indonesian Independence Leader,' *New York Times,* 15 March 1975; 'Men, Matters and Memories,' *Times of India*, 17 April 1955; Feith, *Decline of Constitutional Democracy*, p. 341; Tyabji, *Memoirs of an Egoist*, p. 305.
13. Harris M. Lentz, *Heads of States and Governments Since* 1945 (New York: Routledge, 2013), p. 293; 'Dr. Ali Sastroamidjojo is Dead; Indonesian Independence Leader,' *New York Times*, 15 March 1975.
14. Lentz, *Heads of States and Governments Since 1945*, p. 293.
15. 'Men, Matters and Memories,' *Times of India*, 17 April 1955; Tyabji, *Memoirs of an Egoist*, p. 305.
16. NAA, A1838, 169/1/3 part 1, Some Opinions of Mrs Pandit, 24 April 1954.
17. PMML, JN, file 280 part II, Nehru to Ali Yavar Jung (Cairo), no. 1157-PMH/54, 8 September 1954.
18. PMML, JN, file 282 part I, Tyabji to Commonwealth Secretary, MEA (Subimal Dutt), no. 2/10/CO/54/617, 10 August 1954.
19. Donald Greenlees, *The Origins of Nonalignment: Great Power Competition and Indonesian Foreign Policy 1945–1965* (PhD Thesis, Australian National University, 2018), p. 104.
20. Ibid.
21. Ibid.
22. NAA, A1838, 3002/1 part 1, Visit of the Indonesian Prime Minister to India, undated; 'Methods to Extend Area of Peace Discussed: Nehru,' *Times of India*, 23 September 1954.
23. NAA, A1838, 3002/1 part 1, Visit of the Indonesian Prime Minister to India, undated; A11604, 604/2/2, 'Afro-Asian conference,' attachment to D. J. Munro (AHC New Delhi) to Tange, memorandum 1650, 4 November 1954.
24. PMML, JN, file 282, part I, Tyabji to Commonwealth Secretary, MEA (Subimal Dutt), no. 2/10/CO/54/617, 10 August 1954.

25. PMML, JN, file 282, part I, Dutt's note to the Prime Minister (Nehru) and Secretary General, MEA (Pillai), 13 September 1954.
26. PMML, JN, file 282, part I, Nehru's note to Commonwealth Secretary, MEA (Dutt), 15 August 1954.
27. PMML, JN, file 282, part I, Nehru's note to the Secretary General, MEA (Pillai), 19 August 1954.
28. PMML, JN, file 282, part II, Foreign New Delhi (Dutt) to Indembassy Jakarta (Tyabji), telegram 30566, 16 August 1954; JN, file 282, part I, Tentative Programme of the Visit of His Excellency Ali Sastroamidjojo, undated.
29. NAA, A4232, 1954/New Delhi, 1838, 3002/1 part 1, Crocker to Richard Casey (Australian Minister of External Affairs), despatch 14, 28 September 1954; 'Methods to Extend Area of Peace Discussed: Nehru,' *Times of India*, 23 September 1954.
30. 'Methods to Extend Area of Peace Discussed: Nehru,' *Times of India*, 23 September 1954.
31. PMML, JN, file 282, part I, Tentative Programme of the Visit of His Excellency Ali Sastroamidjojo, undated; NAA, A4232, 1954/New Delhi, Crocker to Casey, despatch 14, 28 September 1954.
32. C. L. M. Penders (ed.), *Milestones on My Journey: The Memoirs of Ali Sastroamijoyo, Indonesian Patriot and Leader* (St. Lucia, Australia: University of Queensland Press, 1979), p. 281. See also NAA, A1838, 3002/1 part 1, Australian Embassy Jakarta to ADEA, savingram 33, 4 October 1954. A1838, 3002/1 part 1, 'India and Indonesia: Meeting of Prime Ministers,' Jakarta despatch 30, 25 September 1954.
33. Penders, *Milestones*, p. 278.
34. PMML, JN, file 283, part II, Nehru to Menon, primin 22465, 29 September 1954. For the text of Nehru's response, see PMML, JN, file 275, part I, Nehru to Ali Sastroamidjojo, 18 August 1954.
35. NAA, A1838, 3002/1, part 1, Visit of the Indonesian Prime Minister to India, undated; NAUK, FO371/117247, DH1011/1, British Embassy Jakarta to FO, despatch 17, 27 January 1955; National Intelligence Estimate 65-55, Possible Developments in Indonesia through 1955, 1 March 1955, CIA Historical Collections, https://www.cia.gov/readingroom/docs/CIA-RDP79R01012A006000030013-0.pdf, accessed 5 August 2020. Expected initially to be held in February 1955, the elections were first postponed to August 1955 and then finally held in December 1955. With regard to the new constitution, this was intended to supersede Indonesia's 1950 provisional charter.
36. NAUK, FO371/117247, DH1011/1, British Embassy Jakarta to FO, despatch 17, 27 January 1955. Since its independence, Indonesia had never held a general election, and its first parliament consisted of appointed members.
37. NAUK, FO371/117247, DH1011/1, British Embassy Jakarta to FO, despatch 17, 27 January 1955; see also 'Indonesia Watches in the Wings,' *Economist*, 17 July 1954; National Intelligence Estimate 65-55: Possible Developments in Indonesia Through 1955, 1 March 1955, CIA Historical Collections, https://www.cia.

gov/readingroom/docs/CIA-RDP79R01012A006000030013-0.pdf, accessed 5 August 2020.
38. J. D. Legge, *Sukarno: A Political Biography* (Singapore: Archipelago Press, 2003), pp. 189–90; NAUK, FO371/117247, DH1011/1, British Embassy Jakarta to FO, despatch 17, 27 January 1955; PMML, JN, file 283, part II, Indembassy Jakarta to Foreign New Delhi, telegram 300, 20 September 1954.
39. PMML, JN, file 283, part II, Indembassy Jakarta to Foreign New Delhi, telegram 300, 20 September 1954.
40. National Intelligence Estimate 65-55: Possible Developments in Indonesia through 1955, 1 March 1955, CIA Historical Collections, https://www.cia.gov/readingroom/docs/CIA-RDP79R01012A006000030013-0.pdf, accessed 15 August 2020.
41. Penders, *Milestones*, pp. 281–2. The attitude of the Indian press was equally lukewarm. On 7 September, *The Hindu* appeared still sceptical about the idea of an Asian-African conference. *The Hindu* wrote that, given the 'odd collection of countries' that might participate in it, it was hard to envisage 'any concrete front emerging from such a gathering.' See NAUK, FO371/111930, D2231/54, Alexander Clutterbuck (British High Commissioner to India) to Viscount Swinton (British Secretary of State for Commonwealth Relations), despatch 101, 3 November 1954.
42. Penders, *Milestones*, p. 281.
43. NAUK, FO371/111930, D2231/48, BHC New Delhi to CRO, telegram 983, 29 September 1954.
44. Penders, *Milestones*, p. 281. This paragraph is largely based on Ali Sastroamidjojo's recollections of events. No memorandum of conversations between Ali Sastroamidjojo and Nehru has been found in the Nehru papers in New Delhi.
45. 'Afro-Asian Co-operation to Ensure Peace,' *Times of India*, 24 September 1954; Penders, *Milestones*, p. 282; NAA, A1838, 3034/11/147 part 1, 'Asian Nations Are Trying to Build a Durable Peace,' *Times of Indonesia*, 27 September 1954.
46. Penders, *Milestones*, p. 282.
47. PMML, JN, file 284, Indel New York (Menon) to Foreign New Delhi (Pillai), telegram 333, 22 September 1954.
48. PMML, JN, file 284, Indel New York to Foreign New Delhi, telegram 33434, 22 September 1954. Organised by the Indian Council of World Affairs at Nehru's urging and held in New Delhi in the spring of 1947, the Asian Relations Conference saw the participation of delegates from twenty-eight independent countries and dependent territories, including a strong contingent of representatives from the Soviet Union's Asian republics. Its membership was predominantly unofficial in its outlook, with independent scholars and representatives of cultural institutions from within and without the Asian region (Ethiopia and Turkey) among the conference's attendees. Key delegations also included government ministers and officials. Australia, New Zealand, Britain, the United States and the Soviet Union sent observers. Although, in principle, the conference's focus was to be on cultural and social matters, as well as political issues such as opposition to colonialism figured prominently. See NAUK, FO 371/116987, 2232/3 D, 'Asian

Conferences 1947–1955,' FO draft paper, 2 December 1955; A. W. Stargardt, 'The Emergence of the Asian System of Powers,' *Modern Asian Studies*, 23:3 (1989), p. 564.

49. Penders, *Milestones*, pp. 281–2.
50. PMML, JN, file 283, part II, Nehru to Menon, primin 22465, 21 September 1954. Pillai, however, told the British that the Indian government, despite its continuing dislike for the Indonesian proposal, had decided to relent in order to 'bolster up [the] present Indonesian Government (which broadly shares Nehru's general outlook and foreign policy) in preparation for [the] Indonesian General Election in 1955.' See NAUK, DO 35/6096, BHC New Delhi to CRO, telegram 893, 29 September 1954.
51. PMML, JN, file 283, part II, Nehru to Menon, primin 22465, 21 September 1954.
52. *SWJN*, II, Volume 27 (New Delhi: Jawaharlal Nehru Memorial Fund, 1984–2015), pp. 443–4. For Nehru's definition of 'area of peace,' see *SWJN*, II/24, p. 565.
53. *SWJN*, II/27, pp. 443–4.
54. PMML, JN, file 285, part I, Note on proposal to hold an Afro Asian conference, 24 September 1954.
55. Wang, *Isolating the Enemy*, ch. 3; Yang Huei Pang, *Strait Rituals: China, Taiwan, and the United States in the Taiwan Strait Crises, 1954–1958* (Hong Kong: Hong Kong University Press, 2019), pp. 80–114.
56. PMML, JN, file 285, part I, Note on proposal to hold an Afro Asian Conference, 24 September 1954.
57. NAA, A1838, 3034/11/147 part 1, 'Nehru's and Sastroamidjojo's Speeches at Banquet in New Delhi,' *P.I. Aneta*, 25 September 1954.
58. Ibid.
59. PMML, JN, file 284, Nehru to C. C. Desai (Indian High Commissioner to Ceylon), no. 688-PMH/54, 23 September 1954.
60. H. W. Brands, *India and the United States: The Cold Peace* (Woodbridge, CT: Twayne Publishers, 1990), p. 83. On Nehru's advisers, see NAA, A1838, 3002/1 part 1, Alan Watt (Australian Commissioner, Singapore) to Crocker, outward telegram 13, 21 October 1954,
61. PMML, JN, file 284, Nehru's note to the Foreign Secretary (R. K. Nehru), 22 September 1954.
62. PMML, JN, file 285, part I, Note on proposal to hold an Afro Asian Conference, 24 September 1954. Nehru also mentioned the promotion of freedom, racialism and economic and cultural cooperation.
63. Nicholas Tarling, '"Ah-Ah": Britain and the Bandung Conference of 1955,' *Journal of Southeast Asian Studies*, 23:1 (1999), p. 78; 'Afro-Asian Talks May Include China, Says Dr. "Jojo,"' *Times of India*, 26 September 1954.
64. PMML, JN, file 285, part I, Note on proposal to hold an Afro Asian Conference, 24 September 1954; see also NAA, A1838, 3002/1 part 1, Australian Embassy Jakarta to ADEA, savingram 33, 4 October 1954.
65. PMML, JN, file 285, part I, Note on proposal to hold an Afro Asian Conference, 24 September 1954.

66. NAA, A1838, 3034/11/147, part 1, 'Premiers' Conference Covered "Matters of Common Concern",' *Times of Indonesia*, 27 September 1954.
67. NAA, A1838, 3034/11/147, part 1, 'India Gives Warm Send-Off to Indonesian Prime Minister,' *P. I. Aneta*, 27 September 1954.
68. Penders, *Milestones*, pp. 281–3.
69. On Ali Sastroamidjojo's views, see NAA, A1838, 3034/11/147, part 1, 'India Gives Warm Send-Off to Indonesian Prime Minister,' *P. I. Aneta*, 27 September 1954. On Palar's views, see NAA, A1838, 3002/1, part 1, Visit of the Indonesian Prime Minister to India, undated.
70. NAA, A4232, 1954/New Delhi, 1838, 3002/1, part 1, Crocker to Casey, despatch 14, 28 September 1954.
71. PMML, JN, file 285, part I, Statement on talks between Nehru and Ali Sastroamidjojo, 25 September 1954.
72. NAA, A1838, 3002/1, part 1, Australian Embassy Jakarta to ADEA, savingram 33, 4 October 1954.
73. NAUK, CO 936/347, Paul Gore-Booth (British ambassador to Burma) to FO, despatch 218, 7 October 1954. In any case, according to Ruslan Abdulgani (Secretary-General, Indonesian Ministry of Foreign Affairs), U Nu told Ali Sastroamidjojo that he agreed to invite China. See NAA, A1838, 3002/1, part 1, Australian Embassy Jakarta to ADEA, savingram 33, 4 October 1954. For the communiqué, see NAA, A1838, 3002/1, part 1, Australian Legation Rangoon to ADEA, savingram 10, 1 October 1954.
74. NAUK, CO 936/347, Gore-Booth to FO, despatch 218, 7 October 1954.
75. Ibid.; NAA, A1838, 3002/1, part 1, Australian Legation Rangoon to ADEA, savingram 11, 8 October 1954.
76. NAUK, FO371/111930, D2231/66, 'Proposed Afro-Asian Conference to Be Held at Djakarta About February/March 1955,' CRO note, 17 December 1954; D2231/66, J. D. Murray (BHC Karachi) to G. Crombie (CRO), 15 November 1955.
77. NAUK, FO371/111930, D2231/63, N. E. Costar (BHC Colombo) to N. Larmour (Office of the British Commissioner-General in Singapore), 3 November 1954.
78. NAUK, FO371/111930, D2231/66, Murray (BHC Karachi) to Crombie (CRO), 15 November 1955.
79. NAUK, FO371/111930, D2231/63A, Indonesia, 9 December 1954; BHC New Delhi to CRO, telegram 983, 29 September 1954.
80. NAUK, FO371/111930, D2231/51, Minute by I. Alexander (FO), 14 October 1954.
81. NAUK, FO371/111930, D2231/45, Roderick W. Parkes (British Embassy Jakarta) to FO, telegram 282, 7 October 1954.
82. PMML, JN, 275, part I, Foreign New Delhi (Nehru) to Indembassy Beijing (Raghavan), Primin 22404, 19 August 1954; JN, 277, part I, Foreign New Delhi (Nehru) to Indembassy Beijing (Raghavan), Primin 22413, 27 August 1954.
83. Extracts from the Press Conference of Prime Minister Jawaharlal Nehru before departure for China, 15 October 1954, doc. 0748, Avtar Singh Bhasin (ed.),

India-China Relations 1947–2000: A Documentary Study, Volume 2 (New Delhi: Geetika Publishers, 2018).

84. PMML, JN, 275, part I, Foreign New Delhi (Nehru) to Indembassy Beijing (Raghavan), Primin 22404, 19 August 1954; JN, 277, part I, Foreign New Delhi (Nehru) to Indembassy Beijing (Raghavan), Primin 22413, 27 August 1954 and Foreign New Delhi (Nehru) to Indembassy Rangoon (Chettur), Primin 22414, 27 August 1954.
85. H. V. R. Iengar to M. O. Mathai, 11 October 1954, doc. 0746, Bhasin, *India-China Relations, Volume 2*.
86. 'India's Trade Pact With China,' *The Scotsman*, 15 October 1954.

7. NEHRU'S VISIT TO CHINA

1. Minutes of Chairman Mao Zedong's Third Meeting with Nehru (4:35 p.m. to 5:30 p.m.), 26 October 1954, WCDA, https://digitalarchive.wilsoncenter.org/document/117828, accessed 10 May 2021.
2. 'Premier Leaves for China,' *Times of India*, 16 October 1954; PMML, JN, file 290, part I, Foreign New Delhi to Indembassy Rangoon, telegram 5913, 14 October 1954; Foreign New Delhi to Indembassy Rangoon, primin 22492, 14 October 1954.
3. 'Premier Leaves for China,' *Times of India*, 16 October 1954.
4. 'Mission to China,' *Times of India*, 16 October 1954.
5. PMML, JN, file 295, part I, Note on Visit to China and Indo-China, 13 November 1954.
6. NAA, A4231, 1954/New Delhi, Walter Crocker (Australian High Commissioner to India) to Richard Casey (Australian Minister of External Affairs), despatch 17, 9 November 1954.
7. 'Mr. Nehru off to China,' *The Times*, 16 October 1954; PMML, JN, file 278, part II, Prime Minister's Visit to China, October 1954; JN, file 289, part I, Devi Dayal to Accountant General, Central Revenues, 12 October 1954.
8. Minutes of Second Meeting between Premier Zhou Enlai and Nehru (3:30 p.m. to 6:30 p.m.), 20 October 1954, WCDA, http://digitalarchive.wilsoncenter.org/document/121747, accessed 5 May 2021; NAUK, FO 371/111963, B10385/2, Paul Gore-Booth (British ambassador to Burma) to Anthony Eden (British Secretary of State for Foreign Affairs), despatch 241, 27 October 1954; NSC Briefing, Prime Minister Nehru's itinerary on China trip, 9 November 1954, CIA Historical Collections, https://www.cia.gov/library/readingroom/docs/CIA-RDP79R00890A000400030020-8.pdf, accessed 15 April 2021.
9. NAUK, 371/110226, FC10385/17A, CRO to various Commonwealth posts, telegram Y 472, 29 October 1954.
10. Tao Wang, *Isolating the Enemy: Diplomatic Strategy in China and the United States, 1953–1956* (New York: Columbia University Press, 2021), Kindle edition, ch. 3; Russell H. Fifield, 'The Five Principles of Peaceful Co-Existence,' *The American Journal of International Law*, 52:3 (1958), p. 506.

11. Wang, *Isolating the Enemy*, ch. 3.
12. NAUK, FO 371/110226, FC10385/17A, CRO to various Commonwealth posts, telegram Y 472, 29 October 1954.
13. NAUK, FO 371/110226, FC10385/11, Humphrey Trevelyan (British Chargé d'Affaires Beijing) to FO, telegram 849, 21 October 1954; FO 371/110226, FC10385/11, New China News Agency, bulletin 1159, 20 October 1954.
14. 'Nehru in Peiping for Crucial Talk,' *New York Times*, 20 October 1954; NAUK, FO 371/110226, FC10385/11, Trevelyan to FO, telegram 849, 21 October 1954; FO 371/110226, FC10385/11, New China News Agency, bulletin 1159, 20 October 1954. K. F. Rustamji, Nehru's chief security officer from 1952 to 1958, put the overall figure at more than a million people. See P.V. Rajgopal (ed.), *I Was Nehru's Shadow: From the Diaries of KF Rustamji, IP, Padma Vibhushan* (New Delhi: Wisdom Tree, 2014), Kindle edition, ch. 8.
15. *SWJN*, II, Volume 27 (New Delhi: Jawaharlal Nehru Memorial Fund, 1984–2015), p. 67.
16. NAUK, FO 371/110226, FC10385/11, Trevelyan to FO, telegram 849, 21 October 1954.
17. *SWJN*, II/27, p. 67; NAUK, FO 371/110226, FC10385/18F, Alexander Clutterbuck (British High Commissioner to India) to CRO, telegram 1096, 4 November 1954; Ramachandra Guha, 'Jawaharlal Nehru and China: A Study in Failure,' *Harvard-Yenching Institute Working Paper Series*, 2011, https://www.harvard-yenching.org/wp-content/uploads/legacy_files/featurefiles/Ramachandra%20Guha_Jawaharlal%20Nehru%20and%20China.pdf, accessed 5 August 2022.
18. NAUK, FO 371/110226, FC10385/18F, Clutterbuck to CRO, telegram 1096, 4 November 1954.
19. Ibid.
20. Ibid.; *SWJN*, II/27, p. 67; PMML, JN, file 295, part I, Note on Visit to China and Indo-China, 13 November 1954; NAA, A4231, 1954/New Delhi, Crocker to Casey, despatch 17, 9 November 1954; *SWJN*, II/27, p. 67.
21. *SWJN*, II/27, pp. 67–8.
22. Gregg Brazinsky, *Winning the Third World: Sino-American Rivalry During the Cold War* (Chapel Hill, NC: University of North Carolina Press, 2017), p. 114.
23. NAUK, FO 371/110226, FC10385/11, Trevelyan to FO, telegram 849, 21 October 1954.
24. Michael M. Sheng, 'Mao and China's Relations With the Superpowers in the 1950s: A New Look at the Taiwan Strait Crises and the Sino-Soviet Split,' *Modern China*, 34:4 (2008), p. 483.
25. Ibid., pp. 483–4; John W. Garver, *China's Quest: The History of the Foreign Relations of the People's Republic* (Oxford: Oxford University Press, 2016), Kindle edition, ch. 4; Shu Guang Zhang, 'Constructing "Peaceful Coexistence": China's Diplomacy Toward the Geneva and Bandung Conferences, 1954–55,' *Cold War History*, 7:4 (2007), p. 520; Gordon H. Chang, 'Nuclear Brink: Eisenhower, Dulles, and the Quemoy-Matsu Crisis,' *International Security*, 12:4 (1988), pp. 96 and 99.

26. Yang Huei Pang, *Strait Rituals: China, Taiwan, and the United States in the Taiwan Strait Crises, 1954–1958* (Hong Kong: Hong Kong University Press, 2019), pp. 80–114.
27. Zhou Enlai cited in Zhang, 'Constructing "Peaceful Coexistence",' p. 520.
28. Ibid.
29. Ibid. That said, Chinese aggressive tactics in the Taiwan Strait continued through late 1954 and early 1955. See Garver, *China's Quest*, ch. 4.
30. On this point, see e.g. Jonathan Ward, 'China-India Rivalry and the Border War of 1962: PRC Perspectives on the Collapse of China-India Relations, 1958–62' (DPhil Thesis, University of Oxford, 2016), p. 48.
31. This account of Nehru's talks with Mao and Zhou is based on declassified Indian and Chinese sources. For an Indian summary record of these conversations see PMML, JN, file 295, part I, Note on Visit to China and Indo-China, 13 November 1954. For the extended Indian record of the Beijing talks, see PMML, JN, file 295, part I and *SWJN*, II/27, pp. 6–40. In a note to his closest advisers on 13 November, Nehru wrote that while 'the detailed records of our conversations in China' were 'not always quite correct,' they nonetheless gave 'a fair idea of what we said to each other.' See PMML, JN, file 295, part I, Nehru's note to FS, CS and JS, 13 November 1954. The Chinese minutes of the talks have been published by the WCDA and are available at http://digitalarchive.wilsoncenter.org
32. PMML, JN, file 295, part I, Summary of Talks Following Formal Call by the Prime Minister on Chairman Mao Tse-Tung, 19 October 1955.
33. Sulmaan Wasif Khan, 'Cold War Co-Operation: New Chinese Evidence on Jawaharlal Nehru's 1954 visit to Beijing,' *Cold War History*, 11:2 (2011), p. 200.
34. Minutes of Chairman Mao Zedong's First Meeting With Nehru (4:30 p.m. to 5:30 p.m.), 19 October 1954, WCDA, https://digitalarchive.wilsoncenter.org/document/117825, accessed 10 August 2019; see also PMML, JN, file 295, part I, Summary of Talks Following Formal Call by the Prime Minister on Chairman Mao Tse-Tung, 19 October 1955.
35. Minutes of Chairman Mao Zedong's Second Meeting with Nehru (7:00 p.m. to 9:30 p.m.), 23 October 1954, WCDA, https://digitalarchive.wilsoncenter.org/document/117815, accessed 10 August 2019; Minutes of Second Meeting Between Premier Zhou Enlai and Nehru (3:30 p.m. to 6:30 p.m.), 20 October 1954, WCDA, https://digitalarchive.wilsoncenter.org/document/121747, accessed 10 August 2019. See also PMML, JN, file 295, part I, Summary of Talks Following Formal Call by the Prime Minister on Chairman Mao Tse-Tung, 19 October 1955.
36. Minutes of Chairman Mao Zedong's Third Meeting With Nehru (4:35 p.m. to 5:30 p.m.), 26 October 1954, WCDA, https://digitalarchive.wilsoncenter.org/document/117828, accessed 10 August 2019.
37. PMML, JN, file 295, part I, Note on Visit to China and Indo-China, 13 November 1954; Summary of talks following formal call by the Prime Minister on Chairman Mao Tse-Tung, 19 October 1955.
38. Minutes of Chairman Mao Zedong's Second Meeting With Nehru (7:00 p.m. to 9:30 p.m.), 23 October 1954, WCDA, https://digitalarchive.wilsoncenter.org/document/117815, accessed 10 August 2019.

39. PMML, JN, file 295 part I, Note on Visit to China and Indo-China, 13 November 1954; JN, file 295, part I, Summary of Talks Following Formal Call by the Prime Minister on Chairman Mao Tse-Tung, 19 October 1955; Minutes of Second Meeting Between Premier Zhou Enlai and Nehru (3:30 p.m. to 6:30 p.m.), 20 October 1954, WCDA, https://digitalarchive.wilsoncenter.org/document/121747, accessed 10 August 2019.
40. PMML, JN, file 295, part I, Note on Visit to China and Indo-China, 13 November 1954.
41. Ibid.; see also *SWJN*, II/27, pp. 11–12; Minutes of Second Meeting Between Premier Zhou Enlai and Nehru (3:30 p.m. to 6:30 p.m.), 20 October 1954, WCDA, https://digitalarchive.wilsoncenter.org/document/121747, accessed 10 August 2019.
42. Minutes of Chairman Mao Zedong's First Meeting With Nehru (4:30 p.m. to 5:30 p.m.), 19 October 1954, WCDA, https://digitalarchive.wilsoncenter.org/document/117825, accessed 10 August 2019. PMML, JN, file 295, part I, Note on Visit to China and Indo-China, 13 November 1954.
43. Minutes of Chairman Mao Zedong's First Meeting With Nehru (4:30 p.m. to 5:30 p.m.), 19 October 1954, WCDA, https://digitalarchive.wilsoncenter.org/document/117825, accessed 10 August 2019. See also PMML, JN, file 295, part I, Summary of Talks Following Formal Call by the Prime Minister on Chairman Mao Tse-Tung, 19 October 1955.
44. *SWJN*, II/27, p. 12; Minutes of Second Meeting Between Premier Zhou Enlai and Nehru (3:30 p.m. to 6:30 p.m.), 20 October 1954, WCDA, https://digitalarchive.wilsoncenter.org/document/121747, accessed 10 August 2019.
45. Minutes of the First Meeting Between Premier Zhou Enlai and Nehru (7:00 p.m. to 11:30 p.m.), 19 October 1954, WCDA, https://digitalarchive.wilsoncenter.org/document/121746, accessed 10 August 2019; Minutes of Chairman Mao Zedong's Second Meeting With Nehru (7:00 p.m. to 9:30 p.m.), 23 October 1954, https://digitalarchive.wilsoncenter.org/document/117815, accessed 10 August 2019.
46. Minutes of Second Meeting Between Premier Zhou Enlai and Nehru (3:30 p.m. to 6:30 p.m.), 20 October 1954, WCDA, https://digitalarchive.wilsoncenter.org/document/121747, accessed 10 August 2019.
47. Minutes of Chairman Mao Zedong's First Meeting With Nehru (4:30 p.m. to 5:30 p.m.), 19 October 1954, WCDA, https://digitalarchive.wilsoncenter.org/document/117825, accessed 10 August 2019.
48. PMML, JN, 295, part I, Minutes of Prime Minister's talks With Chairman Mao on the evening of Saturday 23 October 1954. See also Minutes of Chairman Mao Zedong's Second Meeting With Nehru (7:00 p.m. to 9:30 p.m.), 23 October 1954, https://digitalarchive.wilsoncenter.org/document/117815, accessed 10 August 2019.
49. Minutes of First Meeting Between Premier Zhou Enlai and Nehru (7:00 p.m. to 11:30 p.m.), 19 October 1954, WCDA, https://digitalarchive.wilsoncenter.org/document/121746, accessed 10 August 2019.
50. On this point, see also Khan, 'Cold War Co-Operation,' p. 206.

51. *SWJN*, II/27, p. 15; see also Minutes of Second Meeting Between Premier Zhou Enlai and Nehru (3:30 p.m. to 6:30 p.m.), 20 October 1954, WCDA, https://digitalarchive.wilsoncenter.org/document/121747, accessed 10 August 2019.
52. *SWJN*, II/27, p. 15; see also Minutes of Second Meeting Between Premier Zhou Enlai and Nehru (3:30 p.m. to 6:30 p.m.), 20 October 1954, WCDA, https://digitalarchive.wilsoncenter.org/document/121747
53. Minutes of Chairman Mao Zedong's First Meeting with Nehru (4:30 p.m. to 5:30 p.m.), 19 October 1954, WCDA, https://digitalarchive.wilsoncenter.org/document/117825, accessed 10 August 2019.
54. *SWJN*, II/27, p. 15; see also Minutes of Second Meeting Between Premier Zhou Enlai and Nehru (3:30 p.m. to 6:30 p.m.), 20 October 1954, WCDA, https://digitalarchive.wilsoncenter.org/document/121747, accessed 10 August 2019.
55. Minutes of Second Meeting Between Premier Zhou Enlai and Nehru (3:30 p.m. to 6:30 p.m.), 20 October 1954, WCDA, https://digitalarchive.wilsoncenter.org/document/121747, accessed 10 August 2019; see also *SWJN*, II/27, p. 15.
56. Minutes of Chairman Mao Zedong's First Meeting With Nehru (4:30 p.m. to 5:30 p.m.), 19 October 1954, https://digitalarchive.wilsoncenter.org/document/117825, accessed 10 August 2019; see also *SWJN*, II/27, pp. 10–13. For Mao's strong support of areas of peace and the principles of peaceful coexistence see also Minutes of Chairman Mao Zedong's Third Meeting With Nehru (4:35 p.m. to 5:30 p.m.), 26 October 1954, WCDA, https://digitalarchive.wilsoncenter.org/document/117828, accessed 10 August 2019.
57. *SWJN*, II/27, p. 14; Minutes of Second Meeting Between Premier Zhou Enlai and Nehru (3:30 p.m. to 6:30 p.m.), 20 October 1954, WCDA, https://digitalarchive.wilsoncenter.org/document/121747, accessed 10 August 2019.
58. *SWJN*, II/27, p. 18; Minutes of Second Meeting Between Premier Zhou Enlai and Nehru (3:30 p.m. to 6:30 p.m.), 20 October 1954, WCDA, https://digitalarchive.wilsoncenter.org/document/121747, accessed 10 August 2019.
59. Minutes of Second Meeting Between Premier Zhou Enlai and Nehru (3:30 p.m. to 6:30 p.m.), 20 October 1954, WCDA, https://digitalarchive.wilsoncenter.org/document/121747, accessed 10 August 2019.
60. *SWJN*, II/27, p. 17–18; see also Minutes of Second Meeting Between Premier Zhou Enlai and Nehru (3:30 p.m. to 6:30 p.m.), 20 October 1954, WCDA, https://digitalarchive.wilsoncenter.org/document/121747, accessed 10 August 2019.
61. *SWJN*, II/27, p. 18.
62. PRC FMA 207-00001-04, 13-14, Receiving the Prime Ministers of India and Other Countries and Attending the Asian-African Conference, 9 December 1954, WCDA, http://digitalarchive.wilsoncenter.org/document/114600, accessed 15 August 2019.
63. Minutes of Second Meeting Between Premier Zhou Enlai and Nehru (3:30 p.m. to 6:30 p.m.), 20 October 1954, WCDA, https://digitalarchive.wilsoncenter.org/document/121747, accessed 10 August 2019; *SWJN*, II/27, p. 17.
64. *SWJN*, II/27, p. 17.

65. Ibid., p.16. The Chinese record, however, is more ambiguous on this point, with Nehru being quoted as saying that 'we are in support of this [Indonesian] proposal. We hope this conference can be held. But this conference may not [illegible], because the participating countries have contrary policies.' Later in the memorandum of conversation, Nehru is recorded as saying that the conference would take place. See Minutes of Second Meeting Between Premier Zhou Enlai and Nehru (3:30 p.m. to 6:30 p.m.), 20 October 1954, WCDA, https://digitalarchive.wilsoncenter.org/document/121747, accessed 10 August 2019.
66. *SWJN*, II/27, p. 16.
67. Ibid., pp. 17–18.
68. Ibid., p. 16.
69. NAUK, FO 371/110226, FC10385/17A, CRO to various Commonwealth posts, telegram Y 472, 29 October 1954; FO 371/110226, FC10385/17, Trevelyan to FO, telegram 868, 28 October 1954; Note by Nehru to the Commonwealth Secretary, 7 November 1954, doc. 0765, Avtar Singh Bhasin (ed.), *India-China Relations 1947–2000: A Documentary Study, Volume 2* (New Delhi: Geetika Publishers, 2018).
70. Note by Nehru to the Commonwealth Secretary, 7 November 1954, doc. 0765, Bhasin, *India-China Relations, Volume 2*.
71. NSC Briefing: Sino-Indian Relations, 12 October 1954, CIA Historical Collections, https://www.cia.gov/library/readingroom/docs/CIA-RDP80R01443R000300080002-0.pdf, accessed 10 November 2019.
72. Ibid.
73. Talking Points From Premier Zhou Enlai's Second Meeting With Nehru, 20 October 1954, http://digitalarchive.wilsoncenter.org/document/121740, accessed 10 August 2019. According to the Indian record of the Beijing talks, Nehru stated that 'we must remove fear and this can be done through the Five Principles, but the bona fides must be proved.' *SWJN*, II/27, p. 15.
74. *SWJN*, II/27, pp. 18–20; Talking Points From Premier Zhou Enlai's Second Meeting with Nehru, 20 October 1954, http://digitalarchive.wilsoncenter.org/document/121740, accessed 10 August 2019; Nehru also brought up the question of Nepalese rebel K. I. Singh, who had taken refuge in China and who, according to Nehru, 'had been given encouragement in China.' PMML, JN, file 295, part I, Note on Visit to China and Indo-China, 13 November 1954.
75. *SWJN*, II/27, pp. 18–20; Minutes of Second Meeting Between Premier Zhou Enlai and Nehru (3:30 p.m. to 6:30 p.m.), 20 October 1954, WCDA, https://digitalarchive.wilsoncenter.org/document/121747, accessed 10 August 2019; Khan, 'Cold War Co-Operation,' p. 215.
76. NAUK, FO 371/110226, FC10385/17, Trevelyan to FO, telegram 868, 28 October 1954; *SWJN*, II/27, p. 14; Minutes of Second Meeting Between Premier Zhou Enlai and Nehru (3:30 p.m. to 6:30 p.m.), 20 October 1954, WCDA, https://digitalarchive.wilsoncenter.org/document/121747, accessed 10 August 2019; PMML, JN, file 295, part I, Note on Visit to China and Indo-China, 13 November 1954.

77. PMML, JN, file 295, part I, Note on Visit to China and Indo-China, 13 November 1954; Minutes of Second Meeting Between Premier Zhou Enlai and Nehru (3:30 p.m. to 6:30 p.m.), 20 October 1954, https://digitalarchive.wilsoncenter.org/document/121747, accessed 10 August 2019; *SWJN*, II/27, pp. 17 and 20.
78. Minutes of Second Meeting Between Premier Zhou Enlai and Nehru (3:30 p.m. to 6:30 p.m.), 20 October 1954, WCDA, https://digitalarchive.wilsoncenter.org/document/121747, accessed 10 August 2019; Talking Points From Premier Zhou Enlai's Second Meeting With Nehru, 20 October 1954, WCDA, http://digitalarchive.wilsoncenter.org/document/121740, accessed 10 August 2019; see also *SWJN*, II/27, p. 19.
79. On Nehru's approach to the border question, see for instance Avtar Singh Bhasin, *Nehru Tibet and China* (New Delhi: Penguin, 2021), Kindle edition.
80. Anton Harder, 'Defining Independence in Cold War Asia: Sino-Indian Relations, 1949–1962' (PhD thesis, London School of Economics, 2015), pp. 89–90 and 93.
81. Ibid., pp. 124–5.
82. Minutes of the First Meeting Between Premier Zhou Enlai and Nehru (7:00 p.m. to 11:30 p.m.), 19 October 1954, WCDA, https://digitalarchive.wilsoncenter.org/document/121746, accessed 10 August 2019. Pillai told Trevelyan that while Nehru continued to call for a peaceful settlement, the Chinese side appeared willing to 'recover the coast islands [but not Formosa] by force' without running the 'risk of provoking a conflict.' See NAUK, FO 371/110226, FC10385/17, Trevelyan to FO, telegram 868, 28 October 1954; FO 371/110226, FC10385/18F, Mr. Nehru's Visit to China, 8 November 1954.
83. Minutes of the First Meeting Between Premier Zhou Enlai and Nehru (7:00 p.m. to 11:30 p.m.), 19 October 1954, WCDA, https://digitalarchive.wilsoncenter.org/document/121746, accessed 10 August 2019. See also Khan, 'Cold War Co-Operation,' p. 210.
84. Minutes of Chairman Mao Zedong's Second Meeting With Nehru (7:00 p.m. to 9:30 p.m.), 23 October 1954, https://digitalarchive.wilsoncenter.org/document/117815, accessed 10 August 2019; see also *SWJN*, II/27, pp. 35–40.
85. On Nehru as a possible messenger, see Khan, 'Cold War Co-Operation,' pp. 208–9.
86. Minutes of Chairman Mao Zedong's Third Meeting With Nehru (4:35 p.m. to 5:30 p.m.), 26 October 1954, WCDA, https://digitalarchive.wilsoncenter.org/document/117828, accessed 10 August 2019.
87. Minutes of Fourth Meeting Between Premier Zhou Enlai and Nehru (3:45 p.m. to 4:20 p.m.), 26 October 1954, https://digitalarchive.wilsoncenter.org/document/121749, accessed 10 August 2019.
88. Nehru to Zhou Enlai, 29 October 1954, doc. 0757, Bhasin, *India-China Relations, Volume 2*.
89. NAUK, FO 371/110226, FC10385/17A, CRO to various Commonwealth posts, telegram Y 472, 29 October 1954; PMML, JN, file 295, part I, Note on Visit to China and Indo-China, 13 November 1954.

90. 'There is,' Raghavan added, 'an atmosphere of anticipation of healthy developments in Asia arising out of the visit.' See PMML, JN, file 299, part I, Raghavan to Secretary General (Pillai), 26 November 1954.
91. NAUK, FO 371/110226, FC10385/18C, Clutterbuck to CRO, telegram 1107, 6 November 1954. 'Definitely, the boss,' Nehru added. On Nehru's remark concerning Mao, see FO 371/112197, DL1022/26, Memorandum of Talks With Prime Minister Nehru, 20 November 1954. For Mao's 'lecturing' attitude at times, see also FO 371/110226, FC10385/17, Trevelyan to FO, telegram 868, 28 October 1954.
92. NAUK, FO 371/110226, FC10385/18C, Clutterbuck to CRO, telegram 1107, 6 November 1954.
93. NAUK, FO 371/110226, FC10385/18, Clutterbuck to CRO, telegram 1096, 4 November 1954.
94. Ibid.
95. Ibid.
96. Escott Reid, *Envoy to Nehru* (Delhi: Oxford University Press, 1981), p. 59.
97. NAUK, FO 371/110226, FC10385/18B, Clutterbuck to CRO, telegram 1102, 5 November 1954.
98. NAUK, FO 371/110226, FC10385/18, Clutterbuck to CRO, telegram 1096, 4 November 1954.
99. PMML, JN, file 295, part I, Note on Visit to China and Indo-China, 13 November 1954; NAUK, FO 371/110226, FC10385/17A, CRO to various Commonwealth posts, telegram Y 472, 29 October 1954.
100. Reid, *Envoy to Nehru*, p. 59.
101. NSC Briefing: Nehru's China Trip, 8 November 1954, CIA Historical Collections, https://www.cia.gov/library/readingroom/document/cia-rdp80r01443r000300140023-0, accessed 20 February 2020.
102. NARA, RG 59, Central Decimal Files (CDF) 1950–54, box 2859, 611.91/11-1254, David McK. Key II (Assistant Secretary of State for United Nations Affairs, State Department) to David A. Robertson (Officer in charge of Economic Affairs, Office of Near Eastern Affairs, State Department), Henry A. Byroade (Assistant Secretary of State for Near Eastern, South Asian, and African Affairs, State Department) and Robert R. Bowie (State Department Representative on the National Security Council Planning Board), 12 November 1954.
103. Ibid.
104. NAUK, FO 371/110226, FC10385/18, Clutterbuck to CRO, telegram 1096, 4 November 1954.
105. NAUK, FO 371/110226, FC10385/18/E, Mr Nehru's Impressions of China (note by M. T. Walker), 4 November 1954.
106. PMML, JN, file 295, part II, Nehru to Kailas Nath Katju (Minister for Home Affairs), 15 November 1954.
107. Note by Nehru to the Commonwealth Secretary, 7 November 1954, doc. 0765, Bhasin, *India-China Relations, Volume 2*.
108. NARA, RG 59, CDF 1950–54, box 2859, 611.91/11-154, US Embassy New Delhi to State Department, despatch 2930, 1 November 1954.

109. *SWJN*, II/27, p. 73.
110. U Nu stayed for over 2 weeks, from 30 November to 16 December. See Wang, *Isolating the Enemy*.
111. NAUK, FO 371/115016, FC10379/5, Trevelyan to Eden, 22 December 1954; N. Raghavan to Nehru, 9 December 1954, doc. 0780, Bhasin, *India-China Relations, Volume 2*.
112. N. Raghavan to Nehru, 9 December 1954, doc. 0780, Bhasin, *India-China Relations, Volume 2*.
113. Ibid.
114. NAUK, FO 371/115016, FC10379/5, Trevelyan to Eden, 22 December 1954.
115. Wang, *Isolating the Enemy*.
116. NAUK, FO 371/115016, FC10379/5, Trevelyan to Eden, 22 December 1954.
117. Ibid.; Wang, *Isolating the Enemy*. In so doing, China increased its annual imports of rice from Burma to 150,000–200,000 tonnes.
118. Current Intelligence Bulletin, 14 December 1954, CIA Historical Collections, https://www.cia.gov/library/readingroom/docs/CIA-RDP79T00975A001800390001-9.pdf, accessed 20 February 2020; NAUK, FO 371/115016, FC10379/5, Trevelyan to Eden, 22 December 1954.
119. Liang Zhi, 'Heading Toward Peaceful Coexistence: The Effects of the Improvement in Sino-Burmese Relations from 1953 to 1955,' *Asian Perspective*, 42 (2018), p. 537.
120. Aung Myoe Maung, *In the Name of Pauk-Phaw: Myanmar's China Policy Since 1948* (Singapore: Institute of Southeast Asian Studies, 2011), p. 24.
121. U Nu cited in ibid.
122. Current Intelligence Bulletin, 14 December 1954, CIA Historical Collections, https://www.cia.gov/library/readingroom/docs/CIA-RDP79T00975A001800390001-9.pdf, accessed 20 February 2020.
123. Maung, *In the Name of Pauk-Phaw,* p. 24.
124. Current Intelligence Bulletin, 14 December 1954, *CIA*, https://www.cia.gov/library/readingroom/docs/CIA-RDP79T00975A001800390001-9.pdf, accessed 20 February 2020.
125. Zhi, 'Heading Toward Peaceful Coexistence,' p. 537.
126. Mao cited in Maung, *In the Name of Pauk-Phaw*, p. 24.
127. Ibid.
128. Mao cited in Wang, *Isolating the Enemy*.
129. PRC FMA 207-00001-04, 13-14, Receiving the Prime Ministers of India and Other Countries and Attending the Asian-African Conference, 9 December 1954, WCDA, http://digitalarchive.wilsoncenter.org/document/114600, accessed 10 December 2019. U Nu had already told Indonesian Prime Minister Ali Sastroamidjojo that he supported the inclusion of China in the list of countries to be invited to the Asian-African conference. See PMML, JN, file 290, part I, Communication from the Prime Minister of Indonesia to the Prime Minister of India, handed over by the Indonesian Charge d'Affaires, 13 October 1954.
130. Note by Nehru to the Commonwealth Secretary, 7 November 1954, doc. 0765, Bhasin, *India-China Relations, Volume 2*.

131. NAUK, DO 35/6096, British Embassy Rangoon to FO, 13 January 1955.
132. NAUK, CO 936/348, Note on Talks with 'Colombo Power' Prime Ministers, 18 January 1955.
133. Ibid.
134. NAA, A1838, 3002/1 part 1, Australian Legation Rangoon to ADEA, cablegram 234, 21 December 1954.
135. Critical situations, 16 December 1954, CIA Historical Collections, https://www.cia.gov/readingroom/docs/CIA-RDP91T01172R000300170001-1.pdf, accessed 15 April 2020.
136. Indonesia had concluded an initial trade agreement in late 1953. See Shao Chuan Leng, 'Communist China's Economic Relations with Southeast Asia,' *Far Eastern Survey*, 28:1 (1959), p. 8.
137. PRC FMA 105-00042-03, Zhou Enlai's Conversations With the Ambassadors of India, Indonesia, and Burma, 10 July 1954, WCDA, http://digitalarchive.wilsoncenter.org/document/112439, accessed 1 November 2019; NAA, A1838, 3006/9/5, J. C. G. Kevin (Australian Minister and Chargé d'Affaires to Indonesia) to Arthur Tange (Secretary, ADEA), 5 October 1954.
138. NAA, A1838, 3006/9/5, Kevin to Tange, 5 October 1954.
139. NAUK, FO 371/110251, FC1072/5, Trevelyan to W. D. Allen (FO), 4 October 1954.
140. On Zhou's inability to travel to Indonesia, see PRC FMA 105-00042-03, 78–79, Zhou Enlai's Conversations With the Ambassadors of India, Indonesia, and Burma, 10 July 1954, WCDA, http://digitalarchive.wilsoncenter.org/document/112439, accessed 1 November 2019.
141. NAUK, FO 371/110251, FC1072/4, Trevelyan to Allen, 23 September 1954.
142. PMML, JN, file 292, Indembassy Jakarta to Foreign New Delhi, telegram 34127, 27 October 1954.
143. PRC FMA 207-00085-17, 144–149, Report from the Asia Section, Chinese Foreign Ministry, 'On the Asian-African Conference,' 15 December 1954, WCDA, http://digitalarchive.wilsoncenter.org/document/112442, accessed 1 November 2019.
144. NAUK, FO 371/111930, D2231/68, Minute by W. D. Allen (FO), 25 November 1954.
145. NAUK, FO 371/111930, D2231/68, Minute by Allen, 25 November 1954. On the issue of Chinese participation in a future Asian-African conference, the Chinese government speculated that Ceylon might be contrary to it. On this point, Chinese sources are less clear-cut. See e.g. PRC FMA 207-00085-17, 144–149, Report from the Asia Section, Chinese Foreign Ministry, 'On the Asian-African Conference,' 15 December 1954, WCDA, http://digitalarchive.wilsoncenter.org/document/112442, accessed 1 November 2019; PRC FMA 207-00002-04, 84, 'Report on the Situation of the Bogor Conference,' Cable from the Chinese Embassy in Indonesia, 4 December 1954, WCDA, http://digitalarchive.wilsoncenter.org/document/112441, accessed 1 November 2019; PRC FMA 207-00002-04, 85, Cable from the Chinese Embassy in Indonesia, 'The Prime Ministers of India, Burma, Pakistan, Ceylon are Preparing to Attend the Bogor

Conference,' 6 December 1954, WCDA, http://digitalarchive.wilsoncenter.org/document/115496, accessed 1 November 2019.

146. PRC FMA 207-00085-17, 144–149, Report from the Asia Section, Chinese Foreign Ministry, 'On the Asian-African Conference,' 15 December 1954, WCDA, http://digitalarchive.wilsoncenter.org/document/112442, accessed 1 November 2019; PRC FMA 207-00002-04, 84, 'Report on the Situation of the Bogor Conference,' Cable from the Chinese Embassy in Indonesia, 4 December 1954, WCDA, http://digitalarchive.wilsoncenter.org/document/112441, accessed 1 November 2019.

8. THE BOGOR CONFERENCE

1. PMML, JN, file 306, PM's Note on Afro-Asian Conference: Minute by R. K. Nehru, 20 December 1954.
2. NAUK, FO 371/111930, D2231, Eden's note on conversation with Krishna Menon, 10 December 1954.
3. Ibid.
4. NAUK, FO 371/111930, D2231/74, C. Walker (BHC New Delhi) to G. Crombie (CRO), 9 December 1954.
5. NAUK, FO 371/111930, D2231/71, J. D. Murray (BHC Karachi) to Crombie, 6 December 1954.
6. NAUK, FO 371/111930, D2231/69, CRO to BHC New Delhi, BHC Karachi and BHC Colombo, telegram 216, 26 November 1954.
7. Amit Das Gupta, *Serving India: A Political Biography of Subimal Dutt (1903–1992), India's Longest Serving Foreign Secretary* (New Delhi: Manohar, 2017), pp. 215–17.
8. PMML, JN, file 305, Nehru to Ali Yavar Jung (Indian ambassador to Egypt), primin 22582, 19 December 1954; *SWJN*, Second Series [henceforth II], Volume 27 (New Delhi: Jawaharlal Nehru Memorial Fund, 1984–2015), p. 106, fn 2.
9. *SWJN*, II/27, p. 106. On British misgivings, see NAUK, DO 35/6096, Note of a Conversation Between Anthony Eden and Krishna Menon on 10 December 1954 and PMML, JN, file 305, Conversation Between Sir Anthony Eden and Mr Krishna Menon on 10 December 1954.
10. PMML, JN, file 305, 'Jakarta Conference, December 1954,' note by Subimal Dutt, 17 December 1954.
11. PMML, JN, file 306, part I, Note by Krishna Menon on Prime Minister's Conference in Djakarta, 18 December 1954.
12. Das Gupta, *Serving India*, p. 216. For the American characterisation of Dutt, see NARA, RG 59, CDF, 1955–59, box 2668, 670.901/3-1455, 'Biographic sketches of delegates to the Afro-Asian conference,' US Embassy Jakarta to State Department, A-148, 14 March 1955.
13. Das Gupta, *Serving India*, pp. 215–16.
14. NAA, A1838, 3002/1 part 1, Walter Crocker (Australian High Commissioner to India) to ADEA, cablegram 286, 17 December 1954.

15. G. H. Jansen, *Afro-Asia and Non-Alignment* (London: Faber and Faber, 1966), p. 172; NAA, A11604/2/2, Australian Embassy Jakarta to ADEA, telegram 350, 30 December 1954.
16. PMML, JN, file 306, part I, PM's Note on Afro-Asian Conference, 20 December 1954. On the issue of Asian membership, Nehru also favoured inviting Iran, Nepal, Afghanistan, Iraq, Jordan, Syria, Lebanon, Yemen and Saudi Arabia, but not Formosa.
17. PMML, JN, file 306, part I, PM's Note on Afro-Asian Conference, 20 December 1954.
18. Das Gupta, *Serving India*, p. 217; NAA, A1838, 3002/1 part 1, Crocker to ADEA, cablegram 286, 17 December 1957; NARA, RG 59, CDF 1955–59, box 2668, 670.901/3-1855, US Embassy Jakarta to Department of State, A-150, 18 March 1955.
19. NAA, A1838, 3002/1 part 1, P-I Aneta News Bulletin, 27–28 December 1954; NAUK, CO 936/348, Roderick W. Parkes (British Embassy Jakarta) to Anthony Eden (British Secretary of State for Foreign Affairs), 7 January 1955.
20. 'Colombo Powers in Java Set Wider Stage,' *Western Australian*, 29 December 1954; 'Bogor Talks Prelude to Afro-Asian Unity,' *Times of India*, 1 January 1955.
21. 'Bogor Abounds in Orchids,' *Times of India*, 28 December 1954; Jamie Mackie, *Bandung 1955: Non-Alignment and Afro-Asian Solidarity* (Singapore: Editions Didier Millet, 2005), p. 61. The Bogor presidential palace also provided accommodation for the five leaders. See Roeslan Abdulgani, *The Bandung Connection: The Asia-Africa Conference in Bandung in 1955* (Singapore: Gunung Agung, 1981), p. 21.
22. National Archives of India, New Delhi [henceforth NAI], 1(8) AAC/55, Note of the meeting of the Prime Ministers of the Five Colombo Powers at Bogor in Indonesia on 28 and 29 December 1954; NAUK, CO 396/347, Parkes to FO, telegram 363, 31 December 1954; FO 371/116975, D2231/6, Parkes to FO, telegram 4, 3 January 1955; NARA, RG59, CDF 1955–59, box 2668, 670.901/1-355, Telegram from Djakarta dated January 3; Jansen, *Afro-Asia*, pp. 172–3.
23. NAUK, CO 936/348, Parkes to Eden, 7 January 1955; NAA, A1838, 3002/1 part 2, J. R. Rowland (Australian Chargé d'Affaires to Vietnam) to Arthur Tange (Secretary, ADEA), memorandum 10, 7 January 1955.
24. NAA, A11604, 604/2/2, C. T. Moodie (Australian Legation Rangoon) to Tange, 24 January 1955.
25. Jansen, *Afro-Asia,* pp. 172–73; NAA, A5954, 1412/2, Australian Embassy Jakarta to ADEA, cablegram 350, 30 December 1954. The conference's start date was later brought forward to 18 April due to the Muslim fasting month of Ramadan, which was set to begin on 24 April 1955. On this point, see Mackie, *Bandung 1955*, p. 68 and Naoko Shimazu, 'Diplomacy as Theatre: Staging the Bandung Conference of 1955,' *Modern Asian Studies*, 48:1 (2014), pp. 234–5.
26. NAI, 1(8) AAC/55, Note of the meeting of the Prime Ministers of the Five Colombo Powers at Bogor in Indonesia on 28 and 29 December 1954; NAUK, DO 35/6095, Parkes to FO, telegram 363, 31 December 1954.

27. NAA, A1838, 3002/1 part 2, Rowland to Tange, memorandum 10, 7 January 1955.
28. Jansen, *Afro-Asia*, pp. 175–76; Abdulgani, *The Bandung Connection*, pp. 35–36; PRC FMA 207-00002-04, 94-95, Cable From Peng Di, Situation of the Bogor Conference, 31 December 1954, WCDA, http://digitalarchive.wilsoncenter.org/document/115502, accessed 15 January 2020; NAI, 1(8) AAC/55, Note of the meeting of the Prime Ministers of the Five Colombo Powers at Bogor in Indonesia on 28 and 29 December 1954. On this point, the Indian position was firm. See *SWJN*, II/27, p. 129.
29. Jansen, *Afro-Asia*, pp. 175–6; Abdulgani, *The Bandung Connection*, p. 37; NAUK, CO 396/347, British Embassy Jakarta to FO, telegram 363, 31 December 1954; NAA, A5954, 1412/2, 'The Bogor Meeting of Asian Prime Ministers,' Jakarta Despatch 1, 6 January 1955.
30. NAUK, DO 35/6096, Murray to Crombie, 5 January 1955.
31. PRC FMA 207-00002-04, 100-102, Cable From Peng Di, Third Intelligence Report on the Insider Situation of the Bogor Conference, 6 January 1955, WCDA, https://digitalarchive.wilsoncenter.org/document/115504, accessed 10 March 2020.
32. *SWJN*, II/27, pp. 116–17.
33. NAA, A5954, 1412/2, 'The Bogor Meeting of Asian Prime Ministers,' Jakarta Despatch 1, 6 January 1955; NAUK, CO 396/347, Parkes to FO, telegram 363, 31 December 1954.
34. NAUK, CO 396/347, Parkes to FO, telegram 363, 31 December 1954; NAA, A5954, 1412/2, 'The Bogor meeting of Asian Prime Ministers,' Jakarta Despatch 1, 6 January 1955; A1838, 3002/1 part 2, AHC Karachi to Tange, memorandum 30, 10 January 1955 and A. R. Cutler (Australian High Commissioner to Ceylon) to Tange, memorandum 32, 5 January 1955; NARA, RG 59, CDF 1955–59, box 2668, 670.901/1-355, US Embassy Colombo to Secretary of State, telegram 201, 3 January 1955.
35. NAA, A1838, 3002/1 part 2, AHC Karachi to Tange, memorandum 30, 10 January 1955; Abdulgani, *The Bandung Connection*, p. 37.
36. NARA, RG59, CDF 1955–59, box 2668, 670.901/1-355, Telegram from Djakarta dated January 3.
37. According to this source, 'Ceylon was anxious to revoke the agreement because they wished to receive United States aid and also because of the improved world rice supply position.' Apparently, Burma had 'undertaken to purchase Ceylonese rubber on behalf of Communist China after the rubber-rice is revoked.' Because of this rubber-rice agreement, the United States had denied aid to Ceylon for defying the US-imposed embargo on strategic raw materials to China. NAA, A1838, 3002/1 part 2, R. R. Fernandez (Australian Embassy Jakarta) to Tange, memorandum 1301, 31 December 1954. On the 1952 rubber-rice agreement between Colombo and Beijing, see Shao Chuan Leng, 'Communist China's Economic Relations With Southeast Asia,' *Far Eastern Survey*, 28:1 (1959), p. 7.
38. On the issue of countries to be invited, see NAA, A5954, 1412/2, 'The Bogor Meeting of Asian Prime Ministers,' Jakarta Despatch 1, 6 January 1955; NAUK,

CO 396/347, British Embassy Jakarta to FO, telegram 363, 31 December 1954; Abdulgani, *The Bandung Connection*, p. 30.

39. U Nu cited in Abdulgani, *The Bandung Connection*, p. 31. See also NAA, A1838, 3002/1 part 2, J. C. G. Kevin (Australian Minister and Chargé d'Affaires to Indonesia) to Tange, memorandum 1303, 31 December 1954; A5954, 1412/2, 'The Bogor Meeting of Asian Prime Ministers,' Jakarta Despatch 1, 6 January 1955.
40. Nicholas Tarling, '"Ah-Ah": Britain and the Bandung Conference of 1955,' *Journal of Southeast Asian Studies*, 23:1 (1992), p. 82.
41. PMML, V. K. Krishna Menon Papers [henceforth KM], subject file, 868, Joint Communiqué by the Prime Ministers of Burma, Ceylon, India, Indonesia and Pakistan, 29 December 1954. These countries were Afghanistan, Cambodia, Central African Federation, China, Egypt, Ethiopia, Gold Coast, Iran, Iraq, Japan, Jordan, Laos, Lebanon, Liberia, Libya, Nepal, Philippines, Saudi Arabia, Sudan, Syria, Thailand, Turkey, North and South Vietnam and Yemen.
42. NAUK, CO 936/349, British Embassy Jakarta to FO, telegram 83 14 March 1955; Charles Arden-Clarke (Governor of the Gold Coast) to CO, telegram 132, 15 March 1955; Kwame Nkrumah (Prime Minister of the Gold Coast) to Ali Sastroamidjojo, 17 March 1955.
43. On Nehru's role, see Jansen, *Afro-Asia*, pp. 179–80; NAI, 1(8) AAC/55, Note of the meeting of the Prime Ministers of the Five Colombo Powers at Bogor in Indonesia on 28 and 29 December 1954; NAUK, CO 396/347, British Embassy Jakarta to FO, telegram 363, 31 December 1954; NAA, A1838, 3002/1 part 2, Australian Embassy Jakarta to ADEA, cablegram 2, 3 January 1955.
44. NAA, A1838, 3002/1 part 2, AHC London to ADEA, cablegram 9, 3 January 1955.
45. Abdulgani, *The Bandung Connection*, p. 23.
46. NAUK, CO 396/347, British Embassy Jakarta to FO, telegram 363, 31 December 1954; NAA, A5954, 1412/2, 'The Bogor Meeting of Asian Prime Ministers,' Jakarta Despatch 1, 6 January 1955; NARA, RG59, CDF 1955–59, box 2668, 670.901/1-355, Telegram from Djakarta dated January 3; Jansen, *Afro-Asia*, p. 178.
47. NAA, A1838, 3002/1 part 2, Minute by Crocker, 5 May 1955.
48. NAUK, DO 35/6095, Parkes to FO, telegram 363, 31 December 1954; NARA, RG 59, CDF 1955–59, box 2668, 670.901/1-755, US Embassy Colombo to Secretary of State, telegram 214, 7 January 1955.
49. NAI, 1(8) AAC/55, Note of the Meeting of the Prime Ministers of the Five Colombo Powers at Bogor in Indonesia on 28 and 29 December 1954; NAUK, DO 35/6095, Parkes to FO, telegram 363, 31 December 1954; NAA, A5954, 1412/2, 'The Bogor Meeting of Asian Prime Ministers,' Jakarta Despatch 1, 6 January 1955; Jansen, *Afro-Asia*, p. 178.
50. NAUK, DO 35/6095, Parkes to FO, telegram 363, 31 December 1954.
51. Ibid.; NARA, RG 59, CDF 1955–59, box 2668, 670.901/1-355, US Embassy Colombo to Secretary of State, telegram 201, 3 January 1955; NAI, 1(8) AAC/55, Note of the Meeting of the Prime Ministers of the Five Colombo

Powers at Bogor in Indonesia on 28 and 29 December 1954 and NAI, 1(2) AAC/55, Extract from the fortnightly report for the second half of December 1954 from the Deputy High Commissioner for India in Lahore.

52. NAUK, DO 35/6095, Parkes to FO, telegram 363, 31 December 1954; see also PRC FMA 207-00002-04, 107–108, Cable from Peng Di, Regarding the Situation of the Bogor Conference, 8 January 1955, WCDA, https://digitalarchive.wilsoncenter.org/document/115505, accessed 20 March 2020.
53. NAUK, CO 936/347, British Embassy Jakarta to FO, telegrams 362 and 363, 31 December 1954. For the conference communiqué, see PMML, KM, subject file 868, Joint Communiqué by the Prime Ministers of Burma, Ceylon, India, Indonesia and Pakistan, 29 December 1954.
54. Mackie, *Bandung 1955*, p. 65.
55. NAUK, CO 936/347, British Embassy Jakarta to FO, telegram 362, 31 December 1954.
56. NAUK, DO 35/6096, W. A. C. Mathieson (CO) to J. E. Cable (FO), 28 January 1955.
57. NAA, A1838, 3002/1 part 1, P-I Aneta New Bulletin, 27 and 30 December 1954; NAUK, CO 936/348, Parkes to Eden, 7 January 1955; PRC FMA 207-00002-04, 96-99, Cable from Huang Zhen, Situation Report of the Bogor Conference,2 January 1955, WCDA, https://digitalarchive.wilsoncenter.org/document/115503, accessed 20 March 2020.
58. PMML, JN, file 307, New Delhi to Indel Vientiane, Phnom Penh and Hanoi, 31 December 1954; NAA, A1838, 3002/1 part 2, P-I Aneta New Bulletin, 31 December 1954.
59. *SWJN*, II/27, pp. 116–17.
60. Ibid.
61. Ibid.
62. NAA, A1838, 3002/1 part 2, India Radio News Service, 4 January 1955.
63. NARA, RG 59, CDF 1955–59, box 2668, 670.901/1-355, US Embassy New Delhi to Secretary of State, unnumbered telegram, 3 January 1955.
64. NAUK, FO 371/116975, D2231/17, BHC New Delhi to FO, saving telegram 191, 31 December 1954.
65. Ibid.
66. NAA, A1838, 3002/1 part 2, India Radio News Service, 4 January 1955.
67. NARA, RG 59, CDF 1955–59, box 2668, 670.901/1-355, US Embassy New Delhi to Secretary of State, unnumbered telegram, 3 January 1955.
68. NAA, A1838, 3002/1 part 2, India Radio News Service, 4 January 1955.
69. NARA, RG 59, CDF 1955–59, box 2668, 670.901/1-355, US Embassy New Delhi to Secretary of State, unnumbered telegram, 3 January 1955.
70. 70. NAA, A1838, 3002/1 part 2, India Radio News Service, 4 January 1955.
71. Ibid.
72. NARA, RG 59, CDF 1955–59, box 2668, 670.901/1-355, US Embassy New Delhi to Secretary of State, unnumbered telegram, 3 January 1955.
73. NAA, A1838, 3002/1 part 2, India Radio News Service, 4 January 1955.

74. See for instance PRC FMA 207-00001-04, 13–14, Cable From the Chinese Foreign Ministry, Receiving the Prime Ministers of India and Other Countries and Attending the Asian-African Conference, 9 December 1954, WCDA, https://digitalarchive.wilsoncenter.org/document/114600, accessed 10 March 2020; PRC FMA 207-00085-17, 144–149, Report from the Asia Section, Chinese Foreign Ministry, on the Asian-African Conference, 15 December 1954, WCDA, https://digitalarchive.wilsoncenter.org/document/112442, accessed 10 March 2020; PRC FMA 207-00002-04, 94–95, Cable from Peng Di, Situation of the Bogor Conference, 31 December 31 1954, WCDA, https://digitalarchive.wilsoncenter.org/document/115502, accessed 10 March 2020.
75. NAI, 9(1) FEA/55, Memorandum of Conversation Between Chou En-lai and Raghavan, 17 December 1954.
76. PRC FMA 207-00001-04, 13–14, Cable From the Chinese Foreign Ministry, Receiving the Prime Ministers of India and Other Countries and Attending the Asian-African Conference, 9 December 1954, WCDA, https://digitalarchive.wilsoncenter.org/document/114600, accessed 10 March 2020.
77. PRC FMA 207-00004-03, 22-25, Report from the Chinese Foreign Ministry, Draft of the Tentative Working Plan for Participating in the Asian-African Conference, 16 January 1955, WCDA, https://digitalarchive.wilsoncenter.org/document/113189, accessed 10 March 2020; see also Amitav Acharya, *East of India, South of China: Sino-Indian Encounters in Southeast Asia* (New Delhi: Oxford Academic, 2017), online edition, ch. 4.
78. PRC FMA 207-00004-03, 22–25, Report from the Chinese Foreign Ministry, Draft of the Tentative Working Plan for Participating in the Asian-African Conference, 16 January 1955, WCDA, https://digitalarchive.wilsoncenter.org/document/113189, accessed 10 March 2020.
79. Jian Chen, 'Bridging Revolution and Decolonization: The "Bandung Discourse" in China's Early Cold War Experience,' *Chinese Historical Review*, 15:2 (2008), p. 231.
80. NAA, A1838, 3002/1 part 3, 'China to Attend Asian-African Conference,' *Hsinhua News* attached to W. P. J. Handmer (Australian Trade Commission Hong Kong) to Tange, memorandum 102, 21 February 1955.
81. Zhang, 'Constructing Peaceful Coexistence,' pp. 521–2.
82. PRC FMA 207-00004-01, 1-7, Report from the Chinese Foreign Ministry, Draft Plan for Attending the Asian African Conference, 4 April 1955, WCDA, https://digitalarchive.wilsoncenter.org/document/112896, accessed 20 March 2020; see also Acharya, *East of India, South of China*, ch. 4.
83. PRC FMA 207-00004-01, 1-7, Report from the Chinese Foreign Ministry, Draft Plan for Attending the Asian African Conference, 4 April 1955, WCDA, https://digitalarchive.wilsoncenter.org/document/112896, accessed 20 March 2020; see also Acharya, *East of India, South of China*, ch. 4.
84. On China's view of peaceful coexistence, see for instance Kuisong Yang, 'Changes in Mao Zedong's Attitude Toward the Indochina War, 1949–1973,' *Cold War International History Project Working Paper 34* (Washington, DC: Woodrow Wilson Centre for Scholars, 2002), p. 15, available at https://www.wilsoncenter.org/

sites/default/files/media/documents/publication/ACFB04.pdf, accessed 5 July 2020.

85. Anton Harder, 'Defining Independence in Cold War Asia: Sino-Indian Relations, 1949–1962' (PhD thesis, London School of Economics, 2015), p. 174.
86. Ibid.
87. Chen, 'Bridging Revolution and Decolonisation,' pp. 221 and 226–7.
88. Ibid., p. 222.
89. Ibid., pp. 229 and 239.
90. Mao cited in Jansen, *Afro-Asia*, p. 234.
91. Extracts from the minutes of the Commonwealth Prime Ministers' Conference held in London, 31 January 1955, doc. 0794, Avtar Singh Bhasin (ed.), *India-China Relations 1947–2000: A Documentary Study, Volume 2* (New Delhi: Geetika Publishers, 2018).
92. Extracts from the minutes of the 8th meeting of the Commonwealth Prime Ministers' Conference: 'Long Term Policy in the Far East,' 31 January 1955, doc. 0795, 8 February 1955, Bhasin (ed.), *India-China Relations 1947–2000*. On the ongoing Taiwan Strait crisis, see Michael M. Sheng, 'Mao and China's Relations With the Superpowers in the 1950s: A New Look at the Taiwan Strait Crises and the Sino-Soviet Split,' *Modern China*, 34:4 (2008), pp. 483–8.
93. Extracts from the minutes of the 8th meeting of the Commonwealth Prime Ministers' Conference: 'Long Term Policy in the Far East,' 31 January 1955, doc. 0795, 8 February 1955, Bhasin (ed.), *India-China Relations 1947–2000*.
94. NAI, 1(4) AAC/55, Note by Subimal Dutt, 14 January 1955. Set up in mid-January 1955, the working group included officials from the ministries of External Affairs, Finance, Commerce and Industry, and Education.
95. PMML, JN, file 339, Note on China by T. N. Kaul, Joint Secretary, Ministry of External Affairs, 1955.
96. Lok Sabha Debates (LSD), Vol. II, no. 29, cols. 3887–912, https://eparlib.nic.in/bitstream/123456789/809060/1/pms_01_09_31-03-1955.pdf, accessed 1 December 2019. In February 1955, Iraq and Turkey signed a mutual cooperation pact in Baghdad, which they extended to neighbouring countries. Known as the Baghdad Pact, it eventually included Britain (April 1955), Pakistan (September 1955) and Iran (October 1955). See Sohail H. Hashmi, '"Zero Plus Zero Plus Zero": Pakistan, the Baghdad Pact, and the Suez Crisis.' *International History Review*, 33:3 (2011), p. 528.
97. LSD, Vol. II, no. 29, cols. 3887–912, https://eparlib.nic.in/bitstream/123456789/809060/1/pms_01_09_31-03-1955.pdf, accessed 1 December 2019.
98. Jansen, *Afro-Asia*, p. 191.
99. Robert B. Rakove, *Kennedy, Johnson, and the Nonaligned World* (Cambridge, UK: Cambridge University Press, 2013), p. 7; Minutes of a Meeting, Secretary Dulles' Office, Department of State, Washington, 7 January 1955, doc. 1, *FRUS, 1955–1957, East Asian Security; Cambodia; Laos, Volume XXI* (Washington, DC: GPO, 1990), https://history.state.gov/historicaldocuments/frus1955-57v21/d1, accessed 20 April 2020.

100. See e.g. NARA, RG 306, Country Files, 1953–61, box 16, 'The Conference of Afro-Asian States: Probable Issues and Outcomes,' Department of State Intelligence Report 70, 21 January 1955.
101. NAUK, FO371/111930, D2231/50, FO to British Embassy Addis Ababa, saving telegram 12, 21 October 1954.
102. NAUK, FO 371/116975, D2232/7, Minute by W. D. Allen (FO), 1 January 1955.
103. NAUK, FO371/111930, D2231/50, FO to British Embassy Addis Ababa, saving telegram 12, 21 October 1954; NAUK, FO 371/116975, D2232/7, Minute by Allen, 1 January 1955; Rakove, *Kennedy, Johnson, and the Nonaligned World*, p. 8; Minutes of a Meeting, Secretary Dulles' Office, Department of State, Washington, 7 January 1955, doc. 1, *FRUS*, *1955–1957, XXI*, https://history.state.gov/historicaldocuments/frus1955-57v21/d1, accessed 20 April 2020.
104. For the Eisenhower administration's approach to the Bandung Conference, see Rakove, *Kennedy, Johnson, and the Nonaligned World,* pp. 7–8 and Jason Parker, 'Small Victory, Missed Chance: The Eisenhower Administration, the Bandung Conference and the Turning of the Cold War,' in Kathryn Statler and Andrew Johns (eds), *The Eisenhower Administration, the Third World, and the Globalization of the Cold War* (New York: Rowman and Littlefield, 2006), pp. 153–74.
105. Tao Wang, *Isolating the Enemy: Diplomatic Strategy in China and the United States, 1953–1956* (New York: Columbia University Press, 2021), Kindle edition, ch. 6; Memorandum of a Conversation, Department of State, 10 January 1955, doc. 2, *FRUS*, *1955–1957, XXI*, https://history.state.gov/historicaldocuments/frus1955-57v21/d2, accessed 20 April 2020; Minutes of a Meeting, Secretary's Office, Department of State, Washington, 18 January 1955, doc. 6; *FRUS*, *1955–1957, XXI*, https://history.state.gov/historicaldocuments/frus1955-57v21/d6, accessed 20 April 2020.
106. Circular Telegram from the Department of State to Certain Diplomatic Missions, 25 January 1955, doc. 8, *FRUS*, *1955–1957, XXI*, https://history.state.gov/historicaldocuments/frus1955-57v21/d8, accessed 20 April 2020.
107. Circular Telegram from the Department of State to Certain Diplomatic Missions, 25 February 1955, doc. 23, *FRUS*, *1955–1957, XXI*, https://history.state.gov/historicaldocuments/frus1955-57v21/d23, accessed 20 April 2020.
108. Wang, *Isolating the Enemy*, ch. 6; NAUK, FO371/116975, D2231/34, British Embassy Paris to FO, saving 11, 10 January 1955.
109. NAUK, FO371/116975, D2232/24, 'Afro-Asian Conference,' minute by W. D. Allen (FO), 6 January 1954.
110. Antoine Pinay (French Minister of Foreign Affairs) to various posts, 8 March 1955, doc. 119, in Ministère des Affaires Étrangères, *Documents Diplomatiques Français, 1955, Tome I (1 Janvier–30 Juin)* (Paris: Imprimerie Nationale, 1987).
111. NAUK, CAB 128/28, CC (55) 3rd conclusions, 13 January 1955. However, British ministers agreed 'to discourage the Government of the Central African Federation and the Gold Coast from sending a representative' to Bandung to prevent 'Asian intervention in African affairs.' For the shift in British policy, see also Tarling, 'Britain and the Bandung Conference,' pp. 82–95.

112. Wang, *Isolating the Enemy*, ch. 6; Tarling, 'Britain and the Bandung Conference,' p. 98.
113. Matthew Jones, 'A "Segregated" Asia? Race, the Bandung Conference, and Pan-Asianist Fears in American Thought and Policy, 1954–1955,' *Diplomatic History*, 29:5 (2005), p. 858.
114. Wang, *Isolating the Enemy*, ch. 6; Tarling, 'Britain and the Bandung Conference,' pp. 97–100.

9. THE BANDUNG CONFERENCE

1. NAUK, FO 371/116985, D2231/363, Berkeley Gage (British Ambassador to Thailand) to Harold Macmillan (British Secretary of State for Foreign Affairs), despatch 36, 25 May 1955.
2. G. H. Jansen, *Afro-Asia and Non-Alignment* (London: Faber and Faber, 1966), p. 188; Naoko Shimazu, 'Diplomacy as Theatre: Staging the Bandung Conference of 1955,' *Modern Asian Studies*, 48:1 (2014), p. 235; 'They Want to Have a Freedom Festival,' *Daily Telegraph*, 18 April 1955.
3. Shimazu, 'Diplomacy as Theatre,' p. 238.
4. Ibid., p. 241.
5. Ibid., pp. 237–8.
6. *Het Nieuwsblad voor Sumatra* cited in Brian Russell Roberts and Keith Foulcher, *Indonesian Notebook: A Sourcebook on Richard Wright and the Bandung Conference* (Durham, NC: Duke University Press, 2016), p. 82.
7. Shimazu, 'Diplomacy as Theatre,' p. 237.
8. *Het Nieuwsblad voor Sumatra* cited in Roberts and Foulcher, *Indonesian Notebook*, p. 82.
9. Jansen, *Afro-Asia*, p. 188.
10. NAA, A1838, 3002/1 part 2, A. R. Cutler (Australian High Commissioner to Ceylon) to Arthur Tange (Secretary, ADEA), memorandum 37, 5 January 1955.
11. NAUK, DO 35/6096, British Embassy Rangoon to FO, 13 January 1955.
12. PMML, JN,, file 314, Extract from secret letter no. 1/5/CO/55/2010 dated 14 January 1955 from B. F. H. B. Tyabji (Indian Ambassador to Indonesia) to Subimal Dutt (Commonwealth Secretary, MEA), submitted for information of the Prime Minister; NAI, 1(2) AAC/55, Extract from the fortnightly despatch no. 24 for the period from 16 December to 31 December, received from the Embassy of India, Jakarta, undated. In public, though, the Indian government sought to quell rumours of Indian criticism by instructing Tyabji to convey to the Indonesian government that India 'fully appreciated' the arrangements made for the Indian delegation. See PMML, JN, file 311, Foreign New Delhi (Dutt) to Indembassy Jakarta (Tyabji), telegram 30385, 13 January 1955.
13. NAA, A1838, 3002/1, part 2, Minute by Walter Crocker (Australian High Commissioner to India), 5 May 1955.
14. NAUK, DO 35/6096, Record of Conversation with the High Commissioner of India, 17 January 1955.

15. NARA, RG 59, CDF, 1955–59, box 2668, 670.901/2-1555, Horace Hildreth (US ambassador to Pakistan) to John Foster Dulles (Secretary of State), telegram 1082, 15 February 1955.
16. See e.g. NAI, 1(8) AAC/55, Tyabji to Dutt, no. 2/12/CO/55/2009, 14 January 1955; NAI, 1(2), AAC/55, Extract from the Fortnightly despatch no. 2 for the period from 16 to 31 January 1955, received from the Ambassador of India, Jakarta and extract from the Fortnightly despatch no. 1 for the period from 1 January 1955 to 15 January, received from the Ambassador of India, Jakarta; PMML, JN, file 314, Extract from secret letter no. 1/5/CO/55/2010 dated 14 January 1955 from Tyabji to Dutt, submitted for information of the Prime Minister.
17. NARA, RG 59, CDF 1955–59, box 2668, 670.901/2-1555, Hildreth to Dulles, telegram 1082, 15 February 1955. A high-ranking Pakistani official passed, in strict confidence, an extract of Tyabji's cable to the US ambassador in Karachi. The Pakistanis had received it from a source in India. See NARA, RG 59, CDF 1955–59, box 2668, 670.901/2-1555, Hildreth to Dulles, telegram 1073, 12 February 1955.
18. See e.g. NAUK, FO 371/112223, DL1903/41, Minute by J. E. Cable (FO), 25 November 1954.
19. PMML, JN, file 320, Nehru to Tyabji, 20 February 1955.
20. Ibid.
21. PMML, JN, file 320, Nehru to Ali Sastroamidjojo and Nehru to Sukarno, 20 February 1955.
22. PMML, JN, file 320, Nehru to Ali Sastroamidjojo, 20 February 1955.
23. On the worsening of the Taiwan Strait crisis, see Tao Wang, *Isolating the Enemy: Diplomatic Strategy in China and the United States, 1953–1956* (New York: Columbia University Press, 2021), Kindle edition, ch. 4; Yang Huei Pang, *Strait Rituals: China, Taiwan, and the United States in the Taiwan Strait Crises, 1954–1958* (Hong Kong: Hong Kong University Press, 2019), pp. 116–53.
24. Aware of frequent Indian criticism of the Indonesians, James Cable of the Foreign Office once remarked that the Indians were 'colonial snobs' who 'seldom bother[ed] to conceal their conviction that it is socially more distinguished to have been oppressed by the British than by the Dutch.' NAUK, FO 371/112223, DL1903/41, Minute by J. E. Cable (FO), 25 November 1954.
25. Shimazu, 'Diplomacy as Theatre,' p. 237.
26. Roberts and Foulcher, *Indonesian Notebook*, p. 83.
27. Jansen, *Afro-Asia*, p. 188; 'Conference Area to Be Guarded,' *Hindustan Times*, 14 April 1954.
28. 'Conference Area to be Guarded,' *Hindustan Times*, 14 April 1954.
29. Ibid.; Jansen, *Afro-Asia*, p. 188.
30. Jansen, *Afro-Asia*, p. 188.
31. 'Guns, Flags and Asian Talks,' *Daily Telegraph*, 15 April 1955.
32. Roberts and Foulcher, *Indonesian Notebook*, p. 79.
33. NAUK, FO 371/116983, D2231/319, Oscar C. Morland (British ambassador to Indonesia) to Macmillan, despatch 40, 28 April 1955; see also FO 371/116985,

D2231/366, Report on Asian-African Conference: Bandung, undated (Australian report by K. C. O. Shann).

34. NAUK, FO 371/116983, D2231/319, Morland to Macmillan, despatch 40, 28 April 1955.
35. NAUK, FO 371/116985, D2231/366, Report on Asian-African Conference: Bandung, undated (Australian report by Shann); K. Sarwar Hasan, 'Bandung Memories,' *Pakistan Horizon*, 68: 3/4 (2015), p. 2. Indeed, as Tyabji told Ali Sastroamidjojo, who had criticised Yunus Khan for being 'too dynamic and energetic,' the latter 'had done much in galvanising the whole [conference] organisation.' See PMML, JN, file 335, Tyabji to Dutt, no. 1/5/CO/55, 12 April 1955; see also file 329, part I, Extract from secret D.O. letter no. 1/5/CO/55/1433 dated 25 March 1955 from BFHB Tyabji to the Commonwealth Secretary, MEA. The Secretariat was divided into various sections, including accommodation, transport and protocol.
36. NAUK, FO 371/116975, D2231/35, Asian-African Conference Secretariat Formed, 8 January 1954; C. S. Jha, *From Bandung to Tashkent: Glimpses of India's Foreign Policy* (London: Sangam Books, 1983), p. 63. The Joint Secretariat was headed by Ruslan Abdulgani of Indonesia.
37. NAUK, FO 371/116985, D2231/366, Report on Asian-African Conference: Bandung, undated (Australian report by Shann).
38. NAA, A1838, 3002/1 part 4, Report on the Asian-African Conference by C. P. Fitzgerald, undated; Shimazu, 'Diplomacy as Theatre,' p. 241.
39. PMML, JN, file 335, Tyabji to Dutt, no. 1/5/CO/55, 12 April 1955.
40. Ibid.
41. NAA, A1838, 3002/1 part 3, 'The Asian-African Conference,' *Aneta*, 15 March 1955; Tarling, 'Britain and the Bandung Conference,' p. 101.
42. NAA, A1838, 3002/1, part 4, Report on the Asian-African Conference by C. P. Fitzgerald, undated; Shimazu, 'Diplomacy as Theatre,' p. 241.
43. NAA, A1838, 3002/1, part 3, 'The Asian-African Conference,' *Aneta*, 15 March 1955.
44. Shimazu, 'Diplomacy as Theatre,' p. 237.
45. Ibid.
46. Ibid, p. 238.
47. Roberts and Foulcher, *Indonesian Notebook*, p. 82.
48. 'Thousands Greet Chou En-lai,' *Hindustan Times*, 17 April 1955.
49. Ibid.
50. 'China Seat in U.N. as Talks Issue,' *Sydney Morning Herald*, 17 April 1955; 'Chou Accorded Big Welcome in Jakarta,' *Times of India*, 17 April 1955.
51. 'Thousands Greet Chou En-lai,' *Hindustan Times*, 17 April 1955.
52. 'China Seat in U.N. as Talks Issue,' *Sydney Morning Herald*, 17 April 1955.
53. Roberts and Foulcher, *Indonesian Notebook*, p. 79.
54. Shimazu, 'Diplomacy as Theatre,' p. 245; Roberts and Foulcher, *Indonesian Notebook*, p. 79; NAA, A1838, 3002/1 part 5, Australian Embassy Jakarta to ADEA, cablegram 169, 20 April 1955.
55. Shimazu, 'Diplomacy as Theatre,' p. 254.

56. Ibid., p. 246.
57. NAA, A1838, 3002/1 part 4, China's delegation to Bandung Conference, 15 April 1955; NAUK, FO 371/116980, D2231/215, Humphrey Trevelyan (British Chargé d'Affaires Peking) to FO, telegram 372 and 383, 15 April 1955.
58. PMML, JN, file 333, 'African-Asian Conference,' note by C. S. Jha (Joint Secretary, MEA), 6 April 1955.
59. NAUK, FO 371/116985, D2231/366, Report on Asian-African Conference: Bandung, undated (Australian report by Shann).
60. Steve Tsang, 'Target Zhou Enlai: The "Kashmir Princess" Incident of 1955,' *China Quarterly*, 139 (1994), pp. 766–82, Jamie Mackie, *Bandung 1955: Non-Alignment and Afro-Asian Solidarity* (Singapore: Editions Didier Millet, 2005), p. 68.
61. Tsang, 'Target Zhou Enlai,' pp. 766–82.
62. NAA, A1838, 3002/1 part 5, AHC Colombo to Tange, despatch 4, 6 April 1955, attachment A.
63. On this point, see NARA, RG 59, CDF 1955–59, box 2668, 'The Conference of Afro-Asian States: Probable Issues and Outcomes,' Department of State Intelligence Report, 21 January 1955.
64. NAUK, FO 371/116985, D2231/366, Report on Asian-African Conference: Bandung, undated (Australian report by Shann). Due to the resignation of the Nepalese government, the Nepalese Prime Minister and Foreign Minister did not go in the end. See NAUK, FO 371/116981, D2231/264, British Embassy Kathmandu to P. S. Tomlinson (FO), 14 April 1955.
65. NAUK, FO 371/116981, D2231/264, British Embassy Kathmandu to P. S. Tomlinson (FO), 14 April 1955.
66. Ibid.
67. NAA, A1838, 3002/1 part 5, Australian Embassy Jakarta to ADEA, cablegram 169, 20 April 1955.
68. Ibid.
69. NAUK, FO 371/116981, D2231/298, Ali Sastroamidjojo's speech, undated; Nicholas Tarling, *Britain, Southeast Asia and the Impact of the Korean War* (Singapore: NUS Press, 2005), p. 432.
70. NAA, A1838, 3002/1, part 4, Report on the Asian-African Conference by C. P. Fitzgerald, undated; Mackie, *Bandung 1955*, p. 66; Zhou Enlai's Telegram to the CCP Central Committee and Mao Zedong regarding the Discussion of Political Issues, 30 April 1955, WCDA, https://digitalarchive.wilsoncenter.org/document/121750, accessed 10 April 2020.
71. PMML, JN, file 337, Asian-African Conference, 17 April 1954; NAUK, FO 371/116985, D2231/366, Report on Asian-African Conference: Bandung, undated (Australian report by Shann); DO35/6098, Morland to FO, telegram 140, 20 April 1955; Jansen, *Afro-Asia*, pp. 193–4 and 195; Mackie, *Bandung 1955*, p. 72.
72. NAUK, FO 371/116985, D2231/366, Report on Asian-African Conference: Bandung, undated (Australian report by Shann); NAUK, FO 371/116983, D2231/319, 'Some Impressions of the Bandung Conference,' enclosure to Morland to Macmillan, despatch 40, 28 April 1955.

73. Jansen, *Afro-Asia*, p. 194.
74. Ibid.; NAUK, DO 35/6098, Morland to FO, telegram 152, 21 April 1955; Renaud Sivan (French Ambassador to Indonesia) to Antoine Pinay (French Minister of Foreign Affairs), telegram 168–176, 21 April 1955, doc. 209, *Documents Diplomatiques Français* [henceforth *DDF*], 1955, Tome I (1 Janvier–30 Juin) (Paris: Imprimerie Nationale, 1987).
75. Jansen, *Afro-Asia*, pp. 194–5.
76. Ibid., p. 195; NAA, A1838, 3034/11/147 part 1, Crocker to ADEA, Cablegram 497, 16 September 1961.
77. NAA, A1838, 3002/1 part 4, Report on the Asian-African Conference by C. P. Fitzgerald, undated.
78. Mackie, *Bandung 1955*, p. 72.
79. Ibid., p. 83.
80. NAA, A1838, 3002/1 part 4, Report on the Asian-African Conference by C. P. Fitzgerald, undated; NAUK, DO 35/6098, Morland to FO, telegram 144, 20 April 1955; FO 371/116983, D2231/317, 'Asian-African Conference at Bandung April 1955,' enclosure to Morland to FO, despatch 39, 26 April 1955.
81. NAUK, DO 35/6098, Morland to FO, telegram 152, 21 April 1955.
82. Maurice Couve de Murville (French ambassador to the United States) to Pinay, telegram 2226–32, 20 April 1955, doc. 206, *DDF*, 1955, Tome I (1 Janvier–30 Juin).
83. NAUK, DO 35/6098, Morland to FO, telegram 152, 21 April 1955; FO 371/116983, D2231/317, 'Asian-African Conference at Bandung April 1955,' enclosure to Morland to FO, despatch 39, 26 April 1955; 'Bandung Powers' Pledge to Fight Colonialism,' *Times of India*, 20 April 1955.
84. NAUK, FO 371/116983, D2231/317, 'Asian-African Conference at Bandung April 1955,' enclosure to Morland to FO, despatch 39, 26 April 1955; NAA, A1838, 3002/1 part 4, Report on the Asian-African Conference by C. P. Fitzgerald, undated.
85. NAUK, FO 371/116983, D2231/317, 'Asian-African Conference at Bandung April 1955,' enclosure to Morland to FO, despatch 39, 26 April 1955; NAA, A1838, 3002/1 part 4, Report on the Asian-African Conference by C. P. Fitzgerald, undated.
86. For the text of Zhou's supplementary speech, see NAUK, FO 371/116981, D2231/257C, New China News Agency: Premier Chou En-lai makes supplementary speech, 20 April 1955. On this issue, see NAUK, FO 371/116981, D2231/257C, New China News Agency: Premier Chou En-lai speaks at Asian-African Conference, 20 April 1955; NAA, A1838, 3002/1 part 4, Report on the Asian-African Conference by C. P. Fitzgerald, undated; Sivan to Pinay, telegram 168–76, 21 April 1955, doc. 209, *DDF*, 1955, Tome I (1 Janvier–30 Juin).
87. Zhou Enlai's Telegram to the CCP Central Committee and Mao Zedong regarding the Discussion of Political Issues, 30 April 1955, WCDA, https://digitalarchive.wilsoncenter.org/document/121750, accessed 5 June 2020; Guang Shu Zhang, 'Constructing "Peaceful Coexistence": China's Diplomacy Toward the Geneva and Bandung Conferences, 1954–55,' *Cold War History*, 7:4 (2007), p. 522.

88. NAUK, FO 371/116981, D2231/257C, New China News Agency: Premier Chou En-lai makes supplementary speech, 20 April 1955.
89. Ibid.
90. NAUK, FO 371/116985, D2231/366, Report on Asian-African Conference: Bandung, undated (Australian report by Shann); Mackie, *Bandung 1955*, p. 85.
91. Sivan to Pinay, telegram 177–82, 22 April 1955, doc. 213, *DDF*, 1955, Tome I (1 Janvier–30 Juin); NAUK, FO 371/116985, D2231/366, Report on Asian-African Conference: Bandung, undated (Australian report by Shann); Jansen, *Afro-Asia*, pp. 212–13.
92. NAUK, DO 35/6098, CRO to various posts, telegram 154, 24 April 1954.
93. NAUK, FO 371/116984, D2231/333, 'Colonialism,' enclosure to E. V. Vines (BHC Colombo) to R. C. C. Hunt (CRO), 2 May 1955; Mackie, *Bandung 1955*, p. 87.
94. NAUK, FO 371/116984, D2231/333, 'Colonialism,' enclosure to Vines Hunt, 2 May 1955; Mackie, *Bandung 1955*, p. 87.
95. NAUK, FO 371/116985, D2231/366, Report on Asian-African Conference: Bandung, undated (Australian report by Shann); NAA, A1838, 3002/1, part 4, Report on the Asian-African Conference by C. P. Fitzgerald, undated; Jansen, *Afro-Asia*, pp. 203–4; NAUK, FO 371/116981, D2231/276, Reuters reporting, undated; FO 371/116983, D2231/319, 'Some Impressions of the Bandung Conference,' enclosure to Morland to Macmillan, despatch 40, 28 April 1955; Mackie, *Bandung 1955*, pp. 89–90.
96. P. V. Rajgopal (ed.), *I Was Nehru's Shadow: From the Diaries of KF Rustamji, IP, Padma Vibhushan* (New Delhi: Wisdom Tree, 2014), Kindle edition, ch. 8.
97. NAUK, FO 371/116986, D2231/376, Meeting of the Heads of Delegations, 22 April 1955, 9 a.m. (Thai minutes); Zhou Enlai's Telegram to the CCP Central Committee and Mao Zedong regarding the Discussion of Political Issues, 30 April 1955, WCDA, https://digitalarchive.wilsoncenter.org/document/121750, accessed 5 June 2020.
98. NAUK, FO 371/116986, D2231/376, Meeting of the Heads of Delegations, 22 April 1955, 9 a.m. (Thai minutes).
99. Ibid.
100. Ibid.; Zhou Enlai's Telegram to the CCP Central Committee and Mao Zedong regarding the Discussion of Political Issues, 30 April 1955, WCDA, https://digitalarchive.wilsoncenter.org/document/121750, accessed 5 June 2020. On the question of countries supporting the idea of a new (communist) colonialism, see NAUK, FO 371/116983, D2231/319, 'Some Impressions of the Bandung Conference,' enclosure to Morland to Macmillan, despatch 40, 28 April 1955.
101. NAUK, FO 371/116986, D2231/376, Meeting of the Heads of Delegations, 22 April 1955, 9 a.m. (Thai minutes).
102. NAUK, DO 35/6098, Morland to FO, telegram 176, 25 April 1955.
103. NAUK, DO 35, Colombo to CRO, telegram 181, 27 April 1955; Zhou Enlai's Telegram to the CCP Central Committee and Mao Zedong regarding the Discussion of Political Issues, 30 April 1955, WCDA, https://digitalarchive.wilsoncenter.org/document/121750, accessed 5 June 2020; NAUK, FO

371/116983, D2231/318, Final Communiqué of the Bandung Conference, 4 May 1955.

104. NAA, A11604, 604/2/2, K. C. O. Shann (Assistant Secretary, ADEA and Australian Observer to the Asian African Conference) to ADEA, cablegram 179, 25 April 1955; Mackie, *Bandung 1955*, p. 103.
105. NAUK, DO 35/6098, Morland to FO, telegram 176, 25 April 1955; Mackie, *Bandung 1955*, p. 96.
106. NAUK, FO 371/116983, D2231/319, 'Some Impressions of the Bandung Conference,' enclosure to Morland to Macmillan, despatch 40, 28 April 1955.
107. NAUK, DO 35/6098, Morland to FO, telegram 176, 25 April 1955; FO 371/116983, D2231/318, Final Communiqué of the Bandung Conference, 4 May 1955.
108. NAUK, FO 371/116983, D2231/319, 'Some Impressions of the Bandung Conference,' enclosure to Morland to Macmillan, despatch 40, 28 April 1955.
109. *SWJN*, Second Series [henceforth II], Volume 28 (New Delhi: Jawaharlal Nehru Memorial Fund, 1984–2015), p. 136.
110. Mackie, *Bandung 1955*, p. 96.
111. Jansen, *Afro-Asia*, p. 209; Mackie, *Bandung 1955*, p. 98; NAUK, FO371/116985, D2231/366, Report on Asian-African Conference: Bandung, undated (Australian report by Shann).
112. NAUK, FO371/116985, D2231/366, Report on Asian-African Conference: Bandung, undated (Australian report by Shann).
113. NAUK, FO 371/116986, D2231/376, Meeting of the Heads of Delegations, 22 April 1955, afternoon session (Thai minutes).
114. NAUK, FO 371/116985, D2231/366, Report on Asian-African Conference: Bandung, undated (Australian report by Shann).
115. NAUK, FO 371/116983, D2231/319, 'Some Impressions of the Bandung Conference,' enclosure to Morland to Macmillan, despatch 40, 28 April 1955.
116. NAUK, FO 371/116986, D2231/376, Meeting of the Heads of Delegations, 22 April 1955, afternoon session (Thai minutes).
117. NAUK, FO 371/116986, D2231/376, Meeting of the Heads of Delegations, 23 April 1955, 9.15 a.m. (Thai minutes); Jansen, *Afro-Asia*, p. 210; Mackie, *Bandung 1955*, pp. 98–9; NAUK, FO 371/116983, D2231/319, 'Some Impressions of the Bandung Conference,' enclosure to Morland to Macmillan, despatch 40, 28 April 1955. For Indian views on Malik, Romulo and Jamali, see NAI, 1(16) AAC/55, Ali Yavar Jung (Indian Ambassador to Egypt) to C. S. Jha (Joint Secretary, MEA), 7 April 1955; M. R. A. Baig (Indian Legation, Manila) to D. N. Chatterjee (MEA), 14 February 1955.
118. NAUK, FO 371/116986, D2231/376, Meeting of the Heads of Delegations, 23 April 1955, 9.15 a.m. (Thai minutes); Zhou Enlai's Telegram to the CCP Central Committee and Mao Zedong regarding the Discussion of Political Issues, 30 April 1955, WCDA, https://digitalarchive.wilsoncenter.org/document/121750, accessed 5 June 2020.
119. NAUK, FO 371/116986, D2231/376, Meeting of the Heads of Delegations, 24 April 1955, 4 p.m. (Thai minutes); *SWJN*, II/28, pp. 136–7; H. W. Brands,

The Specter of Neutralism: The United States and the Emergence of the Third World (New York: Columbia University Press, 1989), p. 85; Mackie, *Bandung 1955*, p. 104. For the final communiqué, see NAUK, FO 371/116983, D2231/318, Final Communiqué of the Bandung Conference, 4 May 1955.

120. *SWJN*, II/28, p. 137; NAUK, FO 371/116984, D2231/343, New Zealand Embassy, Washington to New Zealand Department of External Affairs, 26 April 1955.
121. Sivan to Pinay, telegram 226, 27 April 1955, doc. 229, *DDF*, 1955, Tome I (1 Janvier–30 Juin).
122. NAUK, DO 35/6098, Special Summary: Bandung Conference, undated; BHC New Delhi to CRO, telegram 504, 28 April 1955.
123. NAUK, DO 35/6098, Special Summary: Bandung Conference, undated.
124. Ibid.; NAUK, DO 35/6098, BHC New Delhi to CRO, telegram 504, 28 April 1955.
125. NAUK, DO 35/6098, BHC New Delhi to CRO, telegram 504, 28 April 1955.

10. BANDUNG'S AFTERMATH

1. C. Khaliquzzaman cited NAUK, DO 35/6099, Impressions of the Bandung Conference (Australian report by Walter Crocker), undated.
2. NAUK, FO 371/116984, D2231/343, New Zealand Embassy Washington to New Zealand Department of External Affairs, 28 April 1955; FO 371/116984, D2231/345, 'Asian-African Conference: Note by Chancery,' enclosure to Office of Commissioner-General for the United Kingdom in Southeast Asia (Singapore) to FO, 7 May 1955.
3. NAUK, FO 371/116983, D2231/319, 'Some Impressions of the Bandung Conference,' enclosure to Oscar Morland (British Ambassador to Indonesia) to Harold Macmillan (British Secretary of State for Foreign Affairs), despatch 40, 28 April 1955.
4. NAUK, FO 371/116984, D2231/345, 'Asian-African Conference: Note by Chancery,' enclosure to Office of Commissioner-General for the United Kingdom in Southeast Asia (Singapore) to FO, 7 May 1955.
5. NAUK, DO 35/6099, Impressions of the Bandung Conference (Australian report by Crocker), undated.
6. NAUK, FO 371/116985, D2231/350, Roger Makins (British Ambassador to the US) to FO, Saving 256, 12 May 1955.
7. NARA, RG59, CDF, 1955–59, box 2670, 670.901/5-3155, US Embassy Jakarta to Department of State, despatch 537, 31 May 1955.
8. NAUK, FO 371/116896, D2231/373, State Department Intelligence Report 6903, 27 April 1955.
9. NAUK, FO 371/116985, D2231/366, Report on Asian-African Conference: Bandung, undated (Australian report by K. C. O. Shann).
10. NARA, RG59, CDF 1955–59, box 2670, 670.901/5-3155, US Embassy Jakarta to Department of State, despatch 537, 31 May 1955.
11. Ibid.

12. Ibid.
13. NAUK, DO 35/6099, Impressions of the Bandung Conference (Australian report by Crocker), undated.
14. Zhou Enlai cited in Brands, H. W., *The Specter of Neutralism: The United States and the Emergence of the Third World* (New York: Columbia University Press, 1989), p. 114; see also B. K. Nehru, *Nice Guys Finish Second: Memoirs* (Gurgaon, India: Penguin Random House India, 2012), p. 296.
15. NAA, A1838, 3002/1 part 5, CRO to BHC Canberra, telegram 9, 2 May 1955.
16. NAUK, FO 371/116985, D2231/351, British Embassy Beirut to Ivone Kirkpatrick (FO), 9 May 1955.
17. NAUK, FO 371/116985, D2231/354, British Delegation to the UN New York to FO, 15 May 1955.
18. NAUK, FO 371/116985, D2231/357, British Embassy Damascus to FO, 6 May 1955.
19. NAUK, DO 35/6099, Impressions of the Bandung Conference (Australian report by Crocker), undated.
20. PMML, JN, file 341, Nehru to Countess Mountbatten of Burma, 30 April 1955.
21. Ibid.
22. Ibid.
23. Ibid.; NAUK, DO 35/6099, Impressions of the Bandung Conference (Australian report by Crocker), undated.
24. NAUK, DO 35/6099, Impressions of the Bandung Conference (Australian report by Crocker), undated.
25. Ibid.
26. Ibid.
27. NAA, A1838, 3002/1 part 4, *Melbourne Herald*, 21 April 1955.
28. PMML, JN, file 341, Note on the Asian-African Conference at Bandung (by Nehru), 28 April 1954.
29. Tao Wang, *Isolating the Enemy: Diplomatic Strategy in China and the United States, 1953–1956* (New York: Columbia University Press, 2021), Kindle edition, ch. 5; NAA, A1838, 3002/1 part 4, Report on the Asian-African Conference by C. P. Fitzgerald, undated.
30. NAUK, DO 35, 6098, BHC Karachi to CRO, telegram 722, 2 May 1955.
31. Wang, *Isolating the Enemy*, ch. 5; see also Rudra Chaudhuri, 'The Making of an "All Weather Friendship" Pakistan, China and the History of a Border Agreement: 1949–1963,' *International History Review*, 40:1 (2018), p. 46.
32. Naoko Shimazu, 'What is Sociability in Diplomacy?,' *Diplomatica*, *1*:1 (2019), p. 61; see also NAUK, FO 371/116981, D2231/249D, *Asian-African News*, 23 April 1955.
33. NAUK, FO 371/116985, D2231/366, Report on Asian-African Conference: Bandung, undated (Australian report by Shann). For the text of the agreement, see PMML, JN, file 340, Sino-Indonesian treaty on dual nationality question, 25 April 1955.
34. PMML, JN, file 341, Nehru to Countess Mountbatten of Burma, 30 April 1955.

35. NAUK, FO 371/116985, D2231/354, British Delegation to the UN New York to FO, 15 May 1955.
36. NAUK, FO 371/116985, D2231/351, British Embassy Beirut to Ivone Kirkpatrick (FO), 9 May 1955.
37. NAUK, DO 35/6099, Impressions of the Bandung Conference (Australian report by Crocker), undated.
38. Ibid.
39. NARA, RG 59, CDF 1955–59, box 2670, 670.901/5-3155, Arthur B. Emmons (US Embassy Jakarta) to Department of State, despatch 537, 31 May 1955.
40. Renaud Sivan (French ambassador to Indonesia) to Antoine Pinay (French Minister of Foreign Affairs), telegram 199-206, 23 April 1955, doc. 215 and telegram 226, 27 April 1955, doc. 229, *DDF*, 1955, Tome I (1 Janvier–30 Juin) (Paris: Imprimerie Nationale, 1987).
41. NAUK, FO 371/116984, D2231/343, New Zealand Embassy Washington to New Zealand Department of External Affairs, 26 April 1955.
42. NAUK, FO 371/116986, 2231/368 The Afro-Asian conference (paper by the FO Research Department), 5 May 1955.
43. Ibid.
44. PMML, JN, file 341, Nehru to Countess Mountbatten of Burma, 30 April 1955.
45. *SWJN*, Second Series [henceforth II], Volume 28 (New Delhi: Jawaharlal Nehru Memorial Fund, 1984–2015), p. 144; NAUK, DO 35/6098, BHC New Delhi to CRO, telegram 524, 30 April 1955; BHC New Delhi to CRO, saving 50, 28 April 1955; PMML, JN, file 341 Foreign New Delhi (Nehru) to Hicomind London (for Anthony Eden), primin 21121, 29 April 1955; PRC FMA 207-00059-01, Report from the Chinese Foreign Ministry, Comments on the Asian-African Conference from the Participating Countries After the Conference, 10 May 1955, WCDA, https://digitalarchive.wilsoncenter.org/document/114686, accessed 10 November 2020.
46. PMML, JN, file 341, Nehru to Countess Mountbatten of Burma, 30 April 1955.
47. Ibid.; PMML, JN, file 341, Note on the Asian-African Conference at Bandung (by Nehru), 28 April 1954; Foreign New Delhi to Indembassy Jakarta (for Ali Sastroamidjojo), primin 21116, 28 April 1955.
48. PMML, JN, file 340, Nehru to Sardar Swaran Singh (Indian Minister for Works, Housing and Supply), 24 April 1955.
49. NAI, 1(2) AAC/55, Fortnightly despatches nos. 7 and 8 for the period from 1 April to 15 April 1955 and from 16 April to 30 April 1955.
50. PMML, JN, file 341, Nehru to Countess Mountbatten of Burma, 30 April 1955.
51. Ibid.
52. NAUK, DO 35/6099, Impressions of the Bandung Conference (Australian report by Crocker), undated.
53. *SWJN*, II/28, p. 151.
54. PMML, JN, file 341, Note on the Asian-African Conference at Bandung (by Nehru), 28 April 1954.
55. Ibid.
56. Ibid.

57. Ibid.
58. NAUK, DO 35/6099, Impressions of the Bandung Conference (Australian report by Crocker), undated.
59. LSD, vol. IV, part II, 30 April 1955, cols. 6962–74, https://eparlib.nic.in/bitstream/123456789/56077/1/lsd_01_09_30-04-1955_pII.pdf#search=1955%20[1952%20TO%201959]%201955, accessed 10 June 2020.
60. NAUK, FO 371/116985, D2231/354, British Delegation to the UN New York to FO, 15 May 1955; FO 371/116985, D2231/357, British Embassy Damascus to FO, 6 May 1955.
61. NAUK, FO 371/116985, D2231/366, Report on Asian-African Conference: Bandung, undated (Australian report by Shann). According to the *Hindustan Times*, some delegations felt that the Asian-African conference should take place annually. See 'Periodic Meetings of Afro-Asian Nations,' *Hindustan Times*, 17 April 1955.
62. NAUK, FO 371/116985, D2231/366, Report on Asian-African Conference: Bandung, undated (Australian report by Shann).
63. Wang, *Isolating the Enemy*, ch. 5.
64. Summary of the Talks between Premier Zhou and Nehru and U Nu, 16 April 1955, WCDA, http://digitalarchive.wilsoncenter.org/document/114671, accessed 10 November 2021.
65. Ibid.
66. Badr-ud-din Tyabji, *Memoirs of an Egoist. Volume I: 1907 to 1956* (New Delhi: Roli Books, 1988), p. 325.
67. NAI, 1(8), AAC/55, Subimal Dutt (Commonwealth Secretary, MEA) to C. S. Jha (Joint Secretary, MEA), 3 March 1955.
68. 'Leaders Arrive in Bandung for Historic Meet,' *Hindustan Times*, 17 April 1955.
69. Summary of the Talks Between Premier Zhou and Nehru and U Nu, 16 April 1955, WCDA, http://digitalarchive.wilsoncenter.org/document/114671, accessed 10 November 2020.
70. Zhou Enlai's Telegram to the CCP Central Committee and Mao Zedong regarding the Discussion of Political Issues, WCDA, 30 April 1955, https://digitalarchive.wilsoncenter.org/document/121750, accessed 10 November 2020.
71. PMML, JN, file 338, Nehru's note to Dutt and Krishna Menon, 23 April 1955.
72. NAUK, FO 371/116985, D2231/362, Paul Gore-Booth (British Ambassador to Burma) to FO, saving telegram 11, 23 May 1955.
73. PMML, JN, file 338, Nehru's note to Dutt and Menon, 23 April 1955. See also Zhou Enlai's Telegram to the CCP Central Committee and Mao Zedong Regarding the Discussion of Political Issues, WCDA, 30 April 1955, https://digitalarchive.wilsoncenter.org/document/121750, accessed 10 November 2020.
74. NAI, 1(49) AAC/55, Subimal Dutt's note to C. S. Jha, 1 July 1955; Jha's note to Dutt, 12 July 1955; Dutt's note to Jha, 8 October 1955.
75. Mackie, *Bandung 1955*, pp. 108–9; NAUK, FO 371/116987, D2232/3, Asian Conference 1947–1955, 2 December 1955. For the final communiqué see

NAUK, FO 371/116983, D2231/318, Final Communiqué of the Bandung Conference, 4 May 1955.

76. NAUK, DO 35/6099, Impressions of the Bandung Conference (Australian report by Walter Crocker), undated.
77. For a brief account of the five reports, see Guang Shu Zhang, 'Constructing "Peaceful Coexistence": China's Diplomacy Toward the Geneva and Bandung Conferences, 1954–55,' *Cold War History*, 7:4 (2007), pp. 523–4. These dealt with the Taiwan issue, economic cooperation, cultural cooperation, the discussion of political issues and the personalities present at the conference.
78. Zhou Enlai's Telegram to the CCP Central Committee and Mao Zedong regarding the Discussion of Political Issues, 30 April 1955, WCDA, available at http://digitalarchive.wilsoncenter.org/document/121750, accessed 10 November 2020.
79. Zhou Enlai's Report to the CCP Central Committee and Mao Zedong regarding the Cultural Cooperation Issue, 30 April 1955, *WCDA*, https://digitalarchive.wilsoncenter.org/document/121752, accessed 10 November 2020.
80. Ibid.
81. PRC FMA 207-00086-03, Report from the Chinese Foreign Ministry, the Asian-African Conference, April 1955, WCDA, available at http://digitalarchive.wilsoncenter.org/document/112893, accessed 10 November 2020.
82. Gregg Brazinsky, *Winning the Third World: Sino-American Rivalry During the Cold War* (Chapel Hill, NC: University of North Carolina Press, 2017), pp. 106–31; Jian Chen, 'The Tibetan Rebellion and China's Changing Relations With India and the Soviet Union,' *Journal of Cold War Studies*, 8: 3 (2006), p. 83; Qiang Zhai, *China and the Vietnam Wars, 1950–75* (Chapel Hill, NC: University of North Carolina Press, 2000), p. 65.
83. PRC, FMA 107-00065-01, Cable from the Chinese Foreign Ministry, Draft Proposal to Strengthen and Develop Friendly Relations with Asian-African Countries after the Asian-African Conference, 12 July 1955, WCDA, https://digitalarchive.wilsoncenter.org/document/cable-chinese-foreign-ministry-draft-proposal-strengthen-and-develop-friendly-relations, accessed 15 August 2020.
84. Ibid.
85. Ibid.
86. Indonesian Prime Minister Ali Sastroamidjojo visited Beijing in May 1955.
87. PRC, FMA 107-00065-01, Cable From the Chinese Foreign Ministry, Draft Proposal to Strengthen and Develop Friendly Relations With Asian-African Countries After the Asian-African Conference, 12 July 1955, WCDA, https://digitalarchive.wilsoncenter.org/document/cable-chinese-foreign-ministry-draft-proposal-strengthen-and-develop-friendly-relations, accessed 15 August 2020.
88. Ibid.
89. Ibid.
90. Ibid.
91. Andrea Benvenuti, Chien-Peng Chung, Nicholas Khoo and Andrew T. H. Tan, *China's Foreign Policy: The Emergence of a Great Power* (London and New York: Routledge, 2022), p. 123.

92. Zhang, 'Constructing Peaceful Coexistence,' p. 522.
93. Brazinsky, *Third World*, pp. 107 and 131.
94. Ibid., p. 106; 'Communist China's Role in Non-Communist Asia,' NIE 13-2-57, 3 December 1957, CIA Historical Collections, https://www.cia.gov/readingroom/docs/DOC_0001098219.pdf, accessed 20 March 2021.
95. Benvenuti, Chung, Khoo and Tan, *China's Foreign Policy*, p. 123; see also John W. Garver, *China's Quest: The History of the Foreign Relations of the People's Republic* (Oxford: Oxford University Press, 2016), Kindle edition, ch. 4; Zhang, 'Constructing Peaceful Coexistence,' p. 525.
96. Benvenuti, Chung, Khoo and Tan, *China's Foreign Policy,* p. 123; W. A. C. Adie, 'Zhou En-lai on Safari,' *China Quarterly*, 18 (1964), p. 174.
97. Julia Lovell, *Maoism: A Global History* (London: Vintage, 2019), Kindle edition, ch. 6; Benvenuti, Chung, Khoo and Tan, *China's Foreign Policy*, p. 124.
98. Lovell, *Maoism*, ch. 6; Benvenuti, Chung, Khoo and Tan, *China's Foreign Policy*, pp. 123–4.
99. Lovell, *Maoism*, ch. 6; Benvenuti, Chung, Khoo and Tan, *China's Foreign Policy*, p. 124.
100. Zhang, 'Constructing Peaceful Coexistence,' p. 525.
101. Karl Hack, *Defence and Decolonisation in Southeast Asia: Britain, Malaya and Singapore 1941–1968* (London: Curzon Press, 2001), p. 193.
102. Jian Chen, 'Bridging Revolution and Decolonization: The "Bandung Discourse" in China's Early Cold War Experience,' *Chinese Historical Review,* 15:2 (2008), p. 238.
103. For this expression I am thankful to Jonathan Ward. See Jonathan Ward, 'China-India Rivalry and the Border War of 1962: PRC Perspectives on the Collapse of China-India Relations, 1958–62' (DPhil Thesis, University of Oxford, 2016), p. 109.

11. EPILOGUE

1. Krishna Menon cited in Michael Brecher, *India and World Politics: Krishna Menon's View of the World* (London: Oxford University Press, 1968), p. 55.
2. PRC FMA 207-00086-03, Report from the Chinese Foreign Ministry, the Asian-African Conference, WCDA, 1 April 1955, http://digitalarchive.wilsoncenter.org/document/112893, accessed 5 October 2021.
3. Anton Harder, 'Defining Independence in Cold War Asia: Sino-Indian Relations, 1949–1962' (PhD thesis, London School of Economics, 2015), p. 132.
4. Jonathan Ward, 'China-India Rivalry and the Border War of 1962: PRC Perspectives on the Collapse of China-India Relations, 1958–62' (DPhil Thesis, University of Oxford, 2016), p. 114.
5. Ibid.
6. As mentioned earlier, independent India and the PRC had never concluded a formal agreement delimiting their mutual frontier. In the early 1950s, India claimed that its eastern boundary with China was defined by the McMahon Line, which imperial Britain had negotiated with Tibet in 1914. Drawn on a map to a

scale of 8 miles to the inch, it provided no precise delimitation. See A. G. A. M. Noorani, *India-China Boundary Problem, 1846–1947: History and Diplomacy* (New Delhi: Oxford University Press, 2011). In any case, neither the ROC (1912–49) nor the PRC ever recognised it. Chinese maps, instead, depicted the boundary line between India and China as running along the southern foothills of the eastern Himalayas. In the western Himalayas, New Delhi claimed Aksai Chin its own, but China contested such a claim. For a brief discussion of Sino-Indian border claims, see Taylor M. Fravel, *Strong Borders, Secure Nation: Cooperation and Conflict in China's Territorial Disputes* (Princeton, NJ: Princeton University Press, 2008), Kindle edition, appendix.

7. On this point, see also Ward, 'China-India Rivalry,' p. 116.
8. NAUK, FO 371/116986, D2231/373, 'Results of the Bandung Conference: A Preliminary Analysis,' Intelligence report no. 6903 (US paper), 27 April 1955; Lorenz Lüthi, 'Non-Alignment, 1945–1965: Its Establishment and Struggle Against Afro-Asianism,' *Humanity: An International Journal of Human Rights, Humanitarianism, and Development*, 7:2 (2016), pp. 201 and 207.
9. P. V. Rajgopal (ed.), *I Was Nehru's Shadow: From the Diaries of KF Rustamji, IP, Padma Vibhushan* (New Delhi: Wisdom Tree, 2014), Kindle edition, ch. 8.
10. NAI, 1(49) AAC/55, John Kotelawala (Prime Minister of Ceylon) to Gamal Abdel Nasser (Prime Minister of Egypt), 22 September 1955. However, he did so without prior consultation with Ceylon's Colombo partners. See NAI, 1(49) AAC/55, Nehru's note to Secretary General, Foreign Secretary and Commonwealth Secretary (MEA), 15 November 1955.
11. NAI, 1(49) AAC/55, Kotelawala to Nehru, 3 December 1955; Nehru to Kotelawala, 7 December 1955; R. G. Rajwade (Indian Embassy Cairo) to C. S. Jha (Commonwealth Secretary, MEA), do. no. 14(37)/55, 21 November 1955; Ali Yaver Jung (Indian ambassador to Egypt) to Jha, 19 January 1956.
12. NAI, 1(49) AAC/55, Kotelawala to Nehru, 3 December 1955; NAA, A1838, 3002/2 part 2, R. A. Peachey (Acting High Commissioner to Ceylon) to Arthur Tange (Secretary, ADEA), memorandum 1406, 23 November 1955.
13. For the Indonesian rationale as conveyed to Nehru, see NAI, 1(65) AAC/55, Lambertus N. Palar (Indonesian ambassador to India) to Nehru, 16 November 1955.
14. NAUK, FO 371/116986, D2231/387, BHC Karachi to CRO, telegram 1671, 29 November 1955.
15. NAUK, FO 371/116986, D2231/391, BHC Colombo to CRO, telegram 529, 5 December 1955; NAI, 1(49) AAC/55, Kotelawala to Nehru, 3 December 1955.
16. NAI, 1(49) AAC/55, Nehru to Kotelawala, 7 December 1955. See also Nehru's views communicated to the Indonesian government in NAI, 1(65) AAC/55, Nehru's note to Secretary General, Foreign Secretary and Commonwealth Secretary (MEA), 18 November 1955; 1(49) AAC/55, Note by Nehru, Nehru's note to Secretary General, Foreign Secretary and Commonwealth Secretary, 15 November 1955.
17. NAA, A1838, 3002/2 part 2, Asian-African Conference: Note for the Minister, 23 January 1956.

18. NAA, A1838, 3002/2 part 2, Robert W. Furlonger (AHC Karachi) to James Plimsoll (ADEA), 10 January 1956.
19. Ibid.; NAA, A1838, 3002/2 part 2, AHC Karachi to ADEA, memorandum 1435/55, 22 December 1955.
20. NAI, 1(49) AAC/55, Message from U Nu, Prime Minister of the Union of Burma, to Sir John Kotelawala, Prime Minister of Ceylon, sent on 22 December 1955. In early December, U Nu told the British ambassador in Rangoon that he was 'in no hurry for a meeting.' His reluctance 'to have a meeting in Egypt' was due to 'the difficulty about Israel with whom the Burmese must remain on good terms.' He believed 'Israel had made representation to some of the Bandung Government's [sic] about the proposal to meet in Cairo.' He, however, added that 'if there were a general wish to hold the conference,' he would 'probably find it necessary to agree.' NAUK, FO 371/116986, D2231/391, Roderick Sarell (British Embassy Rangoon) to FO, telegram 624, 16 December 1955.
21. NAA, A1838, 3002/2 part 2, Australian Legation Rangoon to ADEA, savingram 24, 28 December 1955.
22. NAI, 1(49) AAC/55, Kotelawala to Dr Burhanuddin Harahap (Prime Minister of Indonesia), 12 January 1956.
23. In early November 1956, Ali Sastroamidjojo requested a meeting of the Colombo group to discuss the Egyptian situation. In New Delhi, the four participating prime ministers also considered the Hungarian crisis. See NAI, 5(1) AAC/56, Indembassy Jakarta to Foreign New Delhi, telegram 43701, 1 November 1956; Joint Statement by the Prime Ministers of Burma, Ceylon, Indonesia and India, 14 November 1956.
24. NAI, 5(1) AAC/56, Attachment to Note by Nehru to Secretary-General, Foreign Secretary and Commonwealth Secretary, 14 November 1956.
25. NAI, 5(1) AAC/56, Note by Nehru to Secretary-General, Foreign Secretary and Commonwealth Secretary and attachment above, 14 November 1956; PMML, JN, file 610, part I, copy of a letter dated 7 April 1958 from S. W. R. D. Bandaranaike, Prime Minister of Ceylon, addressed to the Prime Minister.
26. PMML, JN, file 610, part I, copy of letter dated 7 April 1958 from S. W. R. D. Bandaranaike, Prime Minister of Ceylon, addressed to the prime minister.
27. NAUK, DO 35/8830, 'Neutralism in South and South-East Asia,' Foreign Office Steering Committee paper, 14 March 1960; Cindy Ewing, 'The Colombo Powers: Crafting Diplomacy in the Third World and Launching Afro-Asia at Bandung,' *Cold War History*, 19:1 (2019), pp. 17–18; G. H. Jansen, *Afro-Asia and Non-Alignment* (London: Faber and Faber, 1966), p. 243.
28. Jansen, *Afro-Asia*, p. 243.
29. NAA, A1838, 3002/2 part 2, P. R. Heydon (Australian High Commissioner to India) to Tange, memorandum 658, 10 June 1957; Australian Embassy Washington to ADEA, savingram 30, 12 August 1957; A5462, 2/1/1 part 2, Memcon, Alan Renouf (ADEA) and Robert Hoey (US Embassy Canberra), 9 October 1957; Trevett W. Cutts (ADEA) to Australian Embassy Washington, cablegram 991, 22 October 1957; Jovan Čavoški, 'Distant Countries, Closest Allies: Josip

Broz Tito and Jawaharlal Nehru and the Rise of Global Nonalignment,' *PMML Occasional Paper*, no. 77 (2015), p. 31.

30. PRC FMA 107-00250-06, 51–52, Cable From the Chinese Embassy in Syria, the Situation of Ambassador Chen's Visit to the Syrian Foreign Minister, 11 February 11 1957, WCDA, https://digitalarchive.wilsoncenter.org/document/114822, accessed 5 October 2021.
31. SWJN, Second Series [henceforth II], Volume 24 (New Delhi: Jawaharlal Nehru Memorial Fund, 1984–2015), p. 555.
32. NAA, A1838, 3002/2 part 2, A. J. Eastman (Australian High Commissioner to Ceylon) to Tange, memorandum 159/57, 11 February 1957.
33. PRC FMA 107-00250-06, 49, Cable from the Chinese Foreign Ministry: Main Points of the Discussion Between the Premier and Soekardjo Wiriopranoto, 3 April 1957, WCDA, https://digitalarchive.wilsoncenter.org/document/114704, accessed 5 October 2021.
34. Ibid.
35. Gregg Brazinsky, *Winning the Third World: Sino-American Rivalry During the Cold War*, (Chapel Hill, NC: University of North Carolina Press, 2017), p. 120.
36. Ibid., pp. 120 and 131; Zhihua Shen and Yafeng Xia, 'The Whirlwind of China: Zhou Enlai's Shuttle Diplomacy in 1957 and Its Effects,' *Cold War History*, 10:4 (2010), pp. 517–26.
37. Brazinsky, *Third World*, p. 120.
38. Kuo-kang Shao, 'Chou En-lai's Diplomatic Approach to Non-aligned States in Asia: 1953–60,' *China Quarterly*, 78 (1979), p. 331; Brazinsky, *Third World*, p. 120.
39. Brazinsky, *Third World*, p. 122.
40. Ibid.
41. NAUK, DO 35/6100, BHC Colombo to CRO, telegram 161, 27 November 1957.
42. NAA, A5462, 2/1/1 part 2, Cutts to Australian Embassy Washington, cablegram 936, 22 October 1957.
43. Ibid.
44. Ibid.
45. NAA, A1838, 3002/2, part 3, AHC New Delhi to Tange, memorandum 451, 10 April 1958.
46. NAA, A1838, 3002/2, part 3, AHC New Delhi to ADEA, cablegram 130, 12 April 1958.
47. For the so-called PRRI/Permesta Rebellion in Indonesia in 1958, see for instance Matthew Jones, '"Maximum Disavowable Aid": Britain, the United States and the Indonesian Rebellion, 1957–58,' *English Historical Review*, 114:459 (1999), pp. 1179–216. For the events in Lebanon, see Douglas Little, 'His Finest Hour? Eisenhower, Lebanon, and the 1958 Middle East Crisis,' *Diplomatic History*, 20:1 (1996), pp. 27–54. For the Indian reaction, see Swapna Kona Nayadu, 'In the Very Eye of the Storm: India, the UN, and the Lebanon Crisis of 1958,' *Cold War History*, 18:2 (2018), pp. 221–37.
48. PMML, JN, file 610, part I, copy of letter dated 7 April 1958 from S. W. R. D. Bandaranaike, Prime Minister of Ceylon, addressed to the Prime Minister; Nehru to Finance Minister, 14 April 1958; *SWJN*, II/42, pp. 704–6.

49. NAA, A1838, 3002/2, part 3, AHC New Delhi to ADEA, cablegram 622, 6 December 1959.
50. Ibid. Dutt, now Foreign Secretary, advised Nehru that even an informal 'meeting of few Heads of Government' of the 'Brioni type' would 'antagonise other governments in the Asian-African region and the net result would be further division of opinion among the Bandung countries.' PMML, Subimal Dutt Papers, file 39, Dutt's note to Nehru, 14 December 1959.
51. NAA, A1838, 3016/11/147, part 1, Walter Crocker (Australian High Commissioner to India) to Tange, memorandum 3, 4 January 1959; Lüthi, 'Non-Alignment, 1946–65,' p. 208. Nasser became President in June 1956.
52. Jovan Čavoški, *Non-Aligned Movement Summits: A History* (London and New York: Bloomsbury Academic, 2022), p. 45.
53. Lüthi, 'Non-Alignment, 1946–65,' pp. 201 and 207–8; Aleksandar Životić and Jovan Čavoški, 'On the Road to Belgrade: Yugoslavia, Third World Neutrals, and the Evolution of Global Non-Alignment, 1954–1961,' *Journal of Cold War Studies*, 18:4 (2016), pp. 92–93; Čavoški, *Non-Aligned Movement Summits*, p. 46.
54. Životić and Čavoški, 'On the Road to Belgrade,' p. 93.
55. Ibid.
56. Ibid.
57. L. P. Singh, 'Dynamics of Indian-Indonesian Relations,' *Asian Survey*, 7:9 (1967), p. 657.
58. PMML, JN, file 694, part 1, Nehru's note to Secretary General, Foreign Secretary and Commonwealth Secretary (MEA), 5 November 1959.
59. Nehru cited in Životić and Čavoški, 'On the Road to Belgrade,' p. 94. A few months earlier, in April 1959, he had told Ferhat Abbas, the leader of the Algerian provisional government in exile in Tunis, that 'proposals for holding a new Bandung-type conference had not been considered practicable at present because there were so many tensions among Afro-Asian countries even among Arabs, so many new military regimes and so marked an intrusion of the cold war in Afro-Asian affairs that instead of displaying Afro-Asian strength and unity, such a conference would only emphasise weakness and disagreement.' See *SWJN*, II/48, p. 529. Similarly, he told members of parliament in 1961 that 'although for some years the Chinese and Indonesians had been wanting to have a second Bandung Conference it was his view that such a conference in the present situation would result more in a show of disunity than unity among the participants.' See NAA, A1838, 3002/2, part 3, AHC New Delhi to ADEA, cablegram 226, 26 April 1961.
60. Životić and Čavoški, 'On the Road to Belgrade,' p. 94.
61. Lorenz M. Lüthi, *Cold Wars: Asia, the Middle East, Europe* (Cambridge, UK: Cambridge University Press, 2020), Kindle edition, ch. 11.
62. Lüthi, 'Non-Alignment, 1946–65,' p. 208.
63. Ibid.
64. NAA, A1838, 3002/2, part 3, AHC New Delhi to ADEA, savingram 17, 8 June 1960; Australian Embassy Washington to ADEA, cablegram 1329, 24 May 1960.
65. In November 1959, Nehru, however, agreed with Menon about the desirability of talking privately to a group meeting of Afro-Asian delegations at the United

Nations about Sino-Indian border developments. See PMML, JN, file 694, part I, Indel New York (Menon) to Foreign New Delhi (Nehru), telegram 247, 3 November 1959; Foreign New Delhi (Nehru) to Indel New York (Menon), primin 21170, 4 November 1959.

66. Jovan Čavoški, 'Saving Non-Alignment: Diplomatic Efforts of Major Non-Aligned Countries and the Sino-Indian Border Conflict,' in Amit R. Das Gupta and Lorenz M. Lüthi (eds), *The Sino-Indian War of 1962: New Perspectives* (London: Routledge, 2017), p. 162.
67. Ibid.
68. The wording of some of these criteria, however, was flexible enough to allow countries with a bilateral military agreement or a defence pact with a great power to participate (provided that such agreement or pact would 'not be deliberately concluded in the context of Great Power conflicts'). Similarly, countries that had accepted the presence of foreign military bases on their soil could also participate as long as such a decision had not been made 'in the context of Great Power conflicts.' See NAI, F-III, 102/33/81, Non-aligned summit conferences (1961–1979), undated; Lüthi, 'Non-Alignment, 1946–65,' pp. 209–10; Čavoški, *Non-Aligned Movement Summits*, pp. 47–52.
69. NAUK, FO 371/161226, WP13/287, Michael Creswell (British ambassador to Yugoslavia) to the Earl of Home (FO), despatch 95, 12 September 1961. For a good account of the conference, see for instance Čavoški, *Non-Aligned Movement Summits*, pp. 56–61; Robert B. Rakove, *Kennedy, Johnson, and the Nonaligned World* (Cambridge, UK: Cambridge University Press, 2013), pp. 77–80.
70. NAI, F-III, 102/33/81, Non-aligned summit conferences (1961–1979), undated; Lüthi, 'Non-Alignment, 1946–65,' p. 210; Životić and Čavoški, 'On the Road to Belgrade,' p. 96.
71. NAUK, FO 371/161226, WP13/287, Creswell to Earl of Home, despatch 95, 12 September 1961; see also Annex II to despatch 95 of 1961, Declaration of the Heads of State and Government of Non-Aligned Countries, 12 September 1961.
72. Životić and Čavoški, 'On the Road to Belgrade,' p. 96; Lüthi, 'Non-Alignment, 1946–65,' p. 202.
73. Lüthi, 'Non-Alignment, 1946–65,' pp. 209–10; *Jawaharlal Nehru Letters to Chief Ministers, 1947–1964, Volume 5, 1958–1964* (New Delhi: Jawaharlal Nehru Memorial Fund, 1989), pp. 449–50; NAI, CON/27/61 AFR-I, Josip Broz Tito (President of Yugoslavia) to Nehru, 9 May 1961. On Tito's and Nasser's efforts to talk Nehru into going to Belgrade, see Čavoški, *Non-Aligned Movement Summits*, pp. 53–56.
74. Rakove, *Kennedy, Johnson and the Nonaligned World*, p. 69; Životić and Čavoški, 'On the Road to Belgrade,' p. 95; Cavoški, 'Distant Countries, Closest Allies,' pp. 61–2.
75. Rakove, *Kennedy, Johnson and the Nonaligned World*, pp. 69–70.
76. Čavoški, *Non-Aligned Movement Summits*, p. 53; Čavoški, 'Saving Non-Alignment,' p. 162.
77. Kveder cited in Čavoški, 'Saving Non-Alignment,' pp. 162–3.

78. NAA, A1838, 3034/11/4 part 1, ADEA to all posts, savingram AP115, 19 September 1961; see also Robert B. Rakove, 'The Rise and Fall of Non-Aligned Mediation, 1961–6,' *International History Review*, 37:5 (2015), pp. 995–6.
79. NAA, A1838, 3034/11/147, part 1, Crocker to ADEA, cablegram 497, 16 September 1961.
80. Ibid.
81. Ibid.
82. Čavoški, 'Saving Non-Alignment,' p. 163.
83. Harder, 'Defining Independence,' chapter 4.
84. Jian Chen, 'Zhou Enlai and China's "Prolonged Rise",' in Ramachandra Guha (ed.), *Makers of Modern Asia* (Cambridge, MA: Belknap Press, 2014), Kindle edition, ch. 6; Kuisong Yang, 'Changes in Mao Zedong's Attitude Toward the Indochina War, 1949–1973,' *Cold War International History Project Working Paper 34* (Washington, DC: Woodrow Wilson Centre for Scholars, 2002), https://www.wilsoncenter.org/sites/default/files/media/documents/publication/ACFB04.pdf, pp. 15–19, accessed 5 April 2020; Taomo Zhou, 'Ambivalent Alliance: Chinese Policy Towards Indonesia, 1960–1965,' *China Quarterly*, 221 (2015), pp. 208–28.
85. Andrea Benvenuti, Chien-Peng Chung, Nicholas Khoo and Andrew T. H. Tan, *China's Foreign Policy: The Emergence of a Great Power* (Abingdon, UK and New York: Routledge, 2022), p. 73.
86. Ibid.
87. Ibid.
88. See Speech at a Meeting of the Representatives of Sixty-Four Communist and Workers' Parties, 18 November 1957, WCDA, https://digitalarchive.wilsoncenter.org/document/96211/download, accessed 5 October 2021.
89. Jian Chen, 'Bridging Revolution and Decolonization: The "Bandung Discourse" in China's Early Cold War Experience,' *Chinese Historical Review*, 15:2 (2008), p. 237; Zhihua Shen and Yafeng Xia, *Mao and the Sino-Soviet Partnership, 1945–1959: A New History* (Lanham, MD: Lexington Books, 2015).
90. Mao cited in Chen, *Mao's China*; Qiang Zhai, 'Coexistence and Confrontation: Sino-Soviet Relations after Stalin,' in Klaus Larres and Kenneth Osgood (eds), *The Cold War After Stalin's Death* (New York: Rowman and Littlefield 2006), p. 183. For the term, 'smile diplomacy,' see Laurent Cesari, *Le Problème Diplomatique de l'Indochine 1945–1957* (Paris: Les Indes Savantes, 2013), p. 290.
91. Benvenuti, Chung, Khoo and Tan, *China's Foreign Policy*, p. 74.
92. Chen, 'Zhou Enlai and China's "Prolonged Rise",' ch. 6.
93. Ibid.
94. Jian Chen, 'The Tibetan Rebellion and China's Changing Relations With India and the Soviet Union,' *Journal of Cold War Studies*, 8:3 (2006), p. 84.
95. Chen, 'Zhou Enlai and China's "Prolonged Rise",' ch. 6; Jun Niu, '1962: The Eve of the Left Turn in China's Foreign Policy,' *CWIHP Working Paper 48* (Washington, DC: Woodrow Wilson Centre for Scholars, 2005), pp. 9–29, https://www.wilsoncenter.org/sites/default/files/media/documents/publication/NiuJunWP481.pdf, accessed February 2021. According to Niu, however, this

short-lived return to a less strident foreign policy was due not only to Chinese leaders' anxieties over the success or failure of the Great Leap Forward, but also to a variety of foreign policy considerations.

96. Andrew G. Walder, *China Under Mao: A Revolution Derailed* (Cambridge, MA: Harvard University Press, 2015), p. 180–1; Srinath Raghavan, *War and Peace in Modern India* (London: Palgrave Macmillan, 2010), p. 284.
97. Walder, *China Under Mao,* p. 181; Chen, 'Zhou Enlai and China's "Prolonged Rise",' ch. 6; Niu, '1962,' pp. 31–4.
98. Chen, 'Zhou Enlai and China's "Prolonged Rise",' ch. 6.
99. Benvenuti, Chung, Khoo and Tan, *China's Foreign Policy*, p. 108.
100. Xiaoyuan Liu, 'Friend or Foe: India as Perceived by Beijing's Foreign Policy Analysts in the 1950s,' *China Review*, 15:1 (2015), pp. 122–6.
101. Ibid., pp. 122–39, but especially 137.
102. Ibid, p. 137.
103. Chaowu Dai, 'From "Hindi-Chini Bhai-Bhai" to "International Class Struggle" against Nehru: China's India Policy and the Frontier Dispute, 1950-62,' in Amit R. Das Gupta and Lorenz M. Lüthi (eds), *The Sino-Indian War of 1962: New Perspectives* (London: Routledge, 2017), pp. 71, 76 and 80.
104. Harder, 'Defining Independence,' pp. 190 and 194.
105. Ibid., p. 186.
106. Liu, 'Friend or Foe,' p. 137.
107. Ward, 'China-India Rivalry,' pp. 112 and 133.
108. See, for instance, Lüthi, 'Non-Alignment, 1946–65,' pp. 201–23.
109. Deputy Director (Intelligence), Report: The Sino-Indian Border Dispute, Section 1, 2 March 1963, CIA Historical Collections, https://www.cia.gov/readingroom/print/89555, accessed 20 November 2020.
110. NAUK, FO371/127400, FC1631/41, India: Visit of the Chinese Prime Minister, FE 45/11, 28 March 1957. Zhou's stay in India was part of a more than 2-month-long overseas tour that included eight Asian and three European nations. See NAUK, FO371/127400, FC1631/39, Con O'Neill (British ambassador to the PRC) to Selwyn Lloyd (British Secretary of State for Foreign Affairs), 15 February 1957. Zhou was in India from 29 November to 11 December, from 30 December to 1 January, from 24 to 25 January and from 29 to 31 January. In public, however, Zhou's sojourn in India appeared to be a resounding success. Indian crowds greeted him warmly, while the press gave his visit 'widespread and often favourable' coverage. See NAUK, FO371/127400, FC1631/41, India: Visit of the Chinese Prime Minister, FE 45/11, 28 March 1957.
111. NSC Briefing; Chou En-lai's Tour, 6 February 1957, CIA Historical Collections, https://www.cia.gov/readingroom/docs/CIA-RDP79R00890A000800040021-2.pdf, accessed 10 July 2020.
112. *SWJN*, II/36, pp. 594–602; Harder, 'Defining Independence,' pp. 166–8; Brazinsky, *Third World*, p. 123.
113. *SWJN,* II/36, pp. 594–602; On the uprisings in inner (eastern) Tibet, see Melvyn C. Goldstein, *A History of Modern Tibet. Volume 4. In the Eye of the Storm,*

1957–1959 (Oakland, CA: University of California Press, 2019), pp. 36–8; Ben Hillman, 'Tibetans in China: From Conflict to Protest,' in Michael Weiner (ed.), *Routledge Handbook of Race and Ethnicity in Asia* (New York: Routledge, 2021), p. 221. Beijing's 'democratic reforms' included the redistribution of land and the elimination of class enemies.

114. *SWJN*, II/36, p. 602.
115. Ibid., pp. 601, 613, 616; Harder, 'Defining Independence,' p. 171.
116. *SWJN*, II/36, p. 615.
117. Ibid., pp. 588–9 and 621–2; PRC, CFMA 109-01046-02(1), Cable From Zhou Enlai to Mao Zedong and the Central Committee, Discussion With Nehru on the Hungary Issue, 3 December 1956, WCDA, https://digitalarchive.wilsoncenter.org/document/116534, accessed 5 October 2021.
118. PRC, CFMA 109-01046-02(1), Cable From Zhou Enlai to Mao Zedong and the Central Committee, Discussion With Nehru on the Hungary Issue, 3 December 1956, WCDA, https://digitalarchive.wilsoncenter.org/document/116534, accessed 5 October 2021. For Zhou's views on Hungary, see also *SWJN*, II/36, pp. 587–8, 590–2.
119. *SWJN*, II/36, p. 591; PRC, CFMA 109-01046-02(1), Cable From Zhou Enlai to Mao Zedong and the Central Committee, Discussion With Nehru on the Hungary Issue, 3 December 1956, WCDA, https://digitalarchive.wilsoncenter.org/document/116534, accessed 5 October 2021; Harder, 'Defining Independence,' pp. 168 and 174; Brazinsky, *Third World*, pp. 122–3; S. Gopal, *Jawaharlal Nehru: A Biography. Volume Three: 1956–1964* (London: Jonathan Cape, 1984), p. 37.
120. *SWJN*, II/36, pp. 622 and 635.
121. Brazinsky, *Third World*, pp. 122–3.
122. Gopal, *Nehru, 1956–1964*, p. 39.
123. Raghavan, *War and Peace in Modern India*, pp. 244–6; Gopal, *Nehru, 1956–1964*, pp. 33–4; John W. Garver, *China's Quest: The History of the Foreign Relations of the People's Republic* (Oxford: Oxford University Press, 2016), Kindle edition, ch. 6; Request by Department of State for Release of Cia/RR GM 59-3, the China-India Border Dispute, 20 November 1959, CIA Historical Collections, https://www.cia.gov/readingroom/document/cia-rdp79-01006a000100140001-1, accessed 10 August 2021. China, of course, regarded Aksai Chin as part of Tibet and, thus, under its sovereignty.
124. Lorenz M. Lüthi, 'India's Relations With China, 1945–74,' in Das Gupta and Lüthi (eds), *The Sino-Indian War of 1962*, pp. 32–3; Lüthi, *Cold Wars*, ch. 11.
125. *SWJN*, II/38, p. 676.
126. Ibid.
127. Das Gupta, *Serving India*, pp. 326–7; Raghavan, *War and Peace in Modern India*, p. 246; Steven A. Hoffmann, *India and the China Crisis* (Berkeley, CA: University of California Press, 1990), pp. 34–5.
128. *SWJN*, II/38, p. 655; Lorenz M. Lüthi, 'Sino-Indian Relations, 1954–1962,' *Eurasia Border Review*, 3 (2012), pp. 101 and 119; Lüthi, 'India's Relations With China, 1945–74,' p. 33; Raghavan, *War and Peace in Modern India*, p. 246.

129. John W. Garver, 'China's Decision for War with India in 1962,' in Alastair Iain Johnston and Robert S. Ross (eds), *New Directions in the Study of China's Foreign Policy* (Stanford, CA: Stanford University Press, 2006), p. 32.
130. Harder, 'Defining Independence,' p. 174.
131. See chapters 4 and 7 in this book. See also *SWJN*, II/36, pp. 598–601.
132. For the Chinese attitude, see Liu, 'Friend and Foe,' p. 121 and Dai, 'From "Hindi-Chini Bhai-Bhai" to "International Class Struggle" Against Nehru,' pp. 70–3; for the Indian one, see Harder, 'Defining Independence,' pp. 87–93.
133. NAA, A4311, 106/38, AHC New Delhi to ADEA, savingram 49, 20 September 1958.
134. Chen, 'Zhou Enlai,' p. 160; Chen, 'Tibetan Rebellion,' p. 68; Hillman, 'Tibetans in China,' pp. 221–2.
135. Dai, 'From "Hindi-Chini Bhai-Bhai" to "International Class Struggle" Against Nehru,' pp. 68–84.
136. Lüthi, 'Sino-Indian Relations, 1954–1962,' p. 105; Garver, *China's Quest*, ch. 6; Garver, 'China's Decision for War With India in 1962,' pp. 11–17 and 26.
137. Garver, 'China's Decision for War With India in 1962,' pp. 11–12; John W. Garver, 'India, China, the United States, Tibet, and the Origins of the 1962 War,' *India Review*, 3:2 (2004), pp. 10 and 13–14; Bertil Lintner, *China's India War: Collision Course on the Roof of the World* (New Delhi: Oxford University Press, 2018), Kindle edition, ch. 1. According to Garver, Nehru might have turned a blind eye on CIA activities in India's border areas, but if he indeed did so, his aim was 'to create a set of pressures that would induce Beijing to accommodate India's interests in Tibet.' See Garver, 'China's Decision for War With India in 1962,' pp. 24–5. Kenneth Conboy and James Morrison, two former US intelligence operatives, have been more categorical about that, claiming that Nehru knew the broad contours of the programme, but looked the other way. See Kenneth J. Conboy and James Morrison, *The CIA's Secret War in Tibet* (Lawrence, KS: University Press of Kansas, 2002), pp. 95–6 and 155–6. For a much different view, see S. Mahmud Ali, *Cold War in the High Himalayas: The USA, China and South Asia in the 1950s* (New York: Routledge, 2018), Kindle edition. Ali claims that the Indian government fully cooperated with CIA efforts to aid the Tibetan armed resistance. In doing so, however, he fails to provide convincing evidence in support of his claims.
138. Harder, 'Defining Independence,' pp. 196–7 and 201; Raghavan *War and Peace in Modern India*, p. 250; Garver, 'China's Decision for War With India in 1962,' p. 23. In Garver's view, however, India did provide low-key support to non-violent Tibetan resistance.
139. Nehru cited in G. Parthasarathi (ed.), *Jawaharlal Nehru Letters to Chief Ministers 1947–1964* (henceforth *LCM*), *Volume 5 (1958–64)* (New Delhi: Government of India, 1989), p. 240; Lüthi, 'India's Relations With China, 1945–74,' p. 33.
140. Srinath Raghavan, 'A Missed Opportunity? The Nehru-Zhou Enlai Summit of 1960,' in Manu Baghavan (ed.), *India and the Cold War* (Gurgaon, India: Penguin, 2019), p. 107; Lüthi, 'India's Relations With China, 1945–74,' p. 33; Lüthi, 'Sino-Indian Relations, 1954–1962,' pp. 105–6.

141. Lüthi, 'Sino-Indian Relations, 1954–1962,' p. 106; Raghavan *War and Peace in Modern India*, p. 252.
142. Garver, *China's Quest*, ch. 6; Raghavan, 'A Missed Opportunity?,' p. 110; Raghavan *War and Peace in Modern India*, p. 257.
143. *LCM*, *Volume 5*, p. 285; Lüthi, 'India's Relations With China, 1945–74,' p. 33.
144. For Zhou's visit to New Delhi, see Lüthi, 'India's Relations With China, 1945–74,' pp. 33–4; Lüthi, 'Sino-Indian Relations, 1954–1962,' pp. 112–16.
145. Dai, 'From "Hindi-Chini Bhai-Bhai" to "International Class Struggle" Against Nehru,' pp. 76–7. On China's internal situation during the Great Leap Forward and its aftermath, see for instance Walder, *China Under Mao*, pp. 152–99.
146. For the Nehru-Zhou talks in Delhi, see Raghavan, 'A Missed Opportunity?,' pp. 115–20.
147. For a brief discussion of Nehru's motives, see Andrew Bingham Kennedy, *The International Ambitions of Mao and Nehru: National Efficacy Beliefs and the Making of Foreign Policy* (Cambridge, UK: Cambridge University Press, 2012), p. 229. On increasing domestic pressure on Nehru, see Raghavan, *War and Peace in Modern India*, pp. 258–60 and 262.
148. Lüthi, 'Sino-Indian Relations, 1954–1962,' p. 34.
149. P. B. Sinha and A. A. Athale, *History of Conflict With China* (New Delhi: History Division, Ministry of Defence, 1992), p. 68; Raghavan, *War and Peace in Modern India*, pp. 275–6; Kennedy, *The International Ambitions of Mao and Nehru*, pp. 229–30; Garver, 'China's Decision for War With India in 1962,' p. 34.
150. Garver, 'China's Decision for War With India in 1962,' p. 37.
151. Garver, *China's Quest*, ch. 6; Garver, 'China's Decision for War With India in 1962,' p. 42; Raghavan, *War and Peace in Modern India*, p. 285.
152. Garver, *China's Quest*, ch. 6.
153. Lüthi, 'India's Relations With China, 1945–74,' p. 34; Garver, *China's Quest*, ch. 6.
154. For Chinese perceptions and decision-making in the lead-up to the 1962 border war, see Garver, *China's Quest*, ch. 6; Garver, 'China's Decision for War With India in 1962,' pp. 42–56; Dai, 'From "Hindi-Chini Bhai-Bhai" to "International Class Struggle" Against Nehru,' pp. 77–9.
155. A vast literature exists on the 1962 border war. See, for instance, Hoffmann, *India and the China Crisis*; Lintner, *China's India War*; Gerry Van Tonder, *Sino-Indian War: Border Clash, October-November 1962* (Barnsley, UK: Pen and Sword Military, 2018); Neville Maxwell, China's India War (London: Cape, 1970); Raghavan, *War and Peace in Modern India*.
156. On growing Sino-Pakistani ties in the 1960s and beyond, see Rudra Chaudhuri, 'The Making of an "All Weather Friendship" Pakistan, China and the History of a Border Agreement: 1949–1963,' *International History Review*, 40:1 (2018), pp. 41–64. Islamabad became the capital of Pakistan in 1967. Between 1959 and 1967. Pakistan's capital was temporarily transferred to Rawalpindi as Islamabad was being built.
157. Lüthi, 'Non-Alignment, 1946–65,' p. 211.
158. Lüthi, *Cold Wars*, ch. 12; Čavoški, 'Saving Non-Alignment,' pp. 164–5.

159. Čavoški, 'Saving Non-Alignment,' pp. 166–7 and 170–1; Lüthi, *Cold Wars*, ch. 12.
160. Lüthi, *Cold Wars*, ch. 12; Čavoški, 'Saving Non-Alignment,' pp. 171–72.
161. Lüthi, 'Non-Alignment, 1946–65,' p. 211; Lüthi, *Cold Wars*, ch. 12; Eric Gettig, '"Trouble Ahead in Afro-Asia": The United States, the Second Bandung Conference, and the Struggle for the Third World, 1964–1965,' *Diplomatic History*, 39:1 (2015), pp. 128–31.
162. Čavoški, *Non-Aligned Movement Summits*, p. 74; Čavoški, 'Saving Non-Alignment,' p. 160.
163. For a discussion on the divisions between supporters of non-alignment and those of militant Afro-Asianism, see Jansen, *Afro-Asia*, pp. 363–83; see also NAI, F-III, 102/33/81, Non-aligned summit conferences (1961–1979), undated.
164. Čavoški, *Non-Aligned Movement Summits*, p. 74.
165. Lüthi, *Cold Wars*, ch. 11; Rizal Sukma, *Indonesia and China: The Politics of a Troubled Relationship* (London: Routledge, 1999), p. 28.
166. Čavoški, *Non-Aligned Movement Summits*, p. 75.
167. J. D. Legge, *Sukarno: A Political Biography* (Singapore: Archipelago Press, 2003), Kindle edition, ch. 11; Rakove, 'Rise and Fall of Non-Aligned Mediation,' p. 995; John F. Kennedy Presidential Library, Boston, Presidential Papers, National Security Files, Trips and Conferences, box 252A, 'Belgrade, Conference of Non-Aligned Nations [1 of 2],' Belgrade to Secretary of State, telegram 353, 2 September 1961.
168. Rakove, 'The Rise and Fall of Non-Aligned Mediation,' pp. 995–6. Sukarno would later tell the Chinese that '[i]f the non-aligned movement does not oppose imperialism or colonialism, but takes the middle road, it will be nothing more than a tool of imperialism.' Sukarno cited in Taomo Zhou, *Migration in the Time of Revolution: China, Indonesia and the Cold War* (Ithaca, NY: Cornell University Press, 2019), Kindle edition, ch. 7.
169. Čavoški, *Non-Aligned Movement Summits*, p. 54.
170. Ibid.
171. Mao cited in Zhou, *Migration in the Time of Revolution*, ch. 7.
172. Čavoški, *Non-Aligned Movement Summits*, p. 71.
173. Zhou, *Migration in the Time of Revolution*, ch. 7.
174. Jeremy Friedman, *Ripe for Revolution: Building Socialism in the Third World* (Cambridge, MA: Harvard University Press, 2022), Kindle edition, ch. 2.
175. Jeremy Friedman, *The Sino-Soviet Competition for the Third World* (Chapel Hill, NC: University of North Carolina Press, 2015), pp. 28 and 68.
176. Ibid., p. 28.
177. Ibid., pp. 62–3, 84 and 86.
178. Čavoški, *Non-Aligned Movement Summits*, pp. 54 and 76.
179. Zhou, *Migration in the Time of Revolution*, ch. 7; see also NAI, F-III, 102/33/81, Non-aligned summit conferences (1961–1979), undated.
180. The Chinese Ministry of Foreign Affairs cited in Zhou, *Migration in the Time of Revolution*, ch. 7.
181. Čavoški, *Non-Aligned Movement Summits*, p. 73.

182. Taomo Zhou, 'Ambivalent Alliance: Chinese Policy Towards Indonesia, 1960–1965,' *China Quarterly*, 221 (2015), pp. 208–9. On the roots of Sukarno's opposition to Nekolim, see Frederik P. Bunnell, 'Guided Democracy Foreign Policy: 1960–1965. President Sukarno Moves From Non-Alignment to Confrontation,' *Indonesia*, 2 (1966), pp. 37–76.
183. NAA, A1838, 3034/11/4 part 1, ADEA to all posts, savingram AP85, 19 July 1961; A1838, 3002/2, part 3, ADEA to Australian Embassy Washington, saving 101, 5 April 1961; A1838, 3034/11/4 part 1, ADEA to AHC London, savingram 570, 11 September 1961.
184. Zhou Enlai cited in Zhou, *Migration in the Time of Revolution*, ch. 7.
185. Lüthi, *Cold Wars*, ch. 12.
186. Čavoški, *Non-Aligned Movement Summits*, p. 92.
187. Lüthi, *Cold Wars*, ch. 12.
188. Čavoški, *Non-Aligned Movement Summits*, pp. 75–6.
189. Gettig, 'Trouble Ahead in Afro-Asia,' p. 132; Lüthi, *Cold Wars*, ch. 12.
190. Gettig, 'Trouble Ahead in Afro-Asia,' p. 132.
191. Ibid.; Itty Abraham, 'From Bandung to NAM: Non-alignment and Indian Foreign Policy, 1947–65,' *Commonwealth & Comparative Politics*, 46:2 (2008), p. 212.
192. Gettig, 'Trouble Ahead in Afro-Asia,' p. 132.
193. Ibid., pp. 134–5; Rakove, 'The Rise and Fall of Non-Aligned Mediation,' pp. 998–9; on these divisions, see also Čavoški, *Non-Aligned Movement Summits*, pp. 84–9 and NAI, F-III, 102/33/81, Non-aligned summit conferences (1961–1979), undated.
194. Rakove, 'The Rise and Fall of Non-Aligned Mediation,' p. 999.
195. Ibid.
196. Gettig, 'Trouble Ahead in Afro-Asia,' p. 136.
197. Ibid., pp. 144–50.
198. On Nehru's stance in Belgrade, see Čavoški, *Non-Aligned Movement Summits*, p. 60.
199. Gettig, 'Trouble Ahead in Afro-Asia,' p. 151.

CONCLUSIONS

1. Nehru cited in A. Appadorai and M. S. Rajan, *India's Foreign Policy and Relations* (New Delhi: South Asian Publishers, 1985), p. 357.
2. PMML, JN, file 342, part II, 'Interview with the Amir Faisal,' note by Nehru to Secretary General, Foreign Secretary and Commonwealth Secretary (MEA), 5 May 1955.
3. Xiaoyuan Liu, 'Friend or Foe: India as Perceived by Beijing's Foreign Policy Analysts in the 1950s,' *China Review*, 15:1 (2015), p. 121.
4. Nehru cited in Nicholas Tarling, *Southeast Asia and the Great Powers* (London: Routledge, 2011), p. 28.
5. Nehru cited in Lorenz M. Lüthi, 'Sino-Indian Relations, 1954–1962,' *Eurasia Border Review*, 3 (2012), p. 98.
6. M. S. Rajan, *India in World Affairs, 1954–56* (London: Asia Publishing House, 1964), p. 216.

7. S. Gopal, *Jawaharlal Nehru: A Biography. Volume Three: 1956–1964* (London: Jonathan Cape, 1984), p. 38.
8. Anton Harder, 'Defining Independence in Cold War Asia: Sino-Indian Relations, 1949–1962' (PhD thesis, London School of Economics, 2015), p. 143.
9. See e.g. India, Lok Sabha Debates, Volume II, no. 29 (New Delhi: Lok Sabha Secretariat, 1955), cols. 3887–912, https://eparlib.nic.in/bitstream/123456789/809060/1/pms_01_09_31-03-1955.pdf, accessed 20 May 2019; *SWJN*, Second Series, Volume 28 (New Delhi: Jawaharlal Nehru Memorial Fund, 1984–2015), pp. 125–8.
10. H. W. Brands, *India and the United States: The Cold Peace* (Boston, MA: Twayne Publishers, 1990), p. 85; Jessica M. Chapman, *Remaking the World: Decolonization and the Cold War* (Lexington, KY: University Press of Kentucky, 2023), Kindle edition, ch. 2.
11. See Andrea Benvenuti, Review of Ang Cheng Guan, *The Southeast Asia Treaty Organization* (Abingdon, UK and New York: Routledge, 2022), in *H-Diplo Roundtable XXIV-11*, 7 November 2022, https://hdiplo.org/to/RT24-11, accessed 10 July 2023.
12. NAUK, DO 35/5977, Malcolm MacDonald (British High Commissioner to India) to Gilbert Laithwaite (CRO), 6 December 1955.
13. Brian P. Farrell, 'Alphabet Soup and Nuclear War: China and the Cold War in Southeast Asia,' in Malcolm H. Murfett (eds), *Cold War: Southeast Asia* (Singapore: Marshall Cavendish, c2012), pp. 133–4.
14. Letter from the Acting Director of Central Intelligence (Cabell) to the Secretary of State, 12 September 1955, doc. 67, *FRUS, 1955–1957, East Asian Security; Cambodia; Laos, Volume XXI* (Washington, DC: GPO, 1990), https://history.state.gov/historicaldocuments/frus1955-57v21/d67, accessed 5 April 2022.
15. Farrell, 'Alphabet Soup,' pp. 133–4; Karl Hack, *Defence and Decolonisation in Southeast Asia: Britain, Malaya and Singapore 1941–1968* (Richmond, VA: Curzon Press, 2001), pp. 203–4; Damien Fenton, *To Cage the Red Dragon: SEATO and the Defence of Southeast Asia, 1955–1965* (Singapore: National University of Singapore Press, 2012), pp. 63–5.
16. Hack, *Defence and Decolonisation*, p. 205; Farrell, 'Alphabet Soup,' pp. 88 and 94.
17. On some of these divergences, see e.g. Fenton, *To Cage the Red Dragon,* pp. 101–2; Nicholas Tarling, *Britain and the Neutralisation of Laos* (Singapore: National University of Singapore Press, 2011), pp. 2–3; Hack, *Defence and Decolonisation*, pp. 205 and 209; Laurent Cesari, *Le Problème Diplomatique de l'Indochine 1945–1957* (Paris: Les Indes Savantes, 2013), pp. 298–9; Pierre Journoud, 'La France et l'Asie du Sud-Est, de l'Indochine à l'Asean,' in Pierre Journoud (ed.), *L'Évolution du Débat Stratégique en Asie du Sud-Est depuis* 1945 (Paris: IRSEM, 2012), pp. 34–5.
18. Benvenuti, Review of Ang Cheng Guan, *The Southeast Asia Treaty Organization* (Abingdon, UK and New York: Routledge, 2022), in *H-Diplo Roundtable XXIV-11*, 7 November 2022, https://hdiplo.org/to/RT24-11, accessed 10 July 2023.
19. NAUK, DO 35/8830, 'Neutralism in South and South-East Asia,' Foreign Office Steering Committee paper, 14 March 1960.

20. William Henderson, 'The Roots of Neutralism in Southern Asia,' *International Journal*, 13:1 (1957–58), p. 30.
21. Jonathan Ward, 'China-India Rivalry and the Border War of 1962: PRC Perspectives on the Collapse of China-India Relations, 1958–62' (DPhil Thesis, University of Oxford, 2016), p. 111; see also G. H. Jansen, *Afro-Asia and Non-Alignment* (London: Faber and Faber, 1966), p. 227.
22. Diverse factors contributed to the appeal of neutralism, ranging from the prospect of securing economic aid from the two blocs to the widely held (and intensely felt) belief that non-alignment was the only way for Asian nations to safeguard their hard-won independence. On this complex set of reasons, see e.g. Henderson, 'The Roots of Neutralism in Southern Asia,' pp. 30–40; see also NAUK, DO 35/8830, 'Neutralism in South and South-East Asia,' Foreign Office Steering Committee paper, 14 March 1960.
23. Henderson, 'The Roots of Neutralism in Southern Asia,' p. 37–8.
24. Appadorai and Rajan, *India's Foreign Policy and Relations*, p. 357.

SELECTED BIBLIOGRAPHY

Manuscript and Archival Collections

Prime Ministers Museum and Library (PMML), New Delhi

Jawaharlal Nehru Papers

V. K. Krishna Menon Papers

Subimal Dutt Papers

National Archives of India (NAI), New Delhi

Ministry of External Affairs (MEA), Asia Africa Conference Branch files

MEA, Africa Branch files

MEA, AMS Branch files

MEA, FEA Branch files, MEA

MEA. Historical Division Branch files

MEA. South-East Asia Branch files

National Archives of Australia (NAA), Canberra

A1068: Department of External Affairs, correspondence files

A1209: Prime Minister's Department, correspondence files

A1838: Department of External Affairs, main correspondence files

A3094: Department of External Affairs, correspondence files, Washington Embassy, Washington

A4231: Department of External Affairs, despatches from overseas posts

A5452: Department of External Affairs, secret/top secret correspondence files, Washington Embassy

A5954: Department of Defence, Sir Frederick Shedden Collection

A11604: Department of External Affairs, correspondence files, Jakarta Embassy

National Archives of the United Kingdom (NAUK), Kew

CAB 129: Cabinet memoranda

CO 936: Colonial Office and Commonwealth Office, International and General Department and predecessors, original correspondence

DO 35: Dominions Office and Commonwealth Relations Office, original correspondence
DO 133: Commonwealth Relations Office and Successors, High Commission and Consular Archives (India), registered files
DO 201: Commonwealth Relations Office: confidential prints
FO 371: Foreign Office, general correspondence
PREM 11: Prime Minister's Office, 1951–64

National Archives and Records Administration (NARA), College Park, Maryland
RG 59: Department of State Central Files
RG 306: Records of the US Information Agency

John Fitzgerald Kennedy Presidential Library, Boston, Massachusetts
Presidential Papers, National Security Files, 1961–63

Published Government Documents and Documentary Collections

Bhasin, Avtar Singh (ed.), *India–China Relations: 1947–2000: A Documentary Study*, 5 vols. (New Delhi: Geetika Publishers, 2018).

Documents on Canadian External Relations, Volume 20 (1954) (Ottawa: Department of Foreign Affairs and International Trade, 1997), https://www.international.gc.ca/gac-amc/history-histoire/external-relations_relations-exterieures.aspx?lang=eng

Documents Diplomatiques Français [DDF], 1954, 21 July–31 December (Paris: Imprimerie Nationale, 1987).

DDF, 1955, Tome I (1 Janvier–30 Juin) (Paris: Imprimerie Nationale, 1987).

Foreign Relations of the United States (FRUS), 1951, Asia and the Pacific, Volume VI, Part 1 (Washington, DC: GPO, 1977), https://history.state.gov/historicaldocuments/frus1951v06p1

FRUS, 1951, Asia and the Pacific, Volume VI, Part 2 (Washington, DC: GPO, 1977), https://history.state.gov/historicaldocuments/frus1951v06p2

FRUS, 1952–1954, Africa and South Asia, Volume XI, Part 2 (Washington, DC: GPO, 1983), https://history.state.gov/historicaldocuments/frus1952-54v11p2

FRUS, 1952–1954, China and Japan, Volume XIV, Part 1 (Washington, DC: GPO, 1985), https://history.state.gov/historicaldocuments/frus1952-54v14p1

FRUS, 1952–1954, East Asia and the Pacific Volume XII, Part 1 (Washington, DC: GPO, 1984), https://history.state.gov/historicaldocuments/frus1952-54v12p1

FRUS, 1952–1954, East Asia and the Pacific, Volume XII, Part 2 (Washington, DC: GPO, 1987), https://history.state.gov/historicaldocuments/frus1952-54v12p2

FRUS, 1952–1954, Indochina, Volume XIII, Part 1 (Washington, DC: GPO, 1982), https://history.state.gov/historicaldocuments/frus1952-54v13p1

FRUS, 1952–1954, The Near and Middle East, Volume IX, Part 1 (Washington, DC: GPO, 1986), https://history.state.gov/historicaldocuments/frus1952-54v09p1

FRUS, 1955–1957, East Asian Security; Cambodia; Laos, Volume XXI (Washington, DC: GPO, 1990), https://history.state.gov/historicaldocuments/frus1955-57v21

Jawaharlal Nehru Letters to Chief Ministers, 1947–1964 [JNLCM], Volume 2, 1950–52 (New Delhi: Jawaharlal Nehru Memorial Fund, 1985).

JNLCM, Volume 3, 1952–1954 (New Delhi: Jawaharlal Nehru Memorial Fund, 1987).

JNLCM, Volume 4, 1954–1957 (New Delhi: Jawaharlal Nehru Memorial Fund, 1988).

JNLCM,Volume 5, 1958–1964 (New Delhi: Jawaharlal Nehru Memorial Fund, 1989).

Jawaharlal Nehru's Speeches,Volume 3, March 1953–August 1957 (New Delhi: Government of India, 1970).

Lok Sabha Debates (New Delhi: Lok Sabha Secretariat, 1954–1955), https://eparlib.nic.in/handle/123456789/7

Nehru, Jawaharlal, *India's Foreign Policy: Selected Speeches, September 1946–April 1961* (New Delhi: Government of India, 1961).

Selected Works of Jawaharlal Nehru (SWJN), Second Series, 60 volumes (New Delhi: Jawaharlal Nehru Memorial Fund, 1984–2015).

Zhou Enlai, *Selected Works of Zhou Enlai, Volume II* (Beijing: Foreign Languages Press, 1988).

Online Primary Resources

CIA Historical Collections (CIA), https://www.cia.gov/readingroom/historical-collections

Wilson Center Digital Archive (WCDA), https://digitalarchive.wilsoncenter.org/

Books

Abdulgani, Roeslan, *The Bandung Connection: The Asia-Africa Conference in Bandung in 1955* (Singapore: Gunung Agung, 1981).

Acharya, Amitav, *Whose Ideas Matter? Agency and Power in Asian Regionalism* (New York: Cornell University Press, 2009).

———, *East of India, South of China: Sino-Indian Encounters in Southeast Asia* (New Delhi: Oxford Academic: 2017), online edition.

Ali, S. Mahmud, *Cold War in the High Himalayas: The USA, China and South Asia in the 1950s* (New York: Routledge, 2018), Kindle edition.

Ang, Cheng Guan, *Southeast Asia and the Vietnam War* (Abingdon, UK and New York: Routledge, 2010).

———, *The Southeast Treaty Organisation* (New York: Routledge, 2022).

Appadorai, A. and Rajan, M. S., *India's Foreign Policy and Relations* (New Delhi: South Asian Publishers, 1985).

Benner, Jeffrey, *The Indian Foreign Policy Bureaucracy* (Abingdon, UK and New York: Routledge, 2019).

Benvenuti, Andrea, Chung, Chien-Peng, Khoo, Nicholas and Tan, Andrew T. H., *China's Foreign Policy: The Emergence of a Great Power* (Abingdon, UK and New York: Routledge, 2022).

Bhagavan, Manu, *India and the Quest for One World: The Peacemakers* (London: Palgrave Macmillan, 2013).

Bhasin, Avtar Singh, *Nehru Tibet and China* (New Delhi: Penguin, 2021), Kindle edition.

Brands, H. W., *The Specter of Neutralism: The United States and the Emergence of the Third World* (New York: Columbia University Press, 1989).

———, *India and the United States: The Cold Peace* (Woodbridge, CT: Twayne Publishers, 1990).

Brazinsky, Gregg *Winning the Third World: Sino-American Rivalry during the Cold War* (Chapel Hill, NC: University of North Carolina Press, 2017).

Brecher, Michael, *Nehru: A Political Biography* (New York: Oxford University Press, 1961).

———, *India and World Politics: Krishna Menon's View of the World* (London: Oxford University Press, 1968).

Brown, Judith M., *Nehru: A Political Life* (New Haven, CT and London: Yale University Press, 2003).

Cable, James, *The Geneva Conference of 1954 on Indochina* (New York: St. Martin's Press, 1986).

Čavoški, Jovan, *Non-Aligned Movement Summits: A History* (London and New York: Bloomsbury Academic, 2022).

Cesari, Laurent, *Le Problème Diplomatique de l'Indochine 1945–1957* (Paris: Les Indes Savantes, 2013).

Chapman, Jessica M., *Remaking the World: Decolonization and the Cold War* (Lexington, KY: University Press of Kentucky, 2023), Kindle edition.

Chen, Jian, *Mao's China and the Cold War* (Chapel Hill, NC: University of North Carolina Press, 2010), Kindle edition.

Cohen, Stephen P., *India: Emerging Power* (Washington, DC: Brookings Institution Press, 2001).

Conboy, Kenneth J. and Morrison, James, *The CIA's Secret War in Tibet* (Lawrence, KS: University Press of Kansas, 2002).

Crocker, Walter, *Nehru: A Contemporary Estimate* (New Delhi: Penguin Random House India, 2016), Kindle edition.

Das Gupta, Amit and Lüthi, Lorenz (eds), *The Sino-Indian War of 1962: New Perspectives* (London: Taylor & Francis, 2016).

Das Gupta, Amit, *Serving India: A Political Biography of Subimal Dutt (1903–1992), India's Longest Serving Foreign Secretary* (New Delhi: Manhoar, 2017).

———, *The Indian Civil Service and Indian Foreign Policy, 1923–1961* (London: Routledge, 2021).

Dillon, Michael, *Zhou Enlai: The Enigma Behind Chairman Mao* (London: I. B. Tauris, 2019).

Dixit, J. N., *Makers of India's Foreign Policy* (New Delhi: HarperCollins India, 2004).

Dockrill, Saki, *Eisenhower's New-Look National Security Policy, 1953–61* (New York: St. Martin's Press, 1996).

Feith, Herbert, *The Decline of Constitutional Democracy in Indonesia* (Singapore: Equinox, 2006).

Fenton, Damien, *To Cage the Red Dragon: SEATO and the Defence of Southeast Asia, 1955–1965* (Singapore: NUS Press, 2012).

Frankel, Francine, *When Nehru Looked East: Origins of India-US Suspicion and India-China Rivalry* (Oxford: Oxford University Press, 2020), Kindle edition.

Fravel, Taylor M., *Strong Borders, Secure Nation: Cooperation and Conflict in China's Territorial Disputes* (Princeton, NJ: Princeton University Press, 2008).

Friedman, Jeremy, *The Sino-Soviet Competition for the Third World* (Chapel Hill, NC: University of North Carolina Press, 2015).

———, *Ripe for Revolution: Building Socialism in the Third World* (Cambridge, MA: Harvard University Press, 2022), Kindle edition.

Fursenko, A. A. and Naftali, Timothy J., *Khrushchev's Cold War: The Inside Story of an American Adversary* (New York: W. W. Norton & Company, 2010), Kindle edition.

Gaddis, John Lewis, *Strategies of Containment: A Critical Appraisal of Postwar American National Security Policy* (Oxford and New York: Oxford University Press, 1982).

Garver, John W., *China's Quest: The History of the Foreign Relations of the People's Republic* (Oxford: Oxford University Press, 2016), Kindle edition.

Goldstein, Melvyn C., *A History of Modern Tibet. Volume 4. In the Eye of the Storm, 1957–1959* (Oakland, CA: University of California Press, 2019).

Gopal, S., *Jawaharlal Nehru: A Biography. Volume Three: 1956–1964* (London: Jonathan Cape, 1984).

———, *Jawaharlal Nehru: A Biography. Volume Two: 1947–1956* (London: Vintage Digital, 2014), Kindle edition.

Goscha, Christopher E., *Historical Dictionary of the Indochina War (1945–1954): An International and Interdisciplinary Approach* (Copenhagen: NIAS Press, 2011).

Grosser, Pierre, *L'Histoire du Monde se Fait en Asie: Un Autre Vision du XXe Siècle* (Paris: Odile Jacob, 2017), Kobo edition.

Guha, Ramachandra, *India After Gandhi: The History of the World's Largest Democracy* (New York: HarperCollins, 2007).

———, *Makers of Modern Asia* (Cambridge, MA: Belknap Press, 2014), Kindle edition.

Gupta, Sisir, *India and Regional Integration in Asia* (Bombay, India: Asian Publishing House, 1964).

Hack, Karl, *Defence and Decolonisation in Southeast Asia: Britain, Malaya and Singapore 1941–1968* (London: Curzon Press, 2001).

Heimsath, Charles and Mansingh, Surjit, *A Diplomatic History of Modern India* (New Delhi: Allied Publishers, 1971).

Hoffmann, Steven A., *India and the China Crisis* (Berkeley, CA: University of California Press, 1990).

Hopf, Ted, *Reconstructing the Cold War: The Early Years, 1945–1958* (New York: Oxford University Press, 2012).

Jansen, G. H., *Afro-Asia and Non-Alignment* (London: Faber and Faber, 1966).

Jha, C. S., *From Bandung to Tashkent: Glimpses of India's Foreign Policy* (Madras and Hyderabad, India; London: Sangam Books, 1983).

Joyaux, François, *La Chine et le Règlement du Premier Conflit d'Indochine: Genève 1954* (Paris: Publications de la Sorbonne, 1979), Kobo edition.

Kahin, George McTurnan, *The Asian-African Conference, Bandung, Indonesia, April 1955* (Port Washington, NY: Kennikat Press, 1972).

Kaushik, Davendra, *Soviet Relations with India and Pakistan* (New Delhi: Vikas Publications, 1971).

Kavic, Lorne J., *India's Quest for Security: Defence Policies 1947–1965* (Berkeley, CA and Los Angeles: University of California Press, 1967).

Keith, Ronald C., *The Diplomacy of Zhou Enlai* (London: Macmillan, 1989).

Kennedy, Andrew B., *The International Ambitions of Mao and Nehru: National Efficacy Beliefs and the Making of Foreign Policy* (Cambridge, UK: Cambridge University Press, 2012).

Keylor, William, *The Twentieth Century World and Beyond: An International History Since 1900* (Oxford: Oxford University Press, 2006).

Khan, Sulmaan Wasif, *Muslim, Trader, Nomad, Spy: China's Cold War and the People of the Tibetan Borderlands* (Chapel Hill, NC: University of North Carolina Press, 2015).

Kimche, David, *The Afro-Asian Movement: Ideology and Foreign Policy of the Third World* (Jerusalem: Israel Universities Press, 1973).

Kissinger, Henry, *Diplomacy* (New York: Touchstone, 1994).

Kotelawala, John, *An Asian Prime Minister's Story* (London: George G. Harrap & Co. Ltd, 1956).

Legge, J. D., *Sukarno: A Political Biography* (Singapore: Archipelago Press, 2003), Ebook.

Lentz, Harris M., *Heads of States and Governments since* 1945 (New York: Routledge, 2013).

Lintner, Bertil, *China's India War: Collision Course on the Roof of the World* (New Delhi: Oxford University Press, 2018), Kindle edition.

Logevall, Fredrik, *Embers of War: The Fall of an Empire and the Making of America's Vietnam* (New York: Random House, 2012), Kindle edition.

———, *The Origins of the Vietnam War* (London: Routledge, 2013), Kindle edition.

Louro, Michele L., *Comrades Against Imperialism: Nehru, India, and Interwar Internationalism* (New York: Cambridge University Press, 2018).

Lovell, Julia, *Maoism: A Global History* (London: Vintage, 2019), Kindle edition.

Lowe, Peter, *Contending With Nationalism and Communism: British Policy Towards Southeast Asia, 1945–65* (London: Palgrave, 2009).

Lundestad, Geir, *The United States and Western Europe Since 1945: From 'Empire' by Invitation to Transatlantic Drift* (Oxford: Oxford University Press, 2003).

Lüthi, Lorenz M., *The Sino-Soviet Split: Cold War in the Communist World* (Princeton, NJ: Princeton University Press, 2008).

———, *Cold Wars: Asia, the Middle East, Europe* (Cambridge, UK: Cambridge University Press, 2020), Kindle edition.

Mackie, Jamie, *Bandung 1955: Non-Alignment and Afro-Asian Solidarity* (Singapore: Editions Didier Millet, 2005).

Madan, Tanvi, *Fateful Triangle: How China Shaped U.S.-India Relations During the Cold War* (Washington, DC: Brookings Institution Press, 2020), Kindle edition.

Malone, David M., Mohan, C. Raja and Raghavan, Srinath (eds), *The Oxford Handbook of Indian Foreign Policy* (Oxford: Oxford University Press, 2015).

Maung, Aung Myoe, *In the Name of Pauk-Phaw: Myanmar's China Policy Since 1948* (Singapore: Institute of Southeast Asian Studies, 2011).

Maxwell, Neville, *India's China War* (London: Cape, 1970).

McGarr, Paul, *The Cold War in South Asia. Britain, the United States and the Indian Subcontinent, 1945–1965* (Cambridge, UK: Cambridge University Press, 2013).

McMahon, Robert J., *The Cold War on the Periphery: The United States, India and Pakistan* (New York: Columbia University Press, 1994).

——— (ed.), *The Cold War in the Third World* (Oxford: Oxford University Press, 2012). Kindle edition.

Mody, Ashoka, *India Is Broken: And Why It's Hard to Fix It* (New Delhi: Juggernaut, 2023).

Mozingo, David, *Chinese Policy Toward Indonesia, 1949–1967* (Singapore: Equinox Publishing 2007).

Mullik, B. N., *My Years With Nehru, 1948–1964* (Bombay: Allied Publishers, 1972).

Nehru, B. K., *Nice Guys Finish Second: Memoirs* (Gurgaon, India: Penguin Random House India, 2012).

Noorani. A. G. A. M., *India-China Boundary Problem, 1846–1947: History and Diplomacy* (New Delhi: Oxford University Press, 2011).

Pang, Yang Huei, *Strait Rituals: China, Taiwan, and the United States in the Taiwan Strait Crises, 1954–1958* (Hong Kong: Hong Kong University Press, 2019).

Penders, C. L. M. (ed.), *Milestones on My Journey: The Memoirs of Ali Sastroamijoyo, Indonesian Patriot and Leader* (St. Lucia, Australia: University of Queensland Press, 1979).

Pettman, Ralph, *China in Burma's Foreign Policy* (Canberra, Australia: Australian National University, 1973).

Prashad, Vijay, *The Darker Nations: A People's History of the Third World* (New York: New Press, 2007).

Raghavan, Srinath, *War and Peace in Modern India* (London: Palgrave Macmillan, 2010).

———, *Fierce Enigmas: A History of the United States in South* Asia (New York: Basic Books, 2018), Kindle edition.

Rajan, M. S., *India in World Affairs, 1954–56* (London: Asia Publishing House, 1964).

Rajgopal, P. V. (ed.), *I Was Nehru's Shadow: From the Diaries of KF Rustamji, IP, Padma Vibhushan* (New Delhi: Wisdom Tree, 2014), Kindle edition.

Rakove, Robert B., *Kennedy, Johnson, and the Nonaligned World* (Cambridge, UK: Cambridge University Press, 2013).

Ramesh, Jairam, *A Chequered Brilliance: The Many Lives of V. K. Krishna Menon* (New Delhi: Penguin Random House India, 2019), Kindle edition.

Rao, Nirupama, *Fractured Himalaya: India Tibet China 1949–1962* (n. p.: Penguin Books. 2021), Kindle edition.

Ray, Jayanta Kumar, *India's Foreign Relations, 1947–2007* (New Delhi: Routledge, 2011).

Reid, Escott, *Envoy to Nehru* (Toronto, Canada: Oxford University Press, 1981).

Roberts, Brian Russell and Foulcher, Keith, *Indonesian Notebook: A Sourcebook on Richard Wright and the Bandung Conference* (Durham, NC: Duke University Press, 2016).

Ruane, Kevin and Jones, Matthew, *Anthony Eden, Anglo-American Relations and the 1954 Indochina Crisis* (London: Bloomsbury Academic, 2019).

SarDesai, D. R., *Indian Foreign Policy in Cambodia, Laos and Vietnam, 1947–1964* (Berkeley, CA and Los Angeles: University of California Press, 1968).

Shen, Zhihua and Xia, Yafeng, *Mao and the Sino-Soviet Partnership, 1945–1959: A New History* (Lanham, MD: Lexington Books, 2015).

Sherman, Taylor C., *Nehru's India: A History in Seven Myths* (Princeton, NJ: Princeton University Press, 2023), Kindle edition.

Singh, Zorawar Daulet, *Power and Diplomacy: India's Foreign Policies During the Cold War* (New Delhi: Oxford University Press, 2019), Kindle edition.

Sinha, P. B. and Athale A. A., *History of Conflict With China* (New Delhi: History Division, Ministry of Defence, 1992).

Sukma, Rizal, *Indonesia and China: The Politics of a Troubled Relationship* (London: Routledge, 1999).

Tarling, Nicholas, *Britain, Southeast Asia and the Impact of the Korean War* (Singapore: NUS Press, 2005).

———, *Britain and the Neutralisation of Laos* (Singapore: NUS Press, 2011).

———, *Southeast Asia and the Great Powers* (London: Routledge, 2011).

Thien, Ton That, *India and South East Asia: 1947–1960. A Study of India's Foreign Policy Towards the South East Asian Countries in the Period 1947–1960* (Geneva, Switzerland: Librarie Droz, 1963).

Trevelyan, Humphrey, *Worlds Apart: My Experiences in China (1953–5) and the Soviet Union (1962–5)* (n. p.: Lume Books, 2019), Kindle edition.

Tyabji, Badr-ud-din, *Memoirs of an Egoist. Volume I: 1907 to 1956* (New Delhi: Roli Books, 1988).

Van Tonder, Gerry, *Sino-Indian War: Border Clash, October–November 1962* (Barnsley, UK: Pen and Sword Military, 2018).

Wainwright, A. Martin, *Inheritance of Empire: Britain, India and the Balance of Power in Asia, 1938–55* (Westport, CT: Praeger, 1994).

Walder, Andrew G., *China Under Mao: A Revolution Derailed* (Cambridge, MA: Harvard University Press, 2015).

Wang, Tao, *Isolating the Enemy: Diplomatic Strategy in China and the United States, 1953–1956* (New York: Columbia University Press, 2021), Kindle edition.

Westad, Odd Arne, *The Global Cold War: Third World Interventions and the Making of Our Times* (Cambridge, UK: Cambridge University Press, 2005).

———, *Restless Empire: China and the World Since 1750* (London: Vintage Books, 2013).

———, *The Cold War: A World History* (London: Penguin, 2018), Kindle edition.

Wolpert, Stanley, *Nehru: A Tryst with Destiny* (Oxford: Oxford University Press, 1996).

Zachariah, Benjamin, *Nehru* (London: Taylor & Francis, 2004).

Zhai, Qiang, *China and the Vietnam Wars, 1950–1975* (Chapel Hill, NC: University of North Carolina Press, 2000).

Zhou, Taomo, *Migration in the Time of Revolution: China, Indonesia, and the Cold War,* (Ithaca, NY: Cornell University Press, 2019).

Zubok, Vladislav and Pleshakov, Constantine, *Inside the Kremlin's Cold War: From Stalin to Khrushchev* (Cambridge: Harvard University Press, 1996).

Book Chapters

Acharya, Amitav and Tan, See Seng, 'The Normative Relevance of the Bandung Conference for Contemporary Asian and International Order,' in See Seng Tan and Amitav Acharya (eds), *Bandung Revisited: The Legacy of the 1955 Asian-African Conference for International Order* (Singapore: NUS Press, 2008), pp. 1–16.

Ang, Cheng Guan, 'The Bandung Conference and the Cold War International History of Southeast Asia,' in See Seng Tan and Amitav Acharya (eds), *Bandung Revisited: The Legacy of the 1955 Asian-African Conference for International Order* (Singapore: NUS Press, 2008), pp. 27–47.

———, 'Southeast Asian Perceptions of the Domino Theory,' in Christopher E. Goscha and Christian F. Ostermann (eds), *Connecting Histories: Decolonization and the Cold War in Southeast Asia, 1945–1962* (Washington, DC: Woodrow Wilson Center Press, 2009), pp. 301–31.

———, 'China's Influence Over Vietnam in War and Peace,' in Evelyn Goh (ed.), *Rising China's Influence in Developing Asia* (Oxford: Oxford University Press, 2016), Kindle edition, ch. 3.

Ankit, Rakesh, 'India-USSR, 1946–1949: A False Start?,' in Madhavan K. Palat (ed.), *India and the World in the First Half of the Twentieth Century* (New York: Routledge, 2018), pp. 160–88.

Benvenuti, Andrea, 'US Relations with the PRC during the Cold War,' in Andrew T. H. Tan (ed.), *Handbook of US-China Relations* (Cheltenham: Edward Elgar Publishing, 2016), pp. 44–61.

———, 'US Diplomacy in Asia,' in Andrew T. H. Tan (ed.), *Handbook on the United States in Asia: Managing Hegemonic Decline, Retaining Influence in the Trump Era* (Cheltenham, UK: Edward Elgar Publishing, 2018), pp. 34–53.

———, 'Frustrating the Americans and Befriending the Communists: Nehru's Policy in the Early Asian Cold War, 1947–54,' in Brian P. Farrell, S. R. Joey Long and David J. Ulbrich (eds), *From Far East to Asia Pacific: Great Powers and Grand Strategy 1900–1954* (Berlin: De Gruyter Oldenbourg, 2022), pp. 251–79.

Brecher, Michael, 'India's Decision to Remain in the Commonwealth,' *Journal of Commonwealth and Comparative Politics*, 12:1 (1974), pp. 62–90.

Brown, Judith M., 'Jawaharlal Nehru,' in Steven Casey and Jonathan Wright (eds), *Mental Maps in the Early Cold War Era, 1945–68* (London: Palgrave Macmillan, 2011), pp. 200–17.

Čavoški, Jovan, 'Saving Non-Alignment: Diplomatic Efforts of Major Non-Aligned Countries and the Sino-Indian Border Conflict,' in Amit Das Gupta and Lorenz Lüthi (eds), *The Sino-Indian War of 1962: New Perspectives* (London: Routledge, 2017), pp. 160–79.

Chen, Jian, 'China and the Bandung Conference: Changing Perceptions and Representations,' in See Seng Tan and Amitav Acharya (eds), *Bandung Revisited: The Legacy of the 1955 Asian-African Conference for International Order* (Singapore: NUS Press, 2008), pp. 132–59.

———, 'China's Changing Policies Toward the Third World and the End of the Global Cold War,' in Artemy Kalinovsky and Sergey Radchenko (eds.), *The End of the Cold War and the Third World: New Perspectives on Regional Conflict* (New York: Routledge, 2011), pp. 101–21.

———, 'China, Third World, and the Cold War,' in Robert J. McMahon (ed.), *The Cold War in the Third World* (Oxford: Oxford University Press, 2013), Kindle edition.

———, 'Zhou Enlai and China's 'Prolonged Rise',' in Ramachandra Guha (ed.), *Makers of Modern Asia* (Cambridge, MA: Belknap Press, 2014), Kindle edition.

Dai, Chaowu, 'From 'Hindi-Chini Bhai-Bhai' to 'International Class Struggle' Against Nehru: China's India Policy and the Frontier Dispute, 1950–62,' in Amit Das Gupta and Lorenz Lüthi (eds), *The Sino-Indian War of 1962: New Perspectives* (London: Routledge, 2017), pp. 68–84.

Das Gupta, Amit, 'The Indian Civil Service and Indian Foreign Policy,' in Madhavan K. Palat (ed.), *India and the World in the First Half of the Twentieth Century* (London: Routledge, 2018), pp. 134–59.

Farrell, Brian P., 'Alphabet Soup and Nuclear War: China and the Cold War in Southeast Asia,' in Malcolm H. Murfett (ed.), *Cold War: Southeast Asia* (Singapore: Marshall Cavendish, c2012), pp. 128–94.

Fonseca, Rena, 'Nehru and the Diplomacy of Non-Alignment,' in Gordon A. Craig and Francis L. Loewenheim (eds), T*he Diplomats, 1939–1979* (Princeton, NJ: Princeton University Press, 2019), pp. 371–98.

Garver, John W., 'China's Decision for War With India in 1962,' in Alastair Iain Johnston and Robert S. Ross (eds), *New Directions in the Study of China's Foreign Policy* (Stanford, CA: Stanford University Press, 2006), pp. 86–130.

Harder, Anton, 'Promoting Development Without Struggle: Sino-Indian Relations in the 1950s,' in Manu Baghavan (ed.), *India and the Cold War* (Gurgaon, India: Penguin, 2019), pp. 153–77.

Hashmi, Sohail H., "Zero Plus Zero Plus Zero': Pakistan, the Baghdad Pact, and the Suez Crisis,' *International History Review*, 33:3 (2011), pp. 525–44.

Herring, George C., "A Good Stout Effort': John Foster Dulles and the Indochina Crisis, 1954–1955,' Richard H. Immerman (ed.), *John Foster Dulles and the Diplomacy of the Cold War* (Princeton, NJ: Princeton University Press, 1990), pp. 213–33.

———, 'Franco-American Conflict in Indochina, 1950–1954,' in Lawrence Kaplan, Denise Artaud and Mark Rubin (eds), *Dien Bien Phu and the Crisis of Franco-American Relations, 1945–1955* (Wilmington, DE: Scholarly Resources, Inc., 1991), pp. 29–48.

Hess, Gary R., 'Redefining the American Position in Southeast Asia: The United States and the Geneva and Manila Conferences,' in Lawrence S. Kaplan, Denise Artaud and Mark R. Rubin (eds), *Dien Bien Phu and the Crisis in Franco-American Relations, 1954–1955* (Wilmington: Scholarly Resources, 1990), pp. 123–48.

Hillman, Ben, 'Tibetans in China: From Conflict to Protest,' in Michael Weiner (ed.), *Routledge Handbook of Race and Ethnicity in Asia* (New York: Routledge, 2021), pp. 219–30.

Journoud, Pierre, 'La France et l'Asie du Sud-Est, de l'Indochine à l'Asean,' in Pierre Journoud (ed.), *L'Évolution du Débat Stratégique en Asie du Sud-Est depuis* 1945 (Paris: IRSEM, 2012), pp. 13–51, https://www.irsem.fr/data/files/irsem/documents/document/file/1081/EtudeIRSEM14Finale.pdf

Kennedy, Andrew B., 'Nehru's Foreign Policy: Realism and Idealism Conjoined,' in David M. Malone, C. Raja Mohan and Srinath Raghavan (eds), *The Oxford Handbook of Indian Foreign Policy* (Oxford: Oxford University Press, 2015), pp. 91–103.

Logevall, Fredrik, 'The Indochina Wars and the Cold War, 1945–1975,' in Melvyn Leffler and Odd Arne Westad (eds), *The Cambridge History of the Cold War. Volume 2*, (Cambridge, UK: Cambridge University Press, 2010), pp. 281–304.

Long, S. R. Joey, 'Adversaries, Allies and the Shaping of US Grand Strategy: The Eisenhower Administration and the 1954 Geneva Conference,' in Brian P. Farrell, S. R. Joey Long and David J. Ulbrich (eds), *From Far East to Asia Pacific: Great Powers and Grand Strategy 1900–1954* (Berlin: De Gruyter Oldenbourg, 2022), pp. 309–38.

Lüthi, Lorenz, 'India's Relations With China, 1945–74,' in Amit Das Gupta and Lorenz M. Lüthi (eds), *The Sino-Indian War of 1962: New Perspectives* (London: Taylor & Francis, 2016), pp. 29–47.

Mastny, Vojtech, 'The Elusive Détente: Stalin's Successors and the West,' in Klaus Larres and Kenneth Osgood (eds), *The Cold War After Stalin's Death: A Missed Opportunity for Peace* (Lanham, MD: Rowman & Littlefield Publishers, 2006), pp. 3–26.

Menon, Rajan, 'India and Russia: The Anatomy and Evolution of a Relationship,' in David M. Malone, C. Raja Mohan and Srinath Raghavan (eds), *The Oxford Handbook of Indian Foreign Policy* (Oxford: Oxford University Press, 2015), pp. 509–23.

Mukherji, Rahul, 'The Bandung Conference and the Cold War International History of Southeast Asia,' in See Seng Tan and Amitav Acharya (eds), *Bandung Revisited: The Legacy of the 1955 Asian-African Conference for International Order* (Singapore: NUS Press, 2008), pp 160–79.

Nayudu, Swapna Kona, 'The Soviet Peace Offensive and Nehru's India, 1953–1956,' in Manu Baghavan (ed.), *India and the Cold War* (Gurgaon, India: Penguin, 2019), pp. 36–56.

Parker, Jason, 'Small Victory, Missed Chance: The Eisenhower Administration, the Bandung Conference and the Turning of the Cold War,' in Kathryn Statler and Andrew Johns (eds), *The Eisenhower Administration, the Third World, and the Globalization of the Cold War* (New York: Rowman and Littlefield, 2006), pp. 153–74.

Pechatnov, Vladimir, 'Reflections on Soviet Foreign Policy, 1953–1964,' in Helene Carlbäck, Alexey Komarov and Karl Molin (eds), *Peaceful Coexistence? Soviet Union and Sweden in the Khrushchev Era* (Moscow: Centre for Baltic and East European Studies Södertörn University, 2010), pp. 23–44.

Pruessen, Ronald W., 'John Foster Dulles and Decolonization of Southeast Asia,' in Marc Frey, Ronald W. Pruessen and Tan Tai Yong (eds), *The Transformation of Southeast Asia: International Perspectives on Decolonisation* (Singapore: Singapore University Press, 2003), pp. 226–40.

Raghavan, Pallavi, 'Establishing the Ministry of External Affairs,' in David M. Malone, C. Raja Mohan and Srinath Raghavan (eds), *The Oxford Handbook of Indian Foreign Policy* (Oxford: Oxford University Press, 2015), pp. 80–91.

Raghavan, Srinath, 'A Missed Opportunity? The Nehru-Zhou Enlai Summit of 1960,' Manu Baghavan (ed.), *India and the Cold War* (Gurgaon, India: Penguin, 2019), pp. 100–25.

Rutkowski, Marek W., 'Expanding the Area of Peace: India, Colombo Powers and the Geneva Conference of 1954,' in Brian P. Farrell, S. R. Joey Long and David J. Ulbrich (eds), *From Far East to Asia Pacific: Great Powers and Grand Strategy 1900–1954* (Berlin: De Gruyter Oldenbourg, 2022), pp. 339–59.

Tsui, Brian, 'Coming to Terms With the People's Republic of China: Jawaharlal Nehru in the Early 1950s,' in Young-Chan Kim (ed.), *China-India Relations: Geo-political Competition, Economic Cooperation, Cultural Exchange and Business Ties* (Cham, Germany: Springer Publishing, 2020), pp. 15–30.

Warner, Geoffrey, 'Britain and the Crisis Over Dien Bien Phu, April 1954: The Failure of United Action,' in Lawrence Kaplan, Denise Artaud and Mark Rubin (eds), *Dien Bien Phu and the Crisis of Franco-American Relations, 1945–1955* (Wilmington, DE: Scholarly Resources, Inc., 1991), pp. 55–77.

Zhai, Qiang, 'Road to Bandung: China's Evolving Approach to De-Colonization,' in Tomohiko Umaya (ed.), *Comparing Modern Empires: Imperial Rule and Decolonization in the Changing World Order* (Hokkaido, Japan: Slavic-Eurasian Research Centre, Hokkaido University, 2018), pp. 181–206.

Zhang, Guang Shu, 'In the Shadow of Mao: Zhou Enlai and New China's Diplomacy,' in Gordon A. Craig and Francis L. Loewenheim (eds), *The Diplomats, 1939–1979* (Princeton, NJ: Princeton University Press, 2019), pp. 337–70.

Articles

Abraham, Itty, 'From Bandung to NAM: Non-alignment and Indian Foreign Policy, 1947–65,' *Commonwealth & Comparative Politics*, 46:2 (2008), pp. 195–219.

Adie, W. A. C., 'Zhou En-lai on Safari,' *China Quarterly*, 18 (1964), pp. 174–94.

Appadorai, A., 'The Bandung Conference,' *India Quarterly*, 11:3 (1955), pp. 207–35.

Ashton, Nigel John, 'The Hijacking of a Pact: The Formation of the Baghdad Pact and Anglo-American Tensions in the Middle East, 1955–1958,' *Review of International Studies*, 19:2 (1993), pp. 123–37.

Barnes, Robert, 'Between the Blocs: India, the United Nations and Ending the Korean War,' *Journal of Korean Studies*, 18:2 (2013), pp. 263–86.

Benvenuti, Andrea, 'The British Military Withdrawal From Southeast Asia and Its Impact on Australia's Cold War Strategic Interests,' *Cold War History*, 5:2 (2005), pp. 189–210.

———, 'Constructing Peaceful Coexistence: Nehru's Approach to Regional Security and India's Rapprochement with Communist China in the mid-1950s,' *Diplomacy & Statecraft*, 31:1 (2020), pp. 91–117.

———, 'Nehru's Bandung Moment: India and the Convening of the 1955 Asian-African Conference,' *India Review*, 21:2 (2022), pp. 153–80.

Bhardwaj, Sandeep, 'Three Meanings of Colonialism: Nehru, Sukarno, and Kotelawala Debate the Future of the Third World Movement (1954–61),' *Journal of Global History*, (2023), pp. 1–17.

Boquérat, Gilles, 'India's Commitment to Peaceful Coexistence and the Settlement of the Indochina War,' *Cold War History*, 5:2 (2005), pp. 211–34.

Brands, H. W., 'India and Pakistan in American Strategic Planning, 1947–54: The Commonwealth as Collaborator,' *Journal of Imperial and Commonwealth History*, 15:1 (1986), pp. 41–54.

Brecher, Michael, 'Non-Alignment Under Stress: The West and the India-China Border War,' *Pacific Affairs*, 52:4 (1979–1980), pp. 612–30.

Brissenden, Rosemary, 'India's Opposition to SEATO: A Case Study in Neutralist Diplomacy,' *Australian Journal of Politics and History*, 6:2 (1960), pp. 219–32.

Brooks, Jeffrey, 'When the Cold War Did Not End: The Soviet Peace Offensive of 1953 and the American Response,' https://www.files.ethz.ch/isn/19774/OP278.pdf

Bunnell, Frederik P., 'Guided Democracy Foreign Policy: 1960–1965. President Sukarno Moves From Non–Alignment to Confrontation,' *Indonesia*, 2 (1966), pp. 37–76.

Chang, Gordon H., 'Nuclear Brink: Eisenhower, Dulles, and the Quemoy-Matsu Crisis,' *International Security*, 12:4 (1988), pp. 96–123.

Chaudhuri, Rudra, 'The Limits of Executive Power: Domestic Politics and Alliance Behavior in Nehru's India,' *India Review*, 11:2 (2012), pp. 95–115.

———, 'The Making of an 'All Weather Friendship' Pakistan, China and the History of a Border Agreement: 1949–1963,' *International History Review*, 40:1 (2018), pp. 41–64.

Chen, Jian, 'The Tibetan Rebellion and China's Changing Relations With India and the Soviet Union,' *Journal of Cold War Studies*, 8:3 (2006), pp. 54–101.

———, 'Bridging Revolution and Decolonization: The 'Bandung Discourse' in China's Early Cold War Experience,' *The Chinese Historical Review*, 15:2 (2008), pp. 207–41.

Chetty, A. Lakshmana, 'India and Southeast Asia Treaty Organization (S.E.A.T.O.),' *Proceedings of the Indian History Congress*, 42 (1981), pp. 615–23.

Clymer, Clinton, 'The United States and the Guomindang (KMT) Forces in Burma, 1949–1954: A Diplomatic Disaster,' *The Chinese Historical Review*, 21:1 (2014), pp. 24–44.

Dai, Shen-Yu, 'Peking and Rangoon,' *China Quarterly*, 5 (1961), pp. 131–44.

———, 'Peking, Kathmandu and New Delhi,' *China Quarterly*, 16 (1963), pp. 86–98.

Deshingkar, Giri, 'India-China Relations: The Nehru Years,' *China Report*, 27:2 (1991), pp. 85–100.

———, 'The Construction of Asia in India,' *Asian Studies Review*, 23:2 (1999), pp. 173–80.

Dingman, Roger, 'John Foster Dulles and the Creation of the South-East Asia Treaty Organization in 1954,' *International History Review*, 11:3 (1989), pp. 457–77.

Dobbs, C. M., 'The Pact That Never Was: The Pacific Pact of 1949,' *Journal of Northeast Asian Studies*, 4:3 (1984), pp. 29–42.

Ewing, Cindy, 'The Colombo Powers: Crafting Diplomacy in the Third World and Launching Afro-Asia at Bandung,' *Cold War History*, 19:1 (2019), pp. 1–19.

———, '"With a Minimum of Bitterness": Decolonization, the Right to Self-Determination, and the Arab-Asian Group,' *Journal of Global History*, 17:2 (2022), pp. 254–71.

Fifield, Russell H., 'The Five Principles of Peaceful Co-Existence,' *The American Journal of International Law*, 52:3 (1958), pp. 504–10.

Fitzgerald, Stephen, 'China and the Overseas Chinese: Perceptions and Policies, *China Quarterly*, 44 (1970), pp. 1–37.

Friedman, Jeremy, 'Free at Last, Now What: The Soviet and Chinese Attempts to Offer a Road-map for the Post-colonial World,' *Modern China Studies*, 22:1 (2015), pp. 259–92.

Garver, John W., 'India, China, The United States, Tibet, and the Origins of the 1962 War,' *India Review*, 3:2 (2004), pp. 9–20.

Gettig, Eric, "'Trouble Ahead in Afro-Asia': The United States, the Second Bandung Conference, and the Struggle for the Third World, 1964–1965,' *Diplomatic History*, 39:1 (2015), pp. 126–56.

Gupta, K., 'Sino-Indian Agreement on Tibetan Trade and Intercourse: Its Origin and Significance,' *Economic and Political Weekly*, 13:16 (1978), pp. 696–702.

Harder, Anton, 'Compradors, Neo-Colonialism, and Transnational Class Struggle: PRC Relations With Algeria and India, 1953–1965,' *Modern Asian Studies*, 55:4 (2021), pp. 1227–67.

Hasan, K. Sarwar, 'Bandung Memories,' *Pakistan Horizon*, 68:3/4 (2015), pp. 1–8.

Henderson, William, 'The Roots of Neutralism in Southern Asia,' *International Journal*, 13:1 (1957–58), pp. 30–40.

Herring, George and Immerman, Richard, 'Eisenhower, Dulles, and Dienbienphu: 'The Day We Didn't Go to War' Revisited,' *Journal of American History*, 71:2 (1984), pp. 343–63.

Hilger, Andreas, 'Socialist Internationalism, World Capitalism, and the Global South: Soviet Foreign Economic Policy and India in Times of Cold War and Decolonization, 1950s–1960s,' *Journal of World History*, 32:3 (2021), pp. 439–64.

Hoffmann, Steven A. 'Rethinking the Linkage Between Tibet and the China-India Border Conflict,' *Journal of Cold War Studies*, 8:3 (2006), pp. 165–94.

Immerman, Richard, 'Eisenhower, Dulles, and Dienbienphu: 'The Day We Didn't Go to War' Revisited,' *Journal of American History*, 71:2 (1984), pp. 343–63.

Jalal, Ayesha, 'Towards the Baghdad Pact: South Asia and Middle East Defence in the Cold War, 1947–1955,' *International History Review*, 11:3 (1989), pp. 409–33.

Jones, Matthew, "Maximum Disavowable Aid': Britain, the United States and the Indonesian Rebellion, 1957–58,' *The English Historical Review*, 114:459 (November 1999), pp. 1179–1216.

———, 'A 'Segregated' Asia? Race, the Bandung Conference, and Pan-Asianist Fears in American Thought and Policy, 1954–1955,' *Diplomatic History*, 29:5 (2005), pp. 841–68.

Khan, Sulmaan Wasif, 'Cold War Co-operation: New Chinese Evidence on Jawaharlal Nehru's 1954 Visit to Beijing,' *Cold War History*, 11:2 (2011), pp. 197–222.

Leng, Shao Chuan, 'Communist China's Economic Relations With Southeast Asia,' *Far Eastern Survey*, 28:1 (1959), pp. 1–11.

Little, Douglas, 'His Finest Hour? Eisenhower, Lebanon, and the 1958 Middle East Crisis,' *Diplomatic History*, 20:1 (1996), pp. 27–54.

Liu, Xiaoyuan, 'Friend or Foe: India as Perceived by Beijing's Foreign Policy Analysts in the 1950s,' *China Review*, 15:1 (2015), pp. 117–43.

Lüthi, Lorenz M., 'Sino-Indian Relations, 1954–1962,' *Eurasia Border Review*, 3 (2012), pp. 93–119.

———, 'The Non-Aligned Movement and the Cold War, 1961–1973,' *Journal of Cold War Studies*, 18:4 (2016), pp. 98–147.

———, 'Non-Alignment, 1946–65: Its Establishment and Struggle Against Afro-Asianism,' *Humanity: An International Journal of Human Rights, Humanitarianism, and Development*, 7:2 (2016), pp. 201–23.

Mastny, Vojtech, 'The Soviet Union Partnership With India,' *Journal of Cold War Studies*, 12:3 (2010), pp. 50–90.

McGarr, Paul M., "India's Rasputin'? V. K. Krishna Menon and Anglo-American Misperceptions of Indian Foreign Policymaking, 1947–1964,' *Diplomacy and Statecraft*, 22:2 (2011), pp. 239–60.

———, 'The Long Shadow of Colonial Cartography: Britain and the Sino-Indian War of 1962,' *Journal of Strategic Studies*, 42:5 (2019), pp. 626–53.

McMahon, Robert J., 'United States Cold War Strategy in South Asia: Making a Military Commitment to Pakistan, 1947–1954,' *Journal of American History*, 75:3 (1988), pp. 812–40.

———, "The Illusion of Vulnerability': American Reassessments of the Soviet Threat, 1955–1956,' *International History Review*, 18:3 (1996), pp. 591–619.

Mozingo, David, 'The Sino-Indonesian Dual Nationality Treaty,' *Asian Survey*, 1:10 (1961), pp. 25–31.

Mukherjee, Mithi, "A World of Illusion': The Legacy of Empire in India's Foreign Relations, 1947–62,' *The International History Review*, 32:2 (2010), pp. 253–71.

Nayudu, Swapna Kona, 'In the Very Eye of the Storm: India, the UN, and the Lebanon Crisis of 1958,' *Cold War History*, 18:2 (2018), pp. 221–37.

Nuechterlein, Donald E., 'Thailand and SEATO: A Ten-Year Appraisal,' *Asian Survey*, 4:12 (1964), pp. 1174–81.

Patil, Sameer Suryakant, 'India's China Policy in the 1950s: Threat Perceptions and Balances,' *South Asia Survey*, 14:2 (2007), pp. 290–4.

Raghavan, Srinath, 'Sino-Indian Boundary Dispute, 1948–60: A Reappraisal,' *Economic and Political Weekly*, 41:36 (2006), pp. 3882–92.

Rakove, Robert B., 'The Rise and Fall of Non-Aligned Mediation, 1961–6,' *International History Review*, 37:5 (2015), pp. 991–1013.

Ratnapalan, L. M., 'Britain and the Politics of Ceylon, 1948–1961,' *Historical Journal* 59:2 (2016), pp. 541–65.

Roy, Nabarun, 'Assuaging Cold War Anxieties: India and the Failure of SEATO,' *Diplomacy & Statecraft*, 26:2 (2015), pp. 322–40.

———, 'In the Shadow of Great Power Politics: Why Nehru Supported PRC's Admission to the Security Council,' *International History Review*, 40:2 (2018), pp. 376–96.

Ruane, Kevin, 'SEATO, MEDO, and the Baghdad Pact: Anthony Eden, British Foreign Policy and the Collective Defense of Southeast Asia and the Middle East, 1952–1955,' *Diplomacy & Statecraft*, 16:1 (2005), pp. 169–99.

Shao, Kuo-kang, 'Chou En-lai's Diplomatic Approach to Non-aligned States in Asia: 1953–60,' *China Quarterly*, 78 (1979), pp. 324–38.

———, 'Zhou Enlai's Diplomacy and the Neutralization of Indo-China, 1954–55,' *China Quarterly*, 107 (1986), pp. 483–504.

Shen, Zhihua and Xia, Yafeng, 'The Whirlwind of China: Zhou Enlai's Shuttle Diplomacy in 1957 and Its Effects,' *Cold War History*, 10:4 (2010), pp. 513–35.

———, 'Leadership Transfer in the Asian Revolution: Mao Zedong and the Asian Cominform,' *Cold War History*, 14:2 (2014), pp. 195–213.

Sheng, Michael M., 'Mao and China's Relations With the Superpowers in the 1950s: A New Look at the Taiwan Strait Crises and the Sino-Soviet Split,' *Modern China*, 34:4 (2008), pp. 477–507.

Shimazu, Naoko, 'Diplomacy as Theatre: Staging the Bandung Conference of 1955,' *Modern Asian Studies*, 48:1 (2014), pp. 225–52.

———, 'What is Sociability in Diplomacy?,' *Diplomatica, 1*:1 (2019), pp. 56–72.

Singh, L. P., 'Dynamics of Indian-Indonesian Relations,' *Asian Survey*, 7:9 (1967), pp. 655–66.

Stargardt, A. W., 'The Emergence of the Asian System of Powers,' *Modern Asian Studies*, 23:3 (1989), pp. 561–95.

Tarling, Nicholas, "Ah-Ah': Britain and the Bandung Conference of 1955,' *Journal of Southeast Asian Studies*, 23:1 (1999), pp. 74–111.

Thakur, Vineet, 'An Asian Drama: The Asian Relations Conference, 1947,' *International History Review*, 41:3 (2019), pp. 673–95.

Tsang, Steve, 'Target Zhou Enlai: The 'Kashmir Princess' Incident of 1955,' *China Quarterly*, 139 (1994), pp. 766–82.

Tudda, Chris, "Reenacting the Story of Tantalus': Eisenhower, Dulles, and the Failed Rhetoric of Liberation,' *Journal of Cold War Studies*, 7:4 (2005), pp. 3–35.

Vertzberger, Yaacov, 'India's Strategic Posture and the Border War Defeat of 1962: A Case Study in Miscalculation,' *Journal of Strategic Studies*, 5:3 (1982), pp. 370–92.

Wang, Tao, 'Neutralizing Indochina: The 1954 Geneva Conference and China's Efforts to Isolate the United States,' *Journal of Cold War Studies*, 19:2 (2017), pp. 3–42.

Williams, Lea E., 'Sino-Indonesian Diplomacy: A Study of Revolutionary International Politics,' *China Quarterly*, 11 (1962), pp. 184–99.

Wilson, David A., 'China, Thailand and the Spirit of Bandung (Part I),' *China Quarterly*, 30 (1967), pp. 149–69.

———, 'China, Thailand and the Spirit of Bandung (Part II),' *China Quarterly*, 31 (1967), pp. 96–127.

Yang, Kuisong, 'The Theory and Implementation of the People's Republic of China's Revolutionary Diplomacy,' *Journal of Modern Chinese History*, 3:2 (2009), pp. 127–45.

Yechury, Akhila, 'Imagining India, Decolonizing l'Inde Française, c. 1947–1954,' *The Historical Journal*, 58:4 (2015), pp. 1141–65.

Zhai, Qiang, 'China and the Geneva Conference of 1954,' *China Quarterly*, 129 (1992), pp. 103–22.

Zhang, Guang Shu, 'Constructing 'Peaceful Coexistence': China's Diplomacy Toward the Geneva and Bandung Conferences, 1954–55,' *Cold War History*, 7:4 (2007), pp. 509–28.

Zhi, Liang, 'Heading Toward Peaceful Coexistence: The Effects of the Improvement in Sino-Burmese Relations From 1953 to 1955,' *Asian Perspective*, 42 (2018), pp. 527–49.

———, 'Rethinking Sino-Burmese Relations, 1949–1954,' *Social Sciences in China*, 39:2 (2018), pp. 153–68.

Zhou, Taomo, 'Ambivalent Alliance: Chinese Policy Towards Indonesia, 1960–1965,' *China Quarterly*, 221 (2015), pp. 208–28.

Životić, Alexander and Čavoški, Jovan, 'On the Road to Belgrade: Yugoslavia, Third World Neutrals, and the Evolution of Global Non-Alignment, 1954–1961,' *Journal of Cold War Studies*, 18:4 (2016), pp. 79–97.

Book Reviews

Benvenuti, Andrea, Review of Ang Cheng Guan, *The Southeast Asia Treaty Organization* (Routledge, 2022), in *H-Diplo Roundtable XXIV-11*, 7 November 2022, https://hdiplo.org/to/RT24-11

Schlesinger, Rudolf, Review of G. H. Jansen, *Non-Alignment and the Afro-Asian States* (Faber and Faber, 1966), in *Journal of Asian and African Studies*, 3:1 (1968), pp. 140–1.

Unpublished Theses

Greenlees, Donald, 'The Origins of Nonalignment: Great Power Competition and Indonesian Foreign Policy 1945–1965' (PhD thesis, Australian National University, 2018).

Grosser, Pierre, 'La France et l'Indochine (1953–1956): Une 'Carte de Visite en Peau de Chagrin" (doctoral thesis, Institut d'Études Politiques de Paris, 2002).

Harder, Anton, 'Defining Independence in Cold War Asia: Sino-Indian Relations, 1949–1962' (PhD thesis, London School of Economics, 2015).

Thompson, David Mark, 'Delusions of *Grandeur*: French Global Ambitions and the Problem of Revival of Military Powers, 1950–1954' (PhD Dissertation, University of Toronto, 2007).

Wang, Tao, 'Isolating the Enemy: US-PRC Relations, 1953–56' (PhD dissertation, Georgetown University, 2011).

Ward, Jonathan, 'China-India Rivalry and the Border War of 1962: PRC Perspectives on the Collapse of China-India Relations, 1958–62' (DPhil thesis, University of Oxford, 2016).

Unpublished Papers

Mukherjee, Mridula, 'Situating India in Asia: The Nehru Years,' https://src-h.slav.hokudai.ac.jp/rp/publications/no09/09_09_Mukherjee.pdf

Working Papers

Čavoški, Jovan, 'Arming Nonalignment: Yugoslavia's Relations With Burma and the Cold War in Asia (1950–1955),' *Cold War International History Project Working Paper 61* (Washington, DC: Woodrow Wilson Centre for Scholars, 2002), https://www.wilsoncenter.org/publication/arming-nonalignment-yugoslavias-relations-burma-and-the-cold-war-asia-1950-1955

———, 'Distant Countries, Closest Allies: Josip Broz Tito and Jawaharlal Nehru and the Rise of Global Nonalignment,' *NMML Occasional Paper* 77 (New Delhi: Nehru Library and Museum, 2015), available at https://nehrumemorial.nic.in/images/pdf/OCP/HSS/H%20S%20-%2077.pdf

Guha, Ramachandra, 'Jawaharlal Nehru and China: A Study in Failure,' *Harvard-Yenching Institute Working Paper Series* (2011), https://www.harvard-yenching.org/wp-content/uploads/legacy_files/featurefiles/Ramachandra%20Guha_Jawaharlal%20Nehru%20and%20China.pdf

Harder, Anton, 'Not at the Cost of China: New Evidence Regarding US Proposals to the for Joining the United Nations Security Council,' *Cold War International History*

Project Working Paper 76 (Washington, DC: Woodrow Wilson Centre for Scholars, 2002), pp. 1–16, https://www.wilsoncenter.org/sites/default/files/media/documents/publication/cwihp_working_paper_76_not_at_the_cost_of_china.pdf

Niu, Jun, '1962: The Eve of the Left Turn in China's Foreign Policy,' *Cold War International History Project Working Paper 48* (Washington, DC: Woodrow Wilson Centre for Scholars, 2005), pp. 1–36, https://www.wilsoncenter.org/sites/default/files/media/documents/publication/NiuJunWP481.pdf

Yang, Kuisong, 'Changes in Mao Zedong's Attitude Toward the Indochina War, 1949–1973,' *Cold War International History Project Working Paper 34* (Washington, DC: Woodrow Wilson Centre for Scholars, 2002), pp. 1–43, https://www.wilsoncenter.org/sites/default/files/media/documents/publication/ACFB04.pdf

Zhou, Taomo, 'Ambivalent Alliance: Chinese Policy Towards Indonesia, 1960–1965,' *Cold War International History Project Working Paper 67* (Washington, DC: Woodrow Wilson Centre for Scholars, 2013), https://www.wilsoncenter.org/sites/default/files/media/documents/publication/CWIHP_Working_Paper_67_Chinese_Policy_towards_Indonesia_1960-1965.pdf

Podcasts

Westad, Odd Arne, 'The Cold War: A World History,' *LSE Podcasts*, 9 February 2018, https://soundcloud.com/lsepodcasts/the-cold-war-a-world-history

Newspapers and Magazines

*Canberra Times (*Australia)
Daily Telegraph (Australia)
The Economist (UK)
Hindustan Times (India)
Melbourne Herald (Australia)
New Statesman (UK)
New York Times (United States)
Scotsman (United Kingdon)
Sydney Morning Herald (Australia)
Times of India (India)
Times of Indonesia (Indonesia)
Western Australian (Australia)

INDEX

Note: Page numbers followed by '*n*' refer to notes.

ALSO FROM SPEAKING TIGER

WHO IS BHARAT MATA?

On History, Culture and the Idea of India
Writings by and on Jawaharlal Nehru

Edited and with an Introduction by
Purushottam Agrawal

'[A] very comprehensive survey of Nehru's ideas about India—her civilization, traditions and culture. This is a timely volume which will also stand the test of time.'—*The Hindu*

'Who is Bharat Mata, whose victory you wish?' asked Jawaharlal Nehru—a leading light of the Indian freedom movement who would become the country's first prime minister—at a public gathering in 1936. And then he explained: the mountains and rivers, forests and fields were of course dear to everyone, but what counted ultimately were 'the people of India—spread out all over this vast land. Bharat Mata, Mother India, [is] essentially these millions of people, and victory to her [is] victory to these people.' This collection of writings and speeches by and on Nehru shows us the mind—the ideology, born of experience, observation and deep study—behind this democratic and inclusive idea of India. It is a book of particular relevance at a time when 'nationalism' and the slogan 'Bharat Mata ki Jai' are being used to construct a militant and purely emotional idea of India that excludes millions of residents and citizens.

'Who Is Bharat Mata?' contains selections from Nehru's classic books—*An Autobiography*, *Glimpses of World History* and *The Discovery of India*; his speeches, essays and letters from the pre- and post-Independence years; and some of his most revealing interviews. The concluding section of the book comprises reminiscences and assessments of Nehru by his contemporaries—among them, Mahatma Gandhi, Bhagat Singh, Sardar Patel, Maulana Azad, Aruna Asaf Ali, Sheikh Abdullah, Ramdhari Singh Dinkar, Ali Sardar Jafri, Martin Luther King Jr and Atal Bihari Vajpayee.

In this thoughtfully compiled anthology—which also carries an illuminating introduction—Nehru emerges as a remarkable man of ideas and action who had an instinctive understanding of India's civilizational spirit, as also a clear commitment to the scientific temper; and as a leader who, despite the compulsions of politics, remained a democrat.

'[An] outstandingly curated collection…a necessary book such as this could not have come from a better scholar.'
—*Economic and Political Weekly*